I0815235

AN ENCHANTED WORLD

An Enchanted World

THE SHARED RELIGIOUS LANDSCAPE OF LATE ANTIQUITY

MICHAEL L. SATLOW

PRINCETON UNIVERSITY PRESS
PRINCETON & OXFORD

Published by Princeton University Press
41 William Street, Princeton, New Jersey 08540
99 Banbury Road, Oxford OX2 6JX

press.princeton.edu

GPSR Authorized Representative: Easy Access System Europe—Mustamäe tee 50, 10621 Tallinn, Estonia, gpsr.requests@easproject.com

ISBN 9780691256597
ISBN (e-book) 9780691266329

Library of Congress Control Number: 2025938059

British Library Cataloging-in-Publication Data is available

Editorial: Fred Appel, Tara Dugan
Production Editorial: Elizabeth Byrd
Jacket: Ben Higgins
Production: Danielle Amatucci
Publicity: William Pagdatoon
Copyeditor: Lisa Sinclair

Jacket Image: CPA Media Pte Ltd / Alamy Stock Photo

Printed in the United States of America

10 9 8 7 6 5 4 3 2 1

Dedicated to the victims of October 7, 2023
May their memories be for a blessing

CONTENTS

LIST OF FIGURES

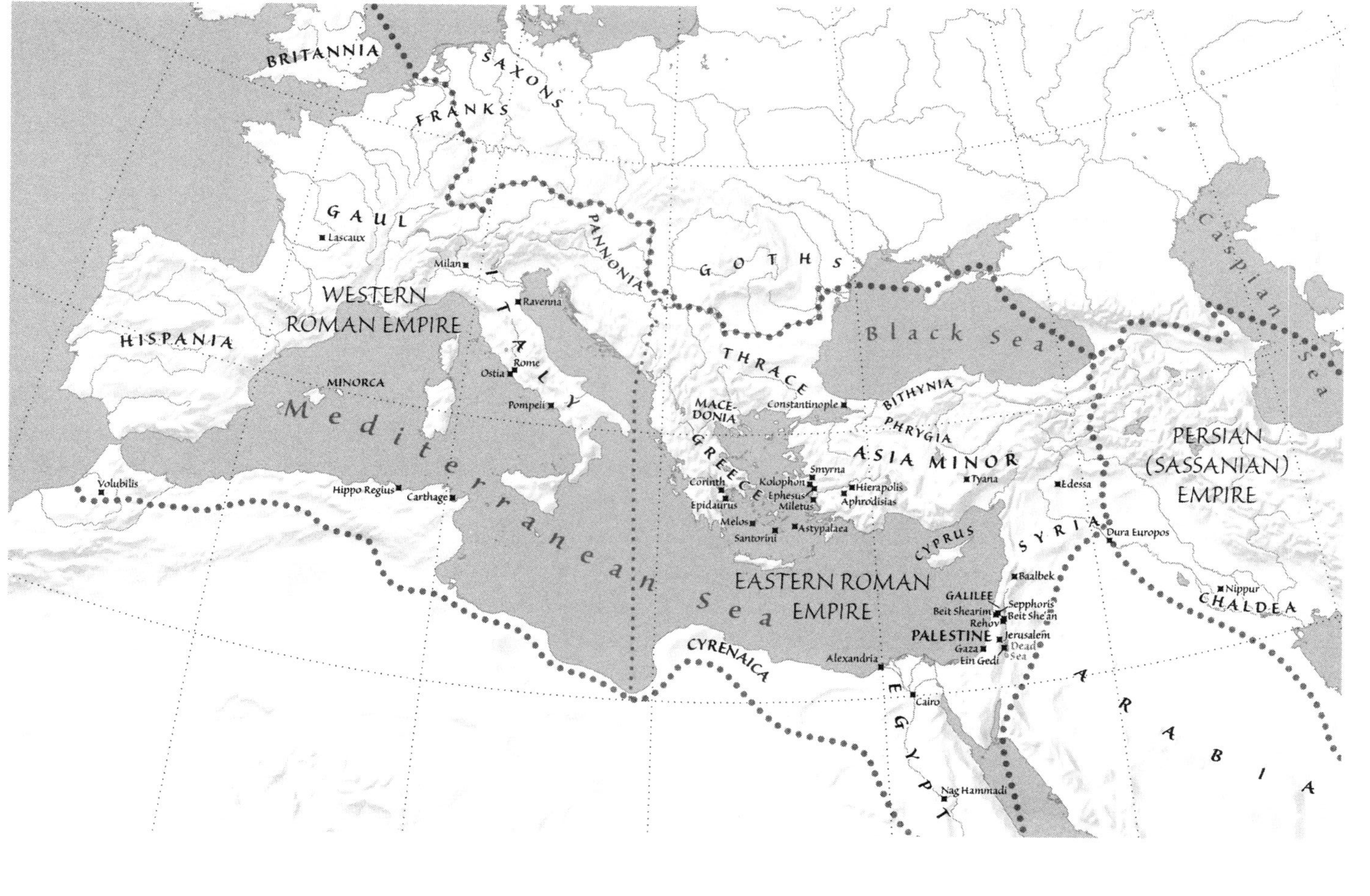

BRITANNIA
SAXONS
FRANKS
GAUL
Lascaux
Milan
WESTERN ROMAN EMPIRE
HISPANIA
MINORCA
ITALY
Ravenna
Rome
Ostia
Pompeii
PANNONIA
GOTHS
Mediterranean Sea
Volubilis
Hippo Regius
Carthage
THRACE
MACE-DONIA
Constantinople
GREECE
Corinth
Epidaurus
Melos
Santorini
Astypalaea
Smyrna
Kolophon
Ephesus
Miletus
Hierapolis
Aphrodisias
Black Sea
BITHYNIA
PHRYGIA
ASIA MINOR
Tyana
Edessa
Caspian Sea
PERSIAN (SASSANIAN) EMPIRE
SYRIA
Dura Europos
CYPRUS
EASTERN ROMAN EMPIRE
Baalbek
GALILEE
Sepphoris
Beit Shearim
Beit She'an
Rehov
PALESTINE
Jerusalem
Gaza
Dead Sea
Ein Gedi
Nippur
CHALDEA
CYRENAICA
Alexandria
Cairo
EGYPT
Nag Hammadi
ARABIA

CONVENTIONS

TRANSLATIONS OF biblical texts follow the New Revised Standard Version. For other texts, if a translation is not noted, the translation is my own. I occasionally transliterate and discuss the original terminology used in these texts. When doing so, I transliterate unsystematically according to what I think would be accessible to a nonspecialist but at the same time comprehensible to a specialist.

Scholars have created a complex notation system for citing ancient texts. The important ones in this book are square brackets and parentheses. Text in square brackets was thought to be part of the original text and supplied by a modern editor. It might, for example, be the text thought to be missing from a damaged inscription. Parentheses are used for editorial additions to a text to make that text more comprehensible.

For the purposes of readability, I usually bundle the sources for a single paragraph into a single note at the end of that paragraph. Many of the claims that I make throughout the book emerge from a long and complicated scholarly discussion, and it would have made the book unwieldy to include the full range of sources behind those discussions. I have thus sought to include only citations of the most important primary source(s) along with references to recent scholarly literature, primarily in English.

When citing an ancient text in its original language, I tend to use the "canonical" reference rather than noting the scholarly edition of the text that I consulted. This should allow for easier location of these references across multiple editions. In cases where there is not a canonical reference system, I note the edition.

Introduction

IN THE fourth century CE, an anonymous woman in the Roman province of Pannonia (now southwestern Hungary) who suffered from elephantiasis went to an expert for help. This expert inscribed a twenty-five-line evocation to "Romulus, the mother Bona," using Greek, Latin, and a series of symbols, on a small silver sheet. This silver sheet was rolled up and placed in a small leather box that the woman presumably carried with her, ultimately to her grave (see figure I.1)[1]

Hundreds, if not thousands, of texts like this survive. They were commissioned by Jews, Christians, and the many others whose religious identity—if they even had one—is ambiguous or unrecoverable. Another example is this one in Coptic (an Egyptian language written in Greek and used by Christians) from the sixth or seventh century CE: "I adjure you with your power and the right hand of the father . . . the son and the authority of the holy spirit, and Gabriel [who] went to Joseph (and) caused him to take Mary for himself as [wife], that you neither delay nor hold back, until you bring to me N daughter of N., and I satisfy my desire with her."[2] The spell, which involves also giving the woman a strong glass of wine to drink, is exactly what it appears to be: an invocation to the Christian Trinity and the archangel Gabriel to let a man lay with a woman he desires. Is it Christian, "pagan," or Christian with "pagan" elements? Does it really matter?

Scholarship often treats texts like these as magical or examples of "popular" or "folk" religion. Combining the names of angels, deities, and all manner of supernatural beings, along with strings of

FIGURE I.1. Silver sheet with engraved inscription evoking "Romulus, the mother Bona," found in Ságvár, Hungary. © Hungarian National Museum Public Collection Centre (inv. MNM-NRIRT-RO 9/1939.4), photo by András Dabasi and Judit Kardos. Used by permission.

incomprehensible (to us) symbols, they are seen as marginal to the "official" religion that took place in temples, synagogues, and churches. In this telling, the writings of intellectuals such as bishops and rabbis shape the primary lens through which we see religion. Their prescribed practices and beliefs, which emphasize behaviors that conform to a particular religious identity (e.g., Jewish or Christian), become central. Religion is about theological, legal, and ritual systems; institutions; and abstract notions, such as "asceticism."

Yet such an approach misses something that was absolutely central to the lives of most people in Late Antiquity (ca. 200–600 CE), when both rabbinic Judaism and Christianity were in formation. Most people thought that the world was thick with supernatural beings, who were as real and had as much (if not more) agency as any person. To get by in the world required being on good terms with the right supernatural beings and able to ward off the bad ones. Being on good terms, in turn, required constant attention. It was unthinkable to go through an ordinary day without cultivating these relationships, whether in short prayers or invocations, the use of amulets, or offerings and sacrifices. This was an enchanted world, full of real if invisible beings. In this sense, "religion"—as a field of knowledge and practice that could be disembedded from the everyday practice of life—loses meaning. Interaction with the supernatural infused nearly every aspect of everyday life, and everyday life would grind to a halt without such interaction.

This book begins with the premise that the story of religion in Late Antiquity is best told not as a story of "Judaism" and "Christianity," abstract systems being actively molded at the time, but as a story of how people thought about and interacted with the invisible world. This is an approach that scholars today refer to as "lived religion." "Lived religion" differs from "popular religion." "Popular religion" implies a relatively stark division between the elite, official, institutional, and correct practice of religion and the more superstitious, magical, incoherent, and thereby worse, practices of the masses. While a "lived religion" approach also focuses on what people are actually doing, it does so in a nonjudgmental and more capacious way. We are not interested here in separating proper from improper religious practice, or the "masses" from the elite, but in trying to assess how individuals of all types encountered the supernatural world. Most people cared more about effective results than religious boundaries. Religious boundaries meant little when it came to healing a sick child, warding off a plague, or seducing a love interest.[3]

When seen in this way, rather than as a story about traditions like "Judaism," "Christianity," and "paganism," the religious history of Late Antiquity becomes not a linear story of triumph or continuity or doctrines and institutions but instead a lurching account of how humans sought to navigate a dangerous and uncertain world. While bishops, rabbis, and Roman priests were creating and enforcing identities and their boundaries, many historians today believe that they had very limited reach and influence. Social relations between people of different ethnicities, or devotees of different deities, were certainly not always smooth in Late Antiquity. Yet neighbors who venerated different deities were for the most part united by basic human fears and a set of assumptions about supernatural beings and the way that they acted in the world.

Adopting this approach involves a significant conceptual shift in the way that most of us think about religion. Many of the words that we so often use to tell these stories—words that come precisely from the intellectuals in Late Antiquity seeking to create boundaries between distinctive traditions—obscure more than they elucidate. What does "religion" mean in a world where the existence of and need for relationships with supernatural beings were simply taken for granted? When we speak of "Judaism" or "Christianity," to whose systems are we referring? "Paganism" is such a vague and inherently (intentionally) pejorative term that it is practically useless in understanding how people related to the supernatural world. For these reasons, I rarely use these terms in this book. Jews, Christians, Greeks, and Romans—actual human beings—appear frequently throughout this book, but the "systems" that label them do not.

Similarly, I find "magic" and "superstition" to be mostly unhelpful categories. Terms like this can be found in Hebrew, Greek, and Latin, where they are used almost exclusively to denigrate targeted practices. There is little consistency in how such labeling was used, and it is clear that many of the practices that an elite group might label as magic were considered by most to be simply a part of the normal toolkit for communication with invisible beings. For example, we possess scores of texts that seek to raise the dead, yet many texts written by rabbis, bishops, and Roman elite recoil at the idea of necromancy and forbid it. Since one person's magic is another's religion, the term is best used sparingly and precisely.

What Is "Late Antiquity"?

This book concerns a period I have called "Late Antiquity." Most scholars understand this period to span somewhere between the third and seventh centuries CE. In most common scholarly usage, however, it denotes more than a specific time span. It also refers to a specific area (the Roman Empire, with some overlap to the Persian Empire as well) and even culture. Like many chronological labels, it has a history and an agenda. Briefly outlining both helps to situate this book in history and historiography.

Before "Late Antiquity," in the world of Roman historians, there was simply the "Late Roman Empire," the "Byzantine world," or even the "early Middle Ages." Each evokes a different historical narrative. The "Late Roman Empire," for example, taps into a narrative of the decline of Rome, as reflected principally in its political structure. Rome's political and literary "golden age," in this narrative, occurred in the period of the Republic, which ended in 27 BCE, when Octavian (later Augustus) began to consolidate his power. By the mid-third century CE, the period of decline had begun. Economic instability, increasing reliance on mercenaries, and ossified bureaucracies marked the beginning of the Late Roman Empire. Spiritually, Romans entered, as E. R. Dodds called it, an "age of anxiety," which set the scene for the spread of Christianity. Almost a century later, the Empire would split into a Western Empire, based in Rome, and an Eastern Empire, based in Constantinople. Some scholars thus use the term "the Byzantine period" to describe the Eastern Empire from the early fourth century CE. The Western Empire comes to an end with the successive sacks of Rome in 410 and 455. In the West, this is the end of antiquity, and the medieval period begins. Meanwhile, the Islamic invasions begin to eat away at Byzantium beginning in the seventh century. Constantinople would finally fall in 1453.[4]

If, from a Roman historian's perspective, the late Empire pointed to a period of decline, in the eyes of Christian historians it was a time of triumph. For early Christians, the birth of Christ ended history. A new, timeless, era had begun. Except, of course, to all appearances it hadn't. Christian writers struggled with this; whether and to what extent most other Christians did is an interesting but unanswerable question. For these Christian intellectuals, though, Constantine's legalization of Christianity in 313 CE (the Edict of Milan) decisively demonstrated that Christianity does, in fact, have a history. The Edict of Milan, in their telling, ushered in an age of Christian triumph. Christians, who increasingly had power and developed legislation that promoted their goals and agendas, had triumphed over the Jews and pagans, not because they were more powerful and luckier but because they were right and better.

Meanwhile, Jewish historians were telling an altogether different story. Prior to 70 CE, the Jewish polity was centered around the Temple in Jerusalem, the house of the Judean god YHWH. Judea had already lost their political independence to the Romans in 6 CE after the failure of the reign of the sons of King Herod but actively rebelled against Rome in 66 CE. In 70 CE, the Romans had put down the rebellion and torched the Temple. As if to punctuate their success, they brutally suppressed a second, smaller uprising that occurred between 132 and 135 CE, known as the Bar-Kokhba rebellion.

The destruction of the Temple meant different things to different historians. To the ancient Christian historians, it was a theological sign of God's rejection of the Jews. Josephus also saw it as a divine punishment for sins, albeit not a sign of rejection. Modern academic Jewish historians sometimes frame it as a watershed moment in Jewish history. The destruction of the Second Temple ended the Second Temple period (ca. 520 BCE–70 CE) and transformed Judaism from a sacrificial religion to one based on study of the Torah. With the sacrificial system in ruins, a new kind of spiritual authority, the rabbis, quickly rose. From the perspective of modern Jewish historians, this became the "rabbinic period" (ca. 70–620 CE).

The ancient rabbis, though, did not quite see history that way. Rabbinic texts begin to emerge in Roman Palestine (the new name of the province) in the early third century CE, although they are based on earlier sources. Rabbinic texts that date to the fourth to sixth centuries, from Palestine as well as Persia, often see the destruction of the Temple as tragic, but the Jewish story, they assert, is one of continuity. Jewish life was always focused on the Torah and the rabbis in the rabbinic imagination, not the Temple. Its destruction changed little.

It was the rise of the academic study of religion that led to a kind of historiographical reckoning. In the United States, academic departments devoted to the study of religion were increasingly founded beginning in the 1960s. Scholars of early, post–New Testament Christianity were often said to be studying patristics, while those studying rabbinic literature were scholars of rabbinics. By the 1980s, neither group was very happy with how they were being categorized. The words "patristics" and "rabbinics" had a crusty, theological ring to them. Each group of scholars was concerned that the terms bore baggage that hindered their full integration into the secular university. Yet they also largely subscribed to a historical narrative that put them at odds with each other and especially with the Roman historians, who were well integrated into departments of classics and history.

In his influential book from 1978, *The Making of Late Antiquity*, the Roman historian Peter Brown helped to clear a new path. Brown did not invent the term "Late Antiquity," but he was perhaps its most ardent and influential supporter. Rather than being a period of decline and fundamental change, Brown asserted, Late Antiquity was a time of continuity. And rather than "declining," Roman society flourished. Christian thinkers emerged from creatively interacting with traditional Greek and Roman thinkers. Christians continued the classical tradition, albeit in a somewhat different form. "Late Antiquity" thus refers not only to a time (ca. 300–700 CE) and a place (the Roman Empire, with special attention to the Greek- and Syriac-speaking eastern provinces) but also to a narrative and cultural complex. For Brown, there was something distinctive about Late Antiquity that paved a gentler path to the Middle Ages.[5]

The concept of Late Antiquity has been intellectually productive and socially useful. This reconceptualization of the period sparked renewed scholarly interest and ignited a new research agenda. Many scholars of patristics relabeled themselves as scholars of Late Antiquity, which allowed for greater scholarly dialogue with Roman and Jewish historians. The narrative of Christian continuity with the classical tradition helped scholars to situate their work outside of theology and in history and classics.

For scholars of Jewish history, the reception of this term was more complicated. In theory, Late Antiquity is capacious, an ecumenical category that encompasses all ethnicities and religions in a single (if complex) culture, making it attractive to these scholars for the same reasons that it was attractive to scholars of formative Christianity. On the other hand, though, the actual narratives produced under the rubric of Late Antiquity tend to marginalize the Jews. In a narrative of Christian continuity with the Roman classical tradition, Jews tend to be pushed to the side.

My own conception of Late Antiquity emerges from my background as a historian of Jews and Judaism. It thus covers the years 70–620 CE, with special attention to the third through sixth centuries (the rabbinic period). There has been much scholarly discussion, due to its relevance to the question of Christian origins, about whether there was a "common Judaism" when the Jerusalem Temple stood. Less attention has been paid to the time after the Temple's destruction. Jews, I argue, are part of the cultural, social, and religious fabric of Late Antiquity, neither central nor marginal. The evidence they left can thus be seen as reflecting this wider culture, not as the parochial writings of an isolated community. What emerges is a picture of a shared spiritual landscape. Whatever fault lines ran through Late Antiquity—and there were many and they were deep—there were also common understandings of the relationship between humans and divine agents. This is the story of Late Antiquity that I seek to tell.

Sources

Most studies of lived religion today rely heavily on survey and ethnographic data. Neither are perfect—people do not always report the truth or even know what they really think, and the observations of the ethnographer are fragmentary, often biased, and filtered through the limited understanding of a single individual. To supplement these sources, or when they are lacking, scholars often use historical archives. Inquisition records from the Catholic Church have provided a particularly rich source for reconstructing the beliefs of those that the church put on trial.

For antiquity, we have none of this. Mostly, we have the literature of the intellectuals, the very people who are often trying to suppress and refigure the more common beliefs and practices we are seeking. Sometimes, when we are lucky, we find explicit descriptions in this literature, usually related for purposes of condemnation. The rabbis, for example, explicitly condemn Jewish practices that they find repellent, and the Christian bishop John Chrysostom inveighs against the Christians in Antioch who prefer to make their oaths in synagogues, because they apparently find them at least as holy as churches. As valuable as these nuggets are, they are relatively few and give little indication of the prevalence of the practices. More often, these texts have to be read "against the grain," or with what scholars call a hermeneutic of suspicion. What is an author attempting to hide or change? For example, both Jewish and Christian literature promote giving money to their respective institutions; this appears to be an attempt to transform a more common, shared notion that alms directly given to the poor bring divine blessings. The problem with this approach, of course, is that the determination of that which remains unstated is never objective and that this form of reading is necessarily somewhat speculative. At the same time, we can be relatively sure that these authors were not hermetically sealed from others and that on some deeper level they share and express more common understandings.[6]

Fortunately, we are not entirely dependent on this literature. Letters and historical documents from antiquity survive, although in small numbers and mostly from Egypt (the Dead Sea Scrolls all predate the period covered in this book). "Spells" (forms of prayer in my telling) written on metal or ceramics survive in decent number. Inscriptions and coins provide different kinds of texts, but both (especially the former) provide data ignored in the literature. Archaeology gives us another window, if often opaque, into everyday life.

While I want to emphasize the fragility of our knowledge and our dependence on (informed) speculation for recovering lived ancient religion, it is also worth emphasizing that almost all ancient history is done in a similar way. Many of us have preconceived narratives of meaning when we encounter some topics, particularly when it comes to religion. One of my goals in this book is to begin to question those preconceptions. Why do you believe what you do? What evidence are you drawing on in constructing your own beliefs? I have always found that one of the rewards of doing ancient history is being constantly challenged with new ways of seeing the world and reconciling what I think I know with actual evidence.

Identities

Recent research in Late Antiquity has tended to focus on religious difference and identity. Those who saw themselves as religious leaders (whether others saw them as such) sought ways of developing stronger group boundaries and identities. An ordinary "Christian," for example, might evoke traditional Roman gods and take oaths in a synagogue without any sense that she was doing anything wrong. The local bishop would most likely disagree. In the fluid world of Late Antiquity such fluidity was the rule rather than the exception, and the strong and consistent attempts by both rabbis and bishops to define Jewish and Christian identities testify to the difficulty of doing so. Recent scholarship has emphasized with great sophistication the strategies by which intellectuals and officials sought to create distinctive religious boundaries.[7]

This approach has shaped modern scholarly narratives of the past. We tell stories about how Christianity did or did not fully separate from Judaism and paganism, or how rabbinic Judaism rose from the ashes of the destruction of the Jerusalem Temple in 70 CE. Our stories deal with abstractions, and they are linear, often stories of the rise or decline of this or that tradition. This is hardly surprising, given the energy and time invested by the intellectual elite who would win the day by creating a massive literature that would tell precisely the story of the uniqueness and truth of their own systems. Many modern accounts cleave closely to the ancient ones, even if they sometimes arrive at different answers. The religious literature of Late Antiquity, written by the intellectuals, constitutes our major source for recovering much of Late Antiquity, and it is hard to break free of the narratives that we have inherited.

The traditional stories that emphasize difference are not only incomplete; they have also proved to be dangerous. They constantly remind us of difference and division and encourage us to separate ourselves from the often evil "other." The history of religious institutions is largely a story of conflict and violence. Yet it is not "religion" that is to blame but the way that we tell its story.

This book tells a different story. I seek to recover and make alive a lost world that crackled with the energy of the supernatural. It is a story that foregrounds that which we share rather than those things that divide us. In some ways, it is a universal story of our most profound human fears and aspirations and how we seek to respond to them. In other ways, it is deeply particularistic, set in the world of the Late Antique Mediterranean and Near East. In both cases, though, it focuses on actual people, be they aristocrats, intellectuals, peasants, children, or slaves. Although accounts of the lives of ordinary (nonelite) women, not to mention their own writings, are sparse, they too cannot simply be ignored. They all believed that supernatural beings existed, that they were agents who could and frequently did act in the world, and that having good relationships with them was vital to success in the world. People called on a wide range of different beings but ultimately recognized that they all lived in the same world, sometimes drawing on the resources of their neighbors in particularly sticky situations.

This story can only be seen by means of comparison. Jews, Christians, Greeks, and Romans lived in a shared world. In many cities in Asia Minor (modern-day Turkey), for example, churches, synagogues, and traditional temples were within a stone's throw of each other. The magnificent synagogue in Sardis was right in the city center. We have abundant evidence of social interaction between people of different identities and ethnicities and the ritual specialists who serviced them all. They lived in the same spiritual landscape. Jews are frequently marginalized in scholarly narratives that either pit Christianity against paganism or show how little Christians moved from their pagan roots. Yet there were many Jews scattered throughout the Mediterranean basin and the Near East, and they left a rich literature that testifies to common beliefs and practices.

Outline

The book opens with an overview of Late Antiquity in chapter 1, which provides the history and context. Chapter 2 discusses religious identities in Late Antiquity, arguing that they tended to be fluid, subjective, and perspectival. This leads us into the shared understanding of the divine realm and invisible beings discussed in chapter 3. Different ethnic groups had different divinities, but nearly all had a similar understanding of how supernatural agents worked. In chapter 4 I discuss the literate elite, specifically those, like rabbis and Church Fathers, who sought to systematize religious identities and whose writings form the bulk of our sources. They had far less power and influence than they would have liked. Chapter 5 shows the ways in which individuals sought to cultivate relationships with supernatural agents. These relationships were seen as crucial to dealing with a dangerous and uncertain world. Many of these relationships did not need to be mediated, but as chapter 6 shows, there were many specialists or ritual experts who could help with activities such as dream interpretation and amulet writing. Chapters 7 and 8 address the related topics of sacred place and sacred time. Here we look at common understandings and practices relating to places (e.g., temples, synagogues) and times (e.g., holidays, birthdays).

The story that this book tells is urgently needed in a world full of hostile divisions. Mistrust and hostility often taint the relationships between secular and religious people, to say nothing of those of different faiths. Violence on behalf of religion has a long pedigree, and it is not likely to go away soon. But what if we were able to reframe what we meant by "religion" to include more room for tolerance and, above all, empathy? What if we were able, simply as individuals, to capture a bit more of the enchantment felt by our ancestors? Could it help us to see our way to a new relationship with the world and those around us?

1

Imagining Late Antiquity

THIS IS a book about lived religion in Late Antiquity. One of the most vexing issues confronting me when writing this book was trying to figure out how to talk about "religion" when the category of "religion," as we typically understand it, only vaguely existed. Relationships with and beliefs about supernatural beings, along with an extraordinarily large and diverse set of rituals and practices used to further them, suffused nearly every aspect of ordinary living. On the one hand, any attempt to isolate distinctly "religious" elements necessarily rips these features out of context. Yet on the other hand, keeping them in context would mean engaging in all aspects of Late Antiquity, which would result in a book that would try anyone's patience.

I have spent my career immersed in Late Antiquity, reading the ancient literary and religious texts in their original languages; poring over archaeological reports; deciphering papyri, coins, and inscriptions; sorting through modern scholarly reconstructions (as well as creating my own); and thinking about what life would have been like in that world. Most readers of this book, I recognize, have not. The goal of this chapter is to provide an understanding of the world we are about to enter. I can offer here only the most schematic sketch of what that world looked, sounded, and smelled like. To do that, I must ask you to join me in an imaginative exercise.

FIGURE 1.1. Tombstone of the son of Megalos, Zoar, 455 CE. Translation: "This is the tombstone . . . Son of Megalos(?), who died on the Sabbath, the twenty-fifth day of the month of Tevet, in the first year of the sabbatical year cycle, in the year three hundred and eighty-six after the destruction of the Temple. Peace." © The Israel Museum (accession number 90.26.12); translation: The Israel Museum, https://www.imj.org.il/en/collections/395637-0. Used by permission.

Let's start by time-traveling to a city in the eastern part of the Roman Empire. Maybe it is February in the year 416 CE. Of course, if you actually lived then, you wouldn't know it by that date. If you were a Jew living near Jerusalem, you might date it using a Hebrew month, the year in the seven-year sabbatical cycle, and the number of years since the destruction of the Temple (dating from the "creation of the world" came later). A Greek in the same area would use a Greek month and a year from the founding of the Roman province of Arabia, in 106 CE. A Christian might date much like the Greek but also indicate the day of the week according to Christian reckoning. Official documents would use the regnal year. In Egypt, for civil matters, the year of the indication (which follows a nine-year cycle) might be noted. In the same city, people reckoned time quite differently for different purposes.

Our first stop would be the forum or *agora*. Hellenistic cities—those founded or remodeled after the conquests of Alexander the Great around 320 BCE—did not have a uniform plan, but some buildings and institutions were almost always found within them. The agora was the city's center. It would be home to many of the city's most important civic buildings (e.g., where the council, or *boule*, met) and important temples (although these were also often located on an acropolis, a hill by the city that also would have had defensive buildings). When the Romans conquered these cities, mainly in the second and first centuries

BCE, they remade them along more of a grid pattern. Instead of an agora, Romans had a forum. The Roman forum had a plan and purpose similar to the agora, so often when the Romans renovated a city they would transform the existing agora into a forum. In such cases, it stood at the intersection of the two main roads, one running north–south (*cardo maximus*) and the other east–west (*decumanus maximus*). Roman administrative and civic offices would be housed in the forum, along with additional temples dedicated to Roman gods, including the reigning imperial family.[1]

What we would notice first, especially on market days, is the commercial activity. According to Roman sources, market days were held every ninth day; rabbinic sources assume them to occur twice a week. There was, undoubtedly, great local variation. Imagine the bustle on these days! Farmers would bring their vegetables and animals to the square, setting up in stalls or on the ground. Animals purchased live might be brought directly to a butcher for slaughter, perhaps in the temples or the side streets. There would be street performers and buskers. The rabbis imagine that the Torah was read in the square on such days, but there is no corroborating evidence that this really happened. The aristocracy might be present in the law courts and administrative buildings, but the shopping and bartering was done by their slaves and other household staff, mixing with the other plebs. Men and women would eye each other, thinking of matches for themselves or their children. Edicts, often engraved on bronze tablets, were posted, but since very few could read, there were readers to publicize new and important ones. The square contained many other inscriptions, carved on stone or set in floor mosaics, in Greek and Latin. Quite a few of these memorialized the rich patrons of the city, but there were also laws, calendars, and texts dealing with other civic matters. Many of the people we will meet in these pages, such as scribes, astrologers, and priests, would be hawking their skills.[2]

Most people purchased their goods with metal coins. Imperial authorities regulated the type of metal, its purity, and its iconography, but there were often regional variations. Coins were almost always stamped with legends in Greek or Latin, often mentioning the reigning emperor.

FIGURES 1.2A, 1.2B. Gold solidus of Justinian I, Constantinople, 538–545. Justinian holds an orb with a cross, representing his sovereignty. ANS 1977.158.1027. Images courtesy of the American Numismatic Society.

They might feature pictures of emperors, local gods, or architectural features (e.g., a temple) of the city. They thus served as ideal vehicles for imperial propaganda. There were no distinctively Jewish coins officially minted in Late Antiquity. From the fourth century on, coins tended to use less "pagan" iconography, haltingly (but far from commonly) replacing it with the symbol of the *chi-rho*. Due to regional differences in currency, the markets were also full of money changers who could convert change into the local coinage (for a fee, of course).[3]

The market was loud, colorful, smelly, and dirty. Even on non-market days, the cities, particularly in hotter locations, would be full of the smell of animals, animal manure, and whatever came out of the public latrines. More developed cities had water installations and sewers to allow for cleaning of these public spaces, but they still emitted quite a stench. There was a cacophony of different languages. Long after Rome had conquered the Greek cities, its citizens continued to speak Greek along with local dialects. The Jews of Palestine often spoke one dialect of Aramaic while the Jews of the Persian Empire spoke another; very few in either place spoke Hebrew. Christians spoke Coptic and Syriac in addition to Greek. Latin would be heard less often in cities (and rarely in the countryside) in the East. Its use was mainly confined to Roman administrative and military centers.

We might also notice the legal proceedings in the agora/forum. Larger cities had basilicas, Roman buildings where formal cases were heard. Such cases came with the trappings of the Roman legal system,

FIGURE 1.3. Public latrine, Beit Shean, Israel. © Michael L. Satlow.

which was available to all Roman citizens (most free inhabitants of the Roman Empire were citizens after 212 CE). The parties often had advocates and argued before official Roman magistrates. The magistrates had legal advisors and commanded soldiers who could enforce decisions. Criminal cases would take place in such a forum, but for most people this environment was expensive and scary. "Be wary of the government, because they only bring a person near when it suits their own needs," as one rabbi says. Most civil disputes were handled through a process like our binding arbitration. Disputants chose an arbiter they trusted, perhaps an imperial or civic official or magistrate, a member of the clergy, a lawyer, or just an "elder" that the parties recognized as fair. Such arbitrated judgments were only peripherally connected to actual Roman law, as understood by Roman jurists. Market days in particular were good times for such arbiters to make a coin, as they charged for their services. If disputants were unhappy with a judgment, they always had the right (if Roman citizens) to litigate further in the official Roman courts.[4]

We have already noticed the temples, but let's take a closer look. By 416 CE, temples were in decline. A series of decrees issued by the Christian imperial authorities sought to ban "pagan" worship and animal sacrifice. These mostly proscribed individuals from making sacrifices or entering the temples, on pain of a financial penalty; they steered gingerly around the temples themselves. One law from 399 CE orders that temples in rural areas be dismantled, although we know from archaeological evidence that this was largely ignored. Even the most Christian of emperors were not keen on destroying urban temples since such an act could result in civic unrest. A law from 408 CE acknowledges the gap between imperial desire and what was practical. Ordering that the "images" (*simulacra*) be torn from the temples, the law plaintively goes on to say, "We recognize that this regulation has been very often decreed by repeated sanctions." These simulacra were cult statues that stood in the heart of the temples; they were the "idols" or images of the gods that brought the divine power to earth. In the courtyard of the temple was usually an altar and other implements for sacrifices. In an urban center that still had functioning temples, we may have seen inhabitants bringing animals into the temple for slaughter and sacrifice. Cooked meat might also be distributed to the people in the case of public festivals held despite the prohibitions.[5]

Some of these temples, though, were decommissioned by the fifth century CE. Their cultic objects were removed, and their wealth was confiscated by the state. They may have been repurposed into public spaces, although we have little idea how they were used. Some were abandoned or were damaged or destroyed through mob action. Christian monks would occasionally tread where the emperors were afraid to, taking matters into their own hands and damaging temples. Some of these temples were converted to churches, but before the sixth or seventh centuries churches or other visible signs of Christianity in the forums were relatively uncommon.[6]

Departing the forum, we would soon encounter the *gymnasium*, which was central to the operation of the Greek city. The Greek *polis*, or city, was among the most important political institutions in the Hellenistic and Roman worlds. It was the polis, rather than the empire, with which most citizens would identify. In theory, a polis was run by its assembly, which consisted of the entire city's free, citizen, adult male population. In practice, power and decision-making was focused on its magistrates and council (boule). These positions were occupied by the richer strata of society, especially the local aristocracy. The gymnasium was an essential institution for maintenance of this political structure. The sons of free adult men, especially those of some means, would often begin their learning with privately hired tutors (pedagogues). They would receive a primary education with a group of students whose parents each paid a teacher. By the time they were eighteen, they were expected to know basic Greek philosophical, rhetorical, and literary texts, especially Homer. At that point they would enter the gymnasium, newly designated as *ephebes*. Traditionally, the gymnasium was the place to train the ephebes as citizen-soldiers. Although the soldier part of the training eroded with the growth of a more professional army maintained by the Empire, ephebes continued to engage in fitness exercises along with more advanced studies.

Gymnasia were primarily a feature of the Eastern (Greek) Roman cities. Since cities in the West were not organized as Greek *poleis*, there was no place for an institution such as the gymnasium. This is not to say that they received an education much different from their compatriots in the East. They were taught by private tutors, largely outside of civic institutions. They probably learned more Latin, although many would also have wanted a more "classical" Greek education. As in the East, there were vernacular dialects that were learned outside of formal education.[7]

Bathhouses were more widespread than gymnasia throughout the Roman Empire. The Romans, rather than the Greeks, developed a "bathhouse culture" and constructed bathhouses in most cities. Some large Roman villas in the countryside had their own bathhouses. Larger bathhouses could be elaborate affairs. A large bathhouse would have several heated rooms, providing several different kinds of wet and dry heat. A furnace would produce the hot air that circulated under the floors in these rooms. They typically also featured a cold plunge, a swimming pool, and an exercise yard and served as social hubs. We know surprisingly little about gender segregation. Large bathhouses may have had separate wings for men and women, while smaller ones may have had separate gender-specific hours or days. There may also have been mixed-gender bathing. Some sources assert that prostitutes would ply their trade at the bathhouses, although they were more typically located at taverns and brothels. Admittance to bathhouses was often free (funded by the municipality or wealthy donors), although there is evidence that individuals could own their own bathhouses and charge for admission. Given the use of big furnaces and elevated floors under which the hot air passed, smaller and less well-funded bathhouses might also not be the safest places. According to the rabbis, one who enters a bathhouse should pray, "May it be your will, YHWH my god, that you save me from this [place] and those similar to it, and do not let ruin or sin come upon me. But if ruin or sin do come upon me, let my death be an atonement for my sins." Upon leaving safely, a person should say, "I give thanks to you, YHWH, who saved me from the fire."[8]

Cities also had buildings devoted to entertainment. Large cities sometimes had a colosseum, similar to a modern-day stadium. Gladiator fights, other public games, and executions would take place in them. Most cities had an amphitheater, which was used both for theater and other forms of entertainment, as well as civic affairs. Horse and chariot races typically took place in a hippodrome. These structures had an oval track about 1,500–2,000 feet long, and the races would usually involve

FIGURE 1.4. Bathhouse hypocaust, Beit Shean, Israel. Hot air would circulate under the floor. © Michael L. Satlow.

several laps around it. In the Roman world in Late Antiquity (especially in the East), the competitors generally belonged to one of two factions, known as the Blues and Greens. Each faction had somewhat fanatical fans, and competitions sometimes erupted into violence. Such violence was rarely solely about sports; as in modern European football, teams mapped to political and civic issues. Orthodox Christians, for example, supported the Blues against the Miaphysite Christians (those who believed that Christ had a single nature rather than both a divine and human nature), who supported the Greens.[9]

As we wander further from the city center, we find more residential areas. Richer families lived in large villas behind gates. Those who were not as well-off lived in one- or two-story buildings constructed around a courtyard. The apartments were used for sleeping and some other domestic activities. They tended to be dark, with windows small enough to allow for visual privacy and to keep out thieves. Oil lamps, usually molded out of clay, were used with wicks to provide light; if the oil was not pure it would create soot and unpleasant odors. (Most people used

FIGURE 1.5. Clay lamp, Israel. The design might evoke a menorah. Photo by Clara Amit, courtesy of the Israel Antiquities Authority (2011–2338). Used by permission.

cheap, unadorned lamps, which are among the most commonly found objects in archaeological excavations.) Thus, much of life's daily rhythms, such as cooking and eating, took place in the courtyards. Women spun and wove—creating textiles that could be sold in the market—in the courtyard as their children played or helped. The courtyard could contain small shrines, altars, or other symbols of devotion. The gods were never far away.

In fact, the gods were scattered through the entire city. Temples came in a stunning array of styles and sizes. Small stand-alone altars, for impromptu sacrifices of grain and small animals, could also be found throughout the city. Images of the deities, "idols," were everywhere.

The prevalence of these "idols caused not a little head-scratching among Jewish and Christian intellectuals. The Christian bishop Tertullian, writing around 200 CE in Latin in Carthage, notes that there is no getting away from them: "But the streets, the market, the baths, the taverns, even our houses, are none of them altogether clear of idols. The whole world is filled with Satan and his angels." Tertullian sought to

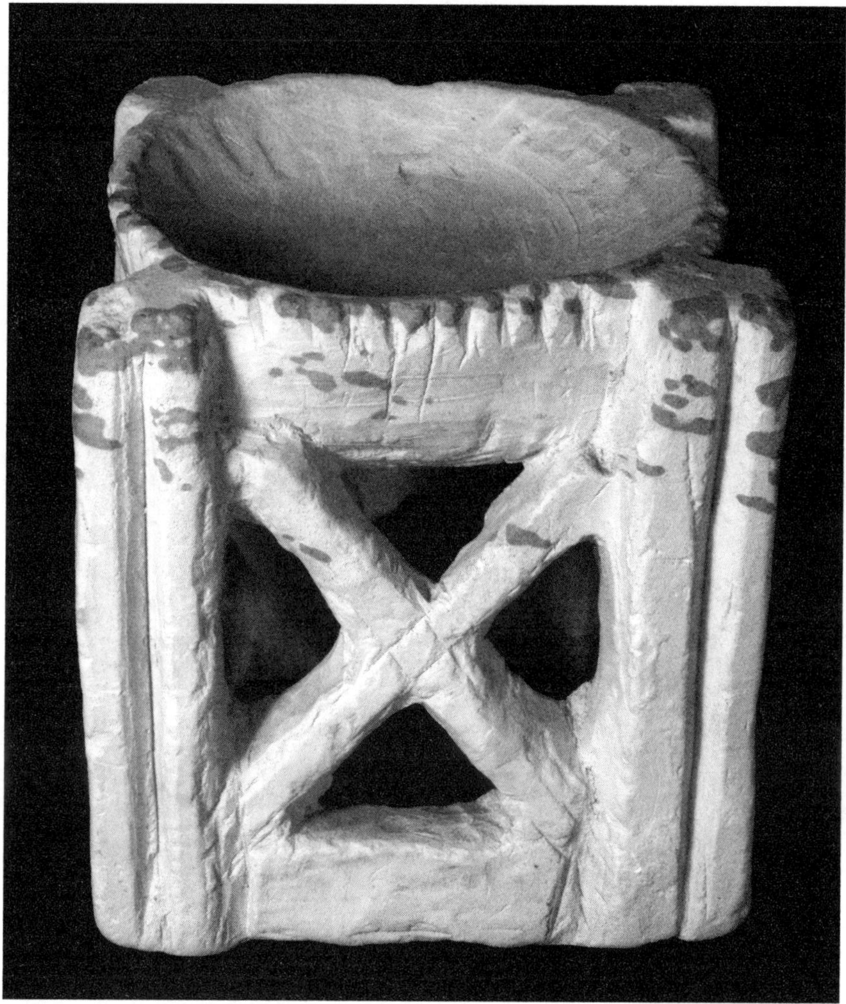

FIGURE 1.6. Altar, Maresha, Israel. The altar is only 13 cm high. Photo by Clara Amit, courtesy of the Israel Antiquities Authority (S-91). Used by permission.

justify how Christians could enter such places. The rabbis engaged in a similar discussion. One strategy that they took was to simply deny that idols were connected to supernatural beings. They were "mere ornamentation," simply decorative objects that did not render a space idolatrous and thereby forbidden. The answers here, though, are less interesting than the question at their root. Jews have long operated in these urban

FIGURE 1.7. Cult figure in niche in shop in Pompeii. Although this dates from the first century CE, such figures were common in ancient cities. © Michael L. Satlow.

spaces. A few may have been uneasy with the statues, but most would likely have ignored them; the rabbis were solving an intellectual problem, not a social one. Most coinage dating from the Hellenistic period onward depicted the traditional gods. The problem may have been more of an issue in Tertullian's Carthage. New Christians, born as Romans who worshipped traditional and indigenous deities, sought to figure out how to live with their new identities in their old worlds.[10]

Even in Late Antiquity, statues, symbols, and images of traditional Greek and Roman gods were more visible than churches and synagogues. Large cathedrals, as in Ravenna and Constantinople, were anomalous. Most indoor Christian worship took place either in private houses and villas or in basilica structures with modest facades. Crosses were scattered in public places, but most obvious and ornate Christian art was placed inside. Synagogues too tended to be basilicas with modest facades. But churches and synagogues had different internal

FIGURE 1.8. Ostia synagogue. Frontal view of the monumental Torah shrine of the "Late Synagogue" (Final Phase, late fifth century CE), extant remains as restored. OSF 02.419, photo by L. M. White. Used by permission, courtesy of L. M. White, UT-OSMAP Excavations.

architectural plans that were distinctive and easily recognizable. Mosaics contained different religious symbols; a Torah niche or ark would occupy a prominent place in a synagogue; and a church would often have a nave, apse, and sometimes a baptistry associated with it.[11]

Processions were common enough that it would not be unusual to run into one. You might encounter a funeral procession, bringing the deceased, wrapped in a shroud, to a cemetery outside of the city, accompanied by mourners reciting dirges. There would be processions on Christian and, at least in some times and places, traditional holy days, of which there were many. Some participants would wave braziers of incense or carry icons, texts, or crosses. Others might follow along with candles, and many would sing prayers. Normally they would end at a holy site.[12]

One space you would not be likely to come across, unless you made the right friends, was a Mithraeum. Often located in caves or under buildings, these places for the worship of Mithras remained secretive. Other gods too were increasingly worshipped out of the public eye as Christian authorities and renegade monks became increasingly bold.

Toward the periphery of the city, you might find a tannery and other industrial facilities. You would not miss the smell. Tanneries, with their abundant use of urine and dung, were so notorious that the rabbis legislated that they be placed downwind of the city and that a wife could demand a divorce from a tanner due to his persistent odor. Tanneries were often located near water facilities, where a variety of other industries that used large amounts of water (e.g., ceramics, dyers) also clustered.[13]

The dead were, ideally, buried outside the city boundaries. There were several types of cemeteries around the cities. Most people were buried simply in unmarked graves. They could be buried in fields set aside for this purpose, or in underground catacombs. Families (not religious communities) were responsible for their own dead. In some communities, Jews tended to be buried with other Jews and Christians with other Christians, but there was surprisingly little regulation or uniformity about burial within such communities. Even in Rome the so-called Jewish catacombs contain many signs of non-Jewish presence and run directly into the complex often called the Christian catacombs (which are themselves hardly uniform). Wealthier families would mark the graves. These markers could be as simple as a painted name in the catacombs or as elaborate as a beautifully carved stone tomb or mausoleum. Such variety could also be found in the rural areas and villas.[14]

FIGURE 1.9. Mithras, born of the rock, wearing a Phrygian cap, found in Rome. The inscription is a dedication to "the mother stone." By permission of the Ministry of Culture—Museo Nazionale Romano (inv. 205827), photo by G. Cargnel, R. D'Agostini, and L. Mandato.

The People

We have little knowledge of the population of the Roman and Sassanian Empires in Late Antiquity. For the Roman Empire, scholars suggest 50–80 million people, but this is a barely informed guess. It is, however, the low density that is striking. Europe today has a population of about 775 million people. In antiquity, the great bulk of the population was concentrated in cities, leaving vast stretches of countryside undeveloped and empty. One would have been able to travel many days in many parts of the Empire, even along the government roads, without seeing a soul.

While the total population density of the Empire was low, in the cities it was remarkably high. For example, Aphrodisias was a walled city in Asia Minor of about 3.5 km^2. Beit Shean, an important city in Roman Palestine, was also walled and contained about 1.6 km^2. Volubilis, the provincial capital of Mauretania Tingitana, was significantly smaller; even the garrison town of Dura Europos was larger, at a bit over 0.5 km^2. By our standards, these are small cities, even when supplemented by the nearby dwellings outside of the city walls. Given our current estimates for the populations of these cities, we arrive at a very rough average of 20,000 people per square kilometer. By way of comparison, my own city, Providence, Rhode Island, has a density of a bit over 4,000 people per square kilometer; Chicago has about 4,500 per square kilometer; Atlanta has 1,400; Milan has 7,500; and Manhattan has 28,000. A typical midsize Late Antique city had a level of activity similar to that of the Upper East Side of Manhattan today.

Upon entering one of these cities, you would first notice slaves. Or perhaps, like most free people in Late Antiquity, you would no longer notice them, despite their ubiquity. The economies of the Roman Empire and its many cities depended on slave labor. Outside of the cities, slaves did most of the agricultural work, and their lives were brutal, miserable, and short. There is a remarkable find in Pompeii of a slave shackled to a wall, unable to flee the toxic gases and volcanic ash. This occurred a bit before Late Antiquity, but we have little reason to doubt that such shackling remained a continuing practice. Urban slaves, except for the prostitutes in the brothels, had it somewhat better. They served aristocratic families in a variety of domestic roles. It seems—but here the evidence is thin—that many families of more modest means (e.g., shopkeepers) also employed a slave or two. Slaves shopped and did domestic household tasks. They may have worn cheaper clothing or had a distinctive look if they were taken captive from a different region, but they otherwise were not visually identifiable as slaves. Some slaves had elevated positions. They would transact business on behalf of their owners or earn extra money for the family as a scribe. Even churches and monasteries owned slaves. It is unclear if they treated them better than average.[15]

Slaves ordinarily did not beg on the streets, which distinguished them from the urban poor. These were the desperate—but free-citizen—day laborers, petty merchants, and prostitutes who lived hand-to-mouth. The plebs were a recognized social class in the Roman Republic, but by Late Antiquity the term had shifted to denote "the masses." In larger cities, many depended on distributions of food and money, financed by the emperor or members of the local aristocracy. Such distributions took place in conjunction with religious festivals or entertainment at the colosseum, amphitheater, or hippodrome. In rural areas, they worked on farms. Many had aristocratic patrons upon whom they depended and to whom they were loyal; in a pinch, these clients served as a security force to defend or advance the interests of the patron. When they died, they were cremated or buried in unmarked graves.

There was then what we would call a "middle class" of merchants, traders, scribes, some military officers, and craftsmen. Many of the simple epitaphs found throughout the Roman Empire were produced by such people. Some landed in this class after they were freed from slavery, while most others followed in their parents' footsteps. They received various degrees of education, as necessary to do their jobs. The "middle" class was hardly middle; it would have been substantially smaller and wealthier than the classes below it. Those who wished to climb socially might seek a gymnasium education, if they could afford to spend those years without earning an income.

In your journey through the city, you were far less likely to see anyone from the aristocracy. There were grades within the aristocracy, but the gulf between them and the "middle" class was vast. At the pinnacle of the social and economic class system was a thin crust of extraordinarily rich men. These men, often senators, inherited great family wealth in the form of land. Whether they lived in or around Rome or Constantinople or in other urban areas, their wealth came from the agricultural goods produced on their vast landholdings, which were scattered throughout the Empire. At any given time, there were under three thousand senators. The emperors regularly gave them additional estates from newly conquered territories. Landowners might then set up villas on their estates. They could also add to their wealth by acquiring the rights to "tax farm" certain areas, a practice whereby they paid a fee to the emperor in return for collecting from the inhabitants whatever taxes would be peacefully tolerated.

The path of one senator is illustrative. Anicius Manlius Severinus Boethius was born into the Anicii family, one of the most storied and wealthy, around 480 CE. He was orphaned when young and adopted by another senator, Quintus Aurelius Memmius Symmachus, who was also extraordinarily rich. Boethius quickly ascended the administrative ranks in the court of Theodoric the Great, the Ostrogothic king from 475 to 526. He served briefly in the position of *magister officiorum* (essentially running Theodoric's kingdom) with his two sons as consuls, before being undercut through court intrigue. He was executed in 524 for treason, although his exact crime is obscure and was quite possibly trumped up. His estate was seized by Theodoric the Great.[16]

Boethius was not just any senator. He wrote works of enduring value. He was a Christian who wrote theological tracts (the church later declared him a martyr), but his real passion was philosophy and other classical subjects, such as logic, music, and mathematics. He knew Greek and translated several classical tracts into Latin. His adopted father, Symmachus, was also an author and, similarly, was executed for treason by Theodoric the Great.

Boethius and Symmachus straddled a line. They were part of the super-elite by virtue of their family, wealth, governmental service, and personal connections to the king. However, they were not only rich aristocrats but also intellectuals. Very few intellectuals emerged from this class. Usually, men in this class spent their time administering affairs of state and increasing their wealth while pursuing more hedonic diversions.

Intellectuals tended to emerge from the next class down. This class, comprising local and provincial nobles and civil and military administrators, was more populous than that of the super-elite but still only a tiny fraction of the total population. Like the super-elite, most of their wealth came through inheritance, agriculture, and what they could get from civil and military administration (including grift). While there was virtually no possibility of movement from this class into that of the super-elite, exceptionally wealthy merchants and traders could find themselves moving up into it. Its members would normally be appointed to the city councils and the magistracies, and they would serve as patrons of those below them. Since there were many local aristocrats, this class was relatively diverse.

One might rub shoulders with or catch a quick glimpse of one of these figures, perhaps on his way to the council building or officiating over a religious ceremony. They were recognizable by their dress, which tended to be more expensive and ornate. They spent most of their time, though, behind closed doors. They socialized and drank not in the local inns and taverns but in their own private villas, attended to by their slaves, who served them wine and imported delicacies. Intellectuals might be more visible in public, but unless they were among the very few who taught public classes, they too would find little reason to go out into the bustle of the city. They had people for that.

We might take this opportunity to peek inside the normally veiled private lives of some of these people. The fundamental political unit in Late Antiquity was the family. The needs and interests of the family—thought of broadly as the clan and its dependents—came before city and empire. We normally see only the upper-crust families in action, making marital alliances and strategic adoptions. Family, though, was the very fabric of society. Further down on the social ladder, family relationships were the only safety net that one had. With most people just a few bad days from utter ruin, having an extended family was vital. A broken leg or flu could otherwise mean the difference between life and death for an entire nuclear family. It was simply expected that the extended family would help its own.

Women and children are, of course, just as much part of the story of Late Antiquity. Yet aside from a few who were either in the very top strata of society or notorious, they are as invisible as the plebs. The tiny shreds of evidence allow only for some broad generalizations. Girls would help around the house with domestic and child-rearing; they rarely received an education. They married in their late teens or early twenties, often to men who were a little older. They settled into a routine of childbearing and child-mourning, with very high infant and child mortality rates. They took care of domestic tasks. In an earlier period, women were associated with the goddess of the hearth (Hestia or Vesta), although by Late Antiquity these goddesses fade away. Unless they were quite affluent, they also might work, either at the loom or selling goods in the market. Most women were not secluded, and they formed friendships with other women. We know of a few truly loving and companionate marriages, all among the upper class, but we do not know how representative they were. Many women died in childbirth, but many also would outlive their husbands. Divorce was available and probably not rare. Remarriage, whether from divorce or widowhood, for both men and women, was relatively common. There was a general preference for marriage within clans (e.g., cousins) to preserve resources.[17]

Did women, children, and slaves develop different kinds of relationships with divine beings? Did they think of them differently? Did they have distinct rituals? I wish that we knew more than we do. Throughout this book we will be attentive to these questions, even if we can rarely offer more than speculative answers.

In each local community, Roman, Greek, Christian, and Jewish families had similar structures. Variations were usually due to class rather than religious identity. Some Christian theological and ideological writing, though, had strong ascetic tendencies that pushed against more common and traditional notions of the family. "If you come to me but will not leave your family, you cannot be my follower," Jesus said (Luke 14:25). Socially, these tendencies led to the development of monastic communities (whose members, nevertheless, sometimes continued to maintain family relationships and even ownership of significant goods). So too they opened space for ascetic "holy" men and women who lived outside of family structures. Such figures, to whom we will return in later chapters, were not exactly new (we see them among earlier Cynics and in Jewish circles), but they did grow to play a more visible social role. Monks, with their separatist and absolute approach, were among the most common instigators of religious violence in Late Antiquity. More often, though, Christian monastics were quite peripheral to the lives of most Christians, not to mention non-Christians.

Returning from your time travel to Late Antiquity, you might reflect on two observations. First, evidence of supernatural beings was everywhere. Most visible may have been the temples and coins, with their ubiquitous representations, but around every corner was an altar, statue of a god, or a small shrine. There were churches and synagogues, mostly discrete but often recognizable. Processions wafting clouds of incense would move around the city, mingled with the smell of sacrificial meat, at least in some cities and at some times. People hawking their expertise as amulet writers and dream interpreters clogged the marketplaces. It would be difficult to walk through the throngs for more than a few minutes without observing an act of communication with the supernatural.

Second, you might be surprised at how difficult it was to distinguish Christians, Jews, and those you might label pagan. They looked and dressed the same, or rather, more accurately, in line with their social stratum. You might assume that the woman offering a dove on a neighborhood altar worshipped a traditional Greek deity, but you would not really be sure. The dream interpreter, astrologer, or amulet maker seemed to be selling to a range of customers, and you might have sworn that the guy who just came out of a church walked into the synagogue down the street. Weren't Jews, Christians, and pagans distinct? Why did these labels seem to matter so little?

Religious identity, as we will see throughout this book, was not irrelevant for the ways in which people interacted with invisible beings, each other, and their neighbors. Nor, though, was it always important. Religious identity was contextual, subjective, and could be worn or discarded strategically, much to the chagrin of rabbis, bishops, and others who sought to build new walls. Before turning in the next chapter to the issue of identity (religious and otherwise) and its relationship to the divine world, though, it is worth simply pausing to consider—to imagine—a world in which those walls were far more porous than we usually think.

2

Religion and Identity in Late Antiquity

WE WILL never know how many synagogues Christians destroyed in Late Antiquity, but it was certainly more than a few. A letter from a bishop of Minorca, a small island to the southeast of Barcelona, describes how in 418 CE a crowd of Christians surrounded the local synagogue, only for it to mysteriously burst into flames. The entire Jewish population of the island, the bishop recounts, became Christians soon after. Hundreds of miles away in southern France, about 150 years after the events in Minorca, another synagogue was razed by Christians, "to the foundations." The Jews converted, with the few recalcitrant stragglers leaving town. Synagogue destructions were common enough that imperial laws were passed that explicitly forbade their destruction. At the same time, the Jews were not always easily cowed. Jews did occasionally rise violently against Christians.[1]

Christians attacked Roman and Greek temples as well. Christian historians gleefully report how Christian mobs, often led by monks, destroyed "pagan" temples. Scholars today think that the Christian authors greatly exaggerate the scale of these attacks, but they did happen, and they had an impact. Although they too were coming under increasing legal pressure in the fifth and sixth centuries, these "pagans" also sometimes fought back.[2]

The focus of this book is on individuals and their experiences negotiating their relationships with the divine realm, not on religious groups

FIGURE 2.1. Epitaph of Licinia Amias, from Rome in the second to third centuries CE. Contains both the traditional notation "D M" and the Christian fish. By permission of the Ministry of Culture—Museo Nazionale Romano (inv. 67646), photo by G. Cargnel and R. D'Agostini.

and their institutions. But it would be misleading to suggest that there were no groups, or that group identity itself did not play a role in lived experience. Group identities could be powerful, and they could sometimes be mobilized for good or for ill. Both rabbis and bishops were struggling during this period to form the borders of their communities: What exactly does it mean to be a Christian or a Jew? What does it mean to be the right kind of Christian or Jew? When, exactly, did group identities matter, and when did they fade into the background?

This chapter departs from the frequent assumption that in Late Antiquity there were three stable religious identities: Jewish, Christian, and pagan. In fact, I want to question our very understanding of "identity." "Identity" was, and still is, rarely stable or objective. Think of your own multiple identities. Some are more relevant than others at certain times. A "woman," for example, is often not one when it comes to legal proceedings in which gender is irrelevant. In another context, somebody might label me as "White" when I hold no such identity. Identity as a category is deeply malleable, and its application is deeply subjective. Identities are intrinsically unstable, and yet they are important to the ways in which we see ourselves and others see us.

This chapter will consider how people in Late Antiquity experienced group identity. We will look at the different modes through which identity was created and how these may have been experienced on the ground. One of the fundamental questions underlying this chapter is that of transregional identity. To what extent, for example, did a Jew in North Africa feel a relationship with a Jew from Palestine or Asia Minor? Would a Christian from Rome be welcome in the Christian community in Persia? Did worshippers of Isis feel a bond, even when they were from very different places and ethnic groups? To get at these questions, I will focus on the major overarching strategies through which group identities were formed in Late Antiquity. Religion, we will see, was not in and of itself a very important basis on which to organize a group. Ethnicity, though, was. In addition to ethnicity, the law created group identities. Being a "Jew," for example, was sometimes a legal determination, although that determination and its ramifications differed substantially in different legal regimes. Finally, whereas ethnicity and legal identities were (at least in theory) outside of individual hands, voluntary associations offered a way in which individuals could declare their own identities.

Ethnicity

Not long ago, a vigorous scholarly debate erupted over how one should translate the Greek word *ioudaios*. Steve Mason, a historian whose research focuses mainly on the Jewish historian Josephus who lived in the first and second centuries CE, argued in an influential article that, against the prevailing custom of translating *ioudaios* as "Jew," it should instead be translated as "Judean," at least when it appears in texts up to around 300 CE. Scholars weighed in on both sides of the debate, often with a kind of outrage that felt out of place for what seemed to be a philological disagreement.[3]

The argument, of course, was never really about a word. It was, rather, a deeper conceptual issue of whether *ioudaioi* (plural, masculine form) are best seen as members of a "religious" community ("Jews") or as a purely ethnic group ("Judean," those from the Roman province of Judea). Mason argued that since there was no category of "religion" in antiquity, it is misleading to identify ioudaioi as "Jews," which to us has religious connotations. Ethnicity, though, was a recognized category of identity in antiquity, and when people—ioudaioi and non-ioudaioi alike—thought of ioudaioi, they thought only of an ethnic group. Although most scholars agree that ethnicity was always a fundamental part of what it meant to be a ioudaios in antiquity, several have argued that the erasure of "Jews" from antiquity would have unwelcome consequences in modern discourse.[4]

Mason's conceptual point is sound, although I continue in this book to use the term "Jews." Many people in antiquity organized themselves and others into ethnicities; ethnic labeling happened from the inside as well as the outside. Ethnic identity was often a primary, even the primary, identity for many. Primarily based on a location (or location of perceived origin), ethnicity dragged along with it many other kinds of associations and expectations, many of which are lost to us today. Generally, Roman writings on Jews tended to stereotype them as hostile to outsiders, worshippers of YHWH, avoiders of pork, circumcisers, and practitioners of strange customs on Sabbaths and their holidays. Individual Jews or Jewish communities may or may not have done any number of these things. For our purposes, what is important is that being labeled a Jew was an identity, whereas being labeled a "worshipper of YHWH" was not, except to the extent that it brought with it identification as an ethnic Jew (or a Samaritan!).[5]

Modern scholars have long noted that ethnic identities are hardly straightforward or objective; they are constantly changing, contextual, perspectival, and malleable. The little evidence that we have concerning Jews in antiquity certainly falls in line with this observation. In much of

FIGURE 2.2. Glass pendant of an impressed menorah, perhaps an amulet. From Ma'alot Tarshiha. Photo by Clara Amit, courtesy of the Israel Antiquities Authority (1931–286/2). Used by permission.

the Roman Empire, Jews could easily be unrecognizable, free to present themselves as they wanted (within the constraints, of course, of what was known about them). Even within tighter Jewish contexts, issues of ethnic identity were at play. For example, when a Jew sometime between the third and fifth centuries (or those who commissioned the epitaph) proudly declares on his gravestone in Beit Shearim, a Jewish cemetery in Galilee, "Isaac, son of Sassos, from Arabia," in Greek, followed by the month in Hebrew and then his profession, "perfume dealer," again in Greek, what is he really trying to convey? Although he never says that he is "Jewish," based on his name, the location of the grave, and the use of Hebrew, we would clearly consider him so. This supposition would lead us to assume that he lived among Jews, worshipped YHWH, avoided certain nonkosher foods, and observed the Sabbath and other Jewish holidays. Why, though, is he explicitly marked as "Arabian," which, in addition to perhaps being an objective marker of his place of origin, would also have brought a different set of expectations? Similarly, we find that in the so-called Jewish catacombs of Rome (where there is clearly a large concentration of Jewish burials, but where non-Jews appear to have been buried as well), the deceased are rarely explicitly called "Jews," although they do often note communities founded around places of origin. One man, for example, is called, in Greek, the "archon of the synagogue of the Siburesians." The inscriptions testify to several such communities or "synagogues" in Rome, most of them obscure (we do not know who the Siburesians were). Would this person have understood himself as a "Jew" or a "Siburesian"? How would other Jews have regarded him? How about Romans?[6]

There are two added complications in our assessment of how Jews may have experienced their own ethnic identity in Late Antiquity. First, they almost never call themselves "Jews" (ioudaioi/ai, or in Hebrew, *yehudim*). In the Roman catacombs, despite many epitaphs with Jewish symbols (e.g., shofar, menorah), only one calls himself a ioudaios. A few call themselves "Hebrews." Rabbinic literature overwhelmingly refers to their people using "Israel" or "children of Israel," terms that appear very infrequently outside of that literature. Second, although the rabbis explicitly state that proselytes are "like Israel in all respects," several people in predominantly Jewish gravesites across the Empire are explicitly labeled as "proselytes." Are "proselytes," *ioudaioi*, "Hebrews," and "Israel" merely meaningless terminological markers for exactly the same thing? And were any of these identities, whether self-applied or given by outsiders, coterminus with exclusive worship of YHWH?[7]

The question itself is ultimately unanswerable, but I want to suggest that it be framed within a larger context. Jews were but one ethnic group in a very large and ethnically diverse Empire. These ethnic identities, in all of their messy subjectivity and lack of legal significance, were alive and well. Places of origin routinely appear on papyri from Egypt, partly to secure identification of the relevant parties (whose scars and other distinguishing features were noted) but also sometimes suggesting a deeper identity. Greek-speaking peoples (or their descendants) from the same place who found themselves far from home formed communities outside of any legal meaning. They socialized together (perhaps speaking their native dialects), maybe ate ancestral foods (grandma's recipes), and worshipped similar ancestral gods. They would also have attended the worship celebrations of the imperial and city gods—particularly when they were assured a free meal—but they really appealed to the deities with whom they, and their ancestors, were most familiar. Somebody may have had a small wooden cult statue, but they did not need a formal organization or building. Their ancestral deities were part of their identity, but their worship was simply a component of their ethnic identity.[8]

Writing in the first century BCE in defense of a client accused of misappropriating funds from the Jerusalem Temple, the Roman statesman Cicero said in respect to the Jews, "each polity, Laelius, has its own *religio*, and we have ours." *Religio* here is best translated as "sacred rites," or divinities and customary modes of worshipping them. Cicero's point about polities (*civitati*), which references the public and civic worship of deities, might well be extended to ethnicities as well. Ethnic groups were expected to have their own sacred rites for their own gods, and worship of them was uncontroversial as long as it was kept private. This approach extended even to the fringe of the Roman Empire. The so-called barbarian groups like the Franks, Saxons, and Goths were constantly rearranging their own notions of ethnicity in order to address rapidly changing political circumstances. This process of "ethnogenesis," as scholars call it, naturally involved the gods. Arian Christianity—the doctrine that Christ is of a separate substance and subordinate to the Father, which orthodox Christians labeled heretical—became favored in many barbarian circles. Yet with a few exceptions, the Franks and Saxons did not persecute orthodox Christians. People were free to worship, in private, as they wanted.[9]

Some four hundred years after Cicero, the Emperor Julian echoed the same sentiment, also in respect to the Jews, who by this time could no longer be considered a polity: "I wish to show that the Jews agree with the Gentiles (*ethnesin*), except that they believe in only one God. That is indeed peculiar to them and strange to us; since all the rest we have in a manner in common with them—temples, sanctuaries, altars, purifications and certain precepts. For as to these we differ from one another either not at all or in trivial ways."[10] The passage is polemical, and Julian—who would garner the nickname "the Apostate" from the church—was intent on using the example of the Jews to demonstrate the singularity (not in a good way) of the Christians. Nevertheless, despite the hyperbole and perhaps even his misrepresentation of contemporary Jewish practices (it is not impossible that Jews continued to have altars and made sacrifices, but not at all certain either), his primary point is that Jews are an ethnic group much like any other.[11]

Christians, though, were not, at least not for the purposes of this polemic. Indeed, Julian draws on a long Christian discourse that wrestles with self-identity: What exactly is a "Christian" in a world where ethnic identity is primary? Christian intellectuals struggled with this question. Building on one strain of thought in the New Testament, some writers sought a universal, trans-ethnic meaning to Christian identity; this is the one that is perhaps most familiar to us today. That is, Christian identity is in some essential sense different from ethnicity and race and can be overlaid on top of any ethnicity. According to this logic, a Roman can be a Christian, a Carthaginian can be a Christian, a Thracian can be a Christian, and a Judean can be a Christian. It is especially this last example that should give pause. Can a Judean/Jew really be a Christian? In fact, is Christianity really a universal identity distinct from ethnicity?

The truth is that even Christian intellectuals could not break the hold of what Denise Buell, a scholar of Christianity, terms "ethnic reasoning." Many saw Christianity as an identity that did not supplement ethnicity but was an ethnicity in its own right. Twisting the logic of ethnicity almost to its breaking point, some Christians posited that there were three ethnicities in the world: Jewish, Christian, and Greek. Almost no one in antiquity would have thought this was true, although most would have recognized the language and logic. Christians needed to be *something*, and an ethnic group made at least some kind of sense. Such a construction of identity was rhetorically useful in imagining a single united and universal Christian identity, but for most other real-world purposes, it was less so. One anonymous letter probably written around 200 CE, for example, argues that Christians are very much like everybody else, living in their distinct ethnic communities, but that what unites them is their common "citizenship" in heaven. The purpose of such a claim was apologetic. "Christian" identity is private and not in competition with other, more important, identities.[12]

It is difficult to pin down how ordinary Christians understood their own identities, especially specifically as Christians. One might think that in the fifth century, with the increasing power of orthodox Christian bishops in the Byzantine imperial court, a sense of a more united Christian identity would begin to emerge. The limited evidence that we have, though, does not exactly support this. Augustine repeatedly complained that the Christians in North Africa were putting local allegiances—by which he meant some amalgam of civic and ethnic considerations—ahead of their Christian identity. Theological struggles among Christians were connected in complex ways to local ethnic and civic identities. Local communities that already had or were creating an ethnic identity could distinguish themselves by adopting distinct theological positions, as the Goths did with Arianism. In inscriptions, Christians in Asia Minor continue to make note of their civic and ethnic identities throughout Late Antiquity.[13]

Then there were the Christians in the eastern fringe of the Roman Empire and beyond, in the Persian Empire. To outsiders, those who lived in Aramaic-speaking regions of the Near East (except for Jews and sometimes Samaritans) were "Syrian," which was understood as an ethnicity. This seems to have been true even for the Christians of the region, whose churches showed an affinity for the Greek language. The evidence is sparse, but it is plausible that, at least until the fifth century, most Christians would have had some kind of city or "Syrian" identity, which they shared with non-Christians. Beginning in the fourth or fifth century, Christian intellectuals in Edessa increasingly used a local dialect of Aramaic, which developed into Syriac. Within Christian literature, from this point there developed an increasingly robust Syriac Christian identity that included positing a shared ancestor—the biblical Shem—for all Syrians. Here we can see ethnogenesis in operation: local Christians created a Syrian ethnic identity from a Christian perspective that could include both Christians and non-Christians. A Syrian ethnic identity was now rooted in language, a shared ancestor, and a divinity. Many Aramaic-speaking Christians subscribed to such an ethnic identity; there were diverse ways in which people—Christians or not—could adapt and present as "Syrian"[14]

The situation with Christians who lived in the Persian Empire was cleaner. The Church Father Eusebius reports that Constantine sent a letter to Shapur, the king of Persia, asking him to safeguard the community of "Christians." The authenticity of this letter is debated, but even if it is authentic, it is unclear if Shapur would have understood it to denote a "religious" community. Many Christians (or their ancestors) in Persia originally came from the Roman Empire, often as captives. To Persians, their Christianity was much beside the point; they were simply ethnic Romans. As such—and rarely as Christians—they were occasionally persecuted, as Persia was often at war with Rome. The Persians distinguished this ethnic Roman group from the ethnic Jewish group, most of whom had long roots in the region. While scholars used to think that Persians distinguished such communities on the basis of "religion," it is now clearer that ethnicity played a more important role.[15]

Ethnic identity, then, was perhaps the most important organizing principle in antiquity, even (paradoxically) when it was explicitly rejected, as some Christian writers tried to do. Ethnicity was tightly wound with the expectations of worship of particular deities. Hence, when an ethnic Roman whose family and friends considered them Roman worshipped YHWH—which we know occasionally, if rarely, happened—they would be looked upon as odd, if not vaguely threatening. Romans and Jews who began to worship Christ were in many respects not considered "Christians"; they were Romans and Jews who worshipped Christ. Identity was usually in the eye of the beholder.

The Law

Identity, though, could not always be subjective. It could also be a matter for the law, in which case it needed objective markers. Today, in most Western countries, religious identity is not a legal category. The fact, for example, that I am a Jew is legally meaningless to the federal government of the United States (although, oddly, it is recognized in the state of Rhode Island, where such an identity permits me to marry my niece). Between Late Antiquity and the eighteenth century, however, religion was an important legal category, and different religious identities were regulated by law and came with differing rights. The development of this way of thinking largely emerged during Late Antiquity and was very much in flux during that entire period.[16]

Prior to the first century CE, most legal discrimination (good and bad) occurred on the level of ethnicity and was focused on particular and identifiable regions. In 167 BCE, for example, the Seleucid king Antiochus IV punished the Judeans for revolting. His decrees, whether specifically directed at Jewish ritual practices or not (scholars debate this point), were directed at Judeans in Judea, not those who worshipped YHWH outside of Judea. It was common for rulers to communally punish revolting subjects, which necessarily involved giving them a legal identity. This identity, however, was ethnic rather than religious.[17]

It was the destruction of the Jerusalem Temple in 70 CE, however, that led to a shift in thinking. After the destruction of the Temple, Vespasian levied a tax on all Judeans. The structure of this tax, at least in theory, should have resulted in no net financial loss for individuals. When the Temple stood, all Jews, wherever they lived, were expected to make an annual contribution to the Temple. We have little information about the nature of this expectation, though, and the level of compliance and local enforcement by individual Jewish communities. Vespasian shifted the payee of this tax. Instead of going to the Temple, it would now go to the Roman treasury. The Romans established a special government office to ensure its collection. There are surviving receipts from individual Jews in Egypt and evidence that payment lasted at least into the third century.[18]

Such a tax raised a fundamental issue of identity: Who had to pay it? The law now had to identify "Judeans," whether they lived in Judea or abroad. For the most part, the legal answer to this question was that anybody who publicly worshipped as a Jew was legally identified as one and thus was liable to pay the tax. In return, these self-identified Jews were permitted to practice their rites unhindered. Thus, the Roman historian Cassius Dio, writing toward the end of the second century, could state that while the term *ioudaioi* was applied to the residents of Judea, "it applies also to all the rest of mankind, although of different ethnicities, who affect their customs. This race exists even among the Romans." The exception occurred during the reign of Domitian (r. 81–96), who, we are told, was so desperate for income that he enforced collection also from those Jews purely on the basis of ethnicity. The next emperor, Nerva, quickly went back to the old policy.[19]

The effects of this emerging legal definition may have had far-reaching effects. Proselytes, those Romans who abandoned the traditional gods to worship YHWH, were now given legal protection in exchange for paying the tax. While proselytes do not appear as an official category in Roman legal texts from before the fourth century (presumably, a proselyte would officially be a "Jew"), epitaphs and literary references to them abound. Although still relatively few, these proselytes could now be accommodated legally, at least from a Roman perspective.

A second ramification of the Roman attempt to legally define who was a Jew was perhaps a rabbinic attempt to do the same. Prior to the first century, Jews showed little interest in legally defining their identity. It would have been rather obvious if you belonged to the *ethnos* of the Jews. The few exceptional cases were of little practical consequence. The rabbis began to change this, offering both a legal (and ethnically based) definition of Jewish identity—one needs a Jewish mother—and a conversion procedure through which non-Jews could take on Jewish identity. Both may well have been reactions to this Roman legalization of identity.[20]

Yet another ramification may have been the Roman recognition of the Jewish patriarchate. While it is possible that some form of this position existed prior to this time, the Romans gave it official status. Its first holder was Rabbi Judah, a man who was almost certainly more notable in Roman eyes for his rich and noble background than for his rabbinic title. At least in theory, the patriarch exercised some authority over all Jews in the Roman Empire, although the nature of that authority remains murky. A Jewish communal inscription in Asia Minor mentions the office, and both rabbinic and Roman legal sources suggest that Jews from all over the Roman Empire sent funds to the patriarch in Galilee. We do not know if this money was instead of or in addition to the *fiscus Judaicus*, whether there were any enforcement mechanisms for its collection, how many people sent how much, or what it was used for. For Jews to have a connection like this to the patriarchate, though, required some kind of formal understanding of what a "Jew" was.[21]

As Christians increasingly took and asserted legal power in the Empire, they also needed legal definitions of Jewish personhood. After all, a growing number of imperial laws applied to Jews. These laws mostly governed Christian-Jewish relationships and were largely predictable; they sought to lessen Jewish influence and power over Christians. Legislation prohibited marriages between Jews and Christians and the Jewish ownership of Christian slaves. Jews could not convert Christians. Following traditional Roman practice, the law protected Jews from violence. Synagogue destruction remained criminalized, though these laws were not always enforced.[22]

As with the payment of the fiscus Judaicus, Jews had to be legally defined. Yet it is precisely at this point that the legislation becomes vague. Jews are sometimes categorized as part of a *religio*, but as time goes on and into the fifth century, they become part of a *superstitio* or *secta*, terms that are also used by groups disliked by orthodox Christians, such as heretics. We do not know how Roman authorities identified individual Jews in order to apply the law to them. Some cases would have been relatively easy. If, for example, a man who observed Jewish customs, had Jewish parents, and lived among Jews married a Christian, we would expect that if someone (such as the woman's father) brought a legal action against him, the groom would lose. A Jew by birth, though, who did not openly follow Jewish customs would be a more difficult case: Was he really a member of the Jewish superstitio? It is possible that there was an overlap with the financial issues discussed earlier. If a person paid the fiscus Judaicus and/or sent money to the patriarch, perhaps that could have been taken as evidence of Jewish identity in the eyes of the law. One law from 392 CE gives the exclusive right to expel a Jewish member from the superstitio or religio (the law uses both terms!) to the patriarchs and their appointees. By extension, we might expect that the patriarchate also maintained the ability to determine who belonged.[23]

Legal issues around "religious" identity also had an impact on and shaped Christians. In 249 CE, the Roman emperor Decius issued a decree mandating that everyone (except Jews, who traditionally had been excused from such acts due to the antiquity of their customs) sacrifice to the gods and taste the sacrificial meat. Procedurally, they were to bring a written document (probably in duplicate) to the sacrifice, attesting that they had sacrificed, as they always had. A magistrate would administer an oath and certify the document. These documents, known as petitions or *libelli*, are found throughout the Empire. One of these petitions, for example, reads as follows:

> *1st Hand.* To the commission of the village of Alexandru Nesus, chosen to superintend the sacrifices. From Aurelius Diogenes, son of Satabous, of the village of Alexandru Nesus, aged 72 years, with a scar on the right eyebrow. I have always and without interruption sacrificed to the gods, and now in your presence in accordance with the edict's decree I have made sacrifice, and poured a libation, and partaken of the sacred victims. I request you to certify this below. Farewell. I, Aurelius Diogenes, have presented this petition.
>
> *2d Hand.* I, Aurelius Syrus, saw you and your son sacrificing.
>
> *3d Hand.* . . . onos . . .
>
> *1st Hand.* The year one of the Emperor Caesar Gaius Messius Quintus Trajanus Decius Pius Felix Augustus, Epeiph 9 (June 26, 250).[24]

Refusal to obtain such documents could lead to punishment or death. The decree of Decius marks a move toward extending a cultic Roman identity (tied to sacrifice) into the realm of local cultic practice.

Succeeding emperors over the next fifty years must have thought it did a good job doing so, as they continued it. A reinforcing edict that everyone in the Empire was to sacrifice and offer libations "to the idols" was promulgated around 305 CE. It would be repealed only decades later.[25]

It is unclear whether Decius primarily targeted the Christians with this law, although it clearly had a major impact on them. Many Christians purchased forged documentation, causing significant controversy among the bishops. Others sacrificed. A small number of Christians refused and were killed by the Romans; in Christian eyes, they suffered martyrdom. The net effect, however, was to create a legal community: non-Jews who do not sacrifice. Like any persecution, the Decian (and later Diocletian) edicts helped to accelerate group cohesion. Individual worshippers of Christ, whatever their feelings of adherence to a group, now found themselves in the same Roman legal category.[26]

Curiously, even well into the fourth century, as imperial legislation was beginning to draw boundaries between Jews, Christians, and those devoted to the traditional cults, in nearly all contexts the law left Christian identity as fuzzy as Jewish identity. A Jew should not marry a Christian, but there was no legal definition of what it meant to be a Christian. Presumably, this was because being a Christian was seen as a social rather than legal fact, albeit one with legal consequences. Determination of one's Christian identity would be left to the magistrate, who would have used conventional subjective markers, such as whether the individual participated in Christian rituals. One imperial law concerned the case of a Jew who, having a debt, seek to become a Christian in order to escape from it. What it meant to become a Christian in this context is left unstated.[27]

The single context in which the Roman legal codes were very interested in Christian identity was in intra-Christian definition. An entire book, out of sixteen, of the first major Roman law code, the *Codex Theodosianus*, is devoted to clarifying the relationships of religious communities to each other and the state. A great deal of this legislation involves "heretics," thus creating a need to differentiate proper from improper Christians in legal terms. "Catholic Christians" are defined as all those who believe in Christian doctrine as articulated and ordered by a single episcopal bureaucracy. This and similar laws bring into legal existence a Catholic Church as well as other Christian groups, now branded as heretical. For example, there were Christians who believed, following the theory of a man named Montanus, that prophecy was ongoing and could be experienced by women as well as men. A law from 415 CE forbade "Montanists" from meeting or ordaining clerics. Many may not have even known that they were "Montanists" until this law called them something other than "Christian."[28]

The larger point is that the law is not a simple descriptor of group boundaries. It actively creates them. In practice, this was messy. Creating a legal identity, on paper, does little for individual self-identities. Throughout Late Antiquity, imperial laws were applied inconsistently. Most actual legal actions were brought by individuals, not ruling authorities, and both Roman governors and then the magistrates that would adjudicate these cases had a great deal of discretion. Some governors, for example, took the Decian decree more seriously than others. Those magistrates who executed more Christians would have created more group cohesion among those who worshipped in secret. The need for Jews to remit taxes to either the Romans or the Jewish patriarch would similarly have reinforced some level of communal solidarity (perhaps around a common grievance), although undoubtedly to a lesser extent. In locales where Catholic bishops held power, imperial governors would most likely apply more pressure to those groups and individuals identifying with various "heresies" and thus bring more internal cohesion and stronger individual identities to their members. In every community, the application of the laws and the identities that they created or reinforced differed.

Voluntary Association

The modes of identity surveyed above were largely, from the perspective of the individual, involuntary. Ethnicity was conferred mostly by descent. The law sometimes used other criteria for assigning people to groups. While these identities were largely outside of one's control, an individual did have some control over other forms of identity, which could be public or private and formal or informal. As an example of a private, informal identity, one could be an ethnic Jew who privately worships Christ, even while appearing as a Jew to all others. At the other end of the spectrum, one could join a voluntary association, pay its dues, abide by its bylaws, and attend its regular devotional gatherings. Between these two extremes were as many possible ways to establish a voluntary identity around one's choice of deities as there were people. The formal associations are relatively well-documented and much easier to describe.

Throughout both the Greek and Roman worlds, there were many formal voluntary associations. These functioned much like nongovernmental or nonprofit organizations, although they did not register with the government or enjoy official privileges. There was a formal method for joining the group and often mandatory payment of dues. Membership lists were kept, and members were sometimes expected to abide by bylaws. The kinds of associations ranged widely. In 426 CE, for example, a group of bankers in Egypt created an organization that collected guild taxes. Its members swore an oath to respect the group's leaders and come to each other's aid when called upon. An association of worshippers of Dionysus set up a memorial around 250–300 CE to a member in Bithynia (a region near the Black Sea). An association of ironsmiths recorded their sacrifice of a donkey to "the great god," who is otherwise unidentified. In Macedonia in the second to third century CE, an inscription was made over a picture of the goddess Nike, reading, "Marcus Velleius Zosimos, priest of the unconquerable Nemesis, on behalf of the association of gladiators, has made the reliefs of the gods at his own expense."[29]

Not all voluntary associations were configured around the worship of deities, but the ones that were offer a window into how people thought about identities that we might call "religious." Probably the association about which we know the most in terms of logistical details are the Mithraists. Although Mithras was technically a Persian god, the spread of the cultic worship of Mithras appeared to have begun in Rome and Ostia around the first century CE and, by its demise in the fifth century CE, had spread throughout the Roman Empire. Nearly all of what we know about the theology and beliefs of Mithraists derives from archaeological rather than literary remains and is largely speculative. The mythic narrative of Mithras slaying a bull in a cave, with the bull's blood nourishing the earth, was central to the cult. Meetings and rituals would take place in a special Mithraeum, usually located in a cave or a room designed to look like a cave. Their rituals are obscure but would certainly have involved meals, perhaps of sacrifices that they had made.[30]

Initiation was required to join the cult. The process of becoming a full member involved a combination of learning the Mithraic secrets with ritual activities that, on some level, were meant to induce an ecstatic experience. Joining a Mithraic community—which was open only to men—thus required some dedication. Because the cult was relatively private (it never had a public temple or official recognition) but was also never prohibited, initiates probably found it through acquaintances and friends. The cult was most appealing to the sub-elite, although among this group we find both freemen and slaves, soldiers and ordinary citizens. Joining the cult, however, did not seem to eliminate social and class hierarchies, which were replicated in the internal organization of the cult. As one scholar put it, "It was not a religion for failures, the disaffected, social outsiders or the unworldly."[31]

I have been using the term "cult" loosely. Some factors unified different communities of Mithraists. Most visibly, Mithraeums were relatively uniform throughout the Empire. Members most likely shared a similar myth and had similar initiation experiences. Yet there is little evidence for any organization of these individual communities. Would a Mithraist traveling from Rome to Strasbourg or Dura Europos seek out the local Mithraeum? Would he be welcomed? It is not unlikely (although speculative) that he would be, despite the lack of any overarching transregional authority.

To be a Mithraist was thus like being a member of most other voluntary associations. Despite requiring an initiation, it was not an exclusive identity. In their public life, Mithraists also showed proper (and sincere) devotion to other deities. Although most of their ritual activity was shielded from public view, there was nothing awkward or shameful about being identified as a devotee. In that sense, it is difficult to shoehorn the experience of being a devotee of Mithras into the modern conception of "identity."[32]

Yet another group that raises critical questions about "religious identity" is that of the worshippers of "the most high god" (Theos Hypsistos, in Greek). There are about four hundred inscriptions, from the first century BCE to the fourth century CE, that attest to this deity. Some are attached to buildings and altars, which suggests a cult. Aside from these facts, though, scholars debate nearly every aspect of this cult. Do we see in this worship of "the most high god" a kind of "pagan monotheism," or simply normal hyperbolic language also used to laud other Greek gods? If the former, then we might expect its devotees to have an identity like those of Mithraists, although we do not know whether they would have put more emphasis on exclusive worship of this god. Nor do we have any evidence of individuals identifying themselves as "Hypsistosians" or the like, in the same way that devotees of Mithras do not have an independent term of identity. We can identify individuals as devotees only through their dedications to the god.[33]

These complicated cases of religious identity provide a lens through which to also see both Jewish and Christian identity in Late Antiquity. Jews, as we have already seen, established their identity mainly within the framework of ethnicity, complicated by imperial law. But what about those who wished to "join" the Jews, whether on a social and communal level or, in a more limited sense, as adherents of YHWH? Such people often had other ethnic identities and could not easily see themselves as being part of the Jewish ethnos. There thus arose throughout antiquity many confusing "degrees" by which nonethnic Jews could affiliate with the Jewish community and their god. The term "God-fearers" began to appear in the first century CE but continued throughout antiquity and most probably refers to those who quasi-informally identified with the Jewish community. It is unlikely that there was any kind of formal initiation to become a God-fearer, although in one case a monetary donation was necessary to make it onto a donor list.[34]

What, though, did it really mean to "join" a, or the, Jewish community? Many, I suggest, would have seen it as analogous to joining any other voluntary association. There was no single model of organization for local Jewish communities in Late Antiquity. Some may have had a semi-autonomous and formal legal structure, while others, even within a single city, would consist of small "synagogues" (communities that may or may not have also been physical structures). We can be relatively certain that a man joining any of these communities would need to be circumcised. Otherwise, though, communities would largely have determined their own acts of initiation. The rabbis, aware of the variety of different initiation rites in different local Jewish communities, sought to create a standard conversion procedure that included an educational component and ritual immersion in addition to male circumcision. In a sense, they attempted to transform the act of associating with a local Jewish community into an act of becoming part of the Jewish ethnos. Yet, while some rabbis were declaring that a convert is "like an Israelite in all ways," others (or perhaps even the same ones) were developing intermediate positions that did not fully accept them as part of the ethnos.[35]

A trace of how this was playing out on the ground can be found in the relatively small but significant group of inscriptions referring to proselytes. We have found about thirty inscriptions scattered through the Roman world, mostly epitaphs and dating from the first century CE onward, that explicitly identify individuals (in Greek, Latin, and Hebrew) as proselytes. We are uncertain about what this really meant. Do they reflect the judgment of the Jews who controlled the burial site that the deceased was not exactly "one of us"? Or is it a proud declaration of the deceased or his or her family? Scholars tend toward the latter explanation (as do I), but the question remains unsettled.[36]

When it comes to Christians, the issue of identity is particularly interesting, especially given the dramatic shift in their status in the fourth century CE. In the first centuries of the era, Christian identity primarily meant joining a local Christian community. As with non-Jews joining a Jewish community, they saw this principally in terms of joining a voluntary association. As we have already seen, though, Christians had begun to create a sense of identity based on ethnic reasoning, a process that undoubtedly was accelerated by their persecution and identity under Roman law. There was, apparently, a social element to this identity. In

FIGURE 2.3. Epitaph of proselyte from Rome (Via Nomentana). "Irene, foster child (?), proselyte, of a father and mother, Judaean, Israelite. She lived three years, seven months, and one day." Public domain, CC BY-NC-SA 4.0, https://www.judaism-and-rome.org/epitaph-jewish-proselyte-child-cij-i-21.

the early third century, a Christian in Asia Minor, Abercius, noted on his epitaph that during his long trip to and from Rome (initiated by, it seems, a vision), "I found kindred everywhere," using the language of ethnicity.[37]

Abercius never explicitly identified himself either as a Christian or as a bishop, although other sources suggest that he was both. His inscription raises two critical questions. First, was his ability to find "brotherly" hospitality related to his post as bishop, or could any Christian expect to find that? Second, what did it really mean to be a church official in the third century? That is, was a bishop a local post or did it somehow fit into a larger hierarchical organization? While our sources give us no purchase on the first question, the second one directly relates to that of whether there was a transregional institutional hierarchy that strengthened a sense of Christian identity. The answer seems to be negative. In the third century there was beginning to emerge, in some cities, an institutional hierarchy that sought to bring together local churches under a common leadership. Its effectiveness largely depended on the wealth, status, and charisma of the local bishop. For the most part, bishops and other local communal leaders did not have formal contact with their peers until the fourth century.[38]

In the fourth century, though, everything changed when it came to Christian identity. Christ, embodied in the emerging notion of the Trinity, became not only a state divinity but the divinity favored by the emperors. Within the Roman Empire, being Christian was increasingly seen as the default identity. That is, the law was no longer interested in defining an all-embracing Christian identity. At the same time, there was decreasing need for Christians to organize themselves, qua Christians, into groups that looked like voluntary associations. Ironically, perhaps, voluntary associations would continue to be a strategy of identity for the groups that the now "orthodox" Christians labeled as heresies. Just as prior to the fourth century Christians primarily identified as such by joining voluntary associations in response to imperial legislation, now those who saw themselves as true Christians oppressed by (Christian) imperial legislation would continue to meet in voluntary associations.

In Late Antiquity, "religion" per se was not an organizing strategy of identification. Most people identified themselves by means of ethnicity. Law created identities as well. Finally, people joined voluntary associations to take on identities. These identities, like many identities today, were often perspectival, very much in the eyes of the beholder. They could also be fluid and ambiguous. A proselyte, for example, might be a Jew to one person, a Greek to another, and a problem for a Roman magistrate trying to keep his job.

Although nearly all people in antiquity could easily have identified the deities with whom they strove to have good relationships, their sense of what we would call a religious identity was usually weak and secondary. This is why I think the question about the "parting of the ways" between Judaism and Christianity is ultimately not a useful one. Jews and Christians, no less "Judaism" and "Christianity," never formed fully coherent communities. We would do better to ask when Jews of a particular community saw Christians as distinct and why, and vice versa. To the extent that we can even answer those questions for individual communities, I suspect they would differ significantly.

I do not mean to suggest, though, that it was entirely irrelevant. Throughout the rest of this book, I frequently refer to Jews and Christians (although rarely pagans, which was only a pejorative identity created by later Christians). These identities could be quite powerful; charismatic leaders occasionally drove them into conflict with each other. Yet I also think that usually these identities were secondary, hovering somewhere beneath the surface. In engraved epitaphs, for example, we frequently encounter texts that give no hint of religious identity, which we know only from a more crudely drawn cross or menorah, or a misspelled Hebrew word on a Greek or Latin text. Such cases seem almost to be afterthoughts of identity marking. To understand the history of Late Antiquity primarily in terms of these identities obscures more than it elucidates and predetermines the history as one of conflict between groups. When we let those identities recede, though, and see people as less captured by these identities, a much more interesting and colorful world emerges.[39]

3

Belief and Bureaucracy

THE DIVINE WORLD IN LATE ANTIQUITY

IMAGINE A BIG, sprawling bureaucracy, maybe Rome in antiquity, the Vatican in the Middle Ages, or the headquarters of the European Union in Brussels today. Such bureaucracies, employing thousands if not millions, have clear organizational charts that specify in precise and hierarchical detail where everybody stands. These hierarchical charts are usually pyramidal, with a single person or small council at its peak. Yet, as most of us know, the nice, clean lines that describe such an organization's hierarchy are, in practice, rarely neat. Administrators at nearly all levels are often confused about what they have and do not have the authority to do and where responsibility—especially in the case of mistakes—will fall. Personal ambition, jealousy, and the desire to do favors for favorites all quickly blur the lines, and the bigger the bureaucracy the messier it becomes. Now, with that image firmly in place, imagine the supernatural world.

For many people in antiquity, especially in the Roman and Byzantine Empires, there was not much to distinguish the messy hierarchical organization of this world from that of the invisible one. The cosmos was teeming with invisible beings, each of whom had their theoretical place on the org chart, but most of whom also had some limited ability to take their own initiative. YHWH (the Jewish god), Zeus, or Jupiter may sit at the apex in putative control of all, but heaven was a busy and complicated place for Romans, Greeks, Jews, Christians, and others.

There were other beings of differing degrees of divinity with different abilities, evil beings who sometimes reported according to a different org chart, and spirits, all of whom acted in the world and could be called upon to act for or against those on earth.

Scholars, following Jewish and Christian literature (especially from the Middle Ages), have often used the terms "monotheism" and "polytheism" to categorize religions, ancient and modern. In this classification, Judaism, Christianity, and Islam are monotheist and the other religions are polytheist. In certain contexts, such a classification might be helpful. In many others, though, including the world of Late Antiquity, it is misleading. Everybody believed that there were a plethora of invisible beings. While the intellectuals fought about which of these beings could really be called "gods" and which came under other designations (e.g., "angels" or "spirits"), the fight was largely academic. For most people, what mattered was to figure out which beings did what, which ones could help and which ones could harm, and how to effectively communicate with them.

Much as many Americans have a working but somewhat vague knowledge of their federal government (who is the deputy secretary of state and what exactly do they do?), most people in antiquity had a working knowledge of the cosmos and the invisible beings that inhabit it. This knowledge was practical and actionable; one needed to know where to address a sacrifice or prayer. Perhaps surprisingly, people who lived throughout the ancient Mediterranean and Near East through Late Antiquity had a similar understanding of the deep structure of how these beings existed in relationship to each other and the world. Nobody, for example, thought that the spirit of an ordinary woman—and almost nobody in antiquity would deny that there were such spirits—could begin to hurl thunderbolts. Our task in this chapter, then, is to try to get a better understanding of the divine realm as imagined by those who lived in Late Antiquity.

One important caveat is necessary. The intellectuals of Late Antiquity—those philosophers, rabbis, and bishops who devoted great energy to creating and reinforcing (at least in rhetoric) the boundaries of their respective "faiths"—wrote at great length about these invisible beings. Many, particularly among the philosophers and the bishops, sought to create a rational understanding of this cosmic order. What, for example, is the difference between a god and a human, and can one become the other? These discussions create the backbone of what would become known as theology, and we will return to these intellectuals and their writings in the next chapter. Most people, though, would not have really cared how many angels can dance on the head of a pin. They cared far more about more practical things.

The Top

In most people's imagination, there was a single god or small council of gods who sat at the top of the divine hierarchy. For the Greeks, it was the male, fatherly, mercurial king named Zeus, whose veneration Alexander the Great spread with his conquests in the Near East and Asia. The Romans had their own related pantheon of deities, but it was Jupiter Optimus Maximus who emerged on top. Like Zeus, Jupiter Optimus Maximus proved his power by granting victories to those who venerated him, in this case the leaders of the Roman state, and the state repaid him (for a time) by making him the primary state deity. Already in the eighth century BCE, Hezekiah, king of Judah, ascribed his victory over the much mightier Assyrians to YHWH, the four-lettered (in Hebrew) unpronounceable name that our Bibles usually translate as "Lord" or "Jehovah." Hezekiah followed up on this victory with a campaign against the rest of the Judahite pantheon. Ahura Mazda, the supreme deity of Zoroastrians, was the supreme deity of the Persian Empire. In the fourth century CE, Jesus (in whatever relationship to God) catapulted to the top of the Christian divine hierarchy.

Each of these deities played an important political role. A group understood the deity to be protecting it as a collective, and the collective, through its political leaders and institutions, owed devotion to the deity. One of the clearest examples of this dynamic from Late Antiquity was the devotion to Jupiter Optimus Maximus in the city of Rome. Occupying the primary place in the temple of the Capitoline Triad, Jupiter Optimus Maximus was seen as the protector of Rome and the patron of

FIGURE 3.1. Jupiter Optimus Maximus, partially restored. Public domain, CC BY-SA 2.0, https://en.wikipedia.org/wiki/Jupiter_(god)#/media/File:8646_-_St_Petersburg_-_Hermitage_-_Jupiter.jpg.

many of its emperors. Where the civic and military administrations of Rome went, they took the worship of Jupiter Optimus Maximus with them. As a modern scholar, J. Rufus Fears writes, "To the Roman the modern cult of the flag with its pledge of allegiance, national anthems, and monuments like the Lincoln Memorial and the Altare della Patria, would differ in no whit from his practice of cult offerings, hymns, and temples directed to gods of the state."[1]

While in theory, the equivalency between deity and polity is neat, in actual practice it was a great deal messier. This messiness was an intrinsic part of the way in which those in antiquity thought about their gods, even those on the top. It can be seen primarily in the way that Romans and Greeks named them.

Many Greek and Roman deities bore epithets or surnames. Jupiter Optimus Maximus, for example, has a clear, recognizable name that both declares his power as "the best and greatest" and follows the traditional three-name form taken by Roman citizens. But what about Jupiter Feretrius, worshipped in Rome up until the first century BCE; Jupiter Heliopolitanus, the god of the great Roman temple of Baalbek (in modern Lebanon); or any of the other numerous Jupiters attested in literature and inscriptions? Would their worshippers have regarded them as all referring to the same god? The answer to this question is surprisingly unclear. There is some reason to think that, indeed, the god is the same but the epithet changed depending on which aspect of the god was emphasized. Jupiter Tonans, "the thunderer," who is mentioned in Latin literature and who was the god of several temples (at least one in Rome itself), is in this understanding not a god separate from Jupiter. Jupiter Optimus Maximus encompasses all aspects of Jupiter, but that does not mean that each was not worthy of independent worship.[2]

At the same time, though, it seems that in many places these gods were seen as independent deities best understood as new names for local gods. When, in the fourth century BCE, Alexander the Great brought his own patron god, Zeus, to his conquered cities, many assimilated the new deity to their own local god, distinguishing the god with a new epithet. This led to a bewildering array of Zeuses of dubious relationship to each other. Each Zeus was the local god, now simply with a new name. When Rome began conquering these cities, the administrators and army, followed increasingly by some local aristocrats who desired to take advantage of Roman bureaucracy, brought Jupiter into these cities. Yet in most places in the Eastern Roman Empire, Jupiter supplemented rather than supplanted Zeus. Jupiter was seen as another name for the same god, although Zeus's name remained.[3]

This seems confusing because it was, probably deliberately so. The way to a conquered group's heart is never by declaring their god impotent and defeated. And the way to curry favor with new overlords is never to insult and reject their gods outright. Yet an ambiguous, not entirely coherent, understanding of the relationship between all of these presumably "top" gods seemed to work. The Roman imperial authorities, the Greeks, and the indigenous population could look at the same god in the same temple and understand it as they wished. It was a constructive ambiguity.

We are used to thinking of the Jews as different, but they—and their Israelite ancestors—engaged in a similar kind of ambiguity. In the biblical period, the peoples who would assimilate into the Israelite kingdoms would bring their gods with them. This process is reflected in the Hebrew Bible, a complicated anthology of texts produced over centuries in different places, which contains several different names for their god. The frequently occurring term "the Lord God," for example, is a combined single name for what were originally at least two gods.

The desire of Jews to assimilate their god to others seems to have stopped in the Persian and Hellenistic periods. Neither Greek nor Roman intellectuals could fully understand why the Jews would refuse to make such identifications. Varro, a Roman intellectual writing in the first century BCE, thought it was obvious that YHWH was the same as Jupiter. Other non-Jewish intellectuals undoubtedly shared this belief, although we have no evidence of any Jews who did.[4]

The destruction of the Jerusalem Temple in 70 CE (along with the destruction of a different Jewish temple in Egypt also dedicated to YHWH) caused a shift in Jewish thinking about YHWH. Jews continued to consider YHWH as their supreme deity, but now this deity—unlike nearly every manifestation of Jupiter and Zeus—did not have the support of an organized, autonomous polity. That is, YHWH was no longer a "state god." Curiously, it was at this point that Jews found the logic of the Greeks and Romans more appealing. YHWH quickly began to accumulate new names and epithets again. The rabbis use terms such as "sovereign/master of the universe" or "the presence" (in Hebrew, either *shekinah* or *ha-maqom*) as stand-alone designators for YHWH. In their inscriptions, Jews almost never use the Hebrew name YHWH, or its standard Greek translation, *kurios,* instead preferring the Hebrew terms *El* and *Elohim* and the Greek word *theos,* which is the standard Greek translation of *Elohim*—and, not coincidentally, the term frequently used for Zeus.[5]

The reason for this shift in the way that Jews referred to their god, I suggest, is linked to the deity's changed status. There is no reason to think that for most Jews (although for a smaller proportion than before 70 CE) YHWH's ultimate and universal power had changed. But YHWH was no longer connected to an autonomous political apparatus, and on some level that made the deity less of a state, imperial god and more of a "local" one. Elohim and YHWH under these other names became a mashup equivalent to that of a local god, such as Aphrodite (the patron of several cities), an imperial god such as Jupiter, and a specific manifestation of an imperial god, such as Zeus Akraios. This phenomenon, like that of the epithets of the Greek and Roman gods, was not theologically coherent, but it was useful. It may have seemed odd for Jews to refer to YHWH by this name when the god was without a temple or king. At the same time, though, they did not want to attribute defeat or weakness to their deity. Without a central and centralizing patron, the worship of YHWH also fragmented, leading different communities to figure out how to venerate their deity properly on the basis of past tradition, their material contexts and needs, their contextualized reading of earlier texts (such as the Hebrew Bible), and their loose communications with other Jewish communities.

Through the fourth century, the primary Christian god was a work in progress. Like Jews, Christians also had to reconcile their commitment to a single, universal, and universally powerful deity with the fact that their deity too had no state patron. Christians freely used the Greek terms *kyrios* and *theos* in their writings and inscriptions and added to them the name of Jesus. Intellectuals went to great pains to untangle the relationship between these terms, but it is unlikely that most Christians made hard, fast, and consistent distinctions between them. Like the Jewish god, the Christian god—whom not all Christians considered to be identical with the Jewish god—was singular but also (and like Greek and Roman deities) acquired epithets that allowed for a more expansive and nuanced understanding of the deity's unity.[6]

Beginning in the fourth century, Roman emperors adopted the Christian god as the god of the state and slowly but increasingly began to repress other traditional gods. This was less a revolution than an evolution. Roman emperors were always careful to honor all the important gods, although they felt free to pick their own divine patron. In the third century CE, the emperors Elagabalus and Marcus Aurelius favored the sun god, Sol, honoring the deity on imperial coinage. Here again, ambiguity was a plus; a (probably late) fourth-century biographical sketch of Elagabalus equates Sol with Jupiter. Constantine too took up Sol, now under the name Sol Invictus, as his god, putting the god on coins and including visual references to the deity on the Arch of Constantine. (He also designated Sunday as a day of rest in honor of Sol.) Prior to a crucial battle, though, Constantine had a dream or vision (the sources are sparse and biased) that pointed him to the Christian deity. It is possible, although unlikely, that Constantine abandoned Sol for this god; it is more likely that he assimilated the two. While he was much beloved by later Christian bishops, Constantine himself most likely saw no contradiction in venerating a deity that he thought of as Sol-Jesus while not abandoning the other traditional state gods.[7]

The cities of the Roman Empire had concrete, tangible reminders of who was in charge. In Rome, the Forum was surrounded by a shifting array of temples dedicated to the most important deities (at least for a time) of state. Nearly all these temples had a cult image inside under a portico and thus visible from the space of the Forum. These statues were not quite gods, but nor were they simple representations. They were thought of as infused with divinity. These temples were joined by others dedicated to members of the imperial family. In Rome, an

FIGURES 3.2A, 3.2B. Gold solidus of Constantine I, Ticinum, 320–321. Sol is presenting Victory on a globe to the emperor. ANS 1944.100.9594. Images courtesy of the American Numismatic Society.

enormous cult statue of Constantine was dedicated in the fourth century. State activities to honor the god(s) of the temple would take place in front of the temple and thus spill over into the Forum. With even a few sacrifices each year in front of each of the temples, there must have been a hubbub of almost constant reminders of the tight interconnection of the city, the Empire, and the gods, with portions of the sacrifices then also finding their way into the adjacent markets. The Roman Forum served as the model for forums in cities throughout the Empire.[8]

The forum was important through Late Antiquity, with an entirely new one (perhaps the last) being constructed in Constantinople in the fifth century. As imperial authorities increasingly preferred Christianity, they at first gingerly added churches into the forum. Over time, they would build the churches over temples, as they were abandoned or went into disrepair. The symbolism was important. While the phenomenon of the replacement of temples with churches has often been taken as a sign of Christian triumphalism, at least as important was a message of continuity. The god may change, but the role of the god in civic life was to remain much the same.[9]

Only cities had *forums* in the full meaning of the word. Smaller villages and towns often had public squares that amalgamated activities that we would call "political," "social," "judicial," "economic," and "religious." According to the rabbis, an unusually bad drought triggers a ritual that removes the ark (with the Torah scrolls) to the public square, where it becomes the center of communal worship. The square might have little to permanently mark it architecturally (and thus leave no trace for later scholars), but there is little reason to doubt that nearly all towns had one and that it was central for beseeching the supreme deities.[10]

Second in Command

As on earth, so in heaven. Just as we have kings, so too there are singular, sovereign divinities. Just as human kings usually have vice-regents, close seconds, and sycophantic hangers-on, so too do the gods. Jupiter and Zeus reigned at the top of their divine hierarchies, but they were not alone or unchallenged. Both Greek and Roman mythological legends go to great, and inconsistent, lengths to detail the precise relationships between deities. While individuals or groups might subscribe to one or another of these schemes, that precision was not as important as the more general understanding that the supreme deities had seconds who had great powers, were a bit more approachable than the supreme gods, and who, when necessary, could serve as intermediaries to those gods.

These second-in-command deities were still important enough to be intimidating. They were often the gods adopted by cities within the Roman Empire. Whether or not Aphrodite, the god of the city of Aphrodisias in Asia Minor, really was seen as a local god under a different name, or Artemis of Ephesus was "really" the Greek goddess Artemis—both of whom had magnificent temples dedicated to them in their respective cities—they were clearly important gods who nevertheless were slightly lower than the "father" gods. In addition to receiving public honors, such gods also received private devotions, as indicated by many inscriptions commemorating gifts to them.

Despite their reputation for "monotheism," Jews, too, had a shadowy (if contested) tradition of understanding there to be one or more secondary, usually subordinate, deities who served under their supreme deity. The two most prominent figures who appear in this role are Satan and Metatron. Satan is a particularly difficult figure to pin down, as the Hebrew word *satan* can mean a generic "accuser" rather than referring to a single being. When, in the book of Job, "the satan" prods God to test his faithful devotee Job, it is unclear whether a single figure with the name Satan is meant or simply a generic being who is temporarily taking on the role of accusing Job. Jewish literature authored prior to the destruction of the Jerusalem Temple in 70 CE refers to a variety of beings that are functionally equivalent, such as Mastema in the book of Jubilees or Beliel in some of the Dead Sea Scrolls. The book of 1 Enoch associates evil powers with a high-ranking fallen angel.

It is Satan, though, that survives in rabbinic literature. Rabbinic literature treats Satan vaguely, sometimes referring to a singular figure (similar to but much less lurid than the figure that would emerge in later Christian imagination) and sometimes an anonymous accuser. A Palestinian rabbi struggling to understand the figure of Satan in the book of Job captures this vagueness: "Satan, the evil inclination, and the Angel of Death are all the same." On one level, the saying nicely links sin—the result of succumbing to one's "evil inclination"—to death. On another, though, it suggests that Satan is a single, named figure. Other rabbinic sources introduce the idea that one can "confuse Satan" through certain activities. Satan appears as a woman to tempt rabbis (through the evil inclination) and as a pauper to ensnare them in uncharitable deeds. In such stories, Satan is much more than an impartial angelic prosecutor of those who sinned. Satan has power over every day other than Yom Kippur, the Day of Atonement. Satan is said to have his own "angels" who accompany an evil person. There is no evidence that Jews would have seen Satan as a figure equal to YHWH, but many most likely did see him (Satan is gendered as male) as a powerful divine figure who was both subservient to YHWH and charged with controlling those forces associated with sin and death.[11]

YHWH also had other, more benevolent vice-regents. Within the Hebrew Bible, we have only very slight traces of this understanding, which its writers and editors attempted to suppress. Thus, the clearest (and it is admittedly not very clear) biblical expression of this understanding is found in a relatively late biblical text in the book of Daniel. Daniel relates a vision of four beasts, at the end of which he has a vision of "the Ancient One," presumably YHWH, who appears to render judgment: "I saw one like a human being coming with the clouds of heaven. And he came to the Ancient One and was presented before him. To him was given dominion and glory and kingship, that all peoples, nations, and languages should serve him. His dominion is an everlasting dominion that shall not pass away, and his kingship is one that shall never be destroyed" (Daniel 7:13–14). Unfortunately, the book of Daniel leaves this thought dangling, raising several unanswered questions. Who is this "one like a human being" (or, more literally, "son of man")? The belief expressed here—that there is a second power in heaven closely allied with "the Ancient One" who also is in some way closer to human form—also finds expression in several Jewish texts from the Second Temple period. The clearest example is Jesus, to whom later writers apply this text from Daniel, perhaps reflecting the lens through which he was seen during his day.[12]

The idea that there are actually two powers in heaven survived among Jews into Late Antiquity. It is very difficult to ascertain the prevalence of this idea or the extent to which it was seen as "heretical," and by whom. Scholars debate whether it can be found at all in the earliest layer of rabbinic literature. When the rabbis more clearly reference it, beginning in the late third century CE, it is always in order to condemn it. "Rabbinic Judaism, qua orthodoxy," the scholar Daniel Boyarin writes, "is formed precisely out of the rejection of ideas about the godhead that were once widely held in Jewry." These ideas swirled around different characters. One Talmudic text identifies "Akatriel Yah" as "the Lord of Hosts," who sat in the inner chamber of the Jerusalem Temple. Akatriel appears also in a Hekhalot text. (The Hekhalot texts were written in Late Antiquity either by rabbis or by those with close affinity to the rabbis.) Similarly, another Hekhalot text identifies King David with the divine-messiah figure of Daniel 7. The most important of these figures, though, (at least in Babylonia) was undoubtedly Metatron. Called the "lesser (or perhaps "younger") god" in Hekhalot texts, Metatron also appears in rabbinic literature. Some of these references at once acknowledge the power of Metatron as a figure that can easily be confused with the supreme deity and rail against those who would dare to do so.[13]

While we would like very much to put these texts into a wider perspective—how many Jews actually believed that there was a second power in heaven, whatever one called it—the sources are recalcitrant. The quantity and harsh tone of the rabbinic passages, along with the documented history of the idea, might suggest that the rabbis were fighting against a well-entrenched belief. One scholar has suggested that the portraits found in the center of mosaic zodiacs of some ancient synagogues in Palestine represented Metatron. Several spells written or commissioned by Jews also adjure Metatron (often along with YHWH). Whether or not the rabbis hoped to make an impression on Jews who believed in Metatron, though, they also clearly had in their sights emerging beliefs of Christians.[14]

Jewish and Christian understandings that there was some kind of divine vice-regent who bore some resemblance to human beings emerged out of the same matrix. For Christians, the figure was Jesus. The book of Revelation, probably written in the early second century CE by a man who identifies himself as John of Patmos, opens with a vision of "one like the Son of Man, clothed with a long robe and with a golden sash across his chest. His head and his hair were white as white wool, white as snow; his eyes were like a flame of fire" (Revelation 1:13–14). This figure goes on to say, "I am the first and the last, and the living one. I was dead, and see, I am alive forever and ever; and I have the keys of Death and Hades" (1:17–18). Jesus here has not yet been fully assimilated into a notion of the Trinity. At least until the third century, many followers of Jesus saw him much like the figure described by Daniel, a divine being who was second to the supreme deity, now called the Father.

Jesus would, of course, soon rise in the divine hierarchy. Tertullian, a Christian intellectual who lived in the third century CE in Africa, is the first to attempt to form a coherent account of a Trinity that preserves the individuality of the three "persons" and yet makes them all part of a single deity. The Father, Son, and Holy Spirit are "three, however, not in unchangeable condition, but in rank; not in substance, but in attitude; not in office, but in appearance;—but of one nature and of one reality and of one power, because there is one God from whom these ranks and attitudes and appearances are derived in the name of Father and Son and Holy Spirit." Tertullian, who intended to put out a firestorm among Christian intellectuals about the nature of their godhead, just flamed it further, and the Trinitarian controversy continued long past him (and arguably has never stopped). This, however, was a relatively rarefied conversation within the circles of the educated elite that would hardly have been comprehensible to those without deep learning in Stoicism and other Hellenistic philosophical schools. Nor would they have much been interested.[15]

The important point is that most of Jesus's followers saw him as a secondary divinity. Like Aphrodite and perhaps even Metatron, Jesus fit into a nearly universally understood conceptual structure. When Greeks and Romans mocked Christian ideas, their point of attack was not that Jesus was a divine being; they could understand that perfectly well. Instead, they focused on beliefs and activities that struck them as inconsistent, not in accord with their own texts, and sometimes simply silly, such as the idea that a man who was shamefully executed could become a deity. Despite these attacks, though, Christians quickly began to treat Jesus much as other local deities. Images of Jesus—instead of statues of Greek or Roman gods—began to occupy prominent places in churches (which replaced temples); representations of Christ (often in symbolic form, such as the cross), instead of cultic statues, began to appear on imperial coinage after the fourth century; and inscriptions recording dedications were similar to those made in traditional temples, just with Christian symbols and the name of Jesus. Many inscriptions mention Jesus (or Christ, or Jesus Christ) together with the Greek names for God, seemingly making him a secondary figure. Those who were more accustomed to conceptual frameworks of the Greek gods would not have had a problem understanding the seemingly new Christian one.[16]

Throughout Late Antiquity, Christians developed an increasingly elaborate understanding of and role for Satan. The apostle Paul, who mentions Satan rarely, and even then usually in his role as "tempter" of humans into sin, sees him as a worthy apocalyptic adversary. As he says near the end of one of his letters, "The God of peace will shortly crush Satan under your feet" (Romans 16:20). The Gospels, all written toward the end of the first century or the beginning of the second, assign him

FIGURE 3.3. Early picture of Jesus on gold glass from Rome. Probably part of a drinking vessel. British Museum (1863,0727.6). Used with permission.

a much more important role. According to Luke, Jesus says that he "watched Satan fall from heaven like a flash of lightening" (10:18) upon the defeat of the demons. In John, Jesus calls the Jews the spawn of Satan (8:4). The scholar Elaine Pagels says that such statements are, in fact, the key to understanding why early Christian literature focused on Satan. The earliest followers of Jesus, who were primarily Jews, were engaged in a struggle with other Jews that led them, quite literally, to "demonize" their enemies by constructing a binary view of the world. At the same time, there were theological considerations. Christ needs a worthy enemy, who is then cast into a symmetrical, opposite role as leader of the evil beings. Whatever the original impetus behind the elevation of Satan in these early Christian texts, they found a receptive audience. Satan has continued to fill an important role for Christians, even if the reason changed. Sometimes known as the devil, Satan became the Antichrist, scheduled for a showdown with Christ at the end of days.[17]

Angels and Demons

Under the primary and secondary gods are the angels. The Hebrew Bible assumes the existence of such intermediary beings. These angels function primarily as messengers (the literal translation of the Hebrew word) of the divine word, although they sometimes punch above their weight, as when they led the Israelites out of Egypt or actively killed Israel's enemies. The Bible says nothing of their hierarchy, origins, or nature. These were gaps that Jewish writers in the Second Temple period eagerly filled. The author of the tract "The Book of Watchers," now part of a book called 1 Enoch, for example, develops an extensive myth that explains how intermediary beings—invisible, powerful, and yet inferior to God—came into existence. It goes on to explain how they, like the lesser Greek gods, taught humans various skills. The Book of Watchers, in fact, gives a relatively full account of their corporate hierarchy as well, distinguishing the lesser angels from their bosses and the good from the bad. This precise angelology (as scholars call it) was among the most detailed of those that survive from this period, but it was far from the only one. We find angels in the Dead Sea Scrolls, the books of the Apocrypha (which were written by and for Jews), and many other extant texts from the period.[18]

Jewish sources from Late Antiquity contain the names of several angels, but some were more important than others. Rabbinic literature mentions the angels Michael and Gabriel by name and frequently together (and sometimes with Raphael). Michael is called the "great minister," who serves God by sacrificing on the heavenly altar. One rather strange passage tells of an encounter between Gabriel and Dubiel, the angel of the Persians, in which Gabriel shows his mettle. There is no term in Hebrew or Aramaic quite like "archangel" (which derives from a Greek word), but these rabbinic sources do seem to understand some angels as above the others and closer to YHWH. This understanding of an angelic hierarchy within the divine hierarchy extends beyond rabbinic literature. According to one rabbinic passage, God says, "If a person faces trouble, he should not cry out to the angels Michael or Gabriel. But he should cry out to me, and I will immediately answer him." The passage polemicizes against Jews who appealed to angels instead of God. Liturgical poetry and Jewish books of spells elevate a few named angels above the others. Amulets commissioned by Jews specifically name these (and some other) angels.[19]

The named angels are just the tip of the angelic iceberg. Jews in Late Antiquity thought the world was full of these beings, who played an important role in individual and communal life. Rabbis struggled to reconcile this belief with their purer idea of one god. They were careful to insist that angels were created beings and thus unlike the only uncreated being, YHWH, although they could not agree on when they were created (the second or the fifth days of creation are the most popular options for the rabbis). Rabbis debated whether angels were made of fire or water; their relative status compared to human beings; the extent of their power; and the kinds of jobs that God gives them. What they never debated, though, was their existence, and they admitted that angels came in both male and female genders. Rabbis attempted to hem angels in (at least intellectually) and make sure that they were not confused with the one true God. That they existed and were active in the world was obvious.[20]

Several traditions offer evidence of a widespread assumption that angels played a significant role in the world, especially by offering a kind of natural immunity against demons. One midrash (a rabbinic biblical interpretation), for example, focused on the verse describing Jacob's dream that there was a ladder, and "the angels of God were ascending and descending on it" (Genesis 28:12). Why were angels ascending first, the rabbis ask—do they not come from heaven? One possible reason (they offer several possibilities) is that Jacob had left the Land of Israel. Since the angels of the Land of Israel cannot leave that geographical area, there needed to be a changing of the guard of the angels who accompanied him. Another is to teach us that one can take advantage of other people's angels:

> Rabbi Yosi the Galilean says: If you see a righteous man going on a journey and you want to take the same road, advance or delay your journey three days in order that you will go with him on the road, because the angels of peace accompany him, as it is written, "For he will command his angels concerning you [to guard you in all your ways]" (Psalms 91:11). And if you see an evil person going on a journey and you want to go on the same road, advance or delay your journey three days so that you do not go on the same road because the angels of Satan accompany him, as it is written, "[Appoint a wicked man against him,] let an accuser (Satan) [stand on his right]" (Psalms 109:6).

Advice to keep company with good people and to keep one's distance from bad people is, of course, pedestrian. It occurs repeatedly in the Wisdom literature in the Bible, where it is always grounded in the (to us, natural) assumption that good people exert a good influence on us and bad people will either seek to harm us directly or will lead us astray. This passage goes well beyond that naturalistic explanation. Around a good or bad person is a concentrated miasma of good or bad angels. The passage is not meant to be read metaphorically. An average person could expect in an ordinary day to walk among invisible beings, both good and bad. While the rabbis are here unclear about whether they believe that good people become good as a result of the accompanying angels or whether it is their behavior that brings the angels, they walk with a cloud of these good, protecting angels. Since travel in antiquity was dangerous, it would have been worth changing one's itinerary slightly to take advantage of this protective cloud (and to stay away from a harmful one). The verses justify a preexisting belief.[21]

Angels had a counterpart in demons. "They are more numerous than we are and they surround us like the ridge around a field," says one rabbi. Just as Jewish intellectuals developed complex, mythic angelologies that laid out the workings and hierarchies of the angels, so too did they develop complex, mythic demonologies that sought to order and explain the demonic world. Demons hardly appear in the Hebrew Bible, but they do appear frequently in rabbinic literature (particularly the

Babylonian Talmud), often under the names "evil spirits," "spirits," or "destroyers." In rabbinic understanding, demons and other malevolent beings (such as "the evil eye," if this can really be distinguished from demons proper) are relatively passive but territorial beings that are attracted to liminal spaces. Someone wandering into a space where demons live, like a ruin or bathroom (although they can also live in walls or trees), runs a greater risk of being attacked. Discussions in rabbinic literature tend to wind their way back to putting rabbis at their center, so it is not very surprising that they also imagine that demons are particularly attracted to rabbinic spaces and precisely to the people who can best defend against them. Many Jews had a strong notion of the presence of these spirits and felt keenly the need to guard against their evil acts.[22]

The female demons had a particular pull. The most famous named female demon is Lilith, who appears in the Babylonian Talmud and in assorted nonrabbinic texts, especially inscribed bowls. One story in the Babylonian Talmud locates the origin of Lilith—or more precisely, liliths, taking "lilith" as a type of demon rather than a specific named one—in Adam's seminal emissions during the time that he voluntarily refrained from sex with Eve (a nonbiblical detail added by the rabbis) after their banishment from Eden. She attacked men through seduction and women through other means. One inscription on a Babylonian bowl sought protection for a woman from "the affliction demon, from the satan, from the Lilith, from the harm of male idol spirits, and female idol spirits, from the harm of the upper (and) lower female spirit . . . the sorcery of Zanay, the fornicating singing-girl, and the Lilith who ma[ss]acres her own children (and) the child[ren of her companions]," among other malevolent forces. The bowl refers to more than one lilith, making clear a connection of filicide, a classical trope. While evidence for liliths seems confined to Babylonia, other texts from the Mediterranean basin also attest to belief in female demons, who pose a threat to both men and women.[23]

Christians, like Jews, took the existence of angels and demons for granted as real agents who acted in the world. Christian intellectuals, unlike Jewish intellectuals, were also more tightly constrained by the texts of the New Testament. Evagrius and Augustine, two Church Fathers, thought it necessary to approach the topic of angels philosophically, and they each developed competing notions of what an angel was, where they came from, and how they related to humans. For Evagrius, an angel was an intermediate, almost material state of the intellect, able to rise to the divine or to descend to the state of humans or below. For Augustine, angels were forever unchanging, stuck in their close (angels) or distant and fallen (demons) relationship to God.[24]

Christians had a much more robust understanding of angelic hierarchies than did Jews. Christian bishops developed a notion of "archangels." The fourth-century church historian Eusebius, for example, separates between angels, archangels, and divine powers, seeing them all as necessary for God to show his love to humanity. Christians occasionally built shrines dedicated to angels, especially the archangel Michael. The line between such beings and the one true God could be dim. Christian intellectuals, of course, knew the difference. Augustine was careful to note that, as created beings, angels were not appropriate objects of worship; he certainly would have disapproved of shrines devoted to them. A church council in Asia Minor in 363–364 CE explicitly forbade the evocation of angels and prohibited clergy from participating in such "magic." An inscription from Asia Minor that calls upon, as a group and by individual names, the archangels to protect the city of Miletus is probably Christian. Invoking angels (especially "archangels," as they are called in Greek) also occurred within churches, even if those structures were not explicitly dedicated to them. For example, a chancel screen in a church located on the island of Santorini (as it is known today) contains a humble dedication to "Holy and formidable Michael the Archangel" and calls on him to help the members of the family who presumably made a gift. Angelic veneration was an accepted, even expected, activity for some Christians. At the same time, the church elite harshly condemned it.[25]

For Christian ascetics in particular, angels played an important but in many ways secondary role; they defended against demons. When Christian ascetics talked of "the demon of lust," they meant what they said. Demons were real beings, having actual material (if invisible) bodies, who acted to inflame holy men. They were not simply passive creatures who struck out when disturbed but rather agents of Satan actively spreading evil in the world. They were especially attracted to ascetics who were fasting and praying, seeking to lead them astray. It was at that moment, though, that an angelic guide appeared to help combat them. Only with the help of the angelic guide could the battle against the demons be a fair fight, but the guide also did not take matters fully into his own hands. It was the ascetic himself (these battles were almost always discussed from the perspective of male ascetics) who had to engage, using prayer, fasting, and the citation of scripture.[26]

Ascetic understandings of the role that angels and the angelic guide played in individual spiritual development drew on philosophical notions that did not posit a strict dichotomy between good and evil. Many Christians, though, had a more mythic understanding of the nature of the cosmos, one that pitted good against evil. It was from this mythic understanding that the idea emerged, familiar to many today, of Satan leading an army of demons against God and his angels. This was a theologically dangerous line to tread, for it flirted with the idea that there is a force outside of and not controlled by God and thus that God is not all-powerful. Christian intellectuals largely subordinated evil to God. Christian art, which does not portray Satan and demons prior to the sixth century, usually represents them as animals (particularly snakes, goats, bears, and lions) who are subordinate to Christ. A mosaic from a church in Ravenna, for example, depicts Christ flanked by and extending his hand toward a red (good) angel tending sheep while the blue angel (often identified as Satan) has his goats, somewhat lower down. Other portraits show Christ crushing the head of a snake.[27]

Many Christians, though, crossed that theological line, or at least flirted much closer to it. The Christian groups that tend to be lumped together under the rubric of the "Gnostics," whose thought is documented in a trove of papyri found at Nag Hammadi and the extensive and harsh polemics against Valentinus (who lived in the second century CE), posit somewhat different forms of cosmic dualism. In each, though, there is an ongoing struggle between the material (bad) and spiritual (good) forces. The task of each adherent was to help advance the power of the spiritual forces. While more "orthodox" Christian bishops railed against this understanding as too dualistic, more famously the Manicheans took this a step further. For the Manicheans, the world was in its very fabric riven between the forces of good and evil. In the words of the scholar Jason BeDuhn, the Manichean world was "a devastated battlefield roamed by hostile forces." As with the ascetics, defeat of these hostile forces was made possible only with the help of angelic ones.[28]

Like Jews, Christians believed that, assuming they were pure and good enough, angels would accompany them, thus offering a kind of natural immunity against low-level demonic interference. According to the Church Father Eusebius, the presence of angels, archangels, and divine powers was part of the divine plan, an act of God's love for humanity. Unlike animals, humans have these angels "to be their leaders and governors like herdsmen and shepherds," with Christ at their head. This orthodox understanding of the role that angels play in our lives understates how most Christians understood it. Angels were more than guides for the pure; they were actively fighting off the bad and could be implored to take on more important tasks.[29]

Traditional Greeks and Romans also had a well-developed sense of divine intermediaries. Also called "angels" and *daimones,* they were ethereal messengers who acted in the world. Unlike Christian and Jewish angels and demons, they were not consistently thought to promote, respectively, good and evil. The belief in and veneration of these divine intermediaries or messengers of Greek and Roman gods is well attested in both literature and archaeology. Despite having many actual gods to turn to for help (unlike the more constrained pantheon of Jews and Christians), Greeks and Romans also invoked angels, albeit less frequently. In 316 CE, for example, Syrian soldiers serving in a Roman legion in Egypt inscribed a "prayer for the angels." A bit earlier, a lengthier text from Asia Minor records a monetary dedication made in response to a revelation that the god Men Petraeitos Axetenos made through his angel. The "good angel"—an enigmatic figure or number of figures—also regularly makes an appearance in inscriptions.[30]

Heroes and Saints

Angels and daimones were not the only kind of divine intermediaries. As opposed to divine beings that had always been divine, there were humans who became divine. Already in the fourth century BCE, skeptical Greek philosophers had proposed that the myths of all divine beings, in fact, began from the actions of real human beings. This philosophical position, known as euhemerism (after the Greek philosopher most associated with it, Euhemerus) was, however, always marginal. Most Greeks were completely comfortable with the idea that human beings could not only be seen as gods but could also achieve real semidivine status. These "heroes" functioned much like other divine beings. They were venerated, offered sacrifices, and in turn were expected to intercede in human affairs. A few, like Herakles, broke out of their regional origins, but most never did. Every region had its own heroes, venerated at shrines and graves.[31]

The idea that humans could become divine played out differently in the Roman context. From the time of Cicero in the first century BCE, Romans increasingly began to experiment with combining the notion of deification with politics. Cicero himself promoted Pompey as a god. A deified emperor was not exactly seen as a god but as a *divus*, a divine being somewhat lesser than the gods. One of the peculiar Roman quirks of deification, though, was that it was as much a legal status as an ontological state. When the Roman Senate declared a dead emperor a divus (whether a living emperor could be a divus was a hot-button issue), thus allowing the use of the title and the formation of temples dedicated to that divus, the declaration made it so rather than simply acknowledging what actually was. As such, the Senate also could, and sometimes did, strip the previous title/status of divus from those who had it. "Heroization" was not limited to emperors. In the second century, Hadrian deified his lover Antinoos, and the cult spread far and deep.[32]

Another popular deified figure was Apollonius of Tyana (a town in Asia Minor). Apollonius, whose feats were recorded at length by his third-century biographer Philostratus, was a healer and itinerant miracle-worker who lived in the first century CE. According to

Philostratus, "no one ventured to dispute" that Apollonius was immortal, and he thus became semi-divine after his death. Philostratus was not the only one who held this opinion. An epigram incised on a lintel, probably dating to the third or fourth century, similarly praises Apollonius as one whose body is in the tomb but whom heaven has received.[33]

The traditional Greek idea of heroes and the more formal Roman conception of deification both played a role in the evolving notion throughout Late Antiquity that exceptional humans, after their deaths, could become effective heavenly intermediaries and intercessors. The author of the Letter to the Ephesians (possibly, but not necessarily, Paul himself) thought that joining Christ meant also joining "the holy ones" and those of the "household" of God. Later commentators and scholars assume that at least "the holy ones," often translated as "saints," were humans who ascended to participate in the divine spirit but the terms remain murky to us. By the early third century, though, increasing numbers of Christians began to venerate those whom they saw as having been killed for their faith. The direct evidence for this veneration is sparse, but the Martyrdom of Polycarp, a letter telling of the death of the bishop of Smyrna (in Asia Minor) in the second century, relates that Polycarp's remains were deposited in "a fitting place" and prays for the opportunity to celebrate the anniversary of his martyrdom. Origen also assumes that the souls of good people (mainly martyrs) become saints and act as intercessors for us. The conception that martyrs occupy a special place in heaven and can function as intercessors is organically linked to the logic of traditional hero cults. Similarly, although Roman emperors after Constantine were no longer officially deified while living, they took the title *Dominus Noster*, a deliberately ambiguous term meaning "our lord," which became so conventional that on coins it was simply abbreviated "D N." On their deaths, although not victims of martyrdom, some were promoted as "saints." By the fifth century, Church Fathers took the "cult of saints" largely for granted, adding theological rationales to justify it and to bring it under their own umbrella of authority.[34]

Within this cult of saints, Mary occupied a special place. The veneration of Mary, the mother of Jesus, began early, although the exact form it took is murky. One papyrus scrap contains a prayer to Mary to intercede, but its date is questionable. Mary also appears (relatively) prominently in so-called Gnostic texts from Nag Hammadi, which portray her (or, perhaps, Mary Magdalene) as a leader of the apostles and recipient of divine mysteries. A few other narrative texts that circulated prior to the fifth century similarly describe Mary as having special knowledge of cosmic mysteries. Ephrem, a bishop from Syria, lauds her in his hymns. Beginning in the fifth century, though, evidence for Mary's veneration explodes. A church council at Ephesus in 431 CE gives her the Greek title "Theotokos," "God-bearer," despite pockets of theological resistance (how could a human, the bishop Nestorius argued, give birth to a god?). From that point on, ecclesiastical authorities heavily promote her. Mary can be asked to intercede with her Son, with whom she was seen to have exceptional influence. Christians turned to her in increasing numbers, dedicating goods and addressing prayers to her. Women were particularly attracted to her for her help with issues of fertility. Her powers were seen as uniquely efficacious, largely because she was herself unique in the divine hierarchy: born human, literally touched by God during her life, and then becoming divine after death.[35]

Other saints had a more mundane trajectory to sainthood. They began as simple humans who earned, through their own actions, the grace of God. Their actions often, but not always, involved suffering for God's sake; martyrs were, as a matter of course, thought of as saintly. A saint's real power developed after their death. They became portals that connected heaven and earth. Christian intellectuals, particularly those in the philosophical mode, attempted to explain how this happened. While all agreed that the souls of saints appeared in the world, they disagreed widely about how independent and active these souls were. Were they mere phantasms that emanated according to the divine will, or were they really the active souls of the dead? Did they have the power to act in the world or only to serve as intercessors, moving requests up the ladder to those divine beings who could really act on them? As with many such theological issues at that time, the debate was both fierce and largely marginal to the lives of most Christians, who increasingly venerated saints to boost the chance that their own requests would be answered.[36]

The cult of Thecla demonstrates some of the complex dynamics involved in the veneration of saints. In the second century, there appear to have been oral stories of a woman named Thecla circulating in Christian communities in Asia Minor. These stories revolve around her modesty and her willingness to abandon her traditional family to protect her chastity and to follow Paul, even at risk of her own death. Two versions of these stories were preserved in a written tract, *Acts of Paul and Thecla* (or, probably better, just *Acts of Thecla,* as Paul plays a minor and not very inspiring role in the book), that spread quite widely. According to the *Acts of Thecla,* Thecla was saved repeatedly from danger by divine intervention, and although she faced torture and death at several junctures, her own death appears to have been natural. By the early fourth century, the place where she was thought to have been buried had become a shrine and pilgrimage site. Her fame spread, and Church Fathers promoted her story and veneration, emphasizing especially her chastity. Her image appears on *ampullae*—small vessels that held holy oil or water—made for pilgrims to a saint's grave in Egypt. These depictions curiously always pair her with the local male saint Menas, perhaps as a way of taming her (female) power.[37]

Like most early saints, the "real" Thecla is clouded in myth and legend. If she really existed, she may have lived in Asia Minor, perhaps as an early follower of Christ, and broke with her family over the issue of marriage. Locals—maybe mostly women—saw her as a role model, and the site of her grave (or at least what was thought of as the site of her grave) became an important place at which Christians would come to pray, bring gifts, and ask Thecla for intervention. Over time, her story proved useful to the Church Fathers, who saw in her a role model for the female values that they wished to promote. The cult of Thecla was quickly subordinated to the "orthodox" authorities, with a basilica built over her shrine and administered by ecclesiastical authorities. She could be an ascetic model but still not too independent.

Jews in Late Antiquity rarely adopted the term "saint," but that did not stop them from having a functionally equivalent category. Biblical figures, such as Abraham, Isaac, Jacob, Sarah, Rachel, Moses, and Elijah, were thought to be active in the heavens interceding with God on behalf of the Jewish community as well as individual Jews. The rabbis seem to have accepted this reality, even if overall they seemed somewhat uncomfortable with it. When rabbinic prayers evoke these immortal figures, they tend to appeal to God to consider granting a request "for their sake" or in consideration of their "merit." Some scholars have seen in rabbinic literature a relatively coherent theology about how merit functioned. In their understanding, not only did the rabbis have a single, systematic, and coherent understanding of a doctrine of merit, but this doctrine was rational and domesticated, never threatening the monotheistic ideal of a single heavenly power. I am skeptical. While some rabbinic traditions can certainly be read in that way, many seem to be unselfconsciously drawing on a wider set of assumptions that make the ancestors—patriarchs and matriarchs—more dynamic intercessors. Commenting on the story about Jacob wrestling with an angel (Genesis 32:26–33), for example, one rabbi says that God warned the angel that Jacob had five "amulets" in his possession: "his merit, the merit of his father, the merit of his mother, the merit of his grandfather, and the merit of his grandmother." This turned out to be four more merits than Jacob needed; his own merit was sufficient to overcome the angel. "Merit" here functions like an amulet, each one having its own independent power that functions as much more than a remembrance and prod to God to intercede. "The God of Abraham, the God of Isaac, and the God of Jacob" recurs as a frequent phrase within amulets, an evocation of the patriarchs that was thought to have power over evil forces.[38]

For the rabbis, the protective power of ancestral merit derived from women as well as men. The tradition cited above evokes the merit of Sarah and Rebecca against the angel attacking Jacob. It is the merit of Rachel, though, that weaves more prominently through rabbinic literature. Rachel's role as matriarchal intercessionary in rabbinic literature never rises to the level of Mary in Christian literature, but it does seem to be an intersecting development. The rabbis might have sought to promote the "cult of Rachel" (albeit not very hard) both to recover Rachel from increasing Christian appropriation of her as a symbol of the church and as an analogue to Mary. There is sparse evidence from Late Antiquity of Jewish women (or men) appealing to Rachel or to God in her name; I have not found her name in any nonrabbinic texts or evidence for pilgrimages to her tomb, a practice that would become popular beginning in the nineteenth century. Nevertheless, it would not surprise me if such activity took place.[39]

Spirits

There is yet another category of invisible beings, the spirits of the dead. On the whole, these beings do not so much act in the world as provide a shadowy window into the netherworld. A story from the Babylonian Talmud shows how they work:

> Once a pious man gave a *dinar* to a poor man on the day before Rosh HaShanah during a drought. His wife mocked him, and he went and slept in a cemetery. He heard two spirits (*ruḥot*) conversing. One said to her friend, "My friend, come and let's roam the world and we will hear from behind the curtain what calamities come into the world." She said to her friend, "I am not able, since I am buried in a mat of reeds, but you go and what you hear, tell me." She went and wandered and returned. Her friend said to her, "My friend, what have you heard behind the curtain?" She said to her: "I heard that all who sow during the first rains, hail will strike [the crop.]" He [the pious man] went and sowed during the second rains. [The crops] of the whole world were struck, but his [crops] were not struck.[40]

The main plot line of the story is a common one: a person who is himself struggling financially gives money to the poor and ultimately reaps material rewards in this world. In that sense, the presence of the spirits is almost peripheral; their existence must be taken for granted to drive the plot. The Hebrew word for "spirits" is gendered as feminine, so it is a bit unclear here whether these are male or female spirits, or if the spirits themselves have a gender. In any case, the spirits "live" in the cemetery. One remains physically trapped in her grave, although the other seems to be able to take short trips "behind the curtain," that is, to the invisible divine realm, to eavesdrop. The spirits here and in the continuation of the story specifically do not, and do not want to, communicate with humans. The pious man was simply in the right place at the right time.

What exactly is a "spirit," though? The rabbis, following the Bible, tend toward a unitary and material view of the body that, while not always denying the existence of a "soul," locates the essence of the human in his or her flesh. This is why they emphatically emphasize the doctrine that at the end of days humans will be resurrected in the body before they face divine judgment; they could not face judgment as mere souls because the self must be a combination of body and soul. God's breath made the flesh alive (Genesis 2:7) and when that breath departs the flesh is simply flesh. The rabbis never form a single, coherent understanding of the nature of the divine breath, though. Is it simply an animating force, like turning on a toy's power switch? Or is it more like what we mean by a "soul," containing its own personality, consciousness, and agency? On death, does it simply cease, drawn back into the undifferentiated divine, or does it maintain its own individual identity, waiting to be united to its own body? Rabbinic literature contains variations on all of these possibilities.[41]

The story cited above takes an intermediate position, and it is reasonable to assume that it reflects a wide (although probably not universal) Jewish understanding of the spirits. There is no evidence that Jews in antiquity appealed to the souls of dead relatives (except the truly famous biblical ones) to intercede for them with the divine realm, prayed that these souls be treated well, or attempted to communicate with them. Attempts to communicate with the dead could, in fact, flirt with the prohibition against necromancy known already in the Bible; the rabbis certainly took this seriously, although it is less clear if most Jews were even aware of it. There is limited evidence that Jews, like the Israelites before them, continued to "care for" their dead. Such care may have taken the form of small offerings (including graffiti) at a burial site. Some ancient Jewish cemeteries seem to have been designed to accommodate gatherings that might have included family meals by a relative's tomb.[42]

The lack of Jewish evidence is somewhat surprising. Both Greek and Roman societies expended a great deal of energy on the spirits of their friends and ancestors. Most Greek cities housed a wide assortment of voluntary associations devoted specifically to care of the dead. The associations often had constitutions and needed formal legal recognition from Rome. Typically, they would meet regularly (for many, monthly) to take care of the business of collecting dues and, among other things, attending to the funerary needs of their members, such as distributing funds for proper burials, organizing burial processions, and feasting in honor of the dead. While these associations may not have been formed solely for the purpose of caring for the dead, attending to these funerary needs was one of their most important functions. One third-century inscription from Thessalonica records the bequest of a priestess to such an organization, on condition that some of the proceeds are used every year to offer sacrifices "for" (or maybe "to"?) her.[43]

Voluntary associations were not the only or even the most prominent way in which spirits were part of the quotidian lives of ordinary people. Spirits were thought to continue to live in the underworld, although the terms used and what they represented sometimes blurred into each other. One standard Latin term for the dead was *di manes*, the underworld "gods" that the dead were thought to join. The term became so prosaic that it was abbreviated in its plural dative form (*dis manibus*; DM) and appears in thousands of Latin epitaphs. One particularly poignant one from Rome (probably from the second century), for example, reads: "D. M. Calpurnius Trygetus and Calpurnia Hermione, most unhappy parents, (set this up) for Calpurnius Trygetus, a most dutiful son. He lived 10 years, 6 months, 10 days, 11 hours." The son was thought to have joined the relatively undifferentiated spirits of the underworld. There was a relationship between the di manes, the *di penates*, the *lares*, and the *genii*, although the distinctions between them are not always clear. All were venerated in and connected to the household. The di penates and lares were seen in at least some contexts as the spirits of the ancestors of that particular group, whether of a household or a neighborhood (especially in the case of the lares). Each household also venerated the *genius* of the head of the household, the *pater familias* (as well as, since the time of Augustus, the *genius* of the emperor). Niches found in Roman houses in Pompeii were dedicated to the lares. While it is likely that such niches were common in houses at least around Rome, no direct evidence for them has yet been found in other domestic architecture.[44]

The Romans attached great importance to fulfilling obligations to one's elders as a form of *pietas*, and veneration of the di manes and other household spirits undoubtedly was one way in which they did so. There were other, less abstract, reasons to do so as well, though. Di manes can protect the living. In one Latin epitaph from Rome, a man tells his departed wife that as long as she extends his life, he will make offerings to her. A few Roman festivals invited the dead to enter the world of the living to provide continued protection, particularly of the food supply. The di manes could also be evoked more aggressively. In one tablet from the third century, a man calls on the di manes of his dead brother to help him restrain someone else from leaving Italy.[45]

Like Greek intellectuals, particularly the Neoplatonists, Christian intellectuals were developing abstract notions that the soul was the essence of the self and that it participated in some fashion in the divine realm. Some of these thinkers proposed that, upon death, a person's soul became an angel. The fact that, for Christians, these angels had to be judged for their behavior while they were in the flesh raised other theological problems. Did these souls exercise free choice? How, if they were divine, could they choose to do evil? It is difficult to be sure, but I suspect that most nonintellectual Christians would neither have known or much cared about such formulations and debates.[46]

Invisible beings, whether or not they could properly be called "gods" or had powers that we (or those in Late Antiquity) might label as "divine," were real. They had bodies (albeit not necessarily made of flesh) and materiality and acted in the world. Pretty much everybody in Late Antiquity in the Mediterranean basin and the Near East believed this, regardless of "religious" or ethnic identity, education, or socioeconomic level. Jews, Christians, Greeks, Romans, Sassanians, Samaritans, Manicheans, "Gnostics," and Neoplatonists—all lived in a similar world, with similar understandings about its cosmology. There were "supreme" gods, demi-gods, heroes, angels, demons, and spirits involved in the daily workings of life, and how one got along in the world depended on developing and maintaining the proper relationships with them. Jewish and Christian intellectuals, and the state authorities who turned to the latter, episodically tried to create exclusionary religious identities. Sometimes these attempts were successful, but often they fought against powerful headwinds. If a particular being helped my grandmother or my neighbor's sick child, wouldn't I be foolish to ignore it?

4

The Intellectuals and the Making of "Religion"

IN THE late sixteenth century, the Inquisition arrested, for the third and last time, an Italian miller named Domenico Scandella, or Menocchio. Menocchio was unusual in that he was literate and liked to show it off. He was a man of questionable judgment and peculiar views, the very combination that brought him to the attention of the Inquisition. Going far beyond critiquing traditional church institutions and rituals (which he did frequently and loudly), he espoused his own theories of God, creation, and religion. These theories were so outlandish and incoherent that his exasperated inquisitors made repeated efforts to try to understand them. In the telling of the modern historian Carlo Ginzburg, Menocchio's beliefs emerged from a pastiche of books, conversations with visitors, and common European folk ideas. Menocchio's final encounter with the Inquisition, which ended with his execution through burning, suggests that even at this late date, Europe was only superficially Christianized. The rites looked Christian, the coherent theologies were Christian, and the power was in the hands of the church, but most people translated these facts through their own very different lenses. Menocchio himself was surely unusual, but this was in large measure because he had the tools to articulate ideas that were usually hidden from both the church and the historical record.[1]

There must have been "Menocchios" in Late Antiquity, men and women who were largely self-educated and attempted to create webs of meaning. But there is nothing particularly natural or ordinary about infusing normal, taken-for-granted facts of life with coherent meaning. Contrary to the way that many think about religion today, in antiquity there was no more need to theorize the acts that kept one on the good side of supernatural agents than there was to theorize the acts of normal, day-to-day social relations between people. Most people visited by a Roman tax collector would not even think of pondering how that person precisely fit into the vast and complex imperial bureaucracy, no less the theoretical basis of taxation itself. So too, making an offering or a prayer to an angel hardly necessitated any deep thought about whether such an act was compatible with a belief in a single God.

Some people in antiquity, though, devoted a great deal of thought to such matters. They theorized and systematized, sometimes for their own amusement and social prestige and at other times to establish identifiable social communities. In most modern accounts of religion, these systematizers—whether the rabbis or the Church Fathers—play an outsized role. They indeed created extraordinary legacies, bequeathing to us the fundamental outlines of what we know today as Judaism and Christianity. They created enduring hierarchies and institutions and, most importantly for our purposes, a deep literature that survived. Yet, in their day, they were far less well-known and influential, at least as intellectuals.

These intellectuals were almost exclusively male and arose primarily from the lower aristocracy. They came from families that could afford to educate them, and they had the economic means to give them the time for their pursuits. They made up only a tiny slice of the aristocratic class and thus can be seen as a subset of the "elite." As intriguing as it is to imagine, we have little idea of the journey that brought these men, largely expected to take over the responsibilities of managing an estate and attending to civic matters, to intellectual pursuits. Augustine left us the only full (and possibly self-serving) account of such a journey. As he describes it, a deep intellectual and spiritual unrest, grounded by an excellent classical education, finally drove him to the clergy and his writings. Perhaps he was typical.

My goal in this book is to look behind, or beyond, the systems left by these men. Yet these men and their activities are an important part of this story. On the one hand, they left much of the evidence on which this book is based. On the other hand, though, we can see their activities too as part of the same spiritual landscape as that of their brothers, wives, and slaves. They shared similar assumptions about how to communicate with invisible beings, even if they sometimes sought to transform them. In their activities, we can better see how at least some people—the Menocchios of their time—attempted to impose meaning on a disordered set of beliefs and practices.

This chapter will focus on these intellectuals and their strategies of meaning-making. In Late Antiquity, there were three main ways in which such meaning was created: myths, philosophy, and law. The mythmakers developed and promoted myths as a way of imposing meaning on an otherwise disconnected and incoherent supernatural order. The philosophers theorized and systematized, creating the infrastructure of modern Judaism and Christianity. The jurists sought to order and make coherent widely diverse practices. These are, to be sure, heuristic categories; not all meaning-making can be easily slotted into just one of these categories, and individuals could move between them. Nevertheless, their activities help us to better understand the larger environment in which they functioned.

Mythmaking

In the beginning, according to the Hebrew Bible, God was just there. YHWH—one of the many names that the Hebrew Bible uses to refer to God, introduced in Genesis 2:4—is portrayed as having no history or genealogy. In the Middle Ages, Jewish thinkers would develop the Bible's silence about God's history into philosophical propositions about God's eternal nature; God, in this understanding, was never created. Even in antiquity, though, Jewish and Christian thinkers were beginning to contrast YHWH's eternal, unchanging nature to the human-like births and adolescent phases of other gods. The contrast, of course, was invidious, with the "pagan" gods held up to mockery.[2]

In the context of the ancient world, YHWH's lack of a history was, if not quite unique, at least unusual. Most gods in antiquity had a history. Enlil, the Sumerian god of wind who ultimately became the head of the Sumerian pantheon, is the son of the god Anu. He had a tumultuous adolescence in the city of Nippur before humans were created, eventually seducing a young goddess, Ninlil, and creating several other deities with her through intercourse. Zeus, another sky god and the head of the Greek pantheon, had a similar history. He was born from two gods and then, through intrigue and sexual liaisons, made his way to the top. We do not know the parentage of the Canaanite god Baal, but according to Ugaritic stories he had many dalliances with goddesses and struggles for power with other gods, the outcomes of which had severe consequences for humans. Gods were expected to have parents and children, to live and to love in a life-rhythm like humans.[3]

These stories of the gods and their lives are today known as myths. Scholars have long debated the nature of the relationship between ancient myths, belief in gods, and their cult rituals. That is, did the birth of gods in the human imagination and the creation of rituals to honor them arise prior to the myths that explain them both, or did belief, ritual, and myth arise at the same time? When applied to origins, the question is impossible to answer. The extant evidence is too fragmentary, random, and biased to yield a definitive answer, and the truth is that it is hard to imagine what kind of evidence could even yield a definitive answer. We might discover that evidence of a ritual predates the first attestations of a myth, but that would only prove that we have yet to find an earlier attestation. As they say in the business of ancient history, the absence of evidence is not evidence of absence.[4]

What we do know, however, is that well after their origins, myths continued to develop. There is extensive evidence of different versions of what appears to be the same "story" about a god, as well as of the development of those stories. This evidence has led scholars to develop a few different models (or hypotheses) for explaining how a myth—whatever its origin—evolved and spread. According to one model, for example, myths circulate as stories that are ultimately picked up by bards. These bards wandered from community to community, telling stories for their meals and a few nights' lodging. They tweaked their stories to make them more appealing to a particular audience, just as they heard new stories and different versions of the stories that they already knew. The stories might have been used in ritual contexts, but perhaps not—they made good entertainment, as they sometimes still do today.[5]

Ultimately, though, these stories survived not through their oral medium but because scribes recorded them. In antiquity, scribes were first and foremost government functionaries. Unlike bards, who received their financial support from their audiences, scribes developed within the context of government administration and were paid through royal patronage. Their skills—literacy, math, knowledge of different languages—were the skills of government administration. They kept track of the tax rolls, wrote documents for the royal archives, calculated the calendars, and conducted diplomatic missions to foreign-speaking dependencies and enemies. Scribes also served in ancient temples. They were selected for the job based on their lineage (in antiquity, after all, there were no job listing sites) and trained extensively, often with a curriculum of copying texts that were seen as "canonical." Scribes were not the only ones who could read and compose complex literary texts, but they surely constituted most of those who could.[6]

Scribes, like everyone else, knew different stories of the gods, and some they recorded. It is unclear why they originally did this: perhaps the royal or temple authorities wanted archival copies (although this seems unlikely to me). Perhaps (and I think this is more likely) they began to make these copies for themselves, partly to develop their professional skills, partly out of their own curiosity and interest, and partly to show their expertise to other scribes. In any case, once these copies began to be produced, other scribes copied them until the point where they seemed to enter the corpus of canonical texts with which scribes used to train.[7]

Most myths from the Mediterranean basin and the Near East survive in fragments, many on clay tablets. The earliest extended literary record of a myth of the gods comes from the Greek poet Hesiod, in his seventh-century BCE poem the *Theogony*. Although we know little about his life and education, he was probably not a scribe. The poem tells the story of the birth and development of the Greek gods. We do not know whether Hesiod wrote this poem down or whether he dictated it to someone more literate, or for exactly what purpose it was written. Whatever the answers to these questions, though, it became a model of an integrated and synthetic myth. Even the editors of the Hebrew Bible, scribes living a couple of centuries after Hesiod, sought to weave together various myths about YHWH—at least those that they did not censor—into something of a coherent whole.[8]

Mythmaking is a strategy for creating meaning. These scribes and poets, who repeated, modified, and propagated their myths, assumed that their audiences (whoever they might be) already knew about and accepted the existence of the gods that they discussed. The readers and listeners of these myths were given a way to make sense of the cults and rituals in which they participated, with those like Hesiod showing how some of them connected. Myths are narratives that, whether historically, verifiably "true" or not, create a lens through which to see certain persistent features of the world.

Both myths and the process of mythmaking persisted into Late Antiquity (and still persist to the present). References to myths, especially to classical Greek ones, were everywhere. Late Antique cities were filled with coins, statues, mosaics, and wall paintings that alluded to myths. There is some modern scholarly debate on the nature of theater in Late Antiquity, but whether they continued to stage traditional, Greek-style tragedies and comedies or whether most performances centered on mimes, the content almost certainly continued to evoke ancient myths, albeit with new twists.[9]

Jews treated Greek and Roman myths ambivalently. On the one hand, some Jews clearly used images with mythological overtones to adorn their homes, synagogues, and graves. They could not avoid using the coins with their images. They even attended the theater. One Greek inscription marks a section of a theater in Miletus, in Asia Minor, as "Place of the Jews, also called God-fearing." The inscription was apparently complimentary and perhaps was displayed as a result of a donation from the Jewish community. There is little evidence to suggest that elsewhere too Jews avoided attending theatrical productions.[10]

One of the most peculiar finds from the Jewish cemetery at Beit Shearim—one in which a number of rabbis were buried—is a coffin with a depiction of the myth of "Leda and the swan," in which Zeus turns himself into a swan in order to seduce a beautiful young woman. Were the rabbis fans of this particular myth? It is hard to imagine. Rabbis tended to look askance at these myths and their images. Some rabbis forbade the reading of "the books of Homoros" (presumably Homer), other "external books," and in fact all books written in Greek because they would lead to Jews neglecting Torah study; they recognized the draw that these texts had for the educated elite. They knew that Jews could not avoid using coins, but they nevertheless praised as righteous those who never looked at the images stamped on them. A synagogue at Rehov (outside of Beit Shean) contained no images and had a mosaic floor containing a long, technical text (to which there is a parallel in rabbinic literature). Could this have been a space where rabbis who rejected the decorative trends of the day gathered? They justified living in cities, with statues of gods, by declaring those statues "mere ornaments," thus mentally canceling their divine power. The rabbis condemned the theater but also drew from it in their own parables. They rejected the myths that surrounded them, but at heart, the rabbis were realists, recognizing the need to find a way to live within, rather than apart from, cities of mixed populations.[11]

Christians, many of whom throughout Late Antiquity were born into non-Christian families, had a more complicated relationship with traditional myths. Early Christian writers particularly struggled, like their Jewish counterparts, to forge a way of existing in a Roman world full of "pagan" statues. At best, some of these writers argued (following biblical precedents), the statues are mere material, simple sculptures of stone, wood, or metal that are considered "holy" only because somebody declared it to be so. At worst, the statues are the roosting place of daimones, evil spirits that are meant to seduce people away from the true God. As Christians gained both political power and confidence, though, these rhetorical attacks on the statues of the gods became physical ones.

FIGURE 4.1. Bust of Germanicus defaced by Christians. Taking the nose off a statue was especially common. Public domain, CC BY-SA 2.0, https://en.wikipedia.org/wiki/Religious_persecution_in_the_Roman_Empire#/media/File:Bust_of_Gemanicus.jpg.

Although the destruction of temples was, at least for a while, strictly regulated in the law codes, individual Christians went on the offensive. There are numerous reports in literary texts of monks and bishops in particular attacking and defacing or destroying these statues. At some point, though, there was an open season on the statues of the gods.

Early in the fifth century CE in Ephesus, in Asia Minor, an otherwise unknown Demeas not only destroyed a statue of Aphrodite but publicized it by inscribing on the (former) statue's base an account of his destruction and replacement of the statue with a cross, "that victorious, immortal, symbol of Christ." Defacement and destruction of the statues were even ritualized, with some monks publicly destroying them to purify a place for the establishment of a church or monastery.[12]

Not every Christian was "an athlete for Christ" ready to die for their faith; most, in fact, were far from ideologically, or theologically, pure. Many of those who would accept Christ as their god, for example, grew up going to the theater and saw little reason to stop simply because they had turned to a new god. The Church Father Tertullian, writing around the turn of the second century CE in Latin in Carthage, in northern Africa, excoriates these Christians. He lashes out at Christians in his community who saw no conflict between their faith and their attendance at the theater, despite the clear references to "pagan" beliefs and practices at those performances. These Christians were no dolts; they made their own learned arguments that because nowhere does Scripture actually prohibit attendance at the theater, there is no reason to avoid it. After grudgingly admitting that, technically, they are correct, Tertullian pulls a neat, if strained, bit of interpretation to show that Scripture really does prohibit attendance at the theater. David, seen by early Christians as one of the prophets par excellence in the Old Testament, warned against consorting with "impious . . . scorners." This was not a general admonition, according to Tertullian, but a very specific one: David was looking ahead to the plotting of the Jews against Jesus. Tertullian uses his knowledge of the real meaning of Scripture to then make an a fortiori argument. If David prohibited fraternization with Jews, all the more so did he prohibit fraternizing with "heathens," as one would do in the theaters.[13]

About a century after Tertullian made his argument, another North African bishop, Novatian, similarly attacked Christians for attending the theater. Almost two centuries later, John Chrysostom, the bishop of Constantinople, launched exactly the same attack against his own congregation. Chrysostom was particularly incensed that his congregants would attend theatrical productions rather than church. Attacks against the "pagan" theater and its persistent evocation—which would often elicit strong feelings in its audience—became a conventional trope in Christian literature.[14]

Chrysostom is a good example, though, of the complexity of the Christian approach to theater and the classical tradition, which was inseparable from its depictions and understandings of the gods. Chrysostom was known for his own *paideia* or exemplary classical education. His moniker "Chrysostom," or "golden-tongued" in Greek, reflects his training in classical rhetoric. A Christian report that Chrysostom was a star student of the non-Christian rhetor Libanius is plausible, if not verifiable. Christians like Chrysostom so valued a classical education, paideia, that many taught in the gymnasia, the central civic educational institution of the Greek city. The "pagan" emperor Julian, in fact, banned Christians from teaching in the gymnasia out of fear that they were corrupting the youth. Much as those who Tertullian excoriated had no problem attending the theater, many Christians felt no contradiction between their classical education, suffused as it was with mythological associations, and their (often new) faith.[15]

For elite Christians like Chrysostom, such critiques of popular practice were, in fact, foundational; their goal was to create a unique "Christian" identity for the many "Christians" who had no problem with their identities as simply "Romans who believed in Christ." There is nothing new to the rhetorical strategy of creating a religio-ethnic "other" against which to define one own's identity. In this case, classical mythology is positioned as the polar opposite to the ideal Christian life, one of *simplicitas*. Even the quality of simplicitas, that of a simple and plain lifestyle that values interiority over external (and duplicitous) performance, has roots in the classical tradition of *parrhesia*, "frank speech." Members of the Christian elite, that is, adapted classical lines of attack in order to create a bifurcation between "classical" and "Christian."[16]

The Christian elite were not attempting to discredit myth in general, only the wrong kind of myth. "Myths," in the sense that I am using the term here, are narratives that create meanings; they are not necessarily false, and there is nothing necessarily pejorative about the term.

Christians had developed alternative sets of myths well before John Chrysostom. Many stories about Jesus circulated throughout antiquity. Some of these, such as the four Gospels and (some) letters of Paul, eventually found their way into the New Testament, a canon that probably finally came together only in the fifth century CE. Many other literary expressions of Christian myths, though, did not. The so-called Gnostics (an umbrella term for several different Christian sects deemed by the emerging Catholic tradition as "heretical") had a rich set of myths that rejected the place of the Jewish god, YHWH, in the Christian story. Other Christian groups, such as the Marcionites, the Manicheans, and the Montanists, subscribed to somewhat different, if now not entirely recoverable, myths. Epiphanius, an "orthodox" Christian writer in the fourth century, composed a veritable catalog of groups he deemed "heretical" that when read together portray a Christian world with many competing myths. John Chrysostom's own myths were meant to compete not only with classical ones but also with those of other Christians.[17]

So too we find the new, competing Christian myths in art. All surviving Christian art from before the fourth century is from tombs and catacombs and mostly depicts scenes that are also found in Scripture (Old and New Testaments). After Constantine the weight of Christian artistic tradition shifts, both in context and topic. Christian art in cemeteries declines at the same time that art in churches is beginning to rise and disappears almost entirely by the fifth century. Narrative scenes from Scripture are present throughout all of antiquity, but their focus changes. Christian art, especially in churches, begins to emphasize a glorious Christ. The myth seems to be shifting from one of persecution and salvation to one of power and triumph. This is certainly related to the growing political power of Christians within the Roman Empire.

Some of the earliest extant Christian art from a church is from Ravenna, in Italy. The artistic program of the church at Ravenna (now called the Basilica of San Vitale) illustrates the complex swirl of issues around myth and art, power and meaning-making. Ravenna was an important imperial city in Late Antiquity, the seat of the government of the Western Roman Empire. The Basilica was finished in the middle of

FIGURE 4.2. Christ in majesty with angels, San Vitale, Ravenna. Panther Media GmbH/Alamy Stock Photo (R484XC). Used by permission.

the sixth century and adorned with expensive and impressive mosaics. In one, Christ sits on high on the apse, haloed, flanked by angels, and clothed in royal purple. He hands a crown to Saint Vitale, who was known as a martyr. On his other side, one of the early bishops involved in building the church hands the church to Christ. Sitting on the earth, Christ is clearly in control here.

Two other mosaics, also in prominent places, show, though, that Christ is not the only one in control. On one side of the apse is a large mosaic of the Emperor Justinian I, haloed and clothed in purple with his court, another bishop involved in building the church, and his army. Justinian, turning toward Christ, is offering the Eucharist. Across from this mosaic panel is a parallel one with his wife, the Empress Theodora (also haloed), and her court, offering the chalice.

Taken together, these mosaics (and many others in the church) promote a Christian story focused on triumph and power. Justinian I and Theodora (both of whom lived in Constantinople and never visited Ravenna) are players in a divine saga, joining Christ in his rule over the earth. The artistic program of the Basilica of San Vitale advances a very particular vision of a muscular Christianity. God and emperor remain separate; the iconographic similarities point toward a vague conflation of the divine and the human.[18]

The artistic plan at Ravenna would most likely have unsettled, or even upset, Chrysostom. For him, traditional mythological imagery and particularly that connected to the imperial cult stood opposite the new Christian myth (although he would not call it that). The creators of Ravenna's artistic plan were engaged in their own form of mythmaking, one that nodded to and appropriated classical notions of power and the quasi-divine nature of the emperors. Chrysostom had famously fought with local and imperial authorities and the aristocracy of both Antioch and Constantinople due to his condemnation of excessive wealth and the neglect of the poor that he saw in these communities; his myth of Christianity was based on "the blessed poor." Ravenna's message was more conventional for its day. Christian rituals would take place under the watchful gaze of a well-dressed Christ and between depictions of the emperor, the empress, and the imperial court, with a troop of soldiers in the wings. Chrysostom's vision was probably too radical for the local Italian bishops under whose authority the artwork was made—they are, in fact, the only ones explicitly identified with captions in the mosaics (although these captions appear to have been added later). For these bishops, appropriation of classical myths was a safer—and more lucrative—route.[19]

Unlike Christians, who struggled to find the balance between rejection of their own classical past and its appropriation, Jews had a longer mythological past on which to draw. The ways in which they expressed and developed those myths, though, were similarly connected to the larger urban environments in which their intellectuals lived. Jewish art serves as a rather dramatic example of how Jews changed the ways in which they expressed their own myths. Prior to the third century CE, Jews largely avoided representing figures in their art. The Hasmoneans, the successors to the Maccabees who ruled from 162 BCE to 32 BCE, never depicted themselves on their coins, which made them exceptional among rulers in the Hellenistic and Roman worlds. Even King Herod the Great, the "half-Jew" according to Josephus, did not depict himself on his coins, probably for fear of drawing the ire of the Jewish populace. (Not a single image of him survives from antiquity, even in his private fortress and probable place of burial, Herodion.) Jews sometimes adorned their ossuaries with geometrical and vegetal designs but rarely did so with figures of people or even animals.[20]

By the third century CE, at least outside of Palestine, Jews had abandoned their reluctance to represent figures. And when they did, they chose to use them to represent their myths. The synagogue of Dura Europos, a sleepy garrison city in modern-day Syria that sat on the border of Rome and Syria, was covered with painted pictures of scenes known from the Bible. The find was so unexpected that one scholar, Erwin Randall Goodenough, posited that this was a special group of Jews devoted to an allegorical and astral understanding of religion. Today, we know that such representation was not exceptional. Several synagogue mosaics in Palestine, probably dating to the fourth century and later, contain similar scenes. For example, the synagogue at Sepphoris, a booming mixed-population city in Palestine, contains a spectacular mosaic. With a zodiac in the middle, the mosaic features a rendering of the story of the binding of Isaac (Genesis 22); depicts several implements associated with the biblical Tabernacle with a basket of first fruits that, according to Deuteronomy (26:1–11), one is to bring to the Jerusalem Temple; and is crowned by a picture of an ark. There are many other such synagogue depictions; one from Gaza has a beautiful rendition of David and his lyre. Scholars debate how this art is best interpreted. Are the images "mere ornamentation," or are they meant to be read together as making a coherent statement? In any case, it is reasonably clear that the images (which often have helpful captions, labeling the figures) would serve both a didactic function—making ignorant viewers curious about the myths if not quite explaining them—and one that connects those in the space to a mythological past. We do not know whether the choice of decoration was made by those who donated the mosaics (also helpfully noted in inscriptions), some kind of committee appointed by the synagogue community, or the artisans themselves, but whoever made these decisions were themselves evoking narratives of myths as ways of adding meaning to their worship.[21]

Jews also produced and circulated myths in narrative forms. During the Second Temple period, Jews authored literary works of myth. Many of these books describe tours of heaven or other revelatory experiences, in which God explains his secrets to the protagonist. Throughout Late Antiquity that tradition continued in several texts that became known as Hekhalot, or "chambers," literature, so called because the protagonists (usually rabbinic) sometimes ascend to the chambers of the heavenly palace. In truth, the label encompasses a diverse collection of texts that deal loosely with divine "secrets," including especially the use of special (i.e., divine and angelic) names.[22]

Equally obscure are the Jewish apocalypses of Late Antiquity. The book of Zerubbabel, written in Hebrew probably around the seventh century, was one such apocalypse. Zerubbabel is a shadowy figure in the Hebrew Bible. He was sent by the Persians to lead the restored Jewish settlement in Jerusalem in the sixth century BCE (Ezra 3:8; Haggai 1). Like the Second Temple books that vouchsafed a special divine revelation to Enoch, an even more shadowy biblical figure (Genesis 5:21–24), the book of Zerubbabel records the (secret) visions that Zerubbabel received from the divine realm. In these very thinly disguised visions, Zerubbabel is told that the Jewish messiah will rise to fight and defeat the demonic Christian kingdom. By the time it was written, Jews had been subjected to marginalizing imperial laws (that were, however, only sporadically enforced), but at least some were still unafraid to develop new myths against their oppressors. The fact that the Byzantine Empire was on the verge of collapse in the face of the Arab invasions (or perhaps had even fallen by the time this was written) could, of course, have given the authors a bit of courage as well.[23]

We don't know who produced the Hekhalot texts, how they circulated, or who read them. The authors (they survive as collections of texts written by different people) were certainly literate and had knowledge of rabbinic traditions. In a general sense, the Hekhalot texts advance the proposition that things are not what they seem to be; there is a hidden, secret realm. They do not exactly provide recipes for mystical experiences—many of their instructions are so vague and obscure that it is hard to imagine that they are really meant to be followed—as much as they generate in the mind of their readers a new, alternative ontological reality. Such a sense creates both a distinctive worldview and a community of those who feel that they have access to the true reality behind the veil of the visible world.

Jewish intellectuals used yet another literary form in writing their myths. The rabbis developed a new genre of interpretation of the Bible called midrash. Midrash is based on some earlier forms of biblical interpretation that are found in the Dead Sea Scrolls, but it is distinct enough to be considered a truly rabbinic innovation. Midrash begins from the assumption that the biblical text is entirely perfect, holy, and pregnant with meaning. God has allowed the text to continue to reveal God's will, with the meaning buried in words and clauses, not context. That is, an extra letter in a word—what we might consider a spelling or scribal mistake—really is a message from God, left for the rabbis to discover. Midrash is thus primarily a noncontextual way of reading, in which a verse or a word in a verse or even a letter in a word can yield interpretations that have nothing to do with their contexts.[24]

Midrash spins out alternative meanings from Scripture, often cryptically and in fragments. One, for example, struggles with the question of why humans are worthy of receiving the Torah:

> Rabbi Yehoshua ben Levi said: When Moses ascended to the heights, the ministering angels said before the Holy One, blessed be He, "Master of the World, Why is there one born of a woman among us?" He said to them, "He came to receive the Torah." They said before him, "A precious hidden treasure, that you hid away for 974 generations before the world was created, [and now] You want to give it to flesh and blood? As it is stated, 'What is man that You are mindful of him and the son of a man that you attend to him?' [Psalms 8:5]. [And] 'God our Lord, how glorious Your name in all the earth, You have set your glory above the heavens' [Psalms 8:2]."[25]

The heavenly drama continues with God challenging Moses to prove to the angels that the Torah is for humans, not angels (and assuring him that the angels will not destroy him in anger). Moses then cites verses from the Torah to show that they apply only to humans. Can the prohibitions against murder, adultery, and theft apply to angels? he asks them rhetorically. His arguments sway the angels, and they proclaim, "Lord our God, how majestic is Your name in all the earth!" (Psalms 8:10). Won over, the angels then start showering gifts upon Moses. Even the Angel of Death gives him the ability to stop a plague.

To say that Psalm 8, on its surface, refers to this three-way conversation between God, the angels, and Moses would be beyond a stretch. The rabbis have taken this psalm, dismembered it, and out of its pieces have constructed a very powerful meditation on the differences between God, the angels, and humans. Psalm 8 expresses the wonder and awe that God gave lowly humans power over the earth. In its original context, Psalms 8:10—which closes the short psalm—is an exclamation from the view of the narrator. The rabbis, though, transfer it to the mouths of the angels, who now agree with God's judgment to give the Torah (which is nowhere mentioned in the psalm) to humans.[26]

This is but one of hundreds, if not thousands, of such rabbinic texts. Like many, it weaves a statement—or maybe better, gestures toward a statement—about the nature of the world and humankind out of Scripture. It makes no effort at systematic completeness, logical proof, or harmonization with other theological propositions (e.g., the real nature of angels). This midrash is more directed, with a clearer set of lessons, than many, but it too is open-ended. It is a reading of Psalm 8 but makes no claim to be its exclusive reading. It is Rabbi Yehoshua ben Levi's reading: take it or leave it.

In common discourse today, "myths" are often seen as false narratives common among the uneducated. This understanding goes back to Plato. In several passages, Plato contrasts "myth" with logical argument, clearly denigrating the former. While, as is often the case with Plato, his view is actually more complex (or not entirely consistent), the idea that myths are inferior to arguments has persisted, particularly (unsurprisingly) among philosophers. Yet what I have attempted to show here is that myths are narrative forms of creating meaning. They need not be labeled true or false, and they are certainly not to be considered the sole creation and domain of children or the uneducated. Throughout antiquity, the educated elite drew on common stories, but they also freely shaped and deployed them. When people tell, believe, or even argue against myth, they are involved in a process of meaning-making. A myth might originate with "the people" or an educated thinker, and it might be widely disseminated and accepted.[27]

The reception and interplay of myths in Late Antiquity was complex and varied widely. Often, myths that we might see as "competing" easily crossed what we might see as denominational boundaries. Adherents of Jupiter might not question or see as threatening myths involving Isis, Mithras, or even Christ. Wealthier Jews, like their neighbors, may have adorned their homes with scenes from classical mythology and read "the books of Homer." Rabbis rejected such representations in environments they could control (not many, judging from what we have thus recovered archaeologically) and explained them away ("mere ornamentation") in environments they could not. Most Jews might not have seen a conflict, although they developed and promoted their own myths. Christians, even bishops, often found some accommodation between classical myths and their new ones, although this was trickier. For some Christian leaders like John Chrysostom, myths became pointed boundaries: with us or against us.[28]

Philosophy

Myth, and the mythmakers, made meaning through narratives. There were other ways, though, that intellectuals tried to create meaning out of the assortment of gods, rituals, and observations about the world. Myths offered snippets of explanation, but clearly this was not enough for those who sought intellectual coherence and systems. Systematic reflection about, and critique of, the gods went back to the beginning of philosophy itself.

Even before Plato, Greek philosophers began to think critically about the gods. We have only fragments of their writings, ironically preserved by later Christian authors who cited them in order to refute them. Xenophanes of Kolophon criticized anthropomorphic representation of the gods. Diagoras of Melos is termed an "atheist" even in some ancient sources, although his few surviving fragments suggest that he did not completely deny belief in the gods. Several Greek philosophers, most famously Socrates, were hounded for their "impiety." The charge probably does not refer to wholesale rejection of belief in gods but to specific kinds of critiques that threatened to undermine the authority of local gods and their keepers. Epicurus (341–270 BCE), folding his account of the gods into a more all-encompassing philosophical system, did not reject the gods as much as deny that they were involved in human affairs. Later readers (and perhaps contemporary ones as well) were scandalized by this position, which removed the fear of divine punishment as a motive for good behavior. The rabbis would make his name synonymous with one who denied the power of God—it was not a compliment. Horace, the Roman satirist who lived in the first century BCE, contrasted "Jewish" belief with his own Epicureanism. On being told of a temple at which incense melts without fire, he says, "Let Apella the Jew credit that, I don't. I've heard the gods live a carefree life, and if nature works miracles then it isn't the gods gloomily sending them down from their home in the sky."[29]

Only a small minority of ancient philosophers, however, turned their systematization and harmonization of beliefs and rituals about the gods to dangerous critique. Most took the usual belief in a divine world and rationalized it, seeking to develop systems of thought that explained how this world functioned in relation to ours. Aristotle's notion that there was a "first mover," in which the very existence of the cosmos proves that there must have been a force to order it and put it into motion, became popular. Others, such as Stoics, posited that the divine is to be equated with eternal reason, a power that acts upon inert matter. Cicero, who is probably our best surviving example of a Stoic reflection on the nature of the gods from antiquity, attributes to the older Stoic Chrysippus the statement that god is "the force of fate and the necessity of future events." The folding of divine activity into a single "force of fate," though, did not erase for Cicero and those like him the existence of the local gods, who still deserved piety. The civic gods remained important, if not always fully integrated into a larger philosophical account of the divine.[30]

Philosophical reflection on the gods remained important throughout Late Antiquity. The most important classical philosophical movement to emerge in Late Antiquity became known as Neoplatonism. The founder of this school of thought is generally thought to be Plotinus (204/5–270 CE), who was born in Egypt, educated in Alexandria, and then spent much of his life lecturing and writing (presumably in Greek) in Rome. Plotinus saw himself above all as a reader and interpreter of Plato rather than as the creator of a new school or philosophy. His major contribution was to create a reading of Plato that attenuated the division between the three principal metaphysical components, the One, the Intellect, and the Soul. These three components existed, for Plotinus, in a kind of hierarchical relationship. The One is the absolutely simple first cause, uncreated and indescribable. The Intellect is the first derivation of the One, the set of Platonic forms that ground reality as we know it. The Soul is the desire for the Intellect, mediating between it and the senses.[31]

The One stands at the center of Plotinus's reading of Plato: it is the ineffable fount of all being. Plotinus was thus, depending on how one defines the term, a "monotheist," who associated divinity with the One. This was a less radical position than it might appear, despite having been formulated in a world full of gods. There was a long philosophical tradition stretching back to at least Aristotle that posited a first principle—the so-called unmoved mover—upon which everything else depends. The unmoved mover is associated with the divine. The Stoics too had a "monotheistic" conception. Theirs, however, was grounded in a notion of the "active" principle that "providentially governs the universe." This active principle was indestructible and often identified with fire. Aristotelians, Stoics, and (Neo-)Platonists shared the belief that there was a single first, simple, and providential divine force in the cosmos.[32]

For our purposes, what is most interesting about these philosophers is that they saw no contradiction between their own commitments to a single divine principle and the ordinary and traditional beliefs and rituals devoted to the many gods. They did not attempt to fight against the belief in many divine beings but rather to explain these beings in light of their abstract intellectual systems. For Plotinus, there are a multitude of gods, all of whom are part of the One: "He makes many gods, all depending upon himself and existing from him and through him." Different gods are merely different manifestations of the same single god, identical with the driving force of the universe. This was an intellectual strategy used in the nineteenth century to coin the term "Hinduism." Prior to the creation of the notion that many disparate Indic traditions are all actually manifestations that fall under the same umbrella term, there were simply disparate Indic traditions.[33]

Individuals, according to Plotinus, must seek to reunite with the One by opening ourselves up and allowing the One of the universe to unite with the One in each of us. Yet Plotinus and his followers are strangely quiet about how one is to do that. One supposes that they had spiritual exercises and that some may have even experienced out-of-body sensations, but they rarely discuss what they did or how they felt. At the same time, they rarely suggest that the everyday materialistic, and often bloody, practices of providing gifts to the gods are a problem. Porphyry, a student of Plotinus who wrote a tract praising vegetarianism, was the rare voice against sacrifice, advising instead practice of "the knowledge of god," whatever that means exactly.[34]

The vast majority of Neoplatonists harmonized traditional sacrificial practices with their own symbolic understanding of them. One fourth-century CE Neoplatonist about whom we know little, Sallustius, states that "prayers with sacrifices are animated words, the word giving power to life and life animation to the word." The difference between Porphyry and the other Neoplatonists, as they recognized already in antiquity, hinged on the value of human actions (or perhaps, to borrow a later Christian word, "works") for the unification of the self with the One. That is, going beyond even Sallustius's claim, might ritual action in and of itself achieve unification? The earliest full-throated defense of that position was the Neoplatonist philosopher Iamblichus, a student of Porphyry's. In his tract *de mysteriis,* Iamblichus latched onto a word coined some years before, "theurgy," to defend his position that ritual actions are efficacious. Theurgic rites liberate the soul and allow it to reunite with the One. Throughout this tract, Iamblichus somewhat paradoxically provides a rigorous (even if it did not convince all) philosophical justification for a set of activities that are necessary precisely because they point beyond words and description. In another tract, Iamblichus curiously chose to write a biography of Pythagoras, whose mathematical expertise was also understood as a key to unlocking the divine realm. Although Christians (and many modern scholars) would dismiss theurgy as "magic" and "superstition," for writers like Iamblichus and Proclus, the Neoplatonic scholarch under the Emperor Julian, theurgy was anything but; it was, instead, a component of a well-ordered philosophical system. It had the advantage as well of reinvesting traditional practices with new meaning. It was a new defense of an old practice.[35]

In Late Antiquity, philosophy was not the abstruse intellectual practice that it often is today. From its ancient Greek foundations, it was seen as an exercise that allows us to flourish and reach our potential. Yet at the same time, it was and was not a complete "way of life." A few philosophers, like Epicurus and Diogenes the Cynic, were at least remembered to have led lives that made them recognizable as philosophers (or just odd), although this was much less true of their followers in Late Antiquity. Many ancient biographers of philosophers, who were often themselves philosophers, attributed to their subjects special powers, achieved as a result of their embodiment of divinity. Despite the hyperbole, though, some important philosophers did become prominent and influential figures in the imperial courts, and the Late Antique philosopher was expected to defend traditional practices. Famous philosophers were depicted in art; in Aphrodisias, a city in modern-day Turkey, a collection of busts of philosophers and philosophically inclined leaders suggests the existence of a Neoplatonic school. More ordinary followers of philosophers could "convert" to a particular philosophical school, but their outward behaviors would not distinguish them.[36]

Philosophers, whether they performed miracles, got themselves memorialized in a bust, or simply sat and learned in an academy to be forgotten by posterity, were almost all privileged men. The larger and more famous academies, such as at Athens, had significant endowments, but it is unclear, and probably unlikely, that the money went to subsidize mere students. The study of philosophy requires both a previous education and literacy—which were uncommon throughout antiquity and largely (although not exclusively) confined to those with access to resources—and the time to devote to it, free of working at other jobs. As much as they might sometimes valorize the simple life, the philosophers themselves were not from simple families. Nor do we hear in Late Antiquity of former slaves becoming philosophers, as they sometimes did in earlier times.[37]

There were very few women philosophers in Late Antiquity. One ancient author tells of a woman named Hipparchia, who lived around 300 BCE and was married to a Cynic. According to the later biographer, she occasionally showed up their friends in philosophical arguments. More famous was Hypatia, who lived in the fourth century in Alexandria, a mathematician and (possibly) Neoplatonic philosopher. The daughter of another mathematician and academic who (presumably) tutored her, she was murdered by a Christian mob in 415. We do not know whether she was murdered for the content of her teachings, the political standings of her students, or her boldness to teach as a woman, or whether she was simply caught up as collateral damage in a feud that had little to do with her.[38]

Hypatia appears to have had both Christian and non-Christian students. As in the case of myth, the relationship between Christians and philosophy, and traditionally minded philosophers and Christianity, was varied and complex. Already in the second century CE, Justin Martyr tells us that, having been raised a non-Christian, he aspired to study philosophy. Disillusioned, though, by the philosophical method—which did not provide the surety that he sought—he found in Christ a more amenable and secure path. His narrative thus sets up philosophy and Christianity in opposition to each other; one could make either philosophy or Christianity one's "way of life," but not both. About 250 years later, Augustine would follow a roughly similar trajectory. Born in North Africa to a traditional father with some means and status in his community and to a Christian mother, he first pursued training in philosophy and rhetoric. Dissatisfied with this, under the influence of Ambrose with whom he studied in Milan, he turned to the path of Christ.[39]

Yet for all their rhetorical posturing of pitting philosophy against Christianity, both Justin and Augustine never lost the habits of mind they developed as students of philosophy. At the very same time that they were condemning philosophy as a dead end for answering ultimate questions, they wrote very much like philosophers. Using logic, they attempted to create systems of thought to explain and ground the emerging "Christianity" even while denying that logic was sufficient. Rather than rejecting rational discourse as misleading and hopelessly insufficient, they embraced it. As with the Neoplatonists, it was a discourse that required ritual actions to activate.[40]

Augustine's philosophical contribution to the development of Western Christianity is hard to overstate. He brought intellectual coherence to a hodge-podge of different ideas, all the while grounding the parts of this new system of thought in Scripture. Like Plotinus (with whose thought he was probably modestly familiar), Augustine approached philosophy as commentary; out of the scattered and quite unsystematic nuggets of Scripture he wove together a system. Augustine's thought evolved over time, especially in response to other Christian writers with whom he feuded over certain questions, but its core is relatively stable. For Augustine, Scripture provides an account of the human condition (one trapped in sin) and Christianity offers the solution that philosophy alone cannot. The greatest good lies in turning to God, much as the Neoplatonists urged focusing on the One.[41]

Augustine is probably the most important of the Christian philosophers from Late Antiquity, but he was far from the only one. The Christian Platonists, like Origen (ca. 185–253 CE) and Gregory of Nyssa (ca. 335–394 CE), are remembered best in the Christian tradition, even if the church, about three centuries after Origen's death, anathematized ten of his propositions. But we know of many other philosophical Christians from this period. Jerome, who lived in Palestine in the fifth century CE, inveighed against both Jovinian, who argued against the value of chastity, and Helvidius, who argued against the virginity—perpetual or otherwise—of Mary. Augustine wrote against Pelagius, who gave far more power to human free will than he did, and Faustus, who attacked some of the doctrines that came to dominate the church. Jerome's and Augustine's adversaries were not philosophical slouches, and they show an early church teeming with those who wished to have a hand in creating the new Christian doctrine.[42]

The profusion of philosophical debates among Christians at this time, precisely as the imperial authorities were giving more opportunities to Christians for power and advancement within the imperial bureaucracy, was not accidental. Theological controversy was not solely a means to power; there is little doubt that the combatants held their beliefs sincerely. Yet the viciousness of the debate, which far exceeded the broadsides that Greek philosophical schools launched at each other, also suggests that the stakes were higher. One of the most consequential and complex of these debates, for example, was the so-called Arian controversy. As is typical for those condemned by the "orthodox" church, we know little about Arius, an Alexandrian Christian who lived from ca. 256 to 336 CE. His ideas suggest that he had some kind of advanced education that was generally reserved for those (like Augustine) who came from families of means. Arius and his followers advocated a non-Trinitarian Christology. That is, Arius thought that Christ was born of God, having come into being at a later point than God. In a sense, for the Arians, Christ was thus similar to a "high angel" in nature who became flesh. From what we can gather, though, they attributed the same salvific power to Christ, who then died for the sins of humanity. In terms of communal and personal devotion, one could pray to Christ to intercede with the Father, but Christ did not hold the same supreme power as did the Father.[43]

Arius was not a particularly original thinker in this respect. In the late second century, Celsus, a Greek philosopher, wrote an attack on Christianity to which, about seventy-five years later (in 248, shortly before Arius was born), Origen responded. Celsus's main arguments against Christians were social rather than theological, but he did take the opportunity to attack the notion of the Trinity as absurd and inconsistent with a claim of monotheism. Porphyry, a non-Christian philosopher and contemporary of Arius, similarly attacked the Christian doctrine of the Trinity as irrational. These critiques of Celsus and Porphyry were not baseless, and it is certainly possible that they were convincing to many Christians. Arius might, then, have drawn on these contemporary critiques, in effect, answering them in a way that retains the core beliefs of most Christians.[44]

The fact that Arianism, as it came to be known, was the equivalent of a theological conflagration that the church would need centuries to put out also suggests that the critiques against orthodox Christology—that Christ is a separate being yet co-eternal with and of the same "substance" (or nature) as the Father—made sense to many. Through the fourth century, several Roman emperors were Arians, as well as rulers in Spain, North Africa, and the Kingdom of the Lombards (in Italy) into the early Middle Ages. Arianism represented a sensible, arguably more rational alternative to Orthodox Christology.

The route to the orthodox suppression of Arianism was so long and winding—with each group taking whatever opportunities it had to declare the other heretical—that it raises the question of what was really at stake. Who really cared about the true nature of Christ and why, when the bottom-line impact on most people's lives and worship practices would have been minimal? In at least some respects, the Late Antique debate about Christology was a debate among the philosophical elite fighting for what they normally fight for: prestige, money, and power.

Understanding the christological and other abstruse philosophical/theological debates in Late Antiquity as a competition between elites—whether between non-Christians and Christians or among Christians themselves—might allow us to also understand another puzzling phenomenon: the absence of Jews in these debates. Philo, a Jew who lived in Alexandria ca. 20 BCE–50 CE, left an impressive philosophical oeuvre written in Greek, but he was also the last Jew to do so until the Middle Ages. Although some scholars have argued that the rabbis, emerging in the first century CE and having left a voluminous literature written in Hebrew and Aramaic, should be seen as "philosophers," they do not quite fit the mold. Like philosophers, they devoted their time to study and taught literate male members of the elite in disciple circles. They used older texts and traditions (e.g., Scripture for the rabbis and Plato's writing for the Neoplatonists) as a basis for new speculations, which in turn they saw as helping to guide people to the "good life." They promoted themselves as special, even holy, and worthy of emulation. But there the similarities, which are largely superficial, end. The rabbis did constitute a loose network of highly literate men with specialized training, but nobody in Late Antiquity would have called them "philosophers" or their writings "philosophy." In fact, the rabbis themselves sometimes refer to "philosophers" (using the Greek loan word), usually disparagingly and never meaning Jews.[45]

Before turning to the rabbis and their largely legal mode of making meaning, it is worth briefly returning to the question of why Jews (and not just rabbis) were not involved in philosophy as it was understood in Late Antiquity. Some scholars have suggested that traditional Greeks and Romans did not mount philosophical attacks on Judaism because they had a grudging respect for its monotheism and antiquity. Even Porphyry and Julian, neither of whom hesitated to sneer at Jews and Jewish practice, did not attack Judaism on philosophical grounds; they saved their bile for Christianity. I think that these differences, though, are better explained by looking at the more mundane and material situation of these competing philosophers. Greek, Roman, and Christian philosophers were all playing the same game. They did so (at least in part) to gain prestige, fame, fortune, and, given the shifting political landscape of the Roman Empire in Late Antiquity, power. They competed with each other, and the stakes were only partially about the ideas themselves. This was a game, though, that Jews could not play. After the Jewish revolts of the early second century CE, Jewish intellectuals virtually disappear from the Greek-speaking landscape. Jews themselves did not disappear; there is abundant archaeological evidence that they continued to live and thrive throughout the Roman Empire. But they were excluded, or excluded themselves, from participating in philosophy. Philosophers thus may have ignored "Judaism" not because they respected it but because Jewish philosophers were irrelevant. They paid no more attention to Judaism than they did to Mithraism because they had little to gain by doing so.[46]

Law

There is a third way that ancient intellectuals sought to make meaning and systems out of scattered rituals and beliefs: law. Roman emperors, Christian bishops, and Jewish rabbis all created legal "systems" of sorts.

To understand the connection between law and meaning, though, we must first briefly understand how law was understood and functioned in Late Antiquity.

Most Westerners today have a very particular notion of what law is and how it is meant to function. We assume that law is produced by authoritative institutions (or individuals) that have some means (usually coercive) to enforce it. Laws are meant, at least ideally, to be accessible, transparent, and applicable to all. The job of those who apply the laws—usually judges—is to determine, in a given case, the relevant facts and the governing written laws and then to adjudicate a decision based on those laws.

Law in antiquity, though, rarely functioned in this manner. Disputants took their disagreements to local judges or arbitrators who proposed, or imposed, solutions based on their understanding of what was "just." This sense of justice was shaped by the facts, different contextual factors, and past precedents. Since the local judges were often also involved in positions that were responsible for keeping order, their understanding of what was just or fair was shaped by what those around them would accept as just. A judgment that would lead to more disorder because it would have been perceived as unfair would have been counterproductive. Justice keeps and restores order; it is not some abstract principle.

Precedent is an important factor in any system of justice. Over time, community members develop and transmit a memory of past cases that leads to developing expectations of what "fair" outcomes might look like for similar cases. A judge who went against such precedents would risk being seen as arbitrary and unfair, which in turn could lead to the kind of unrest that could cost him his job, or more. At the same time, judges were not bound by precedents: if in a particular case a different verdict would have been thought fair by the majority, judges were free to make it.

From the time of Hammurabi to the Bible and beyond, scribes collected these precedents, smoothed them out, and wrote them down. These collections were training exercises, not authoritative law codes. By copying and working with them, scribes—who were all-purpose governmental officials who could often find themselves working as or advising judges—developed a better understanding of precedents that would help them adjudicate common cases. When they took such a collection and inscribed it on a monument, as they famously did under the reign of Hammurabi, they were not so much providing a reference book (the vast majority could not even read such a monument) as they were making a simple, propagandistic statement that Hammurabi could be trusted to be just. So too the law codes embedded in the Torah proclaim God's justice.[47]

Many centuries had passed from the time of Hammurabi and the development of the Torah to Late Antiquity, but the place of law had largely remained stable. Roman law, *lex,* was expected to be applied in a fair but flexible way. In Late Antiquity, some laws were produced by the imperial court at its own initiative. Most, however, were created in response to the queries of local officials who were facing particularly sticky local situations and did not want to take responsibility for making a wrong decision. Given the breadth and complexity of the civic organization of the Roman Empire, and the natural reluctance of officials to take responsibility for potentially negative outcomes, the stream of requests for legal guidance to the offices of provincial governors as well as the imperial administration was unremitting. The result was the production of much law, most of which was drawn up in an unsystematic and ad hoc fashion.[48]

Roman jurists began to codify and systematize this ad hoc collection of laws in the second century. In his tract *Institutes,* an otherwise unknown jurist named Gaius created a systematic set of principles that he saw as running through Roman laws. Other jurists, such as Paul and Ulpian (early third century), produced legal commentaries. By the end of the third century, there were at least two collections as well of (highly selected) pronouncements of Roman emperors. The reasons for their composition, as well as their organization, remain obscure. As with the past activity of ancient scribes, these early Roman jurists were most likely producing, on their own initiative, works for guidance in creating and administering law rather than actual normative law. Only in the fifth century, with the production of the *Codex Theodosianus,* do we see a major, government-supported effort to collect and systematize Roman laws, to turn Roman *laws* into Roman *Law.*[49]

After nine years of officially sponsored work, the *Codex Theodosianus* was completed in 438. The redactors of the *Codex Theodosianus* organized prior laws, rescripts, and legal commentaries into categories, recording relevant snippets in each category while making no attempt to harmonize them. The sixteen primary categories built on those in previous collections, with separate books devoted to topics such as inheritances, military affairs, taxes (which comprise several categories—clearly a major concern of the government), and felonies. It is the last book, though, that most interests us, on what we would call (and to an extent what it also calls) religion. It does not appear in earlier collections.[50]

Book 16 of the *Codex Theodosianus* shows the alliance of the emerging orthodox church with the imperial government. The primary goal of book 16 is to privilege a particular group of Christians as authentic. It thus first defines those ecclesiastical authorities that are sanctioned, along with their privileges, before discussing "heretics" (that is, other Christians with whom the bishops were competing), apostates, Jews, and "pagans" and their legal disabilities. Under the guidance of the emperor's spiritual advisors, religious identity became, increasingly, a matter of legal concern. Book 16 of the *Codex Theodosianus* was an attempt at systematizing and defining what it meant, for the purposes of imperial treatment, to be "Christian." Given that heretics could meet with the death penalty, it became exceedingly important, at least in theory, to define also what a "heretic" was.[51]

The "at least in theory" part is important because the *Codex Theodosianus,* similar to earlier legal codes, still did not function like a modern law code. Even on the face of it, it was more encyclopedic than a normative guide, containing multiple contradictory legal pronouncements. There is, additionally, abundant evidence that imperial law was only selectively followed. Like other laws throughout antiquity, the *Codex Theodosianus* was not the only or final determinant for a judge when adjudicating a claim. While the bishops behind book 16 were concerned with defining religious identities and the proper "Christian," their victory was incomplete. While they surely wished that the laws that they framed would become normative, they also recognized the limits of law.

Law, that is, was at least as much about creating a discourse through which intellectuals could create meaning as it was a guide for assigning privileges and penalties. A few decades before the *Codex Theodosianus,* a bishop named Epiphanius of Salamis authored a tract called the *Panarion,* which cataloged "heresies." The bishops behind book 16 were in many respects engaged in the same intellectual project as Epiphanius: defining at least for themselves what they thought it meant to be a "Christian." Only they used law to do so.[52]

For the rabbis, who engaged in mythmaking only sporadically and who refrained entirely from systematic philosophy, law became the primary discourse through which they created systematized meaning. In this context, rabbis should be seen, as one scholar put it, as a "subaltern elite," or at least that is how they saw themselves. They were "intellectuals" who sought to preserve and develop their native indigenous knowledge and traditions in the face of the Roman Empire.[53]

A substantial part of these native indigenous traditions consisted of what we might call religious law or custom. Today, we draw a relatively clear line between the concepts of "law" and "custom"; laws are normative whereas customs are not. It was a blurrier line in antiquity, though. The Greek term *nomos,* even when applied to Jewish practices, was squishy and tended to conflate the two. Jews learned about ancestral practices from their parents, grandparents, and neighbors, not intellectuals.[54]

The rabbis set out to systematize this messy situation. They grew up with and saw all around them Jews engaged in a large variety of distinctive practices. It was rarely clear to them whence these customs arose. They noticed that while the vast majority of Jews "observed" the Sabbath, they did so in different ways, depending not so much on individual initiative as on the common practices in that village or city. They saw large gaps between the text of Scripture and actual practice.

This regional variation and lack of clarity bothered few except them. The rabbinic project was an intellectual, not practical, one. They sorted through customs, decided which to preserve and to suppress, organized them according to their own categorical plan, sought to justify them, and determined their authoritative status, all largely as an intellectual exercise. Around 200 CE, at the instigation of Rabbi Judah the Patriarch (at least according to a credible legend), these discussions were edited into a composition known as the Mishnah. The Mishnah would serve as the foundation for rabbinic discussions that stretched for several more centuries, in Palestine and the Persian Empire (called Babylonia in rabbinic texts), that themselves would be redacted into the two Talmuds, the Palestinian Talmud and the better-known Babylonian Talmud.

The Mishnah is organized by topic. There are tractates, for example, that deal with prayer, observing the sabbatical year, the Sabbath, the reading of the Megillah (and Purim, more generally), forming a marriage, dissolving a marriage, contract law, and penal procedure. It thus covers what we would call legal procedure, ritual law, criminal law, and civil law. Much of it discusses purity and sacrifices, which by the time of the rabbis, with the Temple in ruins, were largely theoretical (except for the rules regarding menstrual purity). Like the *Codex Theodosianus*, the Mishnah records sayings of individual rabbis on these topics, only rarely attempting to harmonize them. The Mishnah infrequently attempts to justify rabbinic positions with reference to Scripture; these positions gain their authority (at least according to a slightly later tradition) from their status as part of the "Oral Law," which was thought to have been given by God at Mount Sinai alongside Scripture. The Mishnah has a beginning but not a starting point; it assumes throughout that in reading any individual part of it one already knows all of it. It was composed by and for specialists.

Scholars continue to debate the original purpose of the Mishnah. Was it meant to be an authoritative legal guide, a kind of legal code to be used by judges? Given the inconsistencies and disagreements within the Mishnah, along with the fact that rabbis do not appear to have had much authority or visibility (particularly at the beginning of the third century CE), that interpretation is unlikely. Other scholars have suggested that the Mishnah was created as a kind of textbook for further rabbinic study, an interpretation that helps to explain its cryptic nature as a book by and for "insiders." If we see code and textbook as two poles in a spectrum of legal writing, the *Codex Theodosianus* might fall more toward (but not on) the code side and the Mishnah on the textbook side. This is not to say that one "influenced" the other (the Mishnah is about 150 years earlier than the *Codex Theodosianus*), but the redactors of both were engaged in a similar intellectual project.[55]

The Mishnah is the earliest rabbinic attempt to collect diverse practices and systematize them. It represents a particular kind of juridical meaning-making, in which dealings with the divine are articulated in systems of legal discourse. Throughout Late Antiquity, though, it would be their extensive use of legal discourse in the two Talmuds that distinguished the rabbis from the other intellectuals. For the rabbis, the discussion of law pointed beyond the subject of the laws themselves, toward general ways of thinking about the world. This can sometimes be a difficult point to grasp for those of us who have been raised to think of religion, in the (particularly Protestant) Christian key, as "belief" or philosophy/theology. Leaving aside for the moment the fact that adherence to a set of rituals can create a form of embodied knowledge, legal discourse itself can convey its own set of values. Mira Balberg, a scholar of ancient Judaism, has, for example, shown that the Mishnah's discussions about sacrifice—which were not directly applicable at the time of the Mishnah's redaction—really conveyed values about the importance of community. Law can be a discourse for "thinking with."[56]

Christians increasingly turned to legal discourse, but it remained subordinate to philosophy. They created various rule books (e.g., the Rule of St. Benedict) throughout antiquity, primarily for small, monastic communities, but these sought to lay out norms rather than use law as a discourse of meaning-making. A series of Christian Synods (as they are known prior to the first Council of Nicaea in 325) and then Councils sometimes produced lists of rules, or "canons." These canon lists, like the Mishnah, collect existing (formal) norms and are somewhat aspirational; they were always (and continue to be) disputed. Unlike the Mishnah, though, these rules are presented without disagreement and in no systematic order. As discursive documents, they do not go very far.[57]

The gap between the unsystematic Christian books of canons and rules and book 16 of the *Codex Theodosianus*—as well as the relevant sections of the later, fuller, and more Christian *Codex Iustinianus* (ca. 529–565 CE)—points toward the more general Christian ambivalence about "law." Paul had already contrasted "law" with "spirit," much to the detriment of the former. If the law "kills," can there be any place for laws or rules? Most institutions of any complexity cannot function without formal norms, and Christian monasteries and confederations of Christian communities were no exception, although they not insignificantly tended to avoid labeling those norms "laws." And when the bishops had the chance to further their goals through participation in the formation of imperial laws, how could they refuse? This ambivalence about "law" and legal discourse as opposed to the importance of faith and the "spirit" would continue to dog Christian communities to our own day.

Myth, philosophy (or theology), and law were all ways in which intellectuals of Late Antiquity sought to impose meaning and order on an otherwise unruly set of traditional beliefs and rituals. They are creations, mostly, of intellectual men of means. Today, many admire these men as the founders of Christianity and rabbinic Judaism. Some had actual positions of power, in, for example, the Roman imperial court. The majority, however, did not. In their day, they went largely unnoticed by most people. They presented themselves as central, using rhetoric that is more bombastic or aspirational than it is reflective of their true, marginal place in the world. Once in a rare while we can see a more honest self-reflection, as when the rabbis advise each other not to inform the people of "correct" observance of the Sabbath, since it is better that they violate these laws out of ignorance rather than intentionally. They knew perfectly well that few would heed them.[58]

I have emphasized the material conditions that led to the activities of these intellectuals, mainly the search for prestige, wealth, and power. I do not mean, though, to be reductionist. There is no reason to doubt that men like Porphyry, Augustine, and Rabbi Judah sincerely saw their intellectual activities as paths to the divine. The life of the mind could be a form of piety in its own right. It was, and remains, a path open to relatively few.

Modern accounts often emphasize that the purpose of religion is to explain the world and its natural phenomena assigning it a function between superstition and science. This is a very intellectual understanding of the purpose of religion, though, and it grows out of an identification of "religion" with the activities of the intellectuals discussed in this chapter. On the ground, away from this rarefied elite, undoubtedly others did episodically explain events in their world by recourse to the gods. Most of the time explanation was at best a secondary function. People went about their daily lives in regular communication with invisible beings, mostly asking them for help or trying to keep them away. Whether one identified as a Jew, a Christian, a Greek, or a Roman, most people shared a similar understanding about the nature of the cosmos, their place within it, and the strategies that they needed to negotiate the basic challenges that faced them all. It is to this set of issues that we turn next.

5

Beyond Transaction

MAINTAINING SACRED RELATIONSHIPS IN DAILY LIFE

WHILE WRITING this book, I spent a semester in Rome. I lived up the block from a daily farmers market, and several times a week I would start my day with a trip to my favorite produce, cheese, and sometimes fish stalls. After a few weeks, the owners of the stalls began to recognize me, and we would regularly have short chats in broken English. Often, although not always, they would give me a small gift with my purchase, such as a small bunch of grapes to eat as I shopped, or some parsley or even jam to take home. The gifts, to be sure, were self-serving in encouraging me (successfully) to return, but they also humanized what I had always seen as a strict transaction. In two decades of regular grocery shopping at my home in Rhode Island, I have never received a gift from my local Stop & Shop.

Societies are rarely purely relational or transactional. Usually, there are more complex mixtures of these dimensions, differentiated by context. The lemon and parsley that the fishmonger adds to my order as a "gift" softens and humanizes what is essentially our transactional relationship. Sometimes loving families, on the other hand, draw up legal contracts between their members to formalize property rights. One can easily imagine, with some horror, how a purely transactional or purely relational society might function.

In fact, many intellectuals of the nineteenth and early twentieth centuries did imagine precisely these scenarios, and the pictures they drew were not pretty. Karl Marx, followed by Max Weber, noted the growing alienation that accompanies new economic modes connected to capitalism. Secularization, linked to scientific and rationalistic ways of thinking, drives us ever increasingly toward a transactional world. The French sociologist Marcel Mauss imagined an earlier (and for him, better) time that was far more relational than transactional. For Mauss, at the heart of a relational community was the gift. The gift-giving cycle with its obligatory triad—to give, to receive, and to reciprocate—forms an endless loop that holds communities together.

Late Antiquity was by no means purely relational, but nor was it nearly as transactional as our own world. Up and down the social line, vertically and horizontally, relationships mattered. This way of thinking extended to interactions with the invisible beings all around; they were social relationships, like all others. Gift-giving was a central means for establishing and maintaining these, like other, relationships. Gifts to these beings—whether sacrifices, offerings, or prayers—were usually not seen as transactional "bribes" meant to sway or convince the being to help but rather as a technique to maintain good and healthy relationships. There were certainly transactional elements to some of these pietistic acts, but one would have to have been quite foolish—as Plato pointed out long before—to think that it would be so easy to bring the gods onto one's side.[1]

This chapter will focus on four general strategies used by those in Late Antiquity to maintain their relationships with divine beings. Sacrifices, and other forms of offerings, constitute material gifts. Prayers, spells, and amulets use words to establish lines of communication with the divine. Prognostication is a tool for using one's relationship with the divine world to predict the future. Finally, contagion involves actually making contact with the divine.

The ground covered in this chapter has sometimes been discussed under the rubric of "popular" or "folk" religion. These terms are inherently imprecise. They can refer to what most people are doing or specifically to the beliefs and practices of less wealthy and marginal groups. A more serious problem, though, is that these concepts have traditionally been used to distinguish practices that were looked down upon as superstitious, magical, or otherwise outside the bounds of "official" religion. Primarily for this latter reason, scholars have largely abandoned the terms. Since the scholarly debate about these terms is relevant to how we approach and think about a range of practices (such as spells and amulets), I begin with a brief discussion of the issues at stake.[2]

Magic, Superstition, and Popular Religion

Writers in Hebrew, Greek, and Latin have long sought to distinguish "proper" acts of devotion from improper ones. These writers often have very clear ideas about what distinguishes acceptable worship from "superstition" and "magic." Going a bit deeper into how "magic" has been used in antiquity and is currently used by scholars opens up the complex dynamics that shape how we often think about religion.[3]

The Hebrew Bible uses a variety of terms to indicate activities that we might lump together as "magical," but it has neither a single umbrella term for them nor a set of useful definitions. A "witch" or "sorceress," for example, should be executed, but we do not know what it meant to practice "witchcraft" (*k-sh-p*). Deuteronomy 18:10–11 lumps the witch together with a variety of other characters, translated by the New Revised Standard Version as "diviners," "soothsayers," "enchanters," "charmers," "mediums," "wizards," and "necromancers." Except for the necromancer, there is no record within the Hebrew Bible or literature contemporaneous with it of what these characters do and how they are different from each other. Only the necromancer is described in a story that is often mistitled "the witch of Endor." The woman, who is explicitly labeled a necromancer rather than a witch, summons the ghost of the prophet Samuel at King Saul's request, even though it was Saul himself who sentenced necromancers to death.[4]

The rabbis were in the business of clarifying such cryptic biblical references in order to make them legally actionable. Although they lacked the authority to actually administer the death penalty (along with nearly any punishment in the communities in which they lived), they thought and wrote long and hard about the objective standards that would make a person liable to the punishments prescribed by Scripture. The rabbis, for example, debate at great length what specific actions make someone subject to the penalties (and which penalties) for breaking the Sabbath or idolatry. Yet when it comes to "witchcraft" (*kishuf*) and the other activities suggested by Deuteronomy 18:10–11, the rabbis disappoint. In the Mishnah, they define a witch as "one who does the act," as opposed to "one who grabs the eyes," that is, creates an illusion. A long discussion in the Babylonian Talmud attempts to clarify this passage but largely without success. One story relates that Rabbi Eliezer and Rabbi Akiva were walking together and Rabbi Akiva asked his companion about the planting of cucumbers. Rabbi Eliezer "said a word (or spell) and the whole field was filled with cucumbers." Rabbi Eliezer's action might appear to be kishuf and thus prohibited, the Talmud continues, but no! Because it was said in order to teach a law to Rabbi Akiva, it was permitted.[5]

What becomes clear in this passage and many like it is that the rabbis fully believed that kishuf, necromancy, and the other acts prohibited by Deuteronomy actually worked. Someone could recite a spell and a field could fill with cucumbers—real ones. Spells and amulets really could heal people and thus could freely be used, and the ideal rabbi, according to the rabbis, mastered kishuf and occasionally performed it during his studies. Rabbis could look at or curse a person and they would dissolve, die, or become ill. The rabbis enthusiastically advocated for a wide variety of techniques to protect against an equally wide variety of demons. None of these acts seem to have bothered the rabbis in the slightest.[6]

What, then, for the rabbis, is the kind of kishuf that makes one liable to the death penalty? Predominantly that which falls into the category of "ways of the Amorites." Certain quite specific kinds of kishuf were associated with non-Jews. These qualify for the rabbis as real kishuf, the kind that was prohibited. Thus, were a rabbi and a "heretic" to do exactly the same thing with exactly the same effect, the "heretic" might well be guilty of kishuf and the rabbi not. Women were also associated with kishuf, although not in any consistent or systematic way. Kishuf is defined not only by what they do but also by who they *are*.[7]

Even the more theoretical discussion by the rabbis about kishuf is not very edifying. Kishuf is said to be an act that goes against the heavenly household, which might mean that it creates an unnatural result. If this were the case, though, the line between kishuf and genuine miracles would remain blurry. Another rabbi suggests that such acts are effective only because they draw on demonic powers, but this suggestion is rejected on the basis of scriptural proof texts. There is broader rabbinic agreement that, whatever gives kishuf its power, it is not very effective against righteous people, primarily rabbis.[8]

The Hebrew term *kishuf* roughly overlaps with the Greek term *deisidaimonia* and the Latin *superstitio* and *mageia* (the latter of which is taken from the Greek). These terms all exhibit remarkable flexibility and ambiguity. *Superstitio*, like *kishuf*, was a smear against a person or group who performed a variety of acts relating to the invisible realm, and the Romans tarred liberally with it. Prior to the fourth century, Romans applied the terms to Jews, Christians, and many other Romans. The "wrong" way of venerating the gods, or venerating the wrong beings, was, however, almost never sufficient in and of itself to bring an accusation of superstitio. The label was applied not simply to weirdos but to weirdos who were thought to be dangerous.[9]

The case of the trial of Apuleius provides an intriguing window into not just the flexible meaning of *superstitio* but its actual social use. Lucius Apuleius, a Syrian who lived in the second century and is best known as the author of *The Metamorphoses* (also known as *The Golden Ass*), also wrote an account of a trial he faced. We have no other sources of this trial and Apuleius's account can hardly be seen as disinterested or unbiased, but it is nevertheless revealing. According to Apuleius, he had married the rich mother of a friend of his (at the friend's encouragement). The friend then married, had a change of heart, and with some relatives sued Apuleius, charging that he had won his mother over by illicit means. The accusers do not actually have any hard evidence, so they instead accuse him of several strange practices that point toward superstitio. Apuleius, tellingly, does not deny the practices. He did, indeed, acquire a venomous mollusk and hide the images of strange gods with his portable collection of more traditional ones. While he justified

FIGURE 5.1. Inscribed bronze amulet from Israel with images. Photo by Clara Amit, courtesy of the Israel Antiquities Authority (1938–1091). Used by permission.

(apparently successfully) these practices to the Roman governor and judge as having no connection to superstitio, it is not hard for the reader to see that his strange behavior may have made Apuleius seem a bit odd to his contemporaries (who probably suspected as much simply from reading *The Metamorphoses*). Strange behavior alone, though, would probably never have resulted in a legal, or maybe even informal, charge. The fact that Apuleius was a Syrian was a factor; foreigners, particularly from the East, were more vulnerable. Most of all, though, the plaintiffs settled on superstitio because they could not otherwise find a credible charge.

What is also curious about Apuleius's account is that he suggests that although he was accused of superstitio, the actual legal charge was that he was a *magus*. *Magus* is a term that was typically applied to Persians who engaged in superstitio (as the Romans saw it) but came to be applied to others as well. A magus, predictably, practiced mageia. If all that seems vague and subjective, that is because it is and was in antiquity. Further, it is unclear whether being a magus was, in fact, a criminal offense under Roman law and, if it was, how the term was to be defined. The ambiguity of the term is all the more striking since it appears in Roman legal writings from around 300 CE. A Roman jurist named Paul wrote a legal commentary that was influential, although not authoritative. Commenting on an earlier law that does not explicitly mention superstitio or mageia, he writes, "It is agreed that those guilty of the magic art (*magicae artis conscios*) be inflicted with the supreme punishment, i.e., be thrown to the beasts or crucified. Actual magicians (*magi*), however, shall be burned alive." He goes on to forbid the possession of "magical books." Even the pedantic Paul, though, does not define the magicae artis and the magi. Undefined and objectively undefinable, they allow for a legal means to address social conflicts that smell bad, even if they otherwise seem legal. There are very few legal cases of superstitio and magicae artis in the extant evidence, but most of those that we know about involved, as in the case of Apuleius, foreigners and some issue (or issues) of love, money, and health.[10]

The transition of *superstitio* from a vague but potentially powerful slur that could be used against Christians to one that Christians began to employ against "pagans" and "heretics" was a delicate one. Through the early fourth century, the term *superstitio* began to be used, particularly in imperial legislation, in ways that were even vaguer than usual and that could thus be taken by Christians in one way and "pagans" in another. By the mid-fourth century, though, with Christians having gained more influence in the imperial court (with the exception, of course, of the reign of Julian) and with the processes of legal codification, superstitio was typically lumped with other practices that deviated from an increasingly rigid construction of what it meant to be a proper "Christian."[11]

Greek, Roman, and Christian intellectuals developed much more robust theories of mageia, superstitio, and related terms. The Neoplatonists developed theories they called theurgy. Theurgy involved participating in ritual (and psychological) activities that either animated a divinity's force in its image or incarnated the divinity in a human being, thus allowing it temporarily to talk. Neoplatonists, particularly Iamblichus and Proclus, discuss (although not to the extent and with the consistency that we might like) the mechanisms for theurgy but ultimately root practices that might be seen as part of the magicae artis in the power of the divine. Christian thinkers, though, largely move in exactly the opposite direction. Augustine links everything that he calls "magic" (which becomes for him an umbrella term that includes divination and superstitio) to demons, which also allows him to further solidify the borders of acceptable Christian practice. Augustine's discussion of demons and how they have the power that they do is sophisticated, but ultimately he goes back to the strategy used by Lactantius, a Christian writer who died in 320 CE: "religion" is good worship of the proper god and superstitio is, by definition, false worship.[12]

The words that we translate as "magic" and "superstition" had their uses in antiquity, primarily as vague and pejorative terms used to label the "other" when other words could not easily be found. They could be used as informal slurs or slung in courts of law. Those engaged in such activities rarely, in antiquity, labeled themselves as "magicians" or practitioners of superstitio. Even the theurgists avoided these terms.

Despite these judgmental associations, "magic" continues to circulate as a term that scholars find, or want to find, useful. Most of us intuitively have a sense of what the category might include: amulets, spells, and ritual ceremonies outside the bounds of the church or synagogue. This definition charts out a vast and subjective gray zone. I may very well not see what I am doing as "magic," but the church might. Yet, as one scholar of Jewish magic writes in his sensitive treatment of the problem, it is a "heuristic device—a means to gather together a group of related cultural phenomena, texts, and artifacts." Other scholars, though, have rejected the term as too hopelessly confused to be useful.[13]

In this book, I rarely use the word "magic." It may well be useful for other scholars trying to accomplish different goals. The entire premise of this project, though, is that unless we have good evidence that people on the ground saw an activity as "magical," we should assume that they treated it just as they would any other form of communication with supernatural beings. "Spells," in this way of seeing things, are little different from "prayers."

"Magic" is one of a cluster of labels that fall under the umbrella of "popular religion," as the concept was understood from antiquity forward. Long before Late Antiquity, elite writers recognized that most people practiced "magic" in some form (along with other frowned-upon acts) and therefore that most people were not engaging in proper worship of their deities. Many portions of the Hebrew Bible, for example, polemicize against common Israelite practices. Earlier texts within the Bible use the term "people of the land" (*ame ha-aretz*) neutrally, but it was already emerging as a pejorative term in the fifth century BCE. Early Greek philosophers heaped scorn on those whose views of the gods, and how they functioned, differed from their own. Augustine reported that Varro, a Roman antiquarian who wrote in the first century BCE, sniffed at those who believed in the ridiculous myths about the gods. This was at least one point on which Varro and Augustine himself agreed.[14]

The idea that there were groups of people—most people—who worshipped incorrectly found its way, like magic, into modern scholarly discourse. Sometimes it was termed "popular" or "folk" religion. Such terms were useful in that they conveyed the fact that there was a loose bundle of beliefs and practices that were more widely shared than what we might expect from the literature of the intellectuals. They came, however, with ancient baggage. "Popular" religion was somehow secondary, less sophisticated, bastardized versions of "official" or "pure" religion. The simple adjective "popular" implies that it stands in contrast to another adjective that describes a better type of "religion."

The scholarly movement away from the categories of "popular" or "folk" religion began a few decades ago, especially in descriptions of American religion. In his magnificent book *The Cheese and the Worms*, Carlo Ginzburg experiments with the term "peasant religion" to describe the religion of sixteenth-century Europe. More recently, scholars of classical antiquity are uneasily settling on the term "lived religion." The lived religion approach avoids separating religious communities into different reified groups, instead emphasizing the lived experience of individuals. Lived religion includes peasants and intellectuals, the literate and the illiterate, the rich and the poor, men and women, and the free and the enslaved. Instead of looking at ideologies, institutions, and communities, we might turn our gaze to these individuals and the lives they made for themselves. This approach has only recently been applied to antiquity and is the one that most informs the approach of this book.[15]

Sacrifices and Offerings

Until the late fourth century CE, the paradigmatic act of veneration throughout the Mediterranean and Near East was animal sacrifice. All major imperial and municipal ceremonies involved an animal sacrifice, usually in a temple and usually eaten by the participants. Some of the voluntary associations, such as those devoted to Mithras, similarly made an animal sacrifice a core ritual activity.

Temples were not used solely for public ceremonies. Private individuals could bring animals for sacrifice. A person of means who desired to thank an important god for some good fortune, or propitiate a god for good health or fertility, might bring a sheep or pig to a temple of Jupiter or Aphrodite. The procedures for such sacrifices undoubtedly varied widely but are in nearly all cases obscure: Was the individual on his or her own for the sacrifice, cooking, and butchering? Would there be priests available to assist, and if so, did they take a portion of the cooked meat as payment? What role, if any, did women play in Roman sacrifice? Although the sacrifice would technically be private, it also had a public dimension. Such individual sacrifices could be seen and discussed, thus adding to the individual's honor, status, and perhaps even standing with the emperor.[16]

Animal sacrifices were not only made at temples. Private altars—again, usually among the wealthy—were constructed and used in domestic spaces. Such altars would not usually be large enough for bigger animals, but they could suffice for small animals and birds. The altars in the houses of Pompeii, although a bit earlier than the focus of this book, sometimes contained chicken parts. In the mid-fourth century CE, Emperor Julian commented on continued Jewish "sacrifices" at Passover. That Jews continued to make sacrifices in Late Antiquity after the destruction of the Jerusalem Temple is not inconceivable. An altar in Jordan was dedicated to Theos Hypsistos, "the most high god" and sometimes a term used for YHWH, by a Jewish woman. As Christianity began to push public sacrifice out of the temples and to the margins, traditional (and mostly aristocratic) Romans developed a theory that private individuals could sacrifice on behalf of the public weal. Smaller animals may also have been used in the "nocturnal sacrifices," perhaps conducted at cemeteries, that imperial legislation was keen to prohibit.[17]

Animal sacrifices were tightly connected to meat consumption. Festivals, with their public distribution of sacrificed meat, served as the occasions where larger domestic animals were consumed (game was typically not offered as a sacrifice but would certainly have supplemented the diets of those who could hunt). The impact of the sacrifices, though, could be seen daily. Most cities had butchers and butcher shops, which, to the small extent that we can tell, were often set up close to temples. Animals would have been slaughtered in the temples, and then surplus flesh, both raw and cooked (most often boiled), would have been moved (or maybe sold) to the butcher for sale. Meat was expensive. According to the Price Edict of Diocletian (301 CE), enacted in order to gain control over inflation, one Italian pound (about 0.75

pounds in the American system) of pork cost twelve denarii. To put that in perspective, according to the same edict, the daily wage for a farmworker was twenty-five denarii, which was also the fee for a scribe writing one hundred lines. For a farmworker to spend half of a day's wage on a pound of pork would have been quite an extravagance (we do not know how many "lines" a scribe could write in a day). Such meat also represented a danger to Jews and Christians, who avoided products that had been sacrificed to the gods. Recognizing the problem somewhat belatedly and in response to a communal crisis in Corinth, Paul attempts to walk a delicate line: sacrificial meat has actually been sacrificed to demons and therefore is best avoided. At the same time, if meat is not explicitly identified as coming from a sacrificed animal, there is no harm in partaking of it. Paul appears to assume that nonsacrificial (i.e., profane) meat exists, and thus it is possible that the meat sold in the butcher shops is profane. He, though, also goes beyond that assumption (and the words of Jesus himself), declaring most meat, and food in general, profane. Later Christians apparently adopted this approach as well.[18]

The status of meat in Jewish communities highlights the often-fuzzy line between what might be considered sacrificial (thus "holy") and profane. Rabbinic sources clearly and tightly regulate sacrificial meat. Such meat is God's and can only be eaten by priests (and their households) in a state of purity. Without a temple in Jerusalem, though, this kind of meat, according to the rabbis, cannot exist. That, however, was not an obstacle for Jewish meat consumption. Deuteronomy, whose authors sought to shut down cult sites that competed with the Jerusalem Temple (and thus to limit the availability of sacrificial meat), at the same time recognized the need to provide for meat consumption outside of Jerusalem. Deuteronomy allows those "in any of your communities" to slaughter and eat meat freely, avoiding only the consumption of forbidden animals and the blood of permitted animals. As long as they followed these strictures, Jewish communities would be strictly by the book in their consumption of nonsacrificial animals. There is little reason to think that Jews in locations beyond Jerusalem abstained from occasionally (as their budget and supply would permit) consuming meat. By the time of the destruction of the Jerusalem Temple, Jews had a long tradition of eating profane (although permitted) meat.[19]

In rabbinic literature, all written well after 70 CE, the slaughter of animals and treatment of profane meat for Jewish consumption looks not so profane. Regulations are imposed on who can slaughter the animal, when the animal is slaughtered, and most importantly, how the animal is to be slaughtered. The method of slaughter, a knife drawn across the throat for domestic animals, is identical to the method of sacrificial slaughter, as are some of the defects in the slaughtered animal that could prohibit its consumption. The rabbis were clearly aware of the similarity of their prescriptions for sacrificial and profane slaughter and sought to guard against those who would conflate the two: "One who slaughters [an animal, with the intention of making it] a burnt offering, a peace offering, a provisional guilt offering, a Passover offering, [or] a thanksgiving offering, his slaughter is invalid [and the animal cannot be consumed]. Rabbi Shimon renders the slaughter valid." The rabbis here clearly envision a scenario in which the slaughter crosses the imagined conceptual line from profane to sacred. The rabbis often discuss hypotheticals that have little basis in popular practice, but such a scenario is at least conceivable. A Jew living without a temple but who, due to history and wider context, thinks "sacrificially"—that is, that YHWH deserves proper sacrificial offerings—might well intend for a profane slaughter to have a sacrificial effect.[20]

Larger Jewish communities had meat markets that sold "properly" slaughtered meat. The rabbis frequently mention butchers. One story in the Palestinian Talmud mentions a "*macellum* of Israel," using the Latin term for a meat market. That passage continues with a story of a Jew in Sepphoris, a heavily Jewish city in Palestine, to whom a butcher would not sell meat. The man asked a Roman to buy the meat for him. When the man went back to the butcher to gloat that he was able to get the meat after all, the butcher retorted that he sold the Roman meat that was not properly slaughtered for Jewish consumption. When this case came before a rabbi, the rabbi permitted the meat on the basis that the butcher's statement alone was not disqualifying. This story demonstrates that it was at least conceivable that a butcher would sell to Jews and non-Jews alike, properly and improperly slaughtered meat, and that there could have existed a somewhat laissez-faire don't ask, don't tell policy regarding the status of meat among Jews.[21]

The logic of animal offerings to the deities has always trickled down, from flesh to vegetation. Animal offerings were paradigmatic but probably relatively uncommon compared to the individual offerings of grains, wine, and incense on smaller, private altars. Scattered Roman sources from the first century BCE onward mention such sacrifices quite incidentally, presumably because they were so common and unexceptional that they were barely worthy of note. Greeks and Romans would typically pour out a little wine as an offering to the chthonic gods before drinking. Small incense altars commonly stood in domestic dwellings. Roman villas often contained a niche for their domestic cult images with a stand or incense altar in front of it. Altars would be scattered through many cities, available for personal use.[22]

Jews, for the most part, did not appear to participate in personal sacrifices in the same way. Very few of these personal altars have Jewish names inscribed on them or are otherwise from a context (e.g., synagogue building) that we can clearly identify as Jewish. Yet it is clear that Jews did adapt the logic behind these personal sacrifices. Jewish incense shovels from Late Antiquity survive. Incense shovels had many uses (including simple fumigation) and so by themselves do not demonstrate that Jews were offering incense to supernatural beings, but it is likely that at least some of their owners used them that way. There could be a fine line between throwing a bit of incense into a fire to make the place smell better and thinking of it as a sacrifice. More commonly, Jews—at least in Palestine (we know very little about similar practices by Jews outside of Palestine)—would "sacrifice" by giving foodstuffs to local Jewish priests. Rabbinic sources tightly prescribe how much of exactly what products must be given to the priests, but it is reasonably certain that they were building on common practice. "First-fruits," however defined, were given, as was bread, meat, and wine. The priest's job was to consume these items, most likely, as in the temple, in a state of ritual purity. These gifts to the priests were thus seen as gifts, or

FIGURE 5.2. Synagogue mosaic from Huldah, Israel, with *lulav*, *ethrog*, incense shovel, menorah, and shofar. This cluster of symbols was common in Jewish iconography. The Greek inscription reads, "Blessing to the nation." Photo by Clara Amit, courtesy of the Israel Antiquities Authority (1953–582). Used by permission.

offerings, to God. They were an essential part of the gift-giving cycle that kept the relationship to YHWH active and strong.[23]

Christians too subscribed to the idea that gifts could be given to the divine by transferring material to human agents. The evidence for Christians giving tithes in Late Antiquity is sparse, but there is a rich rhetoric urging Christians to give "offerings"—also known as "blessings"—to monks and other clergy. A variety of such offerings were made, often as part of the service, but one particular kind is worth special note: bread. In the East, churchgoers frequently brought small loaves of bread. Some of these they purchased specifically for this purpose from merchants outside of the churches; these loaves might be stamped with a cross. The loaves were collected and blessed on the altar, after which they appear to have been divided among the clergy. The basic needs of these clergy in the East were provided by a small salary based on rank (in the West, they were supported entirely by a complicated system of offerings), but these bread offerings were a necessary supplement. The important point for our purposes, though, is that these donations of food (along with money) for support of the clergy (and other "holy men") were seen as gifts to God. As with the Jewish priests and rabbis, one path to divine favor went through the stomach of a priest or monk.[24]

Institutionalized communal worship, whether on the imperial, local, or associative levels, was largely controlled by men. This is not to say that women did not participate, whether as direct actors or spectators. Women served as priests in some traditional cults and could serve in any of several (often vaguely defined) official positions in churches, synagogues, and other voluntary associations. They also were commemorated widely as benefactors. But the evidence for women's participation in such environments is dwarfed by the evidence of male participation. Public cultic spaces, much like the intellectual environments, were in Late Antiquity by and large male spaces.[25]

There is some evidence, albeit sparse, that women had more agency to venerate the gods in private spaces. Women often prepared the meals and thus had more opportunity to gift foodstuffs, whether to priests or the poor. Rabbinic texts, for example, show women as the predominant bread-bakers in a household of limited means, and they would be responsible for separating a portion from the dough to give to the priests. Many texts from antiquity portray women as giving food to the poor (particularly itinerant beggars), which was understood as the fulfillment of the divine will. To say that women controlled the veneration of deities within the household would push the evidence too far (although it might still be true), but they were able to exercise a much freer hand there than in the public sphere.[26]

Yet food was only one of many items that could be given to the divine. Money was also commonly given. Coins could be given to those who were thought to have divine access, whether directly or through a more formal process (such as a church collection). They could be used to pay for the building or renovation of a holy place, in which case, if large enough, they could also be publicly commemorated with an inscription that reminded both divine agents and mortals of the donor's gift. Even smaller donations could be pooled. One fifth-century synagogue inscription from Beit Shean (in Roman Palestine) written in

Greek, for example, calls on God to protect a group of anonymous donors for their gifts. Similar formulas commemorating anonymous group donations, were common in synagogues and churches from this time. The same places often also contain inscriptions commemorating names of donors, suggesting that the group donation inscriptions were meant to encourage smaller donations. One did not need an inscription, though, to give coins to the divine via a building. Many synagogues contain coins in their foundations. Ordinary people appear to have deliberately placed them during building or renovations, most likely as "offerings" or gifts to God.[27]

Almost anything could have been, and often was, given as a gift or votive offering. In addition to food and money, one of the most common objects was lamps. Like bread, these could be purchased outside of temples, synagogues, churches, and other places considered holy and then left inside. Archaeological excavations of such sites frequently discover troves of lamps, with some literature and inscriptions indicating that the lamps and other donations needed to be regularly cleaned out to make space for new ones. Such lamps could be humble or ornate, made of clay or metal, and adorned (or not) with decorations and inscriptions. Cemeteries—whether traditional, Jewish, or Christian—also frequently contain lamps that were deposited or arranged in ways that suggest they were not merely used for light.[28]

One object unique to traditional Greek and Roman temples and particularly places associated with healing was terracotta models of body parts. A person whose heel hurt might purchase a model of a foot and give it to Asklepios, the god of healing, by leaving it at his temple. There are models of all kinds of body parts, especially those connected to fertility. Such gifts seem to primarily have been made in thanks for healing, although many also probably reflected the desire to heal. In many of the more popular centers of healing there must have been a brisk trade in such models. There is evidence in Egypt to suggest that Christian women in Late Antiquity used terracotta figurines as votives, perhaps for saints to grant them children and healing.[29]

Jews, Christians, Greeks, and Romans also commonly placed written texts in places they considered holy. There are many examples of

FIGURE 5.3. Lead votive plaque from the Lower Danube region. Sol Invictus, in a chariot, presides. Public domain. Metropolitan Museum of Art (21.88.175), Rogers Fund, 1921. https://www.metmuseum.org/art/collection/search/251147.

semiliterate graffiti directed to the divine scribbled on walls and in caves. Sometimes they mention a name or have a symbol (a cross or menorah are frequent), and only rarely are they specific in their requests ("help me" and "remember for good" are common). Amulets were also regularly deposited at holy places. In cases like this, it is not always clear whether people thought the efficacy was due to the words inscribed on the object or the object itself.[30]

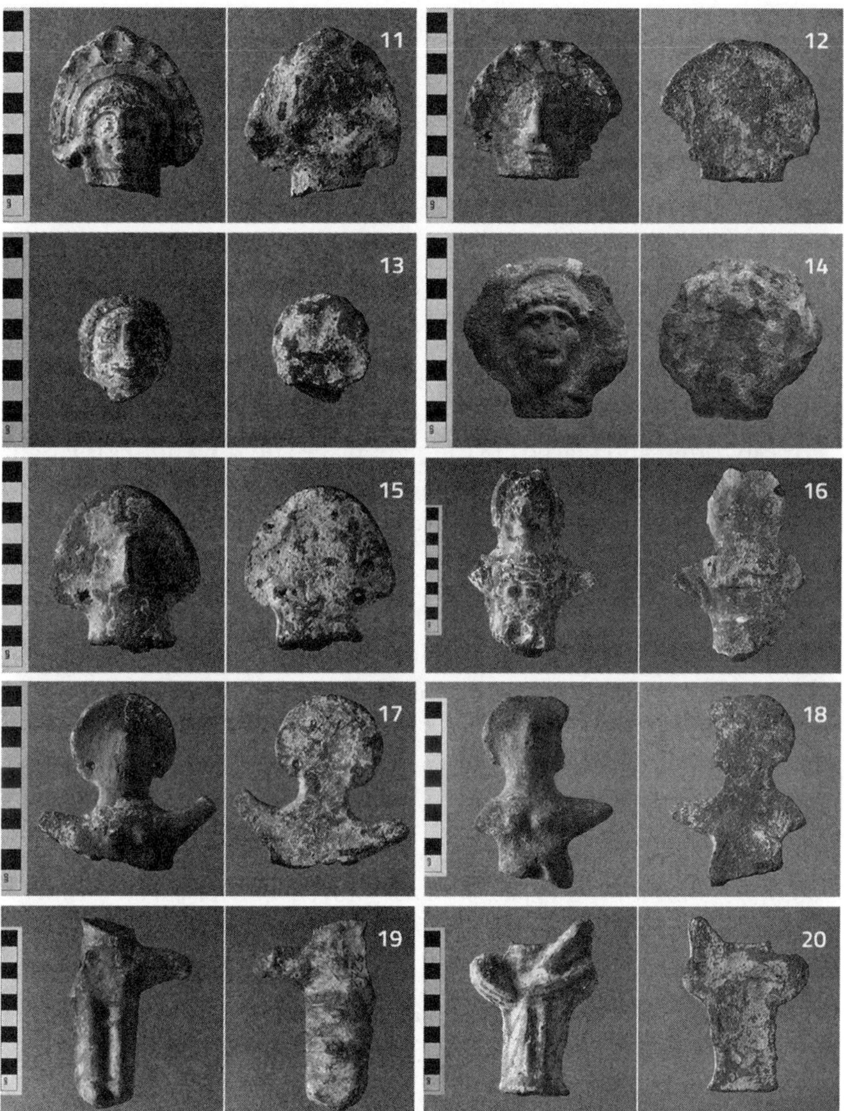

FIGURE 5.4. Collection of Christian terracotta figures from el-Ashmunein in the Museo Egizio, Turin. Public domain, CC BY 4.0, https://rivista.museoegizio.it/article/christian-terracotta-figurines-from-el-ashmunein-in-the-museo-egizio-turin.

Prayers, Amulets, and Spells

Sacrifices and offerings were often nonverbal. The object, rather than the words recited at the ritual (if there were any), was central. Verbal communication, though, was a great deal easier and less costly than making a sacrifice. Simple short statements of thanks or wishes could be directed to a deity many times in a day, or more elaborate requests could be made in communal settings or inscribed on objects.

While some have made a sharp distinction between spells and prayers, I would not. Like prayer, spells are really evocations of divine agents. Like prayer, their effectiveness is enhanced by the right words said (or written and placed) in the right place and time under the right conditions. Also like prayer, there is no guarantee that they will work. In other words, it is difficult (actually, I think impossible) to draw a hard and fast line between spells and prayers. Both are ritualized calls for help to divine agents. The divine agents may, or may not, heed either a spell or a prayer. They were also an ordinary part of everyday life for most people. You might want a spell to help heal a child, provide success at a business dealing, attract a love interest, or hurt an enemy, among many other common desires. Mostly, though, you would probably want a spell, particularly a written one, to protect you from malevolent forces. When the Coptic manual refers to a spell, it uses the Greek word, *euche*. Today, we commonly translate *euche* as "prayer," and it is, in fact, difficult to find awareness in Late Antiquity (except in some of the writings of Christian intellectuals) of any linguistic or conceptual distinction between a "spell" and a "prayer." *Euche*, or its equivalent term in Hebrew, *tefillah*, could refer to any number of verbal utterances directed (directly or indirectly) to any number of entities. What they all share, though, is the desire to communicate with invisible beings.[31]

Prayer, like many of the terms commonly used to discuss religion, is difficult to pin down. It might refer to a specific text or one composed on the spot. It might be recited in a formal, ritualized setting by a learned expert or spontaneously by a peasant. It might be directed toward a deity, a lesser being, or even the community. It might ask for a favor, express thanks for a favor that had been given, or simply express pain or awe. It might be recited publicly in a fashion that was also meant to send a message to the human audience, or privately, even in one's heart. Is an utterance that accompanies a ritual activity a "prayer"? Is a ritual statement meant to perform an action—for example, "you are betrothed to me," "I vow," or "here is the sacrifice"—a "prayer"? For most people in antiquity, the word "prayer" could refer to any of these situations. We might try to sort them by moving through the evidence from more to less formal ways in which people prayed.

Sacrifice sometimes involved the recitation of certain liturgies. These liturgies, as we might expect, were highly formalized, as were the manner and timing of their recitation. To the Roman author Sallust, who said that words without sacrifice are just words, the slightly younger Pliny the Elder seemed to reply that "a sacrifice of victims without a prayer is supposed to be of no effect." These words, as numerous Roman authors mention, were important, and getting them wrong could lead to redoing the sacrifice (much as in 2009 President Barack Obama and Chief Justice John Roberts thought it best to redo the oath of office the next day when the words were fumbled during the formal ceremony). Prayer was also an expected component of Greek veneration of deities, in both public and private contexts. Both Greeks and Romans incorporated the singing of hymns into their prayers as well.[32]

Given the ubiquity of prayer in Greek and Roman contexts, it is striking that we know very little about the actual liturgy recited during public Roman sacrifices. Writing in the second century BCE, Cato does give the texts of several prayers to be recited at different agricultural events. It is unclear, though, whether Cato assumes a private family celebration, a local one (e.g., the village gathers at harvest time), or one to be performed in a central location on behalf of all harvesting communities. It is also unclear whether these ceremonies, with their prayer texts, survived into Late Antiquity.[33]

Greek and Roman prayer was not confined to public gatherings. Greek and Latin sources are replete with references to people praying. Marcus Aurelius, for example, simply assumed that individuals prayed on their own and sought to direct them to purer ways to formulate their prayers. The Neoplatonist philosophers Porphyry, Iamblichus, and

Proclus all robustly defended the utility of prayer and suggested that only those who would deny that the gods exist or that they play any role in our lives would restrain from prayer. Such personal prayer might be entirely private, but when etched on an inscription it could also have a public dimension.[34]

While the Jerusalem Temple stood, Jews also seemed to accompany their sacrifices with verbal declarations. As in the Roman case, however, it is not clear exactly what was said. It is likely that some of the Psalms were recited as part of the sacrificial service. One rabbinic text describes the liturgy that Jewish priests would recite (including the Ten Commandments, the Shema, and the priestly benediction) as part of their preparations for offering the daily communal sacrifice. Otherwise (assuming that the Mishnah offers an accurate description of past temple practice), the sacrifice may have been performed in silence.[35]

The lack of temple liturgy makes the reason for the emergence of Jewish statutory prayer, independent of any sacrifice, somewhat mystifying. But emerge it apparently did. The community that produced the Dead Sea Scrolls in Qumran had a set of liturgical texts that appear to have been recited at particular times. The appearance of statutory prayers, also apparently (we cannot be certain about this) outside of or even replacing sacrifice, is a new development that might have resulted from the growing alienation between the community at Qumran and the authorities in the Jerusalem Temple through the first century BCE. It is also likely that this development drew on the experience of Jews who lived further from Jerusalem. Jews in Egypt and Greece, among other places, had developed regular communal gatherings to recite the Torah and prayers. We know almost nothing about the degree to which those activities were standardized.[36]

According to the rabbis, Jews have an obligation to pray two (or, according to some opinions, three) times each day. They link the obligation, mostly implicitly but sometimes explicitly, to the defunct temple sacrifice. Much as Greeks and Romans increasingly modeled their private sacrifices on the forbidden public ones and understood these private sacrifices as benefiting the community as a whole, so too did the rabbis see regular Jewish prayer. The beneficiary of Jewish statutory prayer was the Jewish people as a whole, not just the individual who prayed.[37]

Jews had synagogues through Late Antiquity, and it is likely that they prayed in them as an organized community. Whether they prayed according to rabbinic prescriptions, or even whether prayer was a central part of what they did in the synagogue (as opposed, for example, to reciting the Torah), is unknown. We also have little insight into individual Jewish prayer at the time. We do not know the number of Jews who prayed regularly or what they said. The rabbis clearly prescribe an order to the prayers and their general themes and the specific language of their last lines but otherwise provide only a hazy picture of the texts of the prayers. The Babylonian Talmud records some individual prayers, but these are never presented as meant for the public.[38]

It is likely that the reason for this was that, aside from the recitation of certain psalms on prescribed days, there was no single, standard liturgy until after the end of Late Antiquity. Jewish liturgical poets authored compositions for use in synagogues that demonstrate that there was fluidity in those services. We can assume that there was a great deal more variety in how individual Jews prayed. Most Jews would have spoken Greek or Aramaic, and it is likely that when they did pray, most of them would have used one of these languages. Evidence for the use or even teaching of Hebrew to Jews outside of rabbinic circles is sparse.

Christians, of course, also engaged in formal and communal liturgies as well as individual prayer. As with Jews, though, it took a while for the communal liturgies to become more consistent across locales. While there was increasing Christian interest in the second and third centuries in both regulating access to the centerpiece of the communal Christian worship service—the Eucharist—and theorizing the meaning and purpose of prayer, Christian prayers were themselves far from uniform. As with Jews, this is readily explicable by the lack of a centralized authority. Very early (scholars used to use the word "primitive") Christian communities founded by Paul could at least turn to a central source—Paul—for guidance. A century after Paul died, they formed a much looser network. Bishops of local communities may have been in touch (by courier-carried letters) with other bishops to remain roughly on the same page in some matters of doctrine and ritual, but this would have tempered rather than eliminated local divergences.[39]

The format and liturgies of formal Christian worship services hardened from the fourth century onward, a result of both increased authority structures within the orthodox church and the increasing role that such liturgy was beginning to play in imperial and civic contexts. As we might expect, in the same way that the grand, imperially financed cathedrals replaced the temples, so too did the Christian mass replace the sacrifice. Although we do not possess a full description of what such a mass looked like until rather late, the evidence does allow us to be relatively confident about its basic outlines. It contained hymns of praise, the recitation of the short, petitionary Lord's prayer, and a sermon. Men and women would participate, although women were probably expected to behave more modestly than the men. At its center, though, was the Eucharist, a ceremony and sharing of food that might be seen as structurally equivalent to the Roman sacrifice. For a new convert to Christianity who was accustomed to watching the sacrifice and sharing in the meat, the pageantry of the mass provided a recognizably symbolic and verbal substitute.[40]

Then there are the many surviving written prayers, or "spells." One Coptic "hoard" (as its editors call it) of spells written sometime from the fourth to sixth centuries exemplifies this practice. The manual is composed of twenty leaves of papyri, written in a few different hands but apparently comprising a single text. It begins with an invocation to God, the angels, and the archangels, all of whom, according to the text, speak Hebrew. It then explicitly refers to this text as a "prayer." Invoking the biblical character of Seth son of Adam (Genesis 4:25), it introduces the master spell, giving general directions for how to recite it: "You are to recite it seven times over some honey and some licorice root. It sets a reminder within you, for ever and ever, in your mind and spirit. Take a hawk's egg and fry it, then eat it over the honey, purifying yourself for forty days until its mind appears to you, in cleanliness and purity for forty days, before you begin (the ritual, with) your garments cleansed." After a few more instructions but before actually giving the spell, the text specifies all the different ways that one should adapt and recite the spell, depending on the situation. For sore ribs, for example, one should recite it over figs and then bind the figs to the patient. For a seizure, it is to be recited over oil used to anoint them. For the safety of a ship, it is to be written on "a clean papyrus" and affixed to the mast. In a master spell, the "father" is invoked and followed by a list of divine names. Most of these are unknown, but some are recognizably Jewish.[41]

Among Christian texts, this one is unusual. It elevates Hebrew, uses Jewish names for God, does not contain specifically Christian names of God (e.g., Jesus), and invokes many figures from the Hebrew Bible. Yet this text was almost certainly written by and for Christians. Coptic (at least in the form used in this manual) was a language that derived from Egyptian and was used almost exclusively by Christians in Late Antiquity. There is no extant text in Coptic that we know was written by Jews. The text has several crosses scattered throughout. The use of indecipherable words (are these names of divinities?) and multiple names at the end are typical of such books and appear meant to elevate its power. This particular text is unusual in its economy: one short spell can serve multiple functions depending on how it is recited. Most manuals—be they Greek, Jewish, or Christian—prescribe different spells for each situation.

When scribes wrote amulets, they may have consulted such manuals, but their work required more than copying a formula and filling in the blanks. Often, for example, they needed knowledge of and access to relatively hard-to-obtain plant and animal material. Sometimes they had to perform certain rituals before or while writing effective texts. Extant amulet texts have overlapping features—for example, particular clauses or divinities invoked—but they are rarely identical to each other or to what is found in the manuals. Scribes made their own decisions about how to formulate incantations. They decided which divine agents to call on and how to do so. They decided whether to include a drawing or lay out the writing in unusual formats. They had to choose (usually within the constraints of availability and cost) a material to write on: for example, a clay shard, a bowl, a piece of papyri or parchment, or a metal tablet. And they probably consulted with the client about the best place to put it. Would it be more effective being worn on the body or buried at the house's threshold?[42]

FIGURE 5.5. Jewish amulet inscribed on bronze, for Sura daughter of Sara, for protection of her unborn child and future descendants. Public domain. Metropolitan Museum of Art (18.84.2a, b), Rogers Fund, 1918. https://www.metmuseum.org/art/collection/search/250668.

Amulets in particular have a tendency to stymie easy classification. Some were clearly connected to Jews and Christians. A Greek amulet, for example, that contains a cross, uses Christian names, invokes Jesus and Michael, and contains citations from the New Testament sits clearly within a Christian community. When we read that a man, Yose son of Zenobia, commissioned a bronze tablet in Aramaic that cited a psalm and called on YHWH to cause the inhabitants of the town to "be suppressed and broken and fallen" before him and then put it into the synagogue wall, we are clearly dealing with a Jewish man in a Jewish community. Most amulets, though, are not as easy to categorize. They

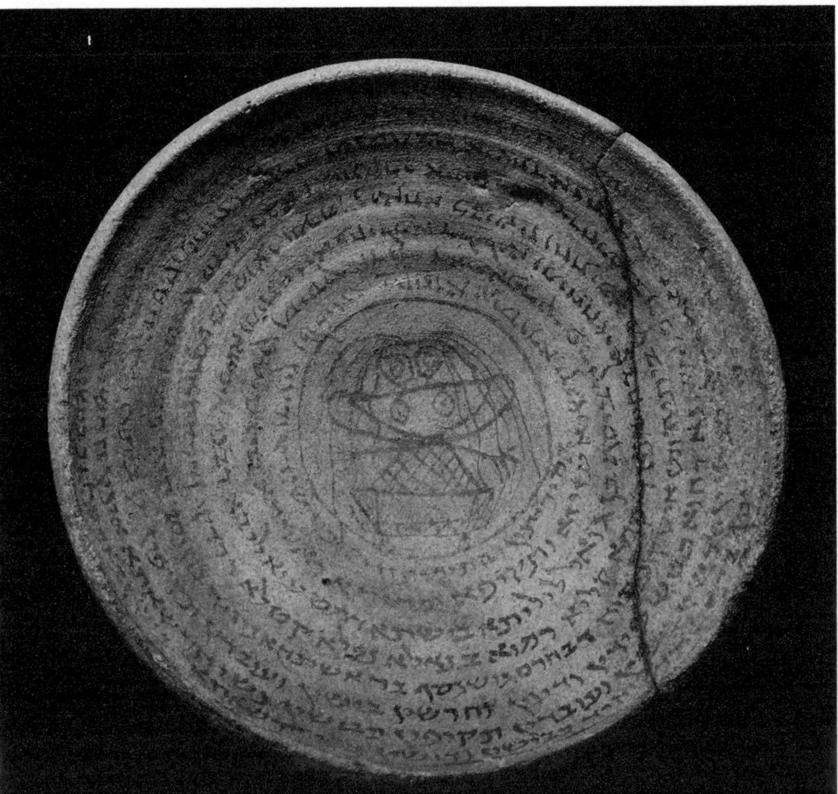

FIGURE 5.6. Incantation bowl from Iraq. Late Antiquity. British Museum (1974,1209.2). Used with permission.

may contain a mix of symbols, languages, names, and divine agents that cross traditional boundaries—one of the very reasons that the Jewish and Christian intellectuals were ambivalent or even hostile to their use. Several of the inscribed bowls found in Iraq, which were probably placed by doors, contain names of rabbis known also in the Talmud (e.g., Rabbi Hanina ben Dosa) alongside the names of spirits and angels and seem to have been written for non-Jewish clients. YHWH, Moses, and Solomon appear in many Greek amulets alongside other non-Jewish deities. This suggests that there was a large amount of improvisation among both scribes and their clients as they drew on what they knew and their experience watching others to find what was most likely to work. For some, the boundaries of "acceptable" prayers to the divine were quite important. Many more, however, had a much looser commitment to such religious borderlines.[43]

Prognostication

Relationships require communication from both sides. The supernatural realm was mostly thought to send its message through material events, such as a good harvest or a plague. There were ways, though, of establishing a more direct channel of communication. The primary reason that one might want to do this was to gain access into the future.

From a very early time, people devised methods of predicting the outcome of uncertain events. Kings employed people who were skilled at reading the patterns of birds or the shape of the liver of a sacrificial animal. (Several terracotta models of livers used to train such professionals are still extant.) Dreams were interpreted, and other unusual "natural" events, such as an early snow or the eruption of a volcano, were seen as signs that were meant to be read. According to the Hebrew Bible, the kings of Israel had prophets in their service, most of whom, we presume, devoted their time to fortune-telling rather than scolding them or pointing out ethical lapses. A ruler would be foolish to embark on a battle or on a risky endeavor without consulting with the appropriate professionals.

The theory of fortune-telling was relatively simple, if not entirely coherent. Divine agents were engaged enough in the affairs of their worshippers that they communicated to them information that they could use to their benefit. The communication, however, was not direct; the gods rarely simply and clearly stated what someone should do in a language that they understood. Oracles were sent through dreams or abnormalities in the natural order, and they needed interpretation. The interpreter, usually what we would call a diviner (although there were many different kinds), guided also by the divine being, would try to translate the communication into a human language. There nevertheless still existed a healthy amount of uncertainty and ambiguity in this process of translation. It was, of course, to the benefit of the diviners to promote the idea that translation was an art rather than a mechanistic science and that the gods were deliberately unclear. There was sometimes much at stake in telling the future for a king (a loss at a battle could be disastrous), and an inaccurate reading of the oracles boded ill for the professional who made it.[44]

One of the most common ways in which the future was communicated was through the movement of the heavenly bodies. These messages were interpreted by astrologers (in antiquity there was no difference between what we would call astrologers and astronomers). The theory behind astrology was that the future was woven into the fabric of the universe and tied to the movement of the stars and planets (which are themselves sometimes seen as divinities or souls). All methods of fortune-telling wrestled with the issue of predeterminism: To what extent could human action influence the outcomes? Astrology, though, grappled with this tension more than most others. Ancient writers on astrology took different positions on the question of whether all human action is predestined or whether we can change presumably predestined outcomes but never came to an answer that was truly satisfying, even to those in antiquity.[45]

Astrology was big business, hardly limited to political officials. Diviners were frequently sought to obtain knowledge from the invisible realm about whether a particular business deal or journey was advisable. The idea of the zodiac was commonly accepted (several representations adorn synagogue floors in Palestine), and papyrus archives from Egypt show Manichaeans and wealthy Christians in Egypt using horoscopes.[46]

Astrology was not the only way to tell the future. Sortilege—which involved the throwing of marked sheep knucklebones (ancient dice)—accomplished similar goals. Around a temple in Phrygia (a region now in western Turkey) stood several large monuments from the second and third centuries whose inscribed texts revealed how it was done. Five knucklebones were thrown, probably all together. Sometimes these were inscribed, but the shape of the knucklebones (each side was different) were in any case correlated with specific values. The dice combination was then located on the text on the monument, each one of which was indexed to a short answer. The answers, as one might expect, were ambiguous. It was up to the ritual expert to interpret how the answer might fit the question. The throw of 1-1-1-1-1, for example, indexes to the following text: "Zeus Olympios. If you see only Chians [i.e., ones]: Zeus will give good thinking to your mind, stranger: he will grant happiness to your work, for which you will give thanks. But appease Aphrodite and the son of Maia [i.e., Atlas]." There was, though, also a do-it-yourself version. Pausanias, who lived in the second century also in Asia Minor, writes that people would come to a shrine dedicated to Herakles (called, though, by a different name), pray in front of the image, roll some knucklebones (which were conveniently laying around), and then consult the inscribed index. Another form of sortilege linked to temples (at least in Egypt) involved "tickets." To submit ticket oracles, a person would give two short written answers, one phrased positively and the other negatively, to the priest, who through divine guidance would choose one to give back. The returned ticket could then also serve as an amulet.[47]

Around the same time, other more portable forms of sortilege developed. This form integrated the question into the luck of the lot. A person would look at a numbered list of questions and pick the most appropriate one. He (the books that we have are addressed to male clients only, although it is of course possible that women also sought assistance in this manner) would then think of a number between one and ten—this is where it was thought that the god intervened—and add it to the number of the question. This new number would then be used as an index that could be looked up in a list of answers.[48]

The importance of a reference text in this process moves us closer toward yet another form of sortilege known as bibliomancy, in which a sacred book was used to deliver oracular answers. The first significant evidence for bibliomancy dates from Late Antiquity, and it appears to have been a preferred form of divination for the Jewish and Christian intellectuals. Although Jews and Christians both used (a different, although overlapping, set of) sacred Scriptures for bibliomancy, the way they used them differed. This difference is, curiously, tied to the way that they wrote and preserved their Scriptures. Christians adopted the codex (that is, like our modern book) as their preferred medium of preservation. A codex can be randomly flipped open. At a particularly difficult juncture in his life, Augustine tells us, he did exactly this, trusting God to take him to a biblical passage that would help him to make a decision. Some Christians combined a more traditional form of sortilege with references to scriptural answers; a few such guides, although ultimately suppressed by the church, survive. Jews, however, used scrolls, which did not lend themselves to that kind of procedure. Instead, according to one story from the Talmud, the bibliomancy took place by means of an innocent child who was learning Scripture. One would ask him about the last passage he learned and take the answer as oracular. It is not clear how widely this was practiced.[49]

Many modern readers might look at these activities with some skepticism: How could people have been so gullible as to think that they worked? It turns out that many intellectuals in antiquity were similarly skeptical. Their skepticism focused more on the ease with which results could be manipulated than with the activity itself. In his novel *The Metamorphoses,* Apuleius skewers a group of soothsaying priests. They doctor the lots so that the same oracular message will come up: "An ox team cleaves the soil for just this reason: Sown grain will sprout abundantly in season." Apuleius goes on to show how the oracle could be applied to any concern. A long passage in the Talmud acknowledges that a dream is like a "letter," a potentially genuine communication from the supernatural (sometimes angelic and sometimes demonic) that needs interpretation. The interpretation, in fact, is more important than the dream; the dream follows its interpretation. There are several ways to game the system for one's advantage. One can "better" a bad dream by assembling three people who declare that the dream is a good one. One can also pay a dream interpreter for a better interpretation. Two rabbis tested this hypothesis by separately relating the same dream, involving a scriptural verse, to the same interpreter, but the one who paid better received a much better interpretation. Even for the rabbis, though, it is also possible that a dream is just a dream, a meaningless impression from events of the day.[50]

Necromancy—raising the dead, often to extract information from them—was a far more fraught way to tell the future. Necromancers are singled out for their loathsomeness in much ancient literature, and most law codes subject them to the death penalty. This may be the result of a kind of anxiety about breaching the division between the living and the dead, which was not as strongly felt about the division between the human and the divine. Another possible reason, which is explicit in imperial law codes, is that the real fear of necromancy was not that the dead would reveal divine secrets but that the client would use the dead to torment his enemies. Whatever the threats and anxieties though, necromancy continued to be practiced, sometimes by or at the behest of the very intellectuals who condemned it. Jews, Christians, and Romans appear to have sought out the dead for a variety of reasons, often with the help of an expert. One of the best places to encounter the dead was, unsurprisingly, in cemeteries, and there is significant evidence that people visited and even slept in them in the hope of communicating with the dead. The Talmud condemns those who fast and then sleep in a cemetery "so that an unclean spirit might rest upon him," which gives enough specificity to suggest that it reflects an actual practice. A Jewish manual of incantations from Late Antiquity (although its date is hard to determine with much certainty) provides a technique to follow at the cemetery: "If you wish to question a ghost; stand facing a tomb and repeat the names of the angels of the fifth encampment (while holding) in your hand a new flask (containing) oil and honey mixed together and say thus: 'I adjure you . . .' When he [i.e., the dead] appears set the flask before him and after this speak your words while holding a twig of myrtle in your hands." The invocation of angels might help to sanitize the practice, distancing it from the demonic realm. Another rabbinic story admits that a necromancer, who himself talks very much like a rabbi, has privileged knowledge, even as the rabbi in the story will not publicly acknowledge it for fear that all will "go astray" after the necromancer.[51]

The Christian relationship with necromancy was similarly ambivalent but was made all the more complex by the understanding of Jesus as having been resurrected. A third-century Christian text condemns the Jews for accusing Christ of having performed necromancy with the cross, a charge it tries vigorously to refute. Jesus is, in fact, portrayed as a necromancer in some Jewish texts, an understanding that might have been informed by some combination of (incomplete) Jewish knowledge of Christian Gospels and stories and observing Christians using crosses as part of their own necromantic activities. It is also possible, though, that the Christian text was also reflecting an intra-Christian polemic and thus portrays one group of Christians condemning another group for using the cross to raise the dead. There is no reason why this text could not actually be engaged in both polemics at once.[52]

Although in the biblical story it is a woman who raises the dead (1 Samuel 28), Jewish and Christian necromancers in antiquity all appear to have been male. So do their clients. Necromancy may have been professionalized, a process that in antiquity frequently involved repackaging knowledge to which women had access or even controlled in order to distance themselves from it. Perhaps men saw necromancy as too important, or too lucrative, to leave to women and sought to reduce their competition.

Contagious Holiness

Calling on the supernatural beings was always risky. It was much safer to strengthen one's relationship to them by simply hanging out with them. There was thus a widespread notion of "contagious holiness," that is, that one could get closer to the supernatural agents through certain kinds of contact.[53]

Throughout Late Antiquity there were competing notions of holiness. One notion connected holiness to ownership. In this model, objects owned by the gods were considered "holy" and thus sacrosanct. This was the model favored by the rabbis and Roman priests, who extensively discussed the formal acts required to transfer ownership of an object to the divine realm, as well as how such objects might return (if ever) back to the profane one. Objects owned by the divine must be treated with appropriate respect, not because they were infused with any special power but because of their property status.[54]

At the same time, though, there existed a wilder, less juridical notion that holiness was a force loose in the world. It would concentrate in certain people, objects, and places and could rub off, as it were, on contact. Among Greeks and Romans, cult statues naturally were seen as having such a potential. Imbued with power, they were placed in special internal rooms in their temples, as much as to protect them as to prevent unauthorized outsiders from incurring divine wrath. Household gods were placed in special niches within homes, and niches in stores would sometimes hold other statues of less powerful gods, all to bring protection to the owners. Intellectuals and jurists who were committed to the notion of holiness based on divine ownership may have looked down on such beliefs.[55]

Jews apparently saw a similar kind of holiness inherent in Torah scrolls. Such scrolls were routinely housed in niches or arks, structures that were like those that housed cult statues. Pictures of them were drawn around graves as a way of harnessing their power to protect the dead.[56]

A rabbinic text captures this sense of holiness:

> The residents of a city who sell a city street, [can] purchase with the proceeds [of the sale] a synagogue. [If they sell] a synagogue, they [can] purchase an ark [for sacred scrolls with the proceeds]. [If they sell] an ark, they [can] purchase dressings [for sacred scrolls with the proceeds]. [If they sell] dressings, they [can] purchase [sacred] scrolls [with the proceeds]. [If they sell sacred] scrolls, they [can] purchase a Torah [with the proceeds].
>
> But: If they sell a Torah, they may not purchase scrolls [of other sacred books]; scrolls—they may not purchase dressings; dressings—they may not purchase an ark; an ark—they may not purchase a synagogue; a synagogue—they may not purchase a street, and so too with any profits [from these sales].[57]

Here the holiness attends even to the value of the holy object, as represented in the proceeds of its sale. There are concentric levels radiating out from the Torah. I doubt that this passage truly reflects what people did, but it does convey what I suspect was a relatively common idea that the Torah was holy and that holiness "catches."[58]

Christians too assumed that certain objects were holier than others and that being near those objects (or directly touching them) made one closer to the divine. Relics are the clearest expression of this

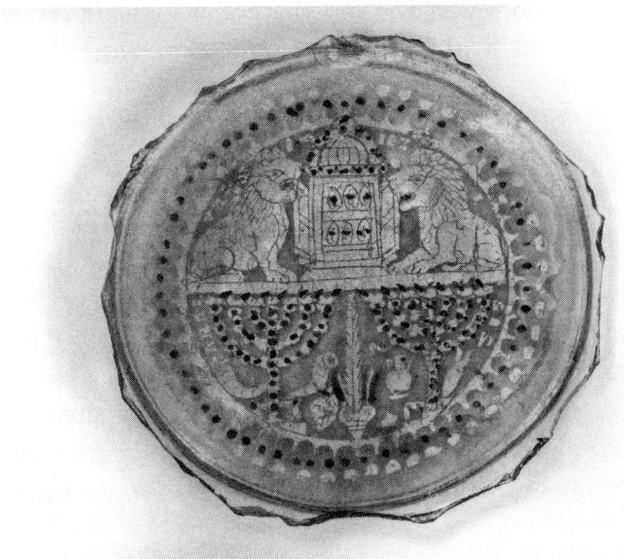

FIGURE 5.7. Gilded glass of a Torah ark with menorahs. Found in Rome, probably fourth century. Photo © Governate of the Vatican City State-Directorate of the Vatican Museums, (inv. 60733). Used by permission.

phenomenon. Christians appear to begin venerating the bones of their saints in the fourth century. Not only the bones were holy, though. Objects that were or had been close to a saint, dead or alive, had also "caught" the holiness of the saint and were venerated in their own right. Sometimes, to avoid exhuming a body, cloth was buried nearby and then, acquiring the body's holiness, could be unearthed, divided, and distributed. Like the Torah scrolls, holiness radiated out from the center.[59]

Relics, though, were not the only place in which Christians materially located holiness. Priests and monks could bless objects, like bread and oil. Called "blessings," they were consumed or brought home by pilgrims and others. We have little information about how ordinary people treated these objects, but it is likely that they were seen as imbued with holiness, particularly if they were acquired during a pilgrimage.[60]

In objects, heaven and earth could meet. Imbued with the force of the supernatural world, an object could radiate holiness. This was a holiness that, as it were, could make everything better. It lent a helping hand to one's communications with the supernatural beings and created an aura that would make it hard for malevolent forces to penetrate.

A world thick with invisible beings presented unlimited opportunities for interaction with them. The ritualized communal worship that we normally associate with "religion" was certainly a part of ordinary life. Such worship, however, played a relatively minor role for most people. Offerings of candles and lamps, alms, blessings over food, a bit of wine spilled on the ground, all were simple quotidian ways of staying in the good graces of supernatural beings. Touching or owning small objects infused with holiness were additional means of staying in tune with these beings.

Humans have evolved with an extraordinary sensitivity to social relationships and hierarchies. We expend vast amounts of energy, often unconsciously, calibrating and strategizing our relationships. We know that relationships are constantly in motion and timing and context are critically important. An action that might improve a relationship in one context might destroy it in another. Even the most stable of relationships requires continual tending.

The same was thought to be true for relationships with supernatural beings. They deserved the same attention as did those with people. An artlessly expressed prayer in an amulet might provoke an undesired reaction. For this reason, sometimes specialists, such as scribes, were needed. Place and timing were also important in these communications, as they are in human ones. These are the topics of the next three chapters.

6

Divine Mediators

SPECIALISTS, ENTREPRENEURS, AND RITUAL EXPERTS

ONE OF John Locke's greatest achievements was to provide a rationale for the separation of religion from business and politics. Locke, an English thinker who lived in the seventeenth century, attempted to carve out a space for public discourse free of religion. Locke essentially invented the idea of the "secular" by limiting what had been the traditional scope of institutional religion and its authorities. Clerics, in Locke's vision, would henceforth tend to the private issues of their congregants' souls, thus allowing politicians and merchants to conduct their affairs free of religious interference. Locke's vision took root. In most Western countries today, there are visible, sometimes quite sharp, lines walling religion off from governance. The head of state in the United Kingdom, for example, is also the head of the Church of England, but the head of government need not be. The idea that religion can be a source for personal enrichment is even more distasteful; in the U.S. tax code, an organization cannot register as "religious" and still operate for profit.[1]

Yet as strong and normalized as this ideology is, we all know that it is pockmarked with exceptions. Even in the United States and France, the two countries with the strictest legal separations between "church" and "state," religion continues to play a critical role in elections and political calculations. Religion, and the pronouncements of religious leaders, motivate voters, while religious institutions work to maximize their political clout. And religion is big business, with a lot of money at stake. Priests, pastors, rabbis, ritual slaughterers, religious schoolteachers—not including all the professionals needed to run and maintain religious facilities, from janitors to accountants—are all paid. In 2023 according to the U.S. Bureau of Labor Statistics, there were some 56,640 clergy employed in the United States, with a median annual wage of $58,920. Since there are over 314,000 places of worship in the United States, this likely undercounts the number of clergy. Religious organizations own vast assets. Businesses that cater to religious sensibilities, such as the enormous Christian literature and music industries or those built to produce and supervise the production of kosher food, are significant economic players. Religion remains a powerful, and often overlooked, economic force.[2]

What is new is not that politics, money, and religion are intertwined but that there should be any expectation that they should not be. Since the dawn of human civilization, people have understood that the ability to provide access to the divine—and to control who gets access—is a valuable service. Sure, it was fine and free for an individual to pray alone wherever and whenever he or she wished, but this was hardly the way for an entire community to relate to their protecting gods. Moreover, private prayer was increasingly seen as unlikely to be as efficacious as an approach to the deities mediated through experts. Mimetic knowledge, the traditions and rituals passed down through families and communities, had its limits. There was always a niche for specialists.

Baruch Spinoza famously revolutionized the approach to the Bible by focusing on the simple question of cui bono: Who benefits? In Spinoza's reading, the Hebrew Bible, and especially the book of Leviticus, was so obviously written for the benefit of the priests that it stood to reason that they wrote it, not God. Moses was indeed behind the Torah, but he cleverly framed the laws that benefit the priests in order to make them palatable to a gullible people. Spinoza's tracts, which saw the Bible in such a purely human and materialistic way, were scandalous enough to lead to opprobrium and ostracization by both Jews and Christians.[3]

Spinoza was too cynical (and his theories of the Bible too flat to survive for long), but he did have a point. Systems that require expert knowledge require experts who have that knowledge. Veneration of the divine, especially on the communal level, was one such system. The experts who were expected to master that knowledge—most of whom would have been born into families that already had standing in those fields—would have a wide range of motives, but among them surely was the desire to retain a decent social and economic standing. They, in turn, would have quite naturally if not always intentionally worked to make their knowledge more complex and inaccessible to elevate their own value and decrease the risk of competition. I want to emphasize that I do not mean this cynically. Many of these experts may well have had only the purest of intentions. They were simply doing what humans do.

In Chapter 4, we discussed one type of expert, the intellectual. The intellectuals, in a sense, won. It is through their writings that we most commonly frame Christianity and Judaism and decide what counts as authentic (i.e., orthodox) and inauthentic (i.e., heretical) expressions of these traditions. As they began to develop through Late Antiquity, though, their eventual victory was far from assured, and the prospect that it might ever happen may well have struck most people—including them—as deeply improbable. They were frequently the least important and most marginal of those who dealt professionally in matters of communicating with the invisible beings.

Later in this chapter, we will return to some of the intellectuals discussed earlier in a different context. First, though, we will survey the varied landscape of these professionals, both those who were connected to organized communities and worked on their behalf and those who had a more entrepreneurial bent, providing paid services to individuals who wanted better access to the divine. The aristocracy, of course, had a vested interest in controlling access to the divine, particularly concerning matters of state. The landscape, though, was awash with many other characters, such as priests and clergy, prophets and necromancers, scribes and ascetics. Each found a niche in the economy of the sacred.

The Aristocracy

While today we commonly separate religious and political functionaries, throughout antiquity they were tightly connected. Aristocratic figures—those with wealth, prestige, and often recognizable political roles—were routinely thought to have special bonds with the deities. Their aristocratic status would lead to their religious roles, which in turn would reinforce their aristocratic status. Rarely, if ever, could a poor person ascend to aristocratic status through their special connections to the divine.

In Late Antiquity, this dynamic is best seen in Rome and the Greek cities of the Mediterranean basin. The Roman political authorities controlled all public cultic activity. Through the period of the Roman Republic, the Senate took it upon itself to decide on whether to admit a deity into the official Roman pantheon—and thus venerate it publicly—or not. Occasionally, it even removed deities from public worship. State religion was directed by the College of Pontifices, at whose head was the *pontifex maximus*. Starting with Augustus, it was the Roman emperor who always bore this title. To make a modern analogy, just as the king of England is head of the Church of England by virtue of being ruling sovereign (and not the reverse), the Roman emperor was the pontifex maximus of Rome. Unlike the king of England, though, the emperor was not shy about making decisions affecting the cult when he so wished. Ultimately, it was his duty and his alone to keep the "peace of the gods." Or, as Cassius Dio said in the late second or early third century CE, "by virtue of being consecrated in all priesthoods, and of their right to bestow most of those positions on others . . . [the emperors] hold in their hands supreme authority over all matters both profane and sacred." It is worth noting that there is no evidence that the emperor, as pontifex maximus, or any of the other *pontifices* (the Latin plural of *pontifex*; mostly nobles appointed by the emperors and the other pontifices), received any specialized training. These were titles that conferred status and some authority in the running of the public cult, but their holders were in no way necessarily experts in how to please the gods.[4]

A similar situation existed in the city cults. Going back to the classical Greek city-state (polis), responsibility for the relationship between the polity and the gods rested with the elected magistrates and city council, or boule. It was the boule, representing the city, that would authorize the public worship of certain deities and not others. The boule also had to officially accept gifts made by individuals to fund public temples and civic celebrations. Enough money changed hands in these transactions that legal penalties were instituted for magistrates who misappropriated funds.[5]

The movement of the Roman Empire toward Christianity beginning in the fourth century brought surprisingly little change to the understanding that it was the emperor and the imperial administration that ultimately had to assure divine favor for the Empire. The emperors, even the Christian ones, continued to take the title of pontifex maximus until the very end of the fourth century. After that, they changed the title to *pontifex inclitus*—"the illustrious pontifex"—in what may have been a small nod to the sensibilities of Christian bishops. As a pontifex maximus, the emperor was officially in charge of the veneration of the traditional deities in Rome. Since they increasingly never visited Rome, the emperors usually delegated this responsibility to the city's principal magistrate. Nevertheless, the title clearly remained symbolically important to the emperors.[6]

Roman emperors shaped their self-understanding around the idea that they were responsible for the peace of the god(s). As we might expect, this was certainly true of Julian in the middle of the fourth century. During his short reign, he embarked on extensive public attempts to mollify the gods, whose neglect he took seriously. Even the Christian emperors, though, were driven by this self-understanding. Nearly every Christian emperor from Constantine onward took it upon himself to convene ecclesiastical synods. In doing so, they were not merely acting as tools of the court bishops. They sincerely felt that they had both a responsibility and something to contribute. They never saw as a hindrance the fact that their own Christian theological understandings might be idiosyncratic and incoherent. They employed Christian bishops, gave them imperial privileges, and paid them from the public treasury (*fiscus*). The public cult—now with Christ at its center—ultimately answered to the pontifex inclitus.

The bishops, though, had other ideas. Christian ecclesiastical hierarchy took shape during the first three centuries of the era. Out of power and drawing on a worldview in which they were persecuted and standing against rather than with imperial authorities, Christian leaders had a hard time wrapping their heads around this new situation. The choice they faced was difficult in every way. Do they allow themselves to be co-opted by the emperor in return for power, influence, and money? Or do they continue to stand against temporal authorities, maintaining purity but risking more persecution and marginalization? Christian leaders took different paths that sometimes put them at odds with each other.[7]

Bishops who did decide to work as part of the Roman administration justified themselves in two ways. First, these officials saw themselves as working not just for the good of Christianity but for the good of the *right* Christianity. All different kinds of Christians saw service in the imperial administration as a way to decisively influence the course of their own ideologies and parties. Most notable in the extant records—almost all written by the ultimately triumphant "orthodox" camp—is the struggle with the Arians. The Arians distinguished themselves by their theological position that Jesus is the son of God, not a "person" of God who is equally co-eternal. (Or perhaps this was the default position, and it was really the emerging orthodox Christians who distinguished themselves.) This understanding, on its face, does make some logical sense from a reading of the Gospels, and it was widespread among Christians. Through the fourth century, several Christian emperors were attracted to this position as well. The orthodox bishops could not fight what they considered to be a heresy from without, and they engaged in the fight at the highest levels of the imperial administration. That this was solely a battle about an abstruse theological position, though, is unlikely. Arians and non-Arians were bound in different social networks that were almost certainly fighting for the perks of power as well.[8]

The second justification, which perhaps was a result rather than a cause of the increasing collaboration between Christian leaders and Roman imperial authorities, was the development of an intellectual framework for understanding the role that the state played for Christians. It was Augustine, writing in the early fifth century, who would most influentially articulate the ideal relationship between Christians and the state. According to Augustine, as long as we live in the present era—having not yet entered into the age of the "city of God"—the state is necessary and deserves our support. It preserves order and provides protection from outside forces (like the Goths, whose sack of Rome in 410 CE was his impetus for writing *The City of God*). The state can certainly be evil, but at its best it can also be an instrument of the divine will, creating a civic order that accords with Christian values. Augustine urged against a theocratic political arrangement in which ecclesiastical authorities took charge of the base matters of governance. At the same time, he left open the opportunity for clergy to cooperate with imperial authorities. For Augustine, the ideal emperor was a deeply believing Christian who, while not a clergy member, would turn to court bishops frequently for advice. The fact that the Emperor Theodosius performed a public penance was particularly impressive to Augustine. Of course, Augustine was writing more for those bishops—giving them leave to give such advice while accepting the perks of imperial office—than for the emperor. Such an approach gave the imperial court (if not the emperor per se) ultimate authority to ensure good relations between the Empire and God. It thus also elevated the standing, power, and prestige of the bishops, who were themselves most frequently from aristocratic families.[9]

Jewish aristocrats also played important roles as divine intercessors, although their story is more complex. For some centuries prior to the destruction of the Jerusalem Temple in 70 CE, Jewish priests—a status inherited from birth through the male line—made up a significant proportion of the Jewish aristocracy in Judea. These priests derived at least some of their wealth from their very role as priests; they received gifts on YHWH's behalf and were not obliged to tithe their agricultural produce. After 70 CE, they continued to play an important communal role by virtue of their traditional roles, inherited wealth, and family prestige.

The patriarch was at the top of some hierarchy, although which one is not entirely clear. The rabbis often regarded the patriarch with deep suspicion or sometimes even scorn. Roman legislation notes that since the cessation of the patriarchate sometime prior to 429 CE, there existed "the Primates of the Jews, who are nominated in the Synhedriis of either of the provinces of Palestine." It is entirely unclear if they, the *primates*, or the sanhedrins, saw themselves or were seen by the larger Jewish community as having any role in communicating with the divine on behalf of the community.[10]

Whatever the powers of the patriarch, they did not extend to Persia. Since Persia was under Sassanian rather than Roman rule, and the patriarch was a Roman office, this is entirely to be expected. There is no information about the exilarch outside of rabbinic texts, which portray an uneasy relationship between rabbis and most of the exilarchs. While it is likely that they had some official status within the Sassanian political system, they had no role mediating between God and the Jewish community of Persia.[11]

Nearly all aristocrats with public offices were free, relatively well-to-do men. In Late Antiquity, there were certainly powerful women living in the imperial court, such as Helena, the pious mother of Constantine, and Theodora, the much beloved (and highly maligned) wife of the Emperor Justinian. They could exercise power, however, only through their influence on the male emperors. Helena did so successfully, as she appears to have been the impetus behind Constantine's ambitious Christian building program (which included the Church of the Holy Sepulchre in Jerusalem). Theodora, perhaps less so. Despite being publicly recognized as a "partner" in Justinian's counsels, she never convinced her husband to support her favored Christian group, the Miaphysites (distinguished by the belief that Jesus Christ had only one nature, a fusion of divine and human), over their opponents, the Chalcedonians. (Scholars today often refer to these groups as the miaphysites and the dyophysites.) In 452 CE, the Chalcedonians declared that Christ had a combined human and divine nature. It is little wonder that the (that is, any) emperor would be attracted to such an understanding; perhaps there was also a bit of Christ in the emperor. Meanwhile, there is no awareness in Jewish sources of even the hair of a possibility that women could assume the office of the patriarchate (matriarchate?) or exilarchate. And despite sayings of Jesus and Paul that lower the divide between men and women, the majority of Christians in positions of real power throughout Late Antiquity also did not seriously discuss the possibility of a woman assuming an ecclesiastical office. If women had power at the top, it was decidedly soft power.[12]

Priests

The men at the top had both the responsibility to assure that the deities continued to favor their people and the power to make radical changes in communal practices, be they the promotion or demotion of a god or the establishment of a new festival. Through Late Antiquity, though, they rarely used this power. This should not be surprising. Public rituals involving the gods have always tended to change very slowly. If it worked for our grandparents—and surely, they were not wrong!—it should work for us. In fact, most political leaders were not particularly knowledgeable about ritual details and left the details of communal ritual performance to experts. The leaders often had some small (but crucial) well-scripted role, which might require them to touch a sacrificial animal in a particular way or recite a short formula, but they would often be coached by experts. These experts, particularly those who administered the communal sacrifices, we usually call "priests."

With the English term "priests," we descend yet again into a terminological thicket. There is no single Latin word that maps closely to our word "priest." There were several different functionaries involved in the Roman sacrificial system. There were pontifices conferred by the emperor, senate, or other ruling body. The "priesthoods" were often ceremonial and came with little or no responsibilities, sometimes given as a marker of status to a municipal benefactor. The Greek terms for priest (*hiereus*) and high priest (*archiereus*) were even vaguer but for the most part came with a similarly honorific character that brought some degree of status. In Aphrodisias, a city in Asia Minor, a couple of men are noted not as "high priests" themselves but as descendants of high priests. A priesthood of this nature could last for a limited period or a lifetime. The holders of these priesthoods were overwhelmingly male, but there were a few examples of women who also served. These priests had the kind of power and discretion that could rarely be used, bound as they were by convention.[13]

About the other priests—the real, nonhonorific ones who had the specialized knowledge about how to conduct sacrifices and who got

FIGURES 6.1A, 6.1B. Silver coin of Aurelian, 270–275, depicting emperor and priest sacrificing at an altar. ANS 1970.165.135. Images courtesy of the American Numismatic Society.

their hands dirty slaughtering and butchering the animal, cooking the parts, distributing the flesh, and mopping up the blood (or assisting those who did)—we know far less. Priestly duties were not honorifics; they were jobs. We do not know if such functionaries generally came to their jobs because their fathers were priests (since there are no mentions or artistic representations of women doing these jobs, it is unlikely—but not impossible—that any were female) or whether they came from more diverse (including slave) backgrounds. We do not even know what such people would be called and if anyone would refer to them in any context with words that come within the lexical field that we call "priest."

On the other hand, we have vast evidence of Jewish priests during Late Antiquity, but we know little about what they did. Jewish priestly status (although not the high priesthood) was always determined through the father's biological line. While the Jerusalem Temple stood, they had defined roles administering the sacrificial system and a position of respect within their communities. The power of the priesthood, though, did not collapse in 70 CE. This is because Jewish priests had always had a role outside of the Jerusalem Temple. At any given time, only a small proportion of priests would be in the Temple (there was some kind of rotation system, but it is unclear how and to what extent it was administered), with the rest living in their own local communities, often far from Jerusalem. Even outside of the Temple, though, there still were still priests who performed cultic functions. Jews who could not easily travel to the Temple still wanted to make sacrifices and give gifts to God. The primary way that they could do this was to give their offerings to the local priests. The destruction of the Temple did not change this.[14]

In Late Antiquity, as before, these offerings were not entirely ad hoc or insignificant. Following biblical prescriptions, the rabbis extensively discussed which products were to be given to the priests (and others, at times) and in what quantities. In addition to first fruits, a bit of every batch of dough and every slaughtered animal was to go to a priest, who would complete the process by eating it, with his household, in a state of ritual purity. These obligations, according to the rabbis, are limited to the geographic area that they define as the "Land of Israel." One striking mosaic inscription from the floor of a synagogue by Beit Shean (in Roman Palestine) details the borders of the area subject to tithing, almost certainly demonstrating that there was at least one Jewish community that took them seriously. While we often do not know when rabbinic texts reflect common practice, it is likely that many Jewish communities, both within the Land of Israel and outside of it, gave gifts to God through their local priests. It is even possible that in the absence of the Jerusalem Temple, this practice intensified. The priests would certainly not have objected.[15]

Local Jewish priests probably could not survive, let alone live well, on what they received from their communities. At the same time, though, such gifts were not insignificant and could have given a real boost to the economic standing of priests in Late Antiquity. Landowning priests would not only receive communal offerings but also be exempt from giving many of them, thus accruing a competitive advantage. This advantage could then be turned into both wealth and status and passed down through families.[16]

The combination of wealth, status, and simple historical memory would help to explain the prominence of priests in Jewish inscriptions from Late Antiquity. Both men and women wanted their priestly status noted on their donation inscriptions and epitaphs. The status is noted for women, although it is often unclear if they are claiming it for themselves or identifying themselves as daughters or husbands of priests, thereby accruing prestige indirectly. Today, Jewish epitaphs commonly note whether the deceased is a priest, which is seen as symbolically prestigious. I am suggesting, though, that in Late Antiquity the prestige was not merely symbolic but linked to real money and power as well.[17]

The fact that "priests" were legible to non-Jews certainly did not hurt their status. Romans and Christians understood Jewish priests as bona fide leaders in the image of their own "priests." When Roman imperial legislation from the fourth century addresses itself to Jewish communal leaders, it frequently includes "priests" (using a couple of different terms) with patriarchs and "fathers of the synagogues." Do the lawgivers here provide evidence that Jewish priests were communal leaders, or are they filtering a vague knowledge that Jewish priests exist through a Christian lens with the result that they assume that Jewish priests play an important role in both communal and synagogue leadership? In either case, such legislation reinforced the wealth and prestige of Jewish priests. In 330 CE, Jewish priests, like other privileged classes, were excused from the duty to fund certain large municipal projects. It is likely—although the evidence is sparse on this point—that the Jews increasingly began to see their priests as the Romans and Christians did. They not only accepted offerings on God's behalf but also were seen as playing (and probably actually did play) an important role in communal leadership and the synagogue.[18]

Jewish priestly privilege and power fostered jealousy and competition, particularly among the rabbis. While the rabbis acknowledged the historic role of the priests and their privileges, some also chafed at what they would have seen as its unfairness. Rabbis saw themselves as learned, toiling in complex intellectual pursuits and engaged in a constant struggle with other rabbis to achieve and keep their prestige. Priests were simply born (an "ascribed status" as opposed to an "achieved" one), and their job was to eat. To the Jewish community in Late Antiquity, a rabbi looked like an odd combination of overachieving jurist and scribe. To the Romans, who would not assign them to the category of "cleric" (which was preserved for "Catholic" ecclesiastical authorities), they were probably "teachers," learned men who deserved some measure of respect but not to the level of priests. Rabbinic literature is by no means "anti-priest," but it does contain a few choice insults. "A *mamzer* [the child produced by certain kinds of illicit, usually incestual, unions] scholar takes precedence over a high priest who is an ignoramus," according to one particularly wishful rabbinic statement. More subtly, the rabbis envision the priests as mere figureheads, necessary to perform certain functions but entirely subordinate in their actions to the rabbis. This was an argument that barely got purchase outside of rabbinic circles.[19]

There are a bewildering number of terms used in Latin and Greek to denote ecclesiastical offices, and the lines between them are not always clear. The term *cleric* or clergy appears in much Latin imperial legislation as a general category. One imperial law from 531 CE concerns "most reverend bishops, as well as presbyters or deacons and subdeacons, and especially monks, although they are not clergymen (*clerici*)." All these officials except for monks, then, appear to be "clergy." Are clergy "priests," though? Just two months before that law, another one mentioned legal privileges for someone who has "priestly privilege" (*sacerdotii praerogativam*): Are such people all "clerics"? When a Greek rescript given in 533 CE refers to the *hiereis* of the "Holy Catholic and Apostolic Church," using the word that was commonly used to designate the "priests" of Roman and Greek temples, is it also referring to the clerici and *sacerdotes*? In other words, what exactly is a Christian "priest"?[20]

Stepping back from terminology helps to clarify the reason behind this ambiguity. Christian ecclesiastical authorities built their political authority as functional replacements for Greek and Roman priests. They may not have burned flesh on temple altars for the good of the emperor and empire, but they did offer the flesh and blood of Jesus on the church altar for similar reasons. They fell into a legible slot in the social order. Christian bishops were themselves sometimes called pontifices, an indication that they were seen, and saw themselves, as fitting into a recognizable social slot. At the same time, Christian leaders wanted to distance themselves as far as possible from those "pagan priests." They coined a variety of new terms, such as *clerici*, to mark that difference.[21]

The fact that priests were primarily oriented toward the *community*, employed by communal bodies and working on behalf of ensuring divine favor on the community as a whole, did not mean that they could not also provide a service, at a price, to individuals. Greek and Roman temples were open to all comers. Individuals could take advantage of a temple that was not at that moment being used for state functions to bring their own offerings. How this concretely worked is not entirely clear: Was there a staff of priests and necessary experts available all the time to accept and process such offerings? Or could anyone approach the altar to slaughter his, her, or their own goat? It seems most likely that even if not directly involved in all private offerings, the priests at least took a small fee for the use of the altar (and perhaps the wood and the cleaning); it could be a side gig. Many Christian priests (*presbyters*) had a similar arrangement in their churches, facilitating the individuals who wanted to make offerings (e.g., lamps) to Christ in order to obtain personal benefit. Several bishops, in fact, commented scornfully on clergy getting rich off commemorative masses.[22]

Prophets

The barrier between the world of mortals and the world of the gods was real but permeable. One of the primary functions of the priests was to facilitate the movement of offerings across this barrier, from the visible to the invisible world. Burning an animal or incense, dedicating a gift to a god, pouring a bit of wine out onto the ground, or even just eating an offering in a state of purity were among the ways that they gave things to the gods. Priests were thus indispensable to the rulers who, ultimately, were tasked with maintaining the peace of the gods. But that permeability went in both directions. Supernatural beings sent guidance on proper behavior back to mortals, especially to those in power. This guidance most often came in the form of ambiguous signs, such as astronomical or meteorological phenomena, the behavior or appearance of animals, or dreams. Anything unusual was a potential sign, and it fell to another set of specialists to interpret it. We will call these specialists prophets, although they, like priests, had a variety of different names depending on their area of expertise.

No ruling court was complete without its prophets. In the earliest of cuneiform documents from Sumer we see them at work, interpreting signs for the rulers. The kings of Israel all had prophets, and in Rome there was the priestly college of the *haruspices*, who, among other duties, interpreted the divine messages that were sent through the appearance of the livers of sacrificed animals. Cicero provides an intriguing if incomplete account of the process of "officially" interpreting a sign in Rome. In 57 BCE, Rome experienced some kind of "rumbling." The Senate declared the noise a "prodigy" (a sign from the gods) and referred it to the haruspices, who then issued a response that ascribed a cause to the noise (divine displeasure at certain Roman behaviors) and, more vaguely, remedies and predictions. As is typical with such interpretations of signs sent from the beyond, this one was itself open to interpretation. From a much earlier time, the great prophets of Israel issued a series of similarly confusing oracular statements that would have been difficult to parse with any precision. In any case, rather than asking the haruspices what they meant, Cicero and his adversaries simply used the response to their own ends.[23]

Due to their potentially sensitive political implications, divine signs and their interpretations were often tightly controlled by the state. As Cicero attests, for an event to be considered a genuine "sign" from the gods it first had to be declared thus by the ruling body. Augustus and his successors were thus very careful about what they allowed to be considered genuine signs and therefore submitted for official interpretation. Romans always looked dimly on "unofficial" signs and their interpretations. Those that they found potentially destabilizing—some coming from Jews and Christians but some from within the Roman ruling elite—they responded to brutally. There was, of course, an obvious sociological reason for this: prophecies could inspire people to act against the interest of the Roman aristocracy. At the same time, though, the fear of unofficial prophecies was linked to a belief that the interpreter of a sign was an active agent in its fulfillment. That is, interpreting a sign was not thought of as a simple human and technical act of translating a divine message. The interpreter himself or herself (there are occasional traces of female prophets, albeit not official Roman ones) was thought to shape and activate the prediction. Even a malicious interpretation had the potential to unleash divine forces from a real sign. Roman officials thus tended to direct their signs to interpreters who they suspected would be sympathetic to their desires.[24]

Emperors, though, did not always get their wishes. The ancient historian Ammianus Marcellinus states that in 363 CE, under Julian, there was a robust infrastructure for identifying and interpreting divine signs. According to Ammianus, the gods sent several signs—correctly and clearly interpreted by the "experts" (*periti*)—that Julian should not invade Parthia. These signs included the premature death of a priest; an earthquake in Constantinople; and consultation of the Sibylline books, ordered by Julian but made by their keepers in Rome. Julian ignored these signs and thus met his early end during the failed invasion. Although Julian himself was decidedly anti-Christian, his use of this infrastructure a mere two years after becoming emperor shows that it had survived earlier Christian rulers. The Christian emperors before and after him were sensitive to the signs sent by God and had in their employment those who could (favorably) interpret them. Constantine's vision of "the cross" before a decisive victory only became significant after it was interpreted. And there was, after all, no dispute between the Christian and non-Christian interpreters that Julian's end was divinely predicted.[25]

The gods did not limit their messaging to rulers. At any given time, the world was full of divine signs, directed at both communities and individuals; one only needed to find and interpret them. Through Late Antiquity, Roman imperial authorities, who were so concerned about unauthorized interpretations of signs that might have political significance, were more relaxed when it came to personal signs. Like the political ones, though, these too required interpretation, and there were many experts who would happily interpret a sign for a coin.

In some places, it was common for private individuals to consult the priests and prophets of a local sanctuary for guidance in interpreting the meaning of a sign or dream. In Asia Minor, for example, there are several inscriptions that commemorate such consultations. These "signs" were often illnesses or physical misfortunes, sometimes accompanied by a dream. The person would then go to the temple to figure out what they did to provoke divine displeasure and commission a "confession stele" to commemorate a happy outcome. For example: "Great is Zeus from Twin Oaks! I, Athenaios, had been punished for a sin committed in ignorance. After I received many punishments a dream demanded a stele, and I wrote down the manifestations of the power of the god."[26] This inscription does not specify the punishments or the sin (many contain one or both), but the rough contours of the underlying scenario are clear. The priests were available to help individuals make sense of unfortunate events, illnesses, or dreams and to accept offerings to set things right with the gods. In this case, the offering may only have been this stele, but sometimes it was also a material or cash donation to the temple.[27]

Taking a trip to a temple to interpret a sign was an ordeal. The trip itself could be expensive. More importantly, though, the outcome was unpredictable and potentially ruinous. A priest, for example, might relay the god's demand for an exorbitant gift. It would be hard to simply walk away from such knowledge, not to mention the social interaction. A safer (if not always truly safe) course of action would be to go to an unaffiliated expert. And fortunately, there were many such experts. Scholars today refer to these experts as "ritual entrepreneurs." They filled many functions (sometimes in the same person), one of which was dream interpretation. They could also cross the borders of "religions" set by the intellectuals and priests. For a fee, many would provide their services to devotees of Artemis, YHWH, or Christ alike.[28]

Dream Interpretation

Of these different types of entrepreneurs, the dream interpreter was the most common. Most of the time, as even specialists from Late Antiquity acknowledge, a dream is just a dream. But sometimes it is a message from the beyond. Individuals who thought that they received such messages would go to a local expert trained to ascertain whether it was indeed a significant dream, and if so, what it meant. At least some of these experts had studied or consulted manuals devoted to dream classification and interpretation. The most complete manual from Late Antiquity to survive was written by a man named Artemidorus of Ephesus in the mid-second century CE. The manual was in part a "scientific" collection of data about dreams and their interpretations gathered from travels through the eastern Mediterranean, along with some theoretical reflections about dream interpretation. Artemidorus stresses that dream interpretation is ultimately contextual and that for an expert to make a correct interpretation he must know the dreamer's personal details. Sometimes these details are critical for knowing whether a dream is to be interpreted auspiciously or not. A dream, for example, of singing in the streets predicts ridicule and disgrace, but only if the dreamer is rich. For a politician to dream about having sex with his willing mother in the missionary position is auspicious (the "mother" is understood as the compliant and willing body politic), but the same dream might not be auspicious for others. Dream interpretation is not something that can be determined mechanically, where one symbol always means the same thing.[29]

Artemidorus emphasizes that dream interpretation is a complex technical skill. He addresses these books to his son and intends them as privileged information. These are the tricks of the trade that his son is not to share. The business of dream interpretation is oddly meritocratic: reputations are built on whether the predictions were thought to have come true. While Artemidorus's manual shows no awareness that Jews or Christians even exist (he does use examples of people dreaming of interactions with traditional Greek gods), much of his interpretive framework could be, and no doubt was, used to interpret those who worshipped other gods as well.

The Babylonian Talmud also contains an extended discussion of dreams and their interpretation that tracks with Artemidorus's manual. Some dreams, according to the rabbis, are meaningless, often just reflecting what the dreamer was thinking about that day. Angels and demons, though, sometimes send dreams; these are the ones that need attention. Dreams can thus qualify as what the Talmud calls a "minor prophecy." They portend the future, particularly whether something good or disastrous will happen to the dreamer. The interpretation of a dream is often dependent on context, particularly the social status of the dreamer. And far from being a neutral or technical event, a dream interpretation can activate the dream.[30]

A long cycle of stories embedded in the Talmud embodies some of the basic tensions of dream interpretation. These stories all involve the interactions of two rabbis, Abaye and Rava, with a dream interpreter, Bar Hedya. The rabbis brought identical dreams to Bar Hedya, but Abaye would pay him for an interpretation and Rava would not. In the first of three sets of stories in this cycle, the two rabbis each related that they dreamed about specific (and the same in each case) biblical verses. Bar Hedya would interpret these favorably for Abaye but inauspiciously for Rava. The next set of dreams are more general, but the pattern remains the same: Abaye receives auspicious interpretations, Rava does not. These interpretations all came to pass. Rava finally began paying Bar Hedya and the interpretations of his dreams and his fortunes changed.[31]

At this point in the cycle, the Talmud cites another story. Once, when Rava and Bar Hedya were together, the latter dropped a book that opened to a page that read (in Hebrew), "All dreams follow the mouth," that is, that they are fulfilled according to their interpretation. Rava, reflecting on the terrible misfortunes he suffered due to Bar Hedya's interpretations, cursed him. Bar Hedya ran to Rome, where, in the final set of stories, he interpreted dreams for members of the emperor's household. He continued only to interpret for those who paid him, which got him in trouble with the Roman government. His end was gruesome.

The basic tension reflected in the Bar Hedya stories revolves around two problems: Could the interpreter just invent an interpretation to maximize his or her own profits? And, given this power, could one who has a dream that was suspected to be inauspicious simply not get it interpreted? The Talmud explicitly raises the second issue and ends up recommending that if one has an ostensibly "bad" dream it be brought to a rabbinic court and declared to be auspicious, reinforcing the declaration with the recitation of several biblical verses. This fits into a more extensive discussion in the Talmud about how to use biblical verses to respond to bad dreams in order to make them into good (or at least no longer bad) omens.

Contrasting this Talmudic story cycle with the manual of Artemidorus also highlights another tension: How culturally specific were dreams and their interpretations? The rabbis, discussing rabbis, dreamed biblical verses, and Bar Hedya was a skilled "interpreter" (*mephasher*, a word also used to denote the interpretation of biblical verses and the solving of thorny legal problems) of these dreams. But is he even meant to be thought of as Jewish? On the one hand, he knows biblical verses (although he does not cite them himself), has a name that could be Jewish Aramaic, knows at least one rabbinic tradition (that the curse of a sage is efficacious), and carries a book written in Hebrew. On the other hand, his name is not necessarily Jewish, he is skilled in the interpretation of more general dreams, and he can insinuate himself within and communicate with the Roman imperial court (in what language?). He is, I think, meant to be a deliberately ambiguous figure who can slip, as dream interpreters can, between different cultural contexts. The only other instance of a person being termed an "interpreter of dreams" in rabbinic literature refers to a Samaritan, another liminal figure who crosses over between Jewish and non-Jewish worlds.[32]

The cultural slipperiness of Bar Hedya is striking since the wider Talmudic context in which these stories appear is not slippery at all. Read as a whole, the Talmud's discussion clearly is arguing for the rabbinic appropriation of dream interpretation. Dreams are to be understood through the lens of Scripture as interpreted by the rabbis. The rabbis offer their own general interpretations, as, for example, when they say that if "in a dream, he has sex with his mother, he should anticipate [gaining] understanding." The rabbis positioned themselves as the dream interpreters for Jews, complete with a set of "traditionally" Jewish strategies for ameliorating bad dreams and interpreting good ones. These strategies, of course, were not "traditional"—there is no indication that Jews responded to bad dreams by reciting scriptural verses prior to this period. Given a choice between consulting Bar Hedya or rabbis (who never actually forbade payment for dream interpretation), I suspect most Jews would have gone with Bar Hedya, whose expertise was proven.

Christians were as interested in dreams as everybody else. Tertullian, a North African Christian writer who lived from around 155 to 220 CE, discusses the nature of dreams in a tract about the soul, *de Anima*. Dreams, he claims, are intrinsically connected to the activities of the soul, which is itself more connected to the beyond during moments of physical sleep. Following conventional ancient wisdom, he classifies most of them as insignificant, informed by thoughts during the day or physical sensations (like those, for example, that arise from eating too many beans). Tertullian compares the soul—which never sleeps—to a gladiator without armor or arms who nakedly flails away. So too our souls are in constant motion, causing us to dream with emotions that have no cause or effect outside of ourselves. Few dreams come from God, and the bulk of those are meant to steer individuals to greater knowledge of God. Only a few of these God-given dreams are truly prophetic and predictive.[33]

Christian writers sometimes relate that they had such predictive or prophetic dreams. Perpetua had a vision that turned out to be a dream that she was certain was sent by God, as did Jerome. But when it comes to dreams, these kinds of divinely sent, predictive, and auspicious dreams are the exception. Most dreams, these writers assert, are sent by demons in order to drive us away from God. Dreams sometimes feature the false "pagan" gods. While we may see this as unsurprising, given the constant barrage of visual and literary images of such gods that most people in an urban environment in Late Antiquity would have encountered, to Christian intellectuals they were a sign of Satan's work. Similarly, the lustful dreams frequently encountered by Christian ascetics, unsurprising to us, must have been the work of the demons. Although acknowledging that dreams could be neutral or even good, these Christian intellectuals largely took a dim and suspicious view of dreaming.[34]

Those who were not part of the Christian elite, though, were more receptive to dreams and their predictive meanings. We have little direct evidence for Christian dream interpretation, probably largely due to the degree that the Christian intellectuals suppressed it. Hippolytus of Rome, writing in the late second or early third century CE, forbade an interpreter of dreams—along with members of some other professions (e.g., pimp, diviner, charioteer)—from being accepted into the church. About two centuries later, despite the opposition of the bishops, Christians were still erecting altars and churches in response to visions of martyrs they saw in their sleep. There are many inscriptions attesting to Greeks making offerings to their gods "at the command of a dream." Christians produced no writing that is comparable to the composition on dreams in the Talmud or Artemidorus's tract, but they continued to dream and saw in those dreams divine messages that they sought to decode. In such cases, the bishops clearly wanted them to turn to them and other episcopal authorities, although it is likely that they also turned to figures like Bar Hedya.[35]

Dream interpreters in Late Antiquity came in different types, but they were all competing against each other. If Asklepios, Jupiter, or the archangel Michael bearing a cross comes to one in a dream, it is not hard to figure out who might best interpret it. Most dreams, though, do not as clearly indicate who might best interpret them. Rabbis argued that Jews, no matter the content of their dreams, should come to them for their interpretation; bishops made the same argument to Christians. While the Greek and Roman temples still stood, their priests, prophets, and other workers too positioned themselves as being best able to provide relief for bad dreams. But it was the entrepreneurs, the Bar Hedyas, who dominated this market.

Astrologers

From the perspective of the state, personal dream interpretation was a relatively benign activity. Other kinds of personal predictive activity, less so. Most politicians and intellectuals throughout antiquity thought astrology and necromancy to be, at best, dubious activities and the experts who facilitated them to be potentially dangerous.

Astrology was a learned skill. The theory behind it is grounded in three basic beliefs. The first is that time has *quality*. That is, moments of time are intrinsically different. The second is that this quality is linked to the movement of the constellations and the planets. Of special interest to astrologers is where the constellations are in the sky and the planets in relation to them. The third is that there is a connection between the quality of the time as indicated in the heavens and what happens here on earth. This connection is sometimes referred to as the doctrine of correspondences. The truth of these propositions was hardly questioned through antiquity or, for that matter, until the early modern period.[36]

The nature of the correspondence was, however, a topic of ancient debate. Was the movement of the astral bodies (in which, according to some, were embodied the gods themselves) the cause of events, or signs of the future? This philosophical problem, of course, is at the heart of all future-telling activities: Are signs of the future deterministic and unalterable? One of the more famous ancient examples that leans toward determinism is that of Oedipus, whose family tried to do everything they could to alter a bad reading of the future only to discover that they facilitated that very outcome. Jewish and Christian intellectuals never denied that there were meanings in the movement of the stars, but they did largely shun deterministic interpretations. The future can be foretold, but acts of piety can change it.[37]

As with dream interpreters, there were learned and less learned astrologers. Expert astrologers would have known not only how to visually recognize what was happening in the heavens but also how to compute the movement of the constellations and stars. One Hebrew manual from Late Antiquity, *Sefer Ha-Razim*, describes how one can ascend through the seven firmaments of heaven, what one will see at each level, and how one should respond. According to its preface, the angel Raziel originally gave this information to Noah, who learned from it the movement of the constellations and what they mean. *Sefer Ha-Razim* is not an astrological manual as we might usually understand the term since it does not detail the correspondences between the quality of time and the meaning of events. It does, though, link astrological phenomena to adjurations of angels and the firmament in which those angels reside. For example, if a man wants to win the heart of a rich woman (the manual entirely assumes a readership of men), he should invoke the angels of the first firmament during the full moon by putting a piece of tin inscribed with an adjuration into a flask containing his sweat and burying it on her doorstep. The manual assumes a ritual expert who has many abilities, including at least some facility with astronomical observations, the names of angels, and scribal skills.[38]

The rabbis very rarely mention astrologers, and when they do, they use a Greek loan word and reduce the position to a pedestrian and frequently incorrect predictor of the future. Despite frequent Roman claims that astrology is "Chaldean," and thus originally practiced in Aramaic, rabbinic literature never uses an Aramaic or Hebrew term that we might translate as "astrologer." The astrologer, even more than the dream interpreter, is mocked, even if the rabbi acknowledges that he (always he) does have the power to accurately predict the future. Even the rabbis never seem to condemn them outright or reject their expert knowledge, and it is likely that other Jews did not have scruples about consulting them. Whether there were specifically Jewish astrologers (as there may have been dream interpreters) is unknown, but it is likely there were.[39]

Christian authorities had a more negative view of astrologers. Already beginning in 357 CE, Roman imperial legislation astrologers get lumped together with soothsayers, diviners, augurs, seers, Chaldeans, and wizards—anyone who consults one is liable for the death penalty. (How often or even whether this was ever enforced is a different question.) The teaching of astrology was banned in 373, and in 409 all astrologers throughout the Roman Empire were to be banished unless they "transfer their faith to the practice of the Catholic religion and never return[ed] to their former false doctrine." While the legislation becomes increasingly severe over time, it is quite possible that astrologers continued to work, with some catering to Christian customers.[40]

Necromancers

Ancient sources mention figures such as "diviners," "dream interpreters," and "astrologers" using different terms, but it was likely that especially in smaller municipalities the same individuals had expertise in more than one of these specializations. There were hazy lines between these activities. One future-telling activity, though, that appears to have had a much clearer boundary was necromancy, the science of telling the future by consulting the dead. Nearly all literary sources from the Late Antique Mediterranean are repelled at the idea of raising the dead. In the seventh century BCE, the Hebrew Bible had already strongly condemned the practice. Greeks and Romans throughout antiquity also legislated against it.[41]

The many prohibitions against necromancy in Jewish, Christian, and Roman imperial law did not eliminate necromancy and necromancers. Some Late Antique texts, even those written by intellectuals (albeit not those whose positions would become normative), unselfconsciously mention the practice of conjuring the dead. Papyruses too attest to the ongoing practice. Rabbinic sources have enough specific references to necromancers and their techniques to suggest that it was ongoing in their communities, despite rabbinic rejection of it. Christian intellectuals may have had a particular aversion to necromancers precisely because necromancy flirts with understandings of Jesus as risen from the dead. Bishops may have felt an acute desire to make sure that their own beliefs and practices were not confused with those of necromancers. This was, in fact, a distinction that seemed not very clear to some Romans.[42]

Given the wide condemnation of the practice, along with severe legal punishments for those who practiced it, it is not particularly surprising that we have little direct evidence for the actual practice of necromancy and its clients and their motives. What does survive, though, is highly suggestive. The rabbis, for example, not only accepted the efficacy of raising the dead but in fact engaged in the very act. One Talmudic account describes the summoning of the dead figures Titus, Balaam, and Jesus to provide advice (mainly about what not to do). In another, a rabbi brings up a body to ascertain its cause of death. Such accounts might best be explained as rabbinic appropriations of accepted practices; most people who engaged in such practices would not have been interested in such questions. We might speculate that people would more often want to raise the dead to ask them questions, or perhaps to enlist their powerful help. Although several inscribed skulls have come to light, the spells on them are like those that are also inscribed on more common objects and do not particularly mention the raising of the dead.[43]

Scribes

Most of the evidence used to reconstruct the history of Late Antiquity—including its "religious" dimension—is textual. On the one hand, this is quite fortunate. Texts yield a much clearer understanding of how individuals thought of and managed their relationships with invisible beings than pictures or archaeology alone. Trying to recover how the prehistoric cave painters of Lascaux related to "divine" forces, for example, is entirely speculative. On the other hand, though, the existence of such a large and diverse number of texts comes with challenges of bias. The texts that survived mostly did so for a reason: they were produced by the elite, literate factions that won. We know about other ancient texts due to random discoveries. The ancient garbage heaps of Egypt, coins, and inscriptions on stone and mosaic have been particularly helpful in adding to our knowledge, but the ad hoc nature of their discovery always raises the question of how representative they are. Yet the biggest bias of all is that relying on texts makes Late Antique Mediterranean religion look textual. That is, it overinflates the importance that texts in general played in people's lives. This is amplified by our own tendency to see religions (especially Christianity and Judaism) as textually based. It is important to remember that most communication between humans and the invisible world was (and probably continues to be across the globe) nontextual, consisting of oral utterances and physical rituals.

Understanding the proper role of scribal expertise and scribes in Late Antiquity requires us first to think about literacy. "Literacy" is a vague word that can indicate skills along a wide spectrum, from knowing how to recognize a name etched on a jug, to writing one's own name on a jug to indicate ownership, to reading, and then writing increasingly complex texts. Since there was no public education, literacy at the upper half of this spectrum was for all intents and purposes limited to those who came from families of some means. These families, if literate themselves, could train their own children (if they could find the time) or could hire teachers at the elementary level. Many abecedaries, etchings of the alphabet on fragments of broken pottery, survive, showing new students practicing how to write. As a student became more proficient, the family

FIGURE 6.2. Limestone ostracon containing vertical columns of a Coptic abecedarium from Egypt. Courtesy of the British Museum, (1899,1016.673/EA31663). Used by permission.

might employ an advanced tutor (or pedagogue) for him (or, more rarely, her). The ability to read and write advanced texts was limited to those who could afford to study into adulthood. Very few people would be able even to read Homer, Virgil, or Scripture. Slightly more people (here we might think, very roughly, of 3–5 percent of the population) had the ability to read longer inscriptions, contracts, documents, and amulets.[44]

Late Antique society thus had a real need for scribes. If somebody wanted to send or read a letter, they went to a scribe. If they wanted to draft and execute a contract or had any official dealings with government authorities (especially around the assessment and collection of taxes), they needed a scribe. If they were involved with legal proceedings (people in Late Antiquity were surprisingly litigious) and like most people could not afford a rhetor—who was better trained to argue a case—then a scribe would suffice. Scribes probably prepared many of the texts that found their way onto inscriptions, via the chiseling of the less literate stonecutters.

Unlike most intellectuals, scribes actually had to work for a living. They usually received their wages from the government and/or private fees given for services. In 301, Diocletian's edict on prices and wages set the scribal fee for 100 lines of high-quality writing at 25 denarii and 100 lines of second-quality writing at 20 denarii; a notary writing a petition was to be paid 10 denarii. For comparative purposes, the same edict set the daily wage of a carpenter or baker at 50 denarii and that of a farm laborer at 25 (plus meals). Wheat and lentils each cost 100 denarii for two gallons, and high-quality olive oil cost 40 denarii for a half-liter. Scribal and notarial work alone could bring, in legal wages, a respectable but by no means extravagant salary (unlike, for example, that of a court advocate, who received 1,000 denarii to plead a case).[45]

Given how ubiquitous scribes were and how much they left to posterity, they are frustratingly hard to pin down. Occasionally, their names can be found on a document—the apostle Paul's scribe, Tertius, mentions himself in the Epistle to the Romans (16:22). More often, though, they remain deep in the background. Most likely, fathers (and maybe mothers in some cases) taught their scribal skills to their sons—and, in the very rare case, daughters. One text mentions a "woman clairvoyant and maker of amulets." We do not know if those amulets were texts or engravings, but it might be telling that she is mentioned to denigrate her; a Christian saint neutralizes her power. We do, however, know of some female scribes.[46]

Aristocratic families would sometimes have their slaves trained to read and write to handle their bureaucratic affairs. Upon release, these freedmen (and perhaps freedwomen could then use these skills to support themselves. We should assume that it would have been rare for other tradespeople who themselves made comparable salaries, like carpenters, to invest money and time to switch professions or train their children to do so. The farmhand or child of a farmhand who became a scribe would have been rare indeed. On the other hand, one could imagine the occasional aristocrat who fell on hard times doing scribal work to support himself.

Scribes also provided a valuable service for those who sought amulets. The production of effective amulets necessitated extensive ritual and scribal expertise. This was expertise that required a professional; few nonprofessionals would have had these abilities. Scribes were not the only people with such expertise, but they were a natural choice. They could access the complex manuals and knew how (or were thought to have known how) to write and format texts correctly. The authors of these amulets remain veiled behind the texts that they survived, but studies of them show that some—although by no means all—exhibit clear signs of having been written by professional scribes. It is tempting to think of this work as "off book" and somewhat secretive, an ordinary scribe who writes tax receipts during the day retiring to do this "magical" work for a bit of side income. More likely, I think, is that it was simply part of their mundane workload, mixed in with the tax receipts, petitions, and contracts. There was nothing particularly secretive or exceptional about the production of such ritual texts.[47]

Holy Men

In 1971, the scholar Peter Brown caused something of a sensation with the publication of a scholarly essay titled "The Rise and Function of the Holy Man in Late Antiquity." On his way, as we have seen, to defining the modern scholarly understanding of "Late Antiquity," Brown made two major arguments. First, in Late Antiquity holiness was increasingly seen as located in exceptional individuals rather than in places. Second, these new "holy men," far from living secluded lives that shunned political engagement, became vital figures in the societies in which they lived and fulfilled many social functions that were necessary in a world in which social relationships were in flux. The essay formed the kernel of Brown's book, *The Cult of the Saints: Its Rise and Function in Latin Christianity*. It also laid the groundwork for Jonathan Z. Smith's more theoretical and influential dichotomy between "locative" religion—in which the divine is confined to or concentrated in a particular place—and "utopian" religion, in which the divine is not confined to a place. Both of these scholars in many ways set the agenda for decades for the study of Late Antiquity.[48]

In 1998, though, Brown gingerly walked back some of what he had written about twenty-five years earlier. During that period, scholars had increasingly been reading ancient texts with a "hermeneutic of suspicion," recognizing that there is often a gap between a historical report and the facts that underlie it. Texts reflect rhetoric and what the authors wanted the reader to know, not necessarily the real social situation. Much of this scholarship emerged from a new interest in women and gender in antiquity, and scholars quickly went from trying to recover the lives of ancient women (the vast majority of whom we know about only through literature written about them by men) to interest in the rhetorical "construction" of these women. It was just not women, though, whose lives were distorted through the rhetoric of representation. Ancient writers used the image of the holy man for their own purposes, thus obscuring the real "holy men." In his earlier writings, Brown had trusted his sources. Now, he was less sure.[49]

Brown's dilemma, whether and how far to trust his sources, encapsulates the problem of discussing the phenomenon of the holy man in antiquity. We have many accounts, across all traditions, of men and women who were seen to have a bit of the divine in them or at least better access to the divine than ordinary mortals. People and communities would turn to them to access the supernatural realm. Some of them were educated and came from wealthier families, but many did not; part of their access to the divine was often seen as a result of their simplicity and distance from "cosmopolitan" life. This is why the holy people themselves never leave any writings; all that we know about them comes from their (mostly) admiring followers. Yet, at the same time, Brown was clearly onto something when he saw the "holy man" as playing a role (though how important a role remains in question) in the societies in which they lived. We can get a clearer picture of these as represented in antiquity, as well perhaps as a tiny glimpse of the real personalities, from the brief consideration of a few examples.

Apollonius of Tyana, who was born in central Asia Minor in the first century CE, had all the trappings that we might normally think belong to a holy man. His third-century biographer Philostratus—who claims to draw on an earlier book of biographical snippets about Apollonius made by one of his contemporary followers, a man named Damis—tells us repeatedly that Apollonius was "godlike," perhaps even a son of Zeus, his birth announced by a thunderbolt. While still young, attracted to the Pythagorean lifestyle, he renounced much of his (significant) inheritance. He ate only the "pure" foods provided by the earth, shunning meat and wine. He renounced all sexual activity and wore clothing so distinctive that it aroused the ire and suspicion of the Roman emperor Domitian. He also had a set of extraordinary powers. He knew the future and could see through the superficial trappings of the visible world. He knew when a person was possessed by a daimon and where satyrs gathered, and he was a superb exorcist. He could become invisible and slip away from trouble. He had extraordinary powers of healing, which he sometimes used to help those who came to him.[50]

Philostratus goes to great pains to let us know what Apollonius was not: a magician or sorcerer. Instead, he was a philosopher with semidivine power whose main strength was his wisdom rather than his supernatural powers. The vast bulk of the biography deals with Apollonius traveling around the eastern Mediterranean, as well as India, gathering and dispensing wisdom. Wherever he went, rulers sought him out, not to benefit from his powers but to learn from him. The emperors Vespasian and Titus were especially keen to learn how they might be good rulers. Apollonius connected wisdom to the proper veneration of the gods. Wherever he went, he visited and often stayed in temples. He regularly offered prayers to the gods and praised a boy for sacrificing every day to Aphrodite. (While Apollonius himself avoided making animal sacrifices, he did not condemn others for doing so.)[51]

The problem, then, is getting through Philostratus to the real Apollonius. Was Philostratus true to his source, Damis, who reliably depicted the real Apollonius? Or was Apollonius really an itinerant healer and "magician," who Philostratus (and maybe Damis before him) attempted to sanitize in order to create a model Pythagorean philosopher? If the latter, would the combination of philosophical wisdom, ascetic behavior, and supernatural powers have been something recognized by Philostratus's third-century readers as a familiar figure, a "holy man," or was this an innovation of Philostratus that would have struck his readers as peculiar? The other mentions of Apollonius, most written toward the end of the third century and beyond, are not useful for recovering the real Apollonius. Most of these later writings about him are heavily colored by theological polemics; he is either praised as an anti-Christian model (although some early Christians did grudgingly praise him as well) or demonized as a sorcerer. A single inscription (probably) mentions him as having a divine origin. Some ancient and modern scholars have portrayed Apollonius as a "Jesus-like" figure, although this involves taking Philostratus's account at face value and devaluing the bulk of his work, which shows him engaged in philosophy.[52]

Whoever the real Apollonius was, though, he—or better, the image of him as portrayed by Philostratus—became a model for a certain kind of Neoplatonist "holy man." Neoplatonists, like Iamblichus, were seen as combining learned philosophical acumen with supernatural powers and were therefore, like Philostratus's Apollonius, sometimes tarred as magicians. We do not need to judge whether that ancient charge is justified or not. Apollonius and his followers linked supernatural powers to the divine realm and gained access to both through a combination of good (and often ascetic and thereby disinterested) behavior, piety, and philosophical study. While more ordinary people would sometimes have come to such a figure for help, these Neoplatonists tended to operate in a more rarefied social world, using their powers to impress each other or to be of service to a sympathetic ruler.[53]

Despite the common assertions in ancient literature (and echoed in Philostratus) that the Jews were different from everyone else, they too had a similar figure of a "holy man." Unlike Greeks, Romans, and Christians, the rabbis never authored biographies, full tracts devoted to the lives of an individual. This, together with other peculiarities of rabbinic literature, makes it exceedingly difficult to piece together the life of any single figure from the biographical snippets scattered across a vast body of literature. The evidence, though, does strongly suggest that similar kinds of people existed both within and outside of rabbinic circles. According to one story in the Mishnah, the community called on a man named "Honi the Circle Drawer" to beseech God for rain—he did such a good job that they then asked him to beseech God to make it stop. The story has parallels outside of rabbinic literature and suggests that Honi had a reputation as having exceptional intercessory power due to his closeness to God. "If you were not Honi, I would excommunicate you" for impudence, says a rabbi in response to the way that he spoke to God. "But what should I do to you, since you sin before God and He does your will for you like a son who sins before his father and [nevertheless the father] does his will?"[54]

There were other Jewish figures in a similar vein to Honi, although their lives and activities are even more shadowy. Rabbinic literature contains several stories of rabbis visiting holy men to seek their assistance with communal matters. Their relationship to the rabbis (or any type of rabbinic-style learning) is often left vague, although they are all noted for their piety and simple living. Another such character, Dosa, is first accused by the rabbis of participating in nonsensical actions before they discover his many righteous deeds. I suspect that the rabbis are here attempting to bring such figures into the rabbinic orbit by associating rabbinically sanctioned actions to them, whether Dosa himself ever actually existed.[55]

Rabbinic stories about rabbinic wonder-workers might provide better, if indirect, evidence for the existence of nonrabbinic Jewish holy men. The rabbis portray several Jewish wonder-workers as rabbis. These rabbis are heavily underdeveloped compared to Apollonius, but they exhibit the same combination of power, behavior, knowledge, and piety. Several rabbis are portrayed, rather matter-of-factly, with most of the powers that Apollonius possessed. They heal, tell the future, scare demons, and kill with a look. Like the Neoplatonists, they do not appear to have been regularly sought out by ordinary people. Instead (in the fantasy world of the rabbis), they dispensed advice to the rulers of Rome and Persia. Just as the rabbis made nonrabbinic Jewish wonder-workers look rabbinic, they claimed that their powers actually belonged to the rabbis.[56]

If the nonintellectual holy man remains a shadowy figure in our sources, he explodes in Christian literature. As Peter Brown noted in his follow-up essay, here we must be cautious: What exactly does the quantity of these literary representations tell us about the number of actual holy men and their importance in their communities? While the authors of these accounts almost certainly exaggerated their importance, such figures undoubtedly played a more important role among Christians than they did among Jews or Romans. One important reason for this is, quite simply, the Jesus myth. Representations of Jesus as a miracle-performing, self-denying, healing, exorcising god in human flesh powerfully expanded imaginative possibilities. If Jesus was such a figure, perhaps others could be as well, although to a lesser degree. Jewish, Roman, and Greek traditional literature never seriously promoted such a myth. The story of Jesus clears a path for the appearance and plausibility of the "holy man."

One of the more interesting examples of how Jesus was used to structure the understanding of the Christian holy man is the account of the life of Symeon the holy fool, who probably lived in the sixth century and spent the most important years of his life in Emesa, a city in modern-day Syria. The primary account, though, comes from Leontios of Neapolis, a Christian bishop who lived about a century later in Cyprus. Leontios's Symeon is a cross between Jesus and Diogenes the Cynic. He is ascetic and performs the typical miracles such as healing, predicting the future, and exorcisms. On the other hand, Symeon performs a series of bizarre actions that evoke those of the Cynics; in Leontios's terminology, he "plays the fool." Some of his actions, like making his entrance into Emesa dragging a dead dog, are left unexplained. Others have a clearer purpose. He breaks a cask of wine in a tavern for seemingly no reason (and is beaten by the owner as a result), but it turns out that in doing so he saved the patrons from drinking wine that had been poisoned by a snake. (It was commonly believed that snakes poisoned liquids that were left in uncovered containers.) He went naked into the women's bathhouse (only to be beaten back by the women) to show that he had no sexual appetite. He pretended to have raped a slave girl in order to spare her from a charge of fornication. "Some of his deeds," Leontios writes, he "did out of compassion for the salvation of humans, and others he did to hide his way of life." Leontios is apologetic enough throughout his account to suggest that he was not making up the story entirely. It is far from clear, though, to what extent it accurately reflected the activities of a real person or drew on accurate sources.[57]

Another Symeon from Syria, known as Symeon the Stylite, is only slightly less eccentric. More precisely, he is known as "Symeon the Stylite the Elder," since there were several Symeons (and others) who through Late Antiquity perched themselves on pillars. Symeon lived in the first half of the fifth century. He was a monk who, according to a contemporary bishop from Syria named Theodoret, was expelled from his monastery due to his eccentric behavior. This behavior led to his increasing reputation for also performing miracles, which in turn attracted pilgrims. The pilgrims, who (according to Theodoret) sought healing and the adjudication of mundane disputes by an impartial holy man, irritated Symeon to the point that he built a platform on a pillar and then proceeded to call it home. This, naturally, made him seem yet more eccentric and thus increased his popularity, drawing more pilgrims and driving him to build ever higher pillars to live on. It was a combination of his ascetic, somewhat eccentric behavior and his reputation as a worker of miracles that led to his appeal as a holy man.[58]

Then there were the "holy women." Several Christian women became known as "holy," yet, as the historian Elizabeth Clark argues, they are depicted quite differently from the aforementioned holy men. They were often (but not globally) depicted as being from aristocratic backgrounds and not working miracles in their lifetimes. The different ways in which these women are depicted raises thorny questions about the relationship between the literary accounts and historical truth. Did the literary authors of these texts, all men writing for men, revise their tales of these women to make their activities more appropriate for women? Or do they more or less reflect the limited paths open to Christian women, even aristocratic ones? One thing, however, is clear: many of these women were ascetics, who had their own independent role in Late Antique society.[59]

Ascetics

Asceticism as a way of life oriented to the divine had long been known among Jews and Christians, but it was always seen as a marginal activity that one did for a limited duration. In the second century, though, some

Christians began to experiment with living a fully ascetic life, often as part of a community of like-minded people. These small ascetic groups often contained both men and women and were located in urban environments. Eventually, they began to attract the attention of the ecclesiastical authorities. Slowly, these groups were brought under increasing institutional control.

The story of Anthony shows this dynamic in action. Anthony founded an ascetic community in Egypt in the late third century. He was perhaps the most important Christian ascetic of his time but not the only one, as communities of ascetics began to develop in several other rural locations throughout the eastern Mediterranean. By the middle of the fourth and into the fifth centuries, segregated communities of Christian ascetics, now tightly controlled by leaders and living by a strict code, developed into the earliest monasteries.[60]

The development and spread of Christian ascetic communities were due to several overlapping factors. One was the intellectual trends of the time, particularly as filtered through some Christian thinkers. The Neoplatonic readings of Plato sharpened his distinction between body and soul. For Plato, the body was a "prison" of the soul, a designation that he appears to have meant more descriptively than judgmentally. That is, for Plato, it is an essential given of the human condition that the soul is encased in the body; this is a theory that he uses to explain various other aspects of what it means to be human. Plato's body was not bad, and he had no conception of the soul "escaping" it except for brief moments. Neoplatonists, though, read Plato differently and thought that we could achieve a condition in which our souls could escape our bodies and reunite with the One. This belief led Porphyry to vegetarianism and other ascetic practices. Christian adaptations of this Neoplatonic devaluation of the body, and their understanding that disciplining the body could lead to the escape of the soul, played a role in the Christian promotion of ascetic practices as spiritually beneficial.[61]

The more mundane quest for power also led to the development of Christian ascetic institutions. One might expect that those choosing to live as ascetics in the desert would also want to withdraw from public life, and for many, that was certainly true. But not for all. Ascetics could also gain a base of followers, attracted by their disciplined lifestyles and the belief that some of them could perform miracles. These followers were not always innocuous. Particularly powerful ascetics—some of whom were seen as "holy men"—could, like bishops, mobilize their followers for political purposes. They could, and sometimes did, instigate riots against traditional temples and non-Christians. These leaders also sometimes had available to them significant monetary resources. Those who joined these institutions were often expected to sign over their belongings. While there is ample evidence from papyrus receipts that many did not fully adhere to this expectation and continued to administer significant material holdings, it is also clear that many rich Christians were attracted to these institutions and enriched their coffers. Ascetics and their institutions offered another path to power that was in tension with more official "ecclesiastical" channels. At times, the bishops and ascetic leaders could work together, but at other times they competed with each other. Messing with an ascetic could have serious repercussions.[62]

The growing prominence of women in these institutions may also have contributed to the growth of Christian asceticism. Wealthier men and women throughout antiquity were expected to marry, procreate, and create a household—the household (rather than, for example, the individual) was seen as the central social unit. For all the normal, diverse, and complicated reasons that still motivate people today, not everyone in antiquity was comfortable with this expectation. Christian asceticism offered a way out for such people, both men and women. Romans, Greeks, and Jews mercilessly mocked these ascetics, but the ideology behind asceticism (i.e., devotion to God) and the presence of a community of like-minded individuals offered an alternative viable path for some. For a woman in particular, this path was both more radical than it was for a man and fraught, as it involved a more visible rebellion against her father. Some of the earliest and most popular Christian martyr stories in the second century revolved around women who renounced the wishes of their families and became ascetics only to be violently tortured and killed for their rebellion. Whether or not these stories are true (in whole or in part) is the subject of significant scholarly disagreement, but they reflect the fears and fantasies of those who produced them. Over time the women attracted to Christian ascetic groups gained power within them; many were widows and had significant financial resources.[63]

These factors also help to explain why Jewish communities in Late Antiquity never developed monastic institutions. Philo, in the first century, had intellectual commitments that denigrated the body and might have led him toward a philosophical stance that, like the Neoplatonists, would have been conducive to asceticism. But Philo appears to have found few Jewish followers. This was in turn probably due less to any intrinsically "Jewish" cultural characteristics or commitment to Scripture than to the more general exclusion of Jews from the philosophical arena. Since Jews never fully (at least, as far as we know, in meaningful numbers) engaged in philosophy, they also did not develop an intellectual infrastructure that could reinforce ascetic institutions. Similarly, Jews who sought power were working under very different conditions from Christians. The social and legal conditions of Jews in Late Antiquity made it difficult, if not impossible, for them to amass political and monetary power in the same way as Christians. There were Jewish ascetics throughout antiquity, but the conditions never supported the development of ascetic institutions.[64]

Other Functionaries

When we think of the individuals who facilitate communication between humans and divine beings we usually think first of clerics and other functionaries associated with buildings and communities, such as priests, pastors, rabbis, and cantors. These roles, and a bewildering array of others, also existed in antiquity, although their roles differed significantly from their modern-day counterparts (when such counterparts existed). For the most part, these were seen as bureaucratic positions within a voluntary organization. The people occupying them rarely derived their main sources of income, or often any income at all, from them.

Probably the most widely used term to denote such functionaries is the Greek word *presbyteros* (plural: *presbyteroi*). The term has the general meaning of "elder" in a bureaucratic sense. One second-century papyrus from Egypt, for example, records a report from the elders of a temple to a local tax farmer. Elders are frequently found in Jewish inscriptions in Late Antiquity as well, in both synagogue and mortuary contexts. A Greek tombstone in Jaffa of a Jew named Isaac, for example, notes that he was "elder of (the synagogue of) the Cappadocians, for Tarsus, linen merchant." The term is inherently ambiguous, and the number of presbyteroi and exactly what they did in any given place varied widely. Sometimes they served as the lay leadership of an organization, while at other times they may simply have been donors honored by the community. Many people thought the title had enough status that they (or their family) chose to include it on their epitaphs. Women too bore titles indicating their role in such institutions, although the emerging orthodox church never formally accepted women as presbyteroi. Attacks by orthodox bishops against "heretical" Christian groups (the Montanists are the most famous) for their ordination of women, though, suggest that the situation on the ground was more fluid. As late as 494 CE women were serving at the altars of some Christian churches.[65]

In Christian institutions, the meaning and role of the presbyteros changed as the position became increasingly integrated into a centralized episcopal hierarchy. Local churches came under the authority of a regional bishop, an *episcopos*, always a man. The bishops would have the authority to attend and vote at synods and would enjoy the many perks granted by imperial law (mainly tax exemptions). Each church grew to have a single presbyteros, a man who reported to the local bishop, rather than a council. The Christian presbyteros was deemed by imperial law to be a "cleric" and thus also enjoyed several legal privileges, if not quite as many as the bishops. Inscriptions that mark the construction or renovation of churches often contain the name of the local bishop but rarely of the presbyteros. In the early fourth century, presbyteroi were forbidden from participating in sexual "immorality" (whatever that means in this context).[66]

Under local presbyteroi were other, lesser clergy whose roles also probably varied according to local custom. Imperial law lists them as deacons, subdeacons, exorcists (*exorcistas*), readers, and sextons. Deacons assisted and sometimes competed with presbyteroi. They, like the presbyteroi, were chosen directly by the local bishops and many became bishops (without first becoming presbyteroi). They seemed to have an organizational structure parallel to the presbyteroi (with an archdeacon serving as the regional head). In Late Antique church inscriptions, individual deacons are mentioned far more often than presbyteroi, although sometimes they appear together (along with the regional bishop). A fifth-century inscription from Evron, in Roman Palestine, for example, lists (in order) the names of the bishop, presbyter, archdeacon, and subdeacon. There were female deacons, although it is unclear if women could serve in other legally recognized clerical positions (other than "most holy virgins," *sacratissimas virgines*, or nuns in modern parlance). They may have had a status and roles like their male counterparts.[67]

In one fundamental way, the organization of synagogue functionaries differed from that of church functionaries: no central organization tried to wrestle them into a hierarchy, and they were of little interest to the imperial administration. Otherwise, though, there are many similarities. Synagogues had a variety of offices whose roles varied, depending on local custom. There were presbyteroi who probably served as the official leadership of the synagogue, which would have been formally organized as a voluntary association. Many synagogues had a "head of the synagogue" (a term that survives in rabbinic sources in Hebrew and in inscriptions in Greek)—some of whom were women—but it is unclear if they served in leadership roles (head of the council of presbyteroi?) or if this was a title honoring a generous benefactor. Some synagogues had a sexton (or, in Hebrew, a *chazzan*), although we do not know what this person did.

We should not project our own images of synagogue life today back into antiquity. There is little evidence, for example, that rabbis had any significant or formal role in the synagogue in Late Antiquity, or that the community employed a chazzan (today referring to a cantor) to run synagogue services. Many synagogues incorporated a niche in which they almost certainly stored a Torah. Whether that Torah was in Hebrew or another language, though, and who read it and how, is far from certain. The rabbis themselves contemplate a case in which nobody in a congregation knew how to lead the prayers or the Torah, perhaps implying that such a case was not uncommon.[68]

One functionary found in both Christian and Jewish communities was the liturgical poet. These poets created new liturgical compositions that were recited in churches and synagogues. Among the most famous are the Christian Romanos and, for Jews, Yannai. Both authored compositions that Christians and Jews recite to this day. We know very few other poets by name, and we have little concrete understanding of their prevalence and how they functioned. That is, were there such poets in every major (or minor) city? Were they paid to compose and, if so, by whom and how much? Yannai produced many versions of a single prayer, which suggests that he was composing liturgy for at least one congregation on a regular basis. (Note that at this time Jewish liturgy may have adhered to a set structure, although the exact prayers and words might have shifted week to week.) Did Yannai recite his own poetry, or was it really meant to be performed by others? The surviving poetry is complex and dense with allusions, and the extent to which they would have been understood is unclear; Christian and Jewish liturgical poets seem to draw on a similar range of techniques and styles. Not all liturgical poetry, though, was highbrow. Augustine wrote a Latin poem against the Donatists because "I wished to familiarize the most lowly people and especially the ignorant and uneducated with the case of the Donatists and to impress it on their memory to the best of my ability."[69]

Ritual authority and expertise—with the two not necessarily linked—came in many shapes. They took different forms in the public and private spheres. Sometimes they were based on political power or wealth, sometimes on knowledge and abilities, and sometimes on a simple intrinsic holiness (presumably granted on the basis of an exceptional life). Knowing whom to consult for what problem and how much to pay was a basic Late Antique life skill. Sometimes, simply consulting the right person was enough. More frequently, though, effectively communicating with the invisible forces depended not just on expertise or authority but also on place and time.

7

The Spiritual Landscape

THERE IS a story told in the Babylonian Talmud about the "wicked" Roman emperor Titus, who polluted and destroyed the Jerusalem Temple in 70 CE. On a ship, presumably at some point after the destruction of the Temple and perhaps on his way back to Rome from Jerusalem, he encountered a dangerous storm. This led him to reason that "the God of these [people] has power only in the water." After all, Titus thinks to himself, YHWH punished two mighty enemies of Israel, Pharaoh and Sisera, by drowning them in water. YHWH is incensed at this skepticism of his universal power and thus decides to punish Titus with the tiny, insignificant gnat, a land-dwelling insect that will enter Titus through his ear and eat its way through his brain until he dies in an incredible state of agony.[1]

For the sake of this argument, we are going to ignore some of the stranger details of this short story, like how Titus knew anything about Israelite history and whether the rabbinic inventors of this story really did not know that according to the Bible (Judges 4–5) Sisera was killed by a stake driven by Yael through his temple, not drowning. At its core, though, this story is about Titus's fatal misperception that YHWH's power is limited to a particular kind of place. To the Late Antique reader or listener, Jewish or not, this "misperception" was completely understandable. Invisible beings were thought to enjoy and frequent some spaces over others. While the rabbis here strongly assert YHWH's universal power, they elsewhere are completely comfortable talking about the deity's preference for some places over others and thus the increased holiness of those places.[2]

Rationally, to us at least, these two tendencies—to see a deity as "everywhere" and all-powerful while asserting that that deity is also local—are in tension. If this tension bothered those in antiquity, though, it did not seem to do so overly much. Ancient sources often blithely assert both the universal and local characteristics of a deity. Most would not have seen a contradiction here. They reconciled an omnipresent divine power with specific and local manifestations, sometimes in many different places at the same time. Jupiter Optimus Maximus was of course present—in body—in his temple on the Capitoline Hill in Rome, just as he was also present in other temples devoted to him (even if he may have been thought to prefer the one in Rome) at the same time as he exercised power throughout the entire world. The same gods were everywhere and somewhere all the time.

Placing the gods and other supernatural beings was important for ritual life. Anyone could venerate almost any supernatural being from anywhere. A devotee of Mercury was no different in this respect from a devotee of YHWH; both thought they could call out to their god from any location. Yet both also knew that communication was stronger in some places than others. If one was to supplicate Mercury, it was better to do it not only with a gift but specifically with one given in a temple devoted to Mercury that contained an actual cult statue of Mercury. To supplicate Pan, a trip to a sacred spring might be in order. For Christians, pilgrimages to sacred sites, particularly to places where Jesus was thought to have done miraculous things, began to take hold as being helpful for boosting one's message. Churches became important portals to the divine. For Jews, the synagogue began to be seen as a "little temple," a quasi-substitute for the destroyed Jerusalem Temple.

The importance of place did not stop at such institutionalized sites. Place mattered for domestic rituals as well. Some places were simply better for certain activities. Bowls that were inscribed with protective prayers could be more effective when placed near the front door of a house, presumably in order to stop the demons before they gained entrance. Many rituals in ancient manuals give importance to the place where they are performed. For example, *Sefer Ha-Razim*, a Late Antique book of spells written in Hebrew, says that to ensure that a particular horse wins a race one must inscribe an amulet and bury it in the correct race lane. According to the scholar Jonathan Z. Smith, place—whether real or imagined—is central to nearly all ritual.[3]

Being in sacred places—that is, places where divine beings are present—requires special deportment. Throughout antiquity, this deportment took the form of purity regulations. "Purity" is a somewhat loose and, today, loaded word. In general, by "purity" we mean "the quality or state of being pure." What, though, does "pure" mean? Put differently, what kinds of blemishes or impurities prevents one from entering into the presence of the divine, and how can one remove them? Are they physical (e.g., being soiled) or moral (e.g., having committed a murder)? Throughout antiquity these questions were posed and debated as well, both between and within different groups. What unites these discussions, though, is that everybody thought that they were critically important. No one (an exaggeration, of course, but close) would think to enter the divine presence while impure. That would be not only rude but also dangerous.

Purity

Any encounter with the divine requires some degree of preparation. The stories of the Hebrew Bible take this for granted. Upon perceiving that YHWH is present in the burning bush, Moses removes his shoes. YHWH specifically commands the Israelites to remain pure—defined, in part, as restraining from sexual intercourse for three days—before the revelation on Mount Sinai. There would be no question about the need for purity in approaching the inner sanctums of the Tabernacle, where the divine presence dwelled. The Torah includes a lengthy tract, probably authored by priests, detailing the complex rules governing purity. According to these rules, purity comes in several types and degrees. Simple contact with a dead body confers the most severe degree of impurity, while contact with some bodily fluids (especially semen and menstrual blood) results in impurity of a lesser degree. Certain kinds of contact with those in a state of impurity can also render one impure. Impurity is clearly seen as contagious and spreads especially well through the medium of liquids. So too, coming out of a state of impurity most often entails ritual actions that involve liquids, such as immersion in water. Food impurity seems to have been of a different nature altogether. While biblical and early postbiblical Jewish texts frequently use the same word, "impurity," to denote forbidden foods, the point seems to be that eating the food is forbidden rather than that touching or consuming the food makes one ineligible to approach the divine presence. Scholars have long struggled to understand and make sense of these quite technical regulations but have still not fully succeeded.[4]

Nor have they fully understood the logic behind what looks to us like a second kind of impurity that we would characterize as belonging more to the realm of morality. Whether people in antiquity at the time of the redaction of the Torah in probably the sixth century BCE distinguished between ritual and moral impurity is less clear. Acts like murder, kidnapping, oppression of the poor, and incest conferred impurity. The biblical texts discuss moral impurity and its consequences more in terms of the community than the individual. We do not know how a murderer, for example, could regain a state of purity that would allow him or her to enter into the presence of the divine.[5]

The purity concerns of the Israelites are well-documented, due to the preservation of the Hebrew Bible, but they were hardly unique. Issues of purity are scattered in cuneiform tablets produced by the neighbors of the Israelites, and they are found in the inscriptions that were sometimes erected at the entrances to Greek temples. These inscriptions were more commonly produced prior to Late Antiquity, but there is good reason to think that similar rules continued to pertain, even in their absence. One first-century inscription base from Ephesus (in Asia Minor) mentions simply that some regular sacrifices made to Demeter and other gods were done so in "great purity." A letter from Egypt, also from the first century, uses the word "defilement" as a synonym for attending a funeral. Romans also typically expected those who entered their temples to be in a state of purity. Even if our sources do not always define exactly what that meant, that does not mean that the practices were not well-known and detailed.[6]

For Jews, after the destruction of the Temple, when YHWH no longer had a place to dwell on earth, purity should logically have lost its importance. That is, if the point of purity is to be in the proper state for standing in the divine presence manifested in the Temple, and there is no longer a temple, then there is no reason to be ritually pure. (There are, of course, other reasons to retain moral purity, as the actions that generate moral impurity remain forbidden.) This, however, is not exactly what happened. Jewish priests (*kohanim*) felt a need to continue their practice of eating their offerings in a state of purity. In the second century CE, many Jews constructed distinctive water installations near places of agricultural production such as threshing areas and olive presses. Some of these water installations served as ritual baths and were probably connected to the giving of tithes to the priests and Levites. A couple of centuries later, private houses in Sepphoris and other cities in Galilee also contained this same kind of stepped pool. While we cannot be certain how they were used (perhaps simply as places to bathe or for female immersion after menstruation), it is at least possible that Jews continued to be concerned about purity, presumably in moments when they thought they were about to enter the divine presence.[7]

Rabbinic sources assume that Jewish purity concerns did not simply cease after the destruction of the Temple. This required something of a shift in thinking about the relationship between the divine presence and place. YHWH had always been seen as both being omnipresent, but in a way that did not (for most Jews) require constant purity, and being "extra-present" in the Jerusalem Temple, a place that did require purity. Without the Jerusalem Temple, the question became where and when YHWH's presence was so imminent that a pure state was required. To some degree, as we will see, the synagogue became such a place. The rabbis—and here it is unclear how representative of other Jews they were—pivoted to a notion of temporary spatiality. That is, YHWH became "extra-present" when invoked; unlike in a temple, this was a temporary presence. To the extent that rabbis saw ordinary meals as a replacement for the sacrificial meals in the Temple, they also saw it as a necessity for diners to have some degree of purity. They did not extend this to the full purity required for entrance into the Temple but limited it to a "purity of the hands," achieved by a simple and intentional handwashing. There was more debate about other ad hoc gatherings, like forming a prayer quorum or studying Torah. Some rabbis saw these gatherings as worthy of a more robust degree of purity than ordinary meals, but others were less certain. These debates probably reflected variation in practice and a general sense of uncertainty among Jews about how to understand purity in a world without a temple.[8]

Purity was a hot-button issue among the earliest Christians. The Gospels are largely in agreement that Jesus put "purity of the heart" at the center of his message and demanded moral purity. They are far less clear about his stance toward various forms of ritual purity. Jesus rejected the kind of impurity conveyed by certain foods, yet the Gospels never portray him eating these formerly forbidden foods. Peter claims that he never ate "impure" foods, and even Paul does not entirely dismiss the utility of Judaeans eating "pure" foods. The New Testament never mentions menstruation and the purity laws associated with it. In one story, Jesus takes for granted the need for ritual purity in the Jerusalem Temple. In another, he seems either to say that ritual purity is not necessary when eating ordinary meals (a position that was far from radical among Jews but seems to have countered some Pharisaic practices) or that ritual purity *alone* when eating is not meaningful. Where exactly Jesus, Paul, Peter, and others among the earliest Christians exactly stood on purity thus remains unclear, but what is clear is that the discourse on purity was important to early Christians as they sought to establish a different identity from Jews.[9]

While the next several generations of Christians often mocked Jewish purity practices (at least as they understood them, which sometimes differed significantly from actual Jewish practice), they too could not and did not want to entirely abandon the notion that only those who were pure could stand in the divine presence. In the sixth century CE, priests were writing to the bishop of Rome asking whether it was permissible to give communion to a man, even a priest, who the night before had had a seminal emission and had not yet washed. The same questions applied to menstruating women. Christians in many places did have some sense that menstruation, sex, and contact with the dead could impart an impurity that prevented one from entering a church or participating in activities considered "holy." Churches often had water

FIGURE 7.1. Baptistery in the Basilica of St. John in Ephesus, Turkey, fifth–sixth centuries CE. Churches often had such installations, with stepped pools in the shape of a cross, next to the main basilica, to be used for baptism rather than ordinary purification. Photo by Bernard Gagnon, CC BY-SA 3.0, https://en.wikipedia.org/wiki/Baptistery#/media/File:Basilica_of_St._John_in_Ephesus_06.jpg.

installations near their entrances to allow parishioners to ritually cleanse themselves before entering the pure space. There just seemed to be something wrong with uniting with the risen Christ while still in a state of ritual impurity, even if completely pure in spirit and soul.[10]

Natural Places

Anomalies are at the heart of most interpretation. In any landscape (in its metaphorical sense) that is thought to be intentional, ordered, and mostly uniform, a disturbance has potential significance. What are we to make of bird behavior that seems out of the ordinary, an unusual looking sheep's liver in a sacrifice, or a disturbing dream? To those in antiquity, as still for many today, these are omens sent from the invisible world and meant to be interpreted. Similarly, when the rabbis or Christian intellectuals encountered an anomaly in Scripture, they saw it as God's signal that meaning was buried underneath. The smoother and more regular the landscape, the more significant the meaning of anomalies.

So too in the physical landscape; people encountered all kinds of anomalies in it, from springs and strange caves to glorious mountains to ancient dinosaur bones or other primitive remains. The logic by which they decided which of these were "interpretable" and which were not, and how one should interpret such a natural sign, is no longer clear to us, but their tendency to see divinity in at least some of these signs is undeniable. In Rome, following Etruscan traditions, things that were struck by lightning had to be purified and buried and were sometimes marked with a special inscription. Sacred springs and mountains were regular features of most landscapes throughout the Mediterranean. The historical trajectory of two such places from Israel, Banias and Mamre, can serve as concrete examples of this relatively common phenomenon.[11]

Banias is in modern-day Israel, in the foothills of the Golan Heights. It is the source of one of the three springs that feed into the Sea of Galilee. Today, the spring gently flows from below a pool, but in antiquity it gushed from a cliff (a later earthquake caused the shift). This unusual feature probably led to early veneration at the site, although there is little evidence for its use prior to the Hellenistic period. By about 200 BCE, residents began to link the site with the deity Pan, who in Greek mythology is associated with shepherds and the wild and who keeps company with the nymphs, who were associated with water. Relatively poor local residents would make trips to the spring to sacrifice, eat, and/or leave small offerings of pottery. A little before the turn of the millennium, Herod had a temple to Augustus installed at the site, and shortly thereafter his son established a new city, Caesarea Philippi, in the plain below. With new buildings at the site, it increased in prestige and attracted a wider regional clientele. These visitors would often leave ceramics as offerings to the gods and would continue to come to the site to dine (perhaps, again, on sacrifices) in the presence of the gods.[12]

According to the archaeologist Andrea Berlin, by the end of the first century CE the site, with its new gleaming buildings and statues, became more of a "showcase" temple that did not attract individual

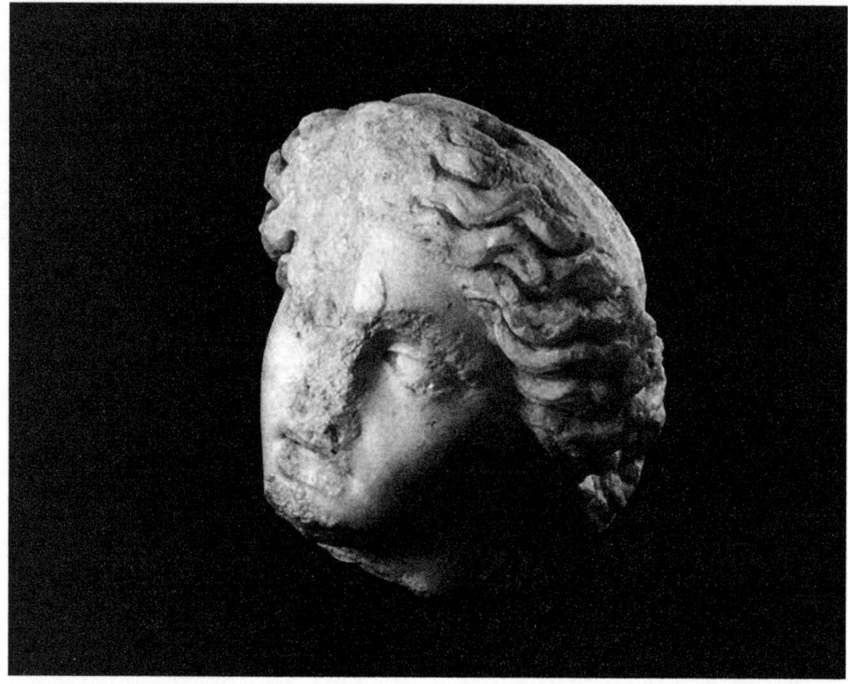

FIGURE 7.2. Head of divine figure. Late Roman, Banias. Photo by Yael Yolovitch, courtesy of the Israel Antiquities Authority (2019–564). Used by permission.

offerings. It is possible that at this time the rituals that took place there were increasingly oriented toward "official" civic functions of Caesarea Philippi and became less welcoming of the more "ordinary" peasants devoted to Pan. In any case, this changed again by the early third century, when new buildings were erected on the site, including a new temple of Pan and the goats. Probably because of this renewed affirmation of the site as a good place to venerate Pan, there was a clear increase in private interest in it. So many visitors brought humble offerings of lamps, in fact, that once the temple filled up a storeroom had to be set aside to hold them. After the fourth century, though, the site was abandoned. Pan's moment, at least in the region of Caesarea Philippi, had passed—perhaps as the result of increased Christianization.[13]

Further south in Roman Palestine, another sacred spring underwent a different kind of transformation. Mamre is located near modern-day

Hebron. This spring never flowed dramatically as did the spring in Banias, but it was notable as an oasis in the Judaean Desert. We do not have evidence for early cultic veneration of the site, although by biblical times it took on importance as the place where three angels appeared to Abraham (Genesis 18:1). By Late Antiquity, the spring had been channeled into a well, and both the supply of water and its sacral character made it an attractive spot for an annual market. It would be a hopeless task to try to disentangle the cultic and mercantile dimensions of this gathering, but what made it especially interesting was its nonparochial nature. According to the church historian Sozomen, the market was attended by Jews, Christians, and "Hellenes" (as he calls them), which created a riotous and diverse atmosphere of ritual. "Some prayed to the God of All," he writes, "while others called upon the angels, offered wine, and sacrificially burned incense, an ox, a ram, a sheep, or a cock." Additional offerings, of lamps, food, coins, and incense, were made at the well itself. We do not know who was doing what (e.g., were Christians sacrificing?), but the mixing of these groups and their practices around the veneration of angels attracted the attention of the Emperor Constantine, who—undoubtedly urged by his bishops—sought to domesticate the site by constructing a Christian basilica there. The locals most likely welcomed the basilica, but it had little impact on their continued use of the site. A sixth-century pilgrim reports that Jews and Christians, separated by a partition, worshipped at the site and continued to make offerings. Christian and Jewish "orthodox" understandings could only partially be imposed on the intrinsic holiness of the place. Mamre was a place where angels gathered, and it was entirely obvious that if one wished to entreat the angels they would hear you better if you were physically close to them than if you were further away.[14]

Banias and Mamre are just two examples of a phenomenon repeated countless times through antiquity: natural sacred sites rarely stayed natural. Throughout the Hellenistic and early Roman periods, and sometimes before, temples and shrines were built on sacred sites, and access was limited by the elite. Most of this activity was already well underway by the time of Late Antiquity, but at Mamre it was not until Constantine's reign that the well around which the angels gathered was put under a church, with access limited by church administrators. Spots on the landscape became intelligible and then sacred due to their anomalous character but human building, and their ascription of mythological and historical events to the site, distanced the site's sacredness from the very reason it was first identified. Nevertheless, and despite the fact that in Late Antiquity there were few pristinely natural sacred sites, there was still a deep belief that place mattered. Destroying the building, as happened with the Jerusalem Temple, did not lessen the holiness of the place, even though there only remained there a desolate rubble or even a garbage pit.[15]

Temples

The gods, or at least the important ones, required a home. Throughout all of antiquity, temples were seen as the dwelling places of the gods, the places that literally housed their presence and power in concentrations greater than outside it. As we have just seen, even the natural dwelling places of the deities were often seen as insufficient. A temple built on such sites not only allowed humans to venerate the deity in a more structured and institutionalized way but also provided a proper dwelling for the deities themselves.

Temples in Late Antiquity had two features that converted them from ordinary buildings into the dwelling place of the god. First, following traditional Roman practice, there was a legal declaration on the part of the Senate (or municipal council) declaring it so. This official legal action essentially, in modern terms, took the property off the tax rolls and transferred it to the possession of the gods. The temples were public buildings, and even Christian public officials took this status, and their obligations to support these buildings, seriously. One inscription from between 375 and 378, for example, records the refurbishment of a temple of Isis by command of the Christian emperors. Private "temples" did not truly exist within a Roman context until, perhaps, well into the fifth century when the state moved its support more decisively to the Christian basilicas.[16]

The second defining feature of a temple was its cult statue. All temples in the Mediterranean and Near East had some material representation of the divinity prominently placed within it. Even the Jerusalem Temple had a set of cherubs and an ark in its innermost chamber, despite the Torah's prohibitions on representing YHWH. Zoroastrians had temples that contained icons of deities but also introduced those connected to fire. Most temples, though, contained statues of the temple's deity. Israelites, then Jews and Christians, mercilessly mocked these statues, to which they would apply the derogatory label "idol." "They have eyes but they cannot see," the Israelite psalmist jeered already around the seventh century BCE (Psalms 115:5). They never let up. In the third century, the Christian Minucius Felix described the stages of manufacturing an idol, noting that at every stage up until the end it is ordinary. And then, "finally, it is a god once man has willed it so and dedicated it accordingly." The point had never been lost on those who made and venerated these statues. A long line of ancient philosophers had more gently pointed out that cult statues were representations of the gods, not the actual gods—a line of argument that Christians would later unironically adopt to justify the placement of statues and icons in churches.[17]

Nevertheless, most Greeks and Romans treated these statues as more than mere representations. Knowing, of course, that a statue was a human creation, they devised ceremonies that invited the deity to dwell within it. The temple without a cultic representation was just a building, and the cultic representation was just a piece of stone or metal without the god's presence within it. Once the deity was safely ensconced, the statue was treated with appropriate veneration and decorum. They were washed and dressed, and when they had to be moved there was a ceremonial procession. If the statue had to be retired, it first needed to be deconsecrated, with the divine invited to leave. They were often buried with respect.[18]

Few would have said that the statue was an actual god, but it was also not simply a hunk of stone. Consecrated statues were independent social agents that connected the world of mortals to that of immortals. They were thought to actually do things, like speak, move, and spit. One scholar describes them as "bionic," pointing also to their characteristics as "amazing, superhuman, surprising." Another scholar has suggested that we understand cultic statues as "avatars," in which the god is present within it while also being elsewhere. Demeter, for example, can be simultaneously present in all her cultic statues while also dwelling in the heavens.[19]

It would have been natural for ordinary Greeks and Romans to assume that a god would be happiest, and thereby in a better mood and more likely to grant favors, when given a beautiful house and statue in which to lodge by the entire civic body. While temples were always used for civic functions, these uses were almost always infrequent, often only a few times a year. On other days, individuals would make use of the temple, bringing gifts, sacrifices, or just a contrite heart to be given or poured out before an appropriate deity. These gifts, as we saw at Banias, could sometimes be so numerous that they periodically had to be moved from the temple proper to sacred storage areas to make room for the incoming. Presumably (although we have little evidence about this), there would have been people on staff at the temple who accepted the offerings on behalf of the gods and, if there was a sacrifice, helped with the logistics, perhaps for a small fee.

The Temple of Asklepios at Epidaurus, a small city about thirteen kilometers southwest of Athens, is an excellent, if atypical, example of the dynamics of sacred space in temples. Asklepios was a demi-god or hero in Greek mythology, a healer with a divine pedigree (son of Apollo) who himself obtained divine status. Already in the classical period Epidaurus was associated with his birthplace, and a sanctuary was built there. Throughout antiquity this was but one of many places in which Asklepios could be worshipped, but it was seen as particularly important to the god. Part of a complex that included a gymnasium, the temple had a civic function and was probably the site of regular ceremonies. For the rest of the year, though, it literally hosted scores of pilgrims. These pilgrims came for healing, often bringing offerings (usually a clay model of the body part they wanted healed), and stayed overnight in the temple, hoping that Asklepios would visit and heal them. The temple, which through its attraction to pilgrims must have been a terrific boon to the local economy, closed in the late fourth century, although the area was transformed into a Christian healing site. Asklepios was everywhere, as well as his temples and cult statues. For many, though, his presence at Epidaurus was seen as more potent and thus offered the greatest likelihood that he would hear one's prayers.[20]

Shrines

Almost by definition, temples in Late Antiquity were civic buildings. There were, however, other built spaces understood as sacred. We might typically refer to them as "shrines," places that were considered holy despite having no role in communal worship. There are scores of such places. Some of them were in the wild and others on private land. Some had permanent caretakers (who, in return for allowing access to the shrine, took a fee from visitors for their services), and others did not. Such places were sometimes associated with a "legible" natural feature that was read as indicating the presence of a god, while others were sites where in the past miracles were thought to have been performed, or where a holy person was buried. For whatever reason, these were considered auspicious sites, places that served as a portal to the divine world, even if the deities were not quite, or always, in residence.[21]

Jews, Greeks, and Romans all had shrines, but none in Late Antiquity took this phenomenon as far as Christians. Beginning in the fourth century, Christians began to put increased importance on places, especially those at which Jesus or other saints were thought to have performed miracles or at which holy people (especially martyrs) were thought to have been killed or buried. Many of these shrines began organically, as local Christians circulated and passed down stories about a particular place. Christians would then visit it for ad hoc prayers or to leave a small offering, such as a (votive) candle. Some of these places were appropriated by imperial Christian authorities or intellectuals. Helena, Constantine's mother, who became a zealous (and/or politically savvy) Christian, herself visited several such places in Palestine and built churches over them. The bishop Eusebius wrote a guide for Christian pilgrims to Palestine, focusing primarily on places mentioned in the Gospels. Such places became far more likely to become the site of churches than those that escaped the notice of powerful clerics. It was important for ecclesiastical authorities to control those places that were considered most holy in order that they not compete with the local churches. The simplest, if not cheapest, way to do this was to build another church at the place and put a cleric in charge.[22]

One reason a shrine might be thought of as a portal to the heavens is because angels congregated there. There were, however, also "countershrines," places where demons congregated. According to most thinking, demons particularly liked public lavatories and bathhouses. Jews and Christians also frequently thought that they were attracted to theaters. The logic here differs from that of shrines. Shrines often acquired their status due to an enduring contagious holiness caused, for example, by the past performance of a miracle or burial of a saint. These countershrines, on the other hand, attracted demons because of what was happening within them. Once the activity ceased or the building was repurposed, the demons would leave. In the interim, people who used such places (most everybody) who were worried about the presence of demons took countermeasures, such as reciting prayers or wearing amulets to repel them. What was certainly clear to everyone, though, was that these were not good places for petitioning the gods. Such requests could easily be intercepted by the demons.[23]

Churches and Synagogues

Churches and synagogues were also considered to be holy spaces. Inscriptions set up within them often use the same phrase, "this holy place." But what was it that made them holy?

This question is easier to answer for churches than synagogues. Several different factors, individually or in combination, could make a church holy. First, churches were often built on sites that had long been considered holy, even well before Jesus walked on earth. A grove sacred to Artemis, or a well in Mamre, would be replaced by a church. While some may have needed additional justification for seeing the church as holy, for many it would have been obvious that this was still a sacred place. Second, it was a place where a miracle was thought to have been performed and hence, by contagion, was and will ever remain a holy place.

Greeks, Romans, and Jews could easily understand these two reasons why a Christian might consider a church to be holy. They had far more difficulty with the third one, that the remains of a dead, usually martyred, saint were buried underneath. For Christians, or at least the intellectuals, these remains were not exactly "human." They had been transformed into a kind of divine substance that remained present in the object and thus opened additional portals to the divine realm. These remains, or relics, would become increasingly important in Christian thought. Ultimately, a proper Catholic church would be required to be built on or possess a relic, whether a piece of bone or something that had been touched by a holy man or woman. The practice, though, was novel and considered odd, even appalling, by many. Corpses were the impurity generators par excellence, and the inclusion of bones in a holy site was seen as a contradiction in terms. The use of other items, such as clothing that had touched a saint, was seen as peculiar but not offensive. There is, after all, no preservation or veneration of the cloak of Asklepios or the sandal of Joshua. Churches were not holy by fiat, simply because they were declared to be on sanctified ground, but because they marked and connected with some other source of holiness, whether a natural place or a relic.[24]

For most people (although not the intellectuals, who drew a polemical distinction), entering a church would have been much like approaching a temple. Although the earliest Christian communities met primarily in people's houses ("house-churches," as scholars call them), during the fourth century, Christians began to build their own places of worship, often supported at least in part by imperial funds. This created a challenge for the architects: What should a church look like? Churches, especially basilicas in which imperial and municipal rites will be conducted, should be grand and fitting for the god, like temples—but to what extent should the architecture mirror temples, with their "pagan" associations and attractiveness to demons? There were also functional differences. Temples, with their open-air altars, were designed around outside space, usually with only porticos to protect participants and onlookers from the elements. Churches, on the other hand, conducted rituals that took longer and required greater participant interaction, such as sermons and receiving communion.

The first imperially financed churches repurposed Roman buildings. Christians tended to stay away from temple architecture, instead using basilica halls, which were rectangular buildings with colonnades that the Romans typically used for legal and business proceedings. This decision was driven mostly by convenience; the buildings were available, could fill the necessary functions, and were not temples. These early circumstances, though, also made the decisions of the architects of later churches much easier. Christians grew to expect that their churches would be basilicas, and the architects delivered.[25]

There were, of course, exceptions, but they were few and tended soon to follow standard models. The problem with building a church in the shape of a basilica is that it was not architecturally distinctive. One might feel, for example, as if one were going into a business meeting or judicial proceeding. This did not, apparently, bother many people (ultimately, the facade, art, and internal furnishings were distinctive and may have mitigated these issues). Some, however, did want to more tightly associate the architecture of the church with a sense of the sacred and, for imperial authorities, grandeur. This evolution is clear in the development of the Hagia Sophia in Constantinople (modern-day Istanbul). The first rendition of the church was as a basilica, built over what appears to be a grave, in the mid-300s. It was destroyed by natural causes and then rebuilt a couple of times before undergoing a complete renovation under Justinian I. This church—which, with modifications, still stands—was consecrated in 537. The Hagia Sophia was a complex of sacred buildings built around the cathedral. The cathedral's plan situated an oval interior, over which loomed a fantastic dome, within a rectangle that was close to a square. Outside buttresses and additions, though, make it difficult to see the basilican layout. The building was meant to demonstrate a new way of configuring Christian sacred space. A similar logic was behind the building of a new, octagonal church in Ravenna, catalyzed by the Christian appropriation of the Pantheon in Rome in 609. Roman Catholic architecture would change again in the Middle Ages, mandating a cross shape to the buildings, but Orthodox Christians retained the distinctive, round shape.[26]

There was never a single architectural model for churches in Late Antiquity. Differences were due to local custom and sensibility, topography, and the availability of human and material resources. Each community had to figure out how to visually mark their holy space as distinctive. The input of the local bishop, who might have had some familiarity with how churches in other communities looked, was a factor but not always the determinative one. Church architecture, though, did begin to develop distinctive features. A church became a recognizable space.

It was not, however, an egalitarian one. Internally, churches reinforced hierarchies. The space around the altar and the use of chancel screens to set it, and the officiants of the service, apart from more ordinary Christians reinforced the social distinction between clergy and others. The richer and more interconnected the church was with imperial and municipal rites, the more it also tended to spatially divide high officials and aristocracy from the poorer masses. Both the church in Ravenna and the Hagia Sophia, for example, had special booths for the imperial family. Textual evidence strongly suggests that there were special places in churches for the other nonecclesiastical aristocracy. There is nothing particularly surprising about the fact that the heavy emphasis on social hierarchy embraced by Rome moved relatively seamlessly to the Christian world. Christians were, for the most part, Romans who happened to believe in Christ. Churches, like temples, were places not only of worship but also of public performances of social distinctions.[27]

No distinction was as pervasive as that between men and women. The early calls of Jesus and Paul to eliminate gender as a basis of social distinctions had little actual traction, even among the Christian elite. There were separate monasteries for men and women, and larger churches contained galleries, where the women sat. Smaller churches may have also seated men and women apart, perhaps even separating them with some kind of portable barrier. In many churches, men and women sat together, but Christian intellectuals did not tire of haranguing women to dress modestly in public, including in churches, and to be as invisible and silent as possible. Richer, aristocratic Christian women clearly wanted, like their husbands, to make their status visible, and it is likely that despite the harangues many continued to do so. Among less privileged women, though, there was probably intense pressure for them to act in a way that reinforced their social subordination to men. The public worship experience for men and women differed, but no woman's voice survives from antiquity to tell us just how.[28]

Churches, like the temples and their images, moved from profane to holy space through a ritual consecration. Evidence does not allow us to reconstruct what the consecration of a church (later called a dedication, to distinguish it from the consecration of the Eucharist and other holy objects) entailed exactly. Eusebius talks vaguely of such ceremonies, mainly describing them as typical church services, albeit with bishops involved and on a more elevated level. The altars came to require additional consecration. Canon law from the early sixth century stated that the altars required anointing before use. The actual ceremony most likely varied by region, but in every case putting holy space into service required some marked moment at which it was transformed from profane or ordinary space.[29]

Just as a building could become a holy church, so too could a church become an ordinary building. The logic behind deconsecration of a space, and particularly a church, is a bit trickier. Churches were often built in places that were thought to be holy, whether due to natural causes or because temples once stood there. That is, a church did not often make an insignificant and random plot of land holy; its location was chosen precisely because people already attached to the immediate area some degree of holiness. When a church was damaged beyond repair, though, or when a town depopulated, what was to be done with such a sanctified space? When Christians desacralized a place on which a Greek or Roman temple once stood, they conceptualized it as an act of "purification" from demons, which they needed to do prior to use of the space. Churches, though, needed a different kind of approach that would (gently) evict the divine presence, in order to avoid (1) offending it through neglect and (2) the possibility of defiling a holy space. Unfortunately, our sources are frustratingly quiet about the rituals and process of deconsecration or, as it is also known, "secularization" of

Christian holy places in Late Antiquity. It certainly involved the transfer of the site's relics to another Christian holy space.[30]

Before the early fourth century, before churches began to replace the public functions (and sometimes even physical location) of temples, Christians met in houses, some makeshift churches, catacombs, and (arguably) cemeteries. For all intents and purposes, they were voluntary associations, and their meeting places resembled those of other such associations. With imperial support, though, and the Christianization of the imperial administration, churches assumed the functions and meaning of Greek and Roman temples. Synagogues, however, underwent a different kind of evolution.

The origin of the synagogue is unclear. From the third century BCE, Jews in Egypt had designated buildings for communal prayer. Nothing of these buildings survives (we know about them through literary references and a couple of inscriptions). Literature from the Second Temple period attests to the existence of synagogues, although the word can refer to buildings or simply congregations that may have had no fixed location. Synagogue buildings were apparently multipurpose places where prayer and reading the Torah might occur as frequently as discussions of communal decisions. These kinds of buildings survive in Palestine in the form of basilicas that can only tentatively be identified as synagogues. Some, however, were designed for a narrower range of activities. One inscription from Jerusalem from the first century CE (the building it came from was not discovered) notes various purposes for the synagogue, including the reading and teaching of the Law and serving as a hostel. Many synagogues had niches in the front to hold Torah scrolls. Today, most scholars reject an older theory that the synagogue must have emerged in the sixth century BCE when the exiled Jews were living in Babylonia. The synagogue really did not take a form that we might recognize as a "synagogue" until Late Antiquity.[31]

Synagogue architecture and understandings of the synagogue began to change in the fourth century CE. Synagogues throughout the Mediterranean began to be more elaborately decorated, often with ornate mosaics. In Palestine, synagogue inscriptions, like church inscriptions, began to refer to the building as a "holy place." Only around the third

FIGURE 7.3. Ruins of synagogue in Sardis (Turkey). The back of the Torah ark is in the foreground. Design Pics Inc/Alamy Stock Photo (FR80JC).

or fourth century CE did Jews begin to see their synagogues as sacred space, a designation that the Hebrew Bible preferred to limit strictly to the Tabernacle or its successor, the Jerusalem Temple (with the occasional divine irruption into the natural world). The rabbis, who were probably more cautious than most Jews when designating a new kind of sacred space, sometimes referred to the synagogue as a "little (or maybe minor) temple." The third-century CE synagogue in Dura Europos, a Roman garrison town on the border with Persia, had walls covered with painted scenes drawn almost entirely from the Hebrew Bible. A century later, synagogues in Palestine also began to feature such artistic representations, often on their floor mosaics.[32]

Many of these synagogue floors have at their center a zodiac, the center of which sometimes contains a figure that looks like Helios. Several of these zodiacs are divided into four quadrants, each of which is represented by the personification of a season. Scholars have long debated how to interpret these zodiacs, whose presence anywhere, but especially in the synagogue, contradicts rabbinic laws. Representations

FIGURE 7.4. Mosaic from a bathhouse in Astypalaea (Turkey). Public domain. https://www.astipalea.com.gr/en.history.html.

of zodiacs, Helios, and the seasons are found, in various combinations, throughout the region in Late Antiquity. The combination of all three of them is unusual outside of synagogues but not completely unattested. A Late Antique floor mosaic from a bathhouse in Astypalaea, an island off the coast of Turkey and now part of Greece, is like those found in these synagogues. I am not sure if this parallel brings us any closer to fully understanding the role that such a representation played in a Palestinian synagogue (or a Greek bathhouse), other than to indicate that the notion of sacred time and the cosmos was generally important throughout the region (see figure 7.4)[33]

The rabbis struggled with the notion of holy space. They tried to reconcile different models of holiness. Is the holiness of a synagogue due to the holiness of the objects (e.g., Torah scrolls) within it? Does God, in some way, own space designated as holy? Or are they thought to be holy because God to some degree actually dwelled within them, as in the Jerusalem Temple? I suspect that most (nonrabbinic) Jews would have chosen this last possibility.[34]

One passage in rabbinic literature illustrates some of the tensions at work. According to the Mishnah, all rabbis agree that a synagogue can be sold. It is, after all, simply a building. Yet, at the same time, the rabbis are not quite willing to abandon the idea that the space has been consecrated. One rabbi states that synagogues must be sold only on condition that the sellers can buy it back (whether for a limited period of time or forever is not stated). Another rabbi limits the purposes to which a former synagogue can be put. One cannot, he says, sell a synagogue if the building will become a bathhouse, tannery (tanning was a very smelly and dirty affair), place of immersion, or lavatory. Even ruined synagogues have permanent restrictions put upon them; those spaces cannot be used for many mundane purposes. Once sanctified—like also the ruins of the Jerusalem Temple—the space cannot be fully deconsecrated.[35]

Evidence about whether Jewish women attended the synagogue, and when they did where they stood or sat, is ambiguous. On the one hand, there are scattered references in rabbinic literature attesting to women attending synagogue. The Palestinian Talmud, for example, records a story of a woman whose husband became angry because she stayed late at synagogue to hear a sermon. Numerous inscriptions in synagogues contain the names of women donors, although that does not necessarily mean that they prayed in the space. According to their excavators, a few synagogues in Galilee had upper galleries that were used by women, although there is little evidence to support this conclusion. We also lack any concrete evidence that men and women prayed in separate sections of the synagogue, as is commonly done today in modern Jewish Orthodox synagogues. There is no extant evidence for the existence of *mechitzot,* barriers that separate men and women. This may mean that women attended synagogue and sat together with men, or that there were gender-separated services; we simply do not know. It is reasonable to expect that there was regional variation in the extent to which women used the synagogues as holy space.[36]

Cemeteries

Temples, churches, and synagogues were all built by communities seeking to facilitate their communication with invisible beings. Some acquired their holiness due to their location at a site that was already thought of as holy, some through the consecrated images or relics within them, and some arbitrarily by fiat. In nearly all cases, though, these constituted spaces that were controlled by specialists and used primarily for communal functions. Cemeteries, on the other hand, were not subject to the same control and served an important function as hallowed spaces in which individuals more commonly sought contact with the invisible beings. While these beings were most often the souls of the dead, they could also include angels and other deities.

In one sense, cemeteries might seem to be peculiar places for such activities. Human remains are quintessentially impure, and the places where such remains rest are often set apart for exactly this reason. Rich Romans, for example, built tombs along the road leading into the city, a situation that caused problems as the city expanded. In Jewish law, contact with human remains or even that which came into contact with human remains could convey a particularly noxious and persistent form of impurity that barred entry into the Temple. Even Christians, who regarded most human bodies whose souls had departed as mere matter like any other (the exception being relics of holy men and women), frequently revered human bodies and the sites at which they were laid to rest.

Yet in another sense, cemeteries were perfectly natural places in which to seek invisible beings. To the extent that people saw the human body as more than mere matter, they also saw human remains and where they were laid as liminal places, in between here and there. What better place to gain access to the beings in the invisible world than through the spirit of a dead relative who you know likes you?

Christians were particularly attracted to the dead as portals to the beyond. This was due in part to their familiarity and comfort with traditional Roman customs, in part, perhaps, to the central role that death and resurrection played in Christian beliefs. Whatever the reasons, however, all through Late Antiquity Christians commonly gathered at graves. These gatherings usually involved a meal, at which, several illustrations from catacombs make clear, the departed were understood to be participating. Areas where Christians were buried frequently also have within them a *mensa* (plural: *mensae*), a stationary table at which the funerary banquets took place at regular intervals. Traditional Roman practices were Christianized. Funerary meals were sometimes uncomfortably combined with Eucharistic masses offered on the mensae. Sometimes a piece of the sanctified bread of the Eucharist was even given to the dead. It did not take long for such practices to spill out from the domestic to the communal. Christians began to gather at the sites where martyrs and other holy people were buried in order to participate in the Eucharist and have a festive meal. Far from being spots of "impurity," these became auspicious places for worship.[37]

Gravesites were not, according to some scholars, secondary and incidental places of Christian worship. They were, in fact, the primary places that Christians went to communicate with their deities. In a provocative and clever book, the Yale historian Ramsey MacMullen used archaeological data to make some very rough estimates of the available standing space of all churches within a given city, with the goal of learning the percentage of the Christian population that could gather in any given space at the same time. Even if his figures are significantly off (as even he admits they could be), it is clear that churches could hold only a small fraction of the Christian population. The rest, MacMullen reasons from archaeological and literary sources, used cemeteries as their principal places of worship. Nor were cemeteries simply secondary and incidental places for Christian worship. They were intentionally designed to facilitate gatherings that were, by their nature, "religious." This is perhaps most clear in the catacombs, many of which are lavishly decorated. Given how much energy and time it took to create these underground complexes, the very fact that they use space so inefficiently—by which I mean that far more dead could fit into the space—also strongly points to their intentional design as places that might be, first and foremost, gathering places for the living.[38]

Christians saw cemeteries as sanctified spaces because they were filled with an unusually high concentration of invisible intermediaries. In the thinking of many, people continued to "live" after their bodies died. After death, these spirits paid special attention to their human remains. Whether they were really present, hovering around a corpse, or were elsewhere but expected offerings and veneration from their human ancestors at the site of their remains was not very important to most people. What was important was that the spirits of ordinary humans could be effective intermediaries or irksome enemies, and the way to maintain friendly relations with them was to pay them homage at the site of their former earthly homes. Masses for the dead were not simply made for the sake of the dead but also—primarily—for the sake of the living who needed these spirits to continue to be effective intermediaries with the divine realm. Extraordinary individuals, whose spirits were promoted into a higher echelon of the cosmic hierarchy and who thus were even more effective intermediaries, were even better to have on one's side. As early as the second century Christians were already beginning to visit the graves of martyrs and saints, doing much what they did by the tombs of their more ordinary ancestors, in order to propitiate these more powerful spirits. The graves of martyrs became prime spots for worship and were increasingly considered holy.[39]

The attraction of Christians to cemeteries made the intellectuals uncomfortable. The method of beseeching the spirits was not so much the issue; the intellectuals themselves also believed that such practices were important and efficacious. The problem instead was the place itself. Christian elite promoted churches—spaces that they built and controlled—as exceptionally holy, and the draw of cemeteries created competition. Fewer Christians in churches meant less revenue collected as part of the offerings, but more importantly, it led to a loss of authority. Cemeteries were spaces not controlled or regulated by ecclesiastical authorities and could thus also be spaces in which nonclerical experts vied for status and power. Church officials thus launched a two-pronged response. First, they inveighed against worship at cemeteries but brought many of the same worship practices—and even the bodies themselves—into churches. One could celebrate the mass for a martyr in the church rather than by his tomb or make a votive offering to one's parents there instead of in the cemetery. Second, when that failed to work, they brought the church to the cemetery or tomb. Many churches were constructed around the tombs of saints, and some areas, such as catacombs, that were difficult to include in a built space were simply decreed in toto to be churches. This was a process, however, that would go on for many centuries, and even to this day the church's victory is incomplete.[40]

A surviving letter by St. Augustine gives a sense of this competition. In 392 CE, Augustine replied to a letter from his colleague Aurelius, bishop of Carthage. Aurelius had written in concern to Augustine that the gatherings at the tombs of saints at times turned into full, drunken parties. This suitably outraged Augustine, who draws on Romans 13:13 to argue that drunkenness is a sin, albeit not the worst one (sexual offenses received that honor), and that drunks should at least "be kept away from the tombs of the sainted dead, from the scenes of sacramental privilege, and from the houses of prayer." Drunkenness in such places is a "plague." Taking the long view, Augustine says that fiery denunciations will make no headway and that only education and gentle exhortations will help to change things. He then offers some more concrete advice:

> Since, however, these drunken revels and luxurious feasts in the cemeteries are wont to be regarded by the ignorant and carnal multitude as not only an honour to the martyrs, but also a solace to the dead, it appears to me that they might be more easily dissuaded from such scandalous and unworthy practices in these places, if, besides showing that they are forbidden by Scripture, we take care, in regard to the offerings for the spirits of those who sleep, which indeed we are bound to believe to be of some use, that they be not sumptuous beyond what is becoming respect for the memory of the departed, and that they be distributed without ostentation, and cheerfully to all who ask a share of them; also that they be not sold, but that if any one desires to offer any money as a religious act, it be given on the spot

> to the poor. Thus the appearance of neglecting the memory of their deceased friends, which might cause them no small sorrow of heart, shall be avoided, and that which is a pious and honourable act of religious service shall be celebrated as it should be in the Church. This may suffice meanwhile in regard to rioting and drunkenness.[41]

Augustine completely accepts the practice of making offerings to the spirits. Even doing so in the cemeteries is acceptable, as long as it is done solemnly (and without drunkenness) and accompanied by gifts to the poor. We do not know if Aurelius—who was fiery by nature and may not have shared Augustine's patience—took his advice or whether he found other ways to tamp down the partying. The very next year, though, a church council in Hippo, Augustine's own city, issued a canon forbidding both the giving of the Eucharist to the bodies of the dead and the baptizing of the dead. Clearly the cemeteries, and the behavior of Christians within them, remained a point of concern.[42]

Christians may have gone further than others in their use of cemeteries as sacred space, but this was more a matter of quality than quantity. Romans thought of human remains as impure and thus did not allow their burial within the sacred boundaries (the *pomerium*) that defined the border of a city. That, however, did not mean that Romans treated human remains casually. Most Romans, who had little or no means, were buried, unmarked, in fields set aside for that purpose. The fields were, presumably (we have little direct evidence for this), owned by the municipality. (Note that the priests purchase the "potters' field" mentioned in Matthew 27:9–10.) Those of significant means might be commemorated with large and expensive monuments conspicuously erected along the roads leading into the city. The families of these deceased paid for both the land and the monument. Others might be buried communally in cemeteries owned by a voluntary organization or individually in small plots tucked around estates or even cities that did not contain pomeriums. Ancient equivalents of the family plots often found on American farms were common.

This practice of burial, which largely left responsibility for each small burial plot to the heirs in perpetuity, raised a thorny problem: Could people later buy these plots and do whatever they wished with them? The idea that later generations could simply plow over the places where their ancestors were buried—or add their own dead to the family tomb or plot—was deeply disturbing to Greeks and Romans alike. Both dealt with the problem in a similar way. Tombs gained their own, "sacred," legal status and thus came under the authority and protection of the state. Originally, the idea that a tomb changes status from private to semi-public probably started with the tomb-owners themselves. Seeking to protect the remains of their ancestors, tomb-owners began to post inscriptions containing both curses and financial penalties for those who disturbed the rest of the dead. These inscriptions are largely formulaic and often specify the exact fine owed by the tomb-violator, to be paid to the polis—an entity that, in the eyes of the tomb-holders, would exist in perpetuity and had the power to enforce the penalty. Whether they wanted it or not, such inscriptions gave municipal authorities a role in the protection of the tombs. Even Nabataean tombs often have such inscriptions.[43]

Once in the business of tomb protection, the state took it seriously. Disturbing the dead became a state crime, subject to severe penalties, which could include being sent to the mines. One law from 356 CE, apparently responding to increasing cases of tomb violation for the sake of salvaging building materials, gives anyone—not just the tomb-owners—the right to begin a legal action against a tomb-violator. Such an action could result in an exorbitant financial penalty. The law contains the following preface: "Those persons who violate the habitations of the shades, the homes, so to speak, of the dead, appear to perpetrate a twofold crime. For they both despoil the buried dead by the destruction of the tombs, and they contaminate the living by the use of this material in building." Tomb-violators are often lumped together with murderers, rapists, and magicians in Roman imperial legislation. Imperial lawmakers could not quite figure out how a tomb could be "sacred," but they used language that came close, as when they say that from time immemorial moving anything from a burial site had been "the next thing to sacrilege."[44]

As the imperial legislators put it, the tombs were special sites because they were the home of the "shades" (*manes*), or spirits, of the dead. This made them particularly important places for Romans when they wanted to honor their ancestors. Romans long observed the *Parentalia*, a multiday festival beginning on February 13 during which families would honor their ancestors. The festival involved offerings to the *manes*, usually in the household but also at the ancestors' tombs, where it was thought that they paid particular attention. Privately, individuals would also seek out help from the *manes* at tombs.[45]

Tombs were also particularly apt places at which to deposit curse tablets. One lead tablet found in the common area of a tomb complex in Greece, for example, calls on the chthonic deities, Violence, Fate, and Necessity (and then, for insurance at the end, another more obscure deity), to punish someone related to the person in the tomb for his role in stealing a garment. While curse tablets were not exclusively found in tombs, depositing them among the dead was clearly a recognized practice, presumably because they would have been thought to have more efficaciously communicated one's desires to the deities.[46]

Jews, despite being more concerned about contracting corpse impurity than were Christians, Romans, or Greeks, nevertheless also attributed "sacred" significance to burial sites. Jews appear to have been more likely than Greeks and Romans to concentrate the burial of their dead, whether in a cemetery, catacomb, or necropolis (a place containing multiple tombs), probably reflecting their desire to limit the spread of impurity. Tomb inscriptions in Palestine sometimes explicitly state that they belong to a family. One passage in the Babylonian Talmud suggests that it is unthinkable that a person would be buried on land that they did not personally own. Yet, as among Greeks and Romans, sources suggest that the community assumed responsibility for maintaining the graves at some point after the families abandoned them.[47]

Jews visited graves for the same reason that everyone else did: they sought to communicate with the spirits who tended to congregate there, usually to ask for their help. One rabbinic story tells a tale of a man who, upon sleeping in a graveyard, overheard spirits conversing. There are several other stories that similarly reflect the belief that the spirits remained close to their bodies. These spirits could be petitioned for help. According to the Babylonian Talmud, for example, one rabbi says that during fast days people visit the cemetery "so that the dead will seek

FIGURE 7.5. Catacombs from Vigna Randanini, Rome. The niches with the bodies would have been sealed, sometimes with an epitaph. Public domain. https://romanjews.com/vigna-randanini-jewish-catacombs-tour.

mercy for us." Elsewhere the Babylonian Talmud recognizes the special status of the cemetery by forbidding frivolity or a series of otherwise ordinary actions within it. The evidence that Jews visited the graves of holy people, whether biblical ancestors, rabbis, or others, is sparse but suggestive. Christian sources claim that, before the Christians themselves took over the site, Jews would visit the putative graves of the Maccabean brothers in Antioch. While the graves of biblical (and rabbinic) heroes such as Rachel, David, and Rabbi Shimon bar Yohai would become sacred sites from the Middle Ages until today, we have little knowledge about whether Jews—whether local or from afar—visited them to seek intervention with the divine.[48]

Archaeological evidence supports the impression of the literary sources that Jews visited ordinary gravesites. A large Jewish necropolis at Beit Shearim (outside modern-day Haifa) and (mainly Jewish but maybe also mixed) catacombs in Rome were designed to accommodate visitors. The necropolis at Beit Shearim contains several cave complexes, into which were carved rooms and places for individual bodies to rest. This complex contains several places that seem to be specifically intended as gathering spaces. Domestic goods (e.g., pots and dishes) were also found at the site. These goods may have been connected to meals held there, although the archaeology is unclear on this issue. The Jewish catacombs in Rome tended to be largely functional; they were narrow, and the tombs cut into them were tightly stacked. Even here, though, people visited, leaving their mark with roughly etched inscriptions, or graffiti. There are a few spaces in the catacombs that, like those at Beit Shearim, were designed to accommodate groups. Some of these places were plastered and painted with decorations. These catacombs had already been looted in antiquity, making it impossible to learn much from the domestic goods found there. The resemblance of these spaces to Christian and Roman ones, however, probably indicates that they were seen and used in a similar way as well.[49]

The gods, and other invisible beings, were everywhere. Or, more precisely, most had the ability to be anywhere at a second's notice, or in more than one place simultaneously. This quality created the possibility in the minds of nearly everyone who lived in antiquity that communication with them could happen anywhere. They were always "on," waiting to hear their names invoked, like an Amazon Echo or an iPhone. At that point, they could decide to come closer to the place where the prayer or request was made, or not. The critical point here is that unlike most modern notions of prayer, in which an omnipresent deity simply hears the prayer from the heavens, the deities in Late Antiquity came down to earth for better hearing. The gods were the agents who moved, not the words of the prayer or the smell of the sacrifices. There were, as always, exceptions, but for the most part, place was presumed to be a factor in communication with the divine.

There were subtle gestures throughout Late Antiquity to change from this "locative" (in the scholar Jonathan Z. Smith's words) notion that communication occurs in place to a more "utopian" idea that assumes that since the divine is omniscient and safely ensconced in heaven, place becomes largely irrelevant. The importance of prayer comes internally, from the heart of the worshipper, as Christian, Jewish, and even sometimes Roman writers emphasize. The Neoplatonists and Gnostics focus on perfection of the self to unify with the divine. Jews, having lost their cultic center, particularly attempted to dislocate the effectiveness of communication with the divine from place. The rabbis frequently promote the idea that the study of Torah or the ad hoc composition of a quorum for prayer brings the divine presence. Palestinian rabbis quite cleverly assign to the entire Land of Israel a special sanctified status, which taps into a locative notion but makes the "place" so large that it basically becomes utopian. Persian rabbis, understandably, pushed back on this notion.[50]

The truth, though, is that despite these gestures and the theoretical possibility that place mattered little when it came to communicating with the divine, it mattered a lot, to pretty much everyone. It was possible to bring the deities to you, but it was also risky. There were places that they actively did not like, and most other places they could take or leave. It would have been a much better bet, with a better chance of positive results, to go to a place where the gods already were, or at least to places that they actively liked.

Individuals chose the optimal places for their requests based on the agent with whom they wanted to communicate, what they wanted from that agent, and, of course, their means. Temples were appropriate for communal worship but were less accessible to individuals. One who sought the intervention of Pan might want to travel to Banias, but if that was too inconvenient, a local temple or even a cult image might suffice. Similarly, a Christian might prefer to go to a church built atop a holy site, but circumstances might steer the individual to the local church or even a cemetery. Jews probably struggled the most with notions of sacred space. Despite rabbinic assurances that place did not matter, such ideas were so ingrained that they sought to create new sacred spaces, particularly in synagogues. Even gravesites could work, though.

Sacred places did much more work for a community than simply serving to facilitate communication with the divine. They replicated and reinforced a variety of social hierarchies as well. Aristocrats demonstrated their wealth and importance by prominently displaying their names on inscriptions, taking important roles in the rituals, and sitting in the best seats. Rituals in these spaces were structured to highlight the authority and importance of priests, clerics, and elders. Women were present these spaces, but in more formal communal contexts the non-aristocratic women were often reminded of their subordinate status. The rare occasions on which women did have opportunities to serve as officiants in a service or take a more active role in the rituals were notable for exactly this reason; they were meant to enact the (partial) reversal of gender roles. Slaves were present in such places, but their enslaved status was almost certainly marked and reinforced by where they sat and what they wore. While in some rare cases sacred spaces did become places where the privileges and social hierarchies temporarily dissolved, most Greeks, Romans, Christians, and Jews would never have encountered such a space.

Effective communication with the invisible beings—communication that brought results—could happen anywhere, but some places were better than others. It could also happen at any time, although, similarly, some times were better than others.

8

Profane and Holy Time

IT WOULD have been hard, anywhere in the Roman Empire, not to notice the *Kalendae Ianuariae*. The *kalends*—the first day—of the month of January had been observed as a festival by Romans for centuries and over time had become a raucous multiday festival. The three-day holiday, capped by a day of revelry, was so joyous that on the fourth day, as people began to return to work, they "prayed to see the same festival again." It was one of the few Roman holidays so pervasive and important that even the rabbis, who studiously avoided discussing most Roman and Christian holidays (although they mention a few in the context of limiting exposure to "idolatry"), speculated about its origin and meaning. The fourth-century bishop John Chrysostom devoted a sermon to the holiday, sputtering in anger at his congregants who seemed to have participated widely in the "demonic" celebrations. Christians, he optimistically thundered, do not need special holidays and should, in fact, reject them. All of time now is a continual feast, in which one day is not more "sacred" than any other.[1]

We will return later to the Kalendae Ianuariae, but for the moment, it is worth thinking about the many complex issues it raises. Everybody knew that timing was no less important than place and method for communicating effectively with invisible beings. John Chrysostom cavalierly dismissed the importance of sacred time, but even he knew that there was no chance he could convince his congregants that sacred days had ceased to exist. The problem, though, was how one could identify a propitious moment: What made one period of time more sacred than another? Was sacred time baked into nature itself and made visible in such signs as the rising and setting of the sun, the movement of the planets, and the phases of the moon? Or was it sacred because some commanding body—the Roman Senate, a city council, God—said it was? Moreover, how did one person's sacred time, such as the Roman Kalendae Ianuariae, layer onto other and competing sacred calendars, such as that of the rabbis? And what was at stake, not only theologically but also in the exercise of power? Groups throughout history, with motives that are not entirely pure, have struggled to control the calendar and its holidays.

Today, when we think of sacred time, we normally think of dates on the calendar, whether a particular day of the week or holiday, marked especially by official days off from work. This was also true in antiquity. People in antiquity were constantly reconciling multiple calendars, especially the festival calendars of Roman imperial authorities, municipalities, and their priests. Scores of such calendars from Late Antiquity, often inscribed on stone or prepared in codex form for individual rich patrons, survive. These festivals would be most palpably experienced in the closing of the law courts (which was, like today's closure of government offices and services, the way holidays were officially recognized) and gatherings accompanied by free refreshments and noisy and sometimes spectacular processions. These were, perhaps like our own official festivals, complicated affairs that intricately linked notions of the sacred with commerce and projections of power and authority.

People in antiquity, though, also experienced sacred time in ways that were less connected to the calendar. Sacred time was an inherent part of the natural order. The cosmos and the motion of the planets were visible signs of time, if only one knew how to read them. Sunrise and sunset, so often dramatically distinguished from the flow of the rest of the day, were clearest. The moon, particularly the full and new moons, was also a visible marker of time. Birth, death, and menstrual cycles—often hard breaks through an individual's life—could hold private significance for individuals and families. It goes without saying that extraordinary weather events and other natural events, such as earthquakes, were also seen as irruptions of the sacred into the undifferentiated flow of profane time.

How people experienced and understood sacred time—how it worked in practice—is among one of the more difficult dimensions of ancient life to recover. While some representations of time survive in inscriptions, calendars, and zodiacs, they can only indirectly reveal how people experienced it. The often-polemical writings of the intellectuals are informative but frequently obscure the more direct experience of sacred time. As we have come to expect, almost nothing survives from antiquity that shows how the non-elite—and especially women, children, and slaves—experienced time. Nevertheless, a careful and critical investigation of the fragments that we do have, bolstered with some informed speculation, can help us to bring into better focus the basic contours of how sacred time "worked" in Late Antiquity.

Astrology: The Cosmos and Time

Today, we distinguish between astronomy and astrology. That distinction, however, only began to emerge (in Europe) in the sixteenth century. By the time of Late Antiquity, many ancient cultures, including the Babylonians and Greeks, had already developed sophisticated models of the movements in the heavens. These models were based on robust observational data and did an excellent job predicting most astral phenomena. What distinguishes this activity from modern-day astronomy, however, is that it was linked to larger conceptual frameworks of the cosmos, time, and the gods. These frameworks, which differed somewhat among different cultures, nearly all assigned cosmic meaning to time; each moment had its own special quality. That quality was determined by the place of the heavenly bodies. Fortunately, since the heavenly bodies were visible, those armed with expert knowledge could read and decipher their meaning. Astrology was the science not simply of observing and predicting the movement of the heavenly bodies but also of understanding what those movements meant for us.

Although the mechanics of determining the meaning of the astral bodies were complex, they were based on two assumptions and a rather simple set of observations. The basic assumption underlying all astrology was that the sky can be meaningfully divided into twelve pie-shaped quadrants. The name of each quadrant followed the dominant constellation within it, that is, the sign of the zodiac. The meaning of any particular moment in time derives from where each of the astral bodies are—that is, in which quadrant of the sky—at a given moment. There are a vast number of potential combinations of where each of the five planets known at that time could be in relation to the constellations and each other. Moreover, the sun (at its rising) and moon also moved through the constellations, albeit at a much faster pace. By Late Antiquity, these observations could be calculated. Experts prepared charts (much as today) with such information and for a fee would use them to help nonexperts understand the meaning of a particular moment.[2]

There was a second assumption, though, that was fundamental to understanding why and how the locations of these astral bodies were meaningful, which was that the planets, sun, and moon were connected to the gods. The word "connected" is deliberately ambiguous. Some thought that these bodies were gods, some that they were visible manifestations of gods, and others simply that they were controlled by divine forces. We might assume that the belief that different gods were associated with, or controlled, the different astral bodies caused great difficulties for those Jews and Christians who rejected the very existence of multiple gods.

Yet that assumption would, by and large, be mistaken. Jewish and Christian intellectuals in Late Antiquity did have reservations about the practice of astrology, but they were rarely based on its presumed "polytheistic" nature. They were, rather, much more concerned with two other issues: the theological threat of determinism and the practical threat to their own authority. The idea that the position of the astral bodies at a particular moment in time—especially at birth—predetermined the future course of events was deeply troubling to intellectuals who assumed that human beings had free will. But even as troubling as this tension was, many of these same intellectuals could not entirely reject the common, prevailing notion that there was in fact a relationship between the position of the astral bodies and human fate. The same rabbis who repeat that "Israel has no sign (*mazal*)," that is, that the planets do not determine the fate of individual Jews, can also state that the length of "life, children, and sustenance do not depend on merit, but on the sign (*mazal*)." So too, a long composition in the Babylonian Talmud alternates between denying that Jews have a fate and asserting that they do: "One [born] on the third day of the week will be a rich and fornicating man." A gloss, clearly meant to lessen the astrological implications of the assertion, adds that this is because, according to Genesis, flora was created on the third day. Christian writers also often had strong theological reservations about astrology and the role it assigns fate, but this was such an engrained concept that few rejected it outright on these grounds alone. Julius Firmicus Maternus, a Roman polymath, wrote both an extensive astrological treatise in the first half of the fourth century and then a polemical tract on "The Error of the Pagan Religions." Even if he converted to Christianity between writing the two tracts (as many scholars think, although without direct evidence), he still never condemned astrology in the latter.[3]

Of more concern both to these intellectuals and to political authorities was astrologers' presence and popularity. Writing from across the spectrum leaves little doubt that astrologers commonly plied their skills and expertise. The Babylonian Talmud regularly calls them "Chaldeans," a term that links their astrological skills to the ancient land of Chaldea and shows them advising commoners and rabbis alike: one rabbi even accepted career advice from an astrologer. At the same time, the rabbis took pains to show that astrological knowledge was inferior to their own. Augustine denounces the "mathematicians" (as astrologers were also commonly called in imperial legislation), whose predictions are false. These condemnations dovetailed with the concerns of Roman political rulers. From at least the time of Augustus, the Romans recognized that "extra-official" astrologers had the potential to pose a risk to the government and the emperor himself. As Christians became increasingly influential in setting imperial legislation, the legislative bans on astrologers began to increase as well. Both the astrologers themselves and their clients were threatened with harsh punishments. The barrage of legislation over close to a century might testify to its relative ineffectiveness.[4]

FIGURE 8.1. Zodiac in mosaic floor in Beit Alpha, Israel, dating to the sixth century CE. Public domain. https://en.wikipedia.org/wiki/Zodiac_mosaics_in_ancient_synagogues#/media/File:Mosaic_Zodiac_from_Synagogue_in_Beit_Alpha,_Israel,_6th_Century_(31858682362).jpg.

Astrological thinking was clearly pervasive. One does not need to look at its condemnation by the elite, though, to drive that point home. Archaeologists have unearthed many representations of the zodiac, in a variety of different contexts. In Late Antique Roman Palestine, we have several depictions of the zodiac found on mosaic floors in synagogues and one literary representation of the zodiac signs in an

FIGURE 8.2. Inscription mentioning the zodiac signs from a synagogue in Ein Gedi, Israel. Image courtesy of Zev Radoven. Used with permission.

inscription, also from a Jewish context. Such zodiacs are like those found in churches and other Greek and Roman contexts throughout the Mediterranean region. Many of these illustrated mosaics label each of the constellations, whether in Greek or Aramaic. Many, including most of those found in synagogues, have at their center a representation of a figure that looks like (or represents) Helios, the sun god.[5]

The presence of Helios—or a Helios-like figure—in the center of synagogue floors has generated extensive scholarly discussion. Early scholars, disturbed by the apparent contradiction between this figure (and others on the zodiac) and their assumption that good, rabbinic Jews would have rejected figural representations, sought either to dismiss the communities that created them as deviant or to label the figures as "merely decorative" and thus of no further importance. Modern scholars have abandoned these apologetic explanations but still disagree about how we are to interpret these zodiac wheels in synagogues (and churches). Are they didactic, meant to teach onlookers about the astrological calendar? Is "Helios" really a representation of YHWH, the God of Israel, or one of YHWH's angels? Or is the entire image meant to convey a general message relating to the structure of the cosmos—or even to serve as a channel between heaven and the cosmos, much as Christian icons do, being objects of devotion in and of themselves?[6]

Images of the zodiac are not the only sign in the material evidence of the importance of astrological thinking. Several calendars survive from antiquity. Some were written in codices for personal use of the elite, but many were inscribed in public places. These calendars came in different forms and served different purposes. Mosaics that show the solar months, along with illustrations of each month, appear in some villas. Some (but not all) allude to the zodiac. The purely textual inscription from the synagogue at Ein Gedi contains a list of the signs of the zodiac followed by a list of the lunar months (see figure 8.2). Many other inscriptions throughout the Roman Empire attempt to synchronize different timekeeping schemes, often noting sacred times and moments of astrological significance. Even the illiterate would likely have recognized the visual representations of the calendar and the very fact that time had a relationship with astrology.[7]

There are many other indications, though, that astrology mattered. Many Christian epitaphs mention fate; they would undoubtedly have horrified Augustine. Some epitaphs mention the deceased's astrological sign. Christian artifacts contain astrological symbols, and at least some Christians commissioned horoscopes. Jewish amulets too sometimes refer to the astrological signs, and some Jewish liturgical poetry is deeply imbued with astrological imagery. Roman commemoration of birthdays was loosely, if not always explicitly, connected to astrological thinking. Romans thought that each man, on birth, received a *genius,* a kind of divine and immortal double of the essential traits of the person. Women also received a *genius,* connected to the goddess Juno (it is not clear if every woman, like a man, received her own individual *genius* or shared the *genius* of Juno). In Late Antiquity, the notion of the *genius* was often conflated with that of the "self" or "soul." A man was expected to make a small offering (usually a libation) to his *genius* on his birthday as well as to other *genii* that were important to his ancestral family on their appropriate days. There is little evidence to gauge whether women made libations on their own birthdays or folded their commemoration of their *genii* in with their observance of Juno. The nature of each *genius,* though, seems linked to the astrological facts of one's birth and possibly one's conception.[8]

Neither Jews nor early Christians seem to have attached much importance to birthdays. Neither group was uncomfortable with the idea of having individual "guardian angels," but the Roman emphasis on supplicating such beings through sacrifice—and its link to the Empire writ large—may have been enough to dissuade them from commemorating birthdays. Both, however, began to commemorate the day of death, a practice that was not unknown in Rome but was also less loaded. For Christians, such days, especially of holy men and women, became auspicious times to supplicate the divine. The anniversary of Polycarp's martyrdom, for example, was observed annually, and early Christian locals observed the anniversaries of the deaths of their favored saints and martyrs. Tertullian condemns widows who do not honor their deceased husbands on the anniversaries of their death, although this is probably due less to the "auspiciousness" of the day than to it being an expression of devotion. We have no evidence until the Middle Ages that Jews attached significance to the anniversaries of deaths.[9]

Visible Time

Time is not only visible in the movement of the planets. Every day, interrupting the subtle and sometimes imperceptible flow of one moment to another, the sun rises and sets. Sunrise and sunset can be quite dramatic. They are remarkable, even magnificent, visual spectacles: brief, blazing moments, especially in the Mediterranean basin. As cyclical special astronomical moments they were ripe for speculation. And, indeed, those who lived in Late Antiquity considered deeply how to understand them and the extent to which they were useful or dangerous.

Sunrise and, to a lesser degree, sunset became times especially important for institutional worship. Romans frequently sacrificed at sunrise, and when the Jerusalem Temple stood, its Jewish priests made two statutory sacrifices each day, one at sunrise and the other toward sunset. Greeks, too, may have favored sunrise as a propitious time to sacrifice, but the evidence is uncertain. This timing was linked quite simply to the visible nature of the sunrise, although later thinkers, seeking to explain the practice, suggested that it was also the moment at which divinities awake.[10]

For the rabbis, the communal sacrifices served as a template for thinking about individual prayer obligations. Prior to the rabbinic period, there do not appear to have been any individual or communal obligations to pray on a regular basis outside of the temple sacrifice. (The Dead Sea community—perhaps the Essenes—may have had such an obligation, but they would represent our only evidence for such a practice.) The rabbis saw individual prayer as a substitute for the communal sacrifice that could no longer be offered, much as the Neoplatonists did when the Christian authorities banned all communal sacrifice. In line with this, the rabbis discuss in great deal who must pray, when, and how. These discussions frequently use the sacrifices as a paradigm. Rabbinic discussion of the correct time for the recitation of the Shema, for example, links back to the times of the priestly watches in the Temple.

As is frequently the case, the rabbinic evidence presents a question: Are they describing a relatively common Jewish practice of regular, statutory, communal, and individual prayer (even one that might emerge throughout Late Antiquity), or are they presenting an image of the world as they imagine it should be? Or, put more simply, did regular Jewish prayer emerge as a substitute for the sacrifices that could no longer be offered? We still cannot answer those questions. There is ample evidence, particularly from outside of Judaea and dating before the destruction of the Temple, for regular Jewish gatherings (that presumably included prayer, although the evidence is not entirely clear) on the Sabbath. The building of synagogues within Palestine exploded in Late Antiquity, yet despite numerous inscriptions found within them, almost all of which commemorate gifts or ask for salvation or health, we have little sense of what people did inside of them. To complicate the picture further, we must remember that few people at that time were literate enough to read a prayer book or wealthy enough to possess one (the first Jewish prayer book was composed in the early Middle Ages). Did individual Jewish boys learn by memory the (rabbinic) prayers in childhood and take care to recite them twice a day, either communally (e.g., in a *minyan*, a group of ten adult males) or individually? Did women?

It is plausible, although by no means certain, that many Jews in Late Antiquity did attend the synagogue on the Sabbath, where they heard a Torah reading, prayers being recited, and perhaps a sermon of some kind. Outside of the Sabbath, we can assume that Jews, like everyone else, prayed, but we cannot know what they prayed, if they did so in a community, or whether they saw in their prayers a replacement for sacrifice. It is likely that they thought that certain periods of the day, especially sunrise and sunset, were auspicious times to pray. In doing so, they may have thought that they were imitating the angels.[11]

The idea that there were certain times of day that were more propitious than others for supplication due to this kind of natural time is not well attested outside of Jewish sources. Christians established standard times for prayer, but they based these on logic and scriptural precedents rather than any correspondence with divine time. The *Apostolic Constitution*, for example, expects that Christians will assemble for worship every day, morning and evening, but gives little reason other than that the body of Christ (as represented by the congregation) remains whole.[12]

There is, however, a remarkable testimony of how at least some Christians experienced sunrise. One Christmas morning in Rome in the mid-fifth century, Pope Leo the Great gave a sermon that focused on how the devil was leading good Christians into false worship. After inveighing against the worship of astral bodies (in the hope that one could change their astrological fate), he turns to those who "worship" the sun:

> From such a system of teaching proceeds also the ungodly practice of certain foolish folk who worship the sun as it rises at the beginning of daylight from elevated positions: even some Christians think it is so proper to do this that, before entering the blessed Apostle Peter's basilica, which is dedicated to the One living and true God, when they have mounted the steps which lead to the raised platform, they turn round and bow themselves towards the rising sun and with bent neck do homage to its brilliant orb. We are full of grief and vexation that this should happen, which is partly due to the fault of ignorance and partly to the spirit of heathenism: because although some of them do perhaps worship the Creator of that fair light rather than the Light itself, which is His creature, yet we must abstain even from the appearance of the observance: for if one who has abandoned the worship of gods finds it in our own worship, will he not hark back again to this fragment of his old superstition, as if it were allowable, when he sees it to be common both to Christians and to infidels?[13]

According to Leo, and there is little reason to doubt him, some Christians in Rome would begin their day by going to a hill at sunrise and praying, facing east. Others, less ambitiously, would simply bow in the direction of the east before entering St. Peter's Basilica. He is not exactly sure what is going through their minds when they do this, but whatever it is, no matter how well-meaning, they should stop because it looks bad. The difference between worship of the sun and worship of the god who made the light is a subtle one that could be totally lost on observers. In a city that still had a significant non-Christian population, against whom Leo was trying to create boundaries, it did not help his cause when non-Christians could not distinguish between Christian ritual practices and their own. Yet to most of these Christians in Rome, this was exactly the point: "our" piety and "your" piety are not all that far apart.

Divine Time

One of the two primary characteristics ancient thinkers sometimes used to distinguish divinities from nondivinities is that they are eternal (the other is that they are now immortal). To live in eternity is, in a sense, to live outside of time, in a state in which nothing changes. The philosophical explication of this concept, both in ancient and modern thinkers, is complicated and not entirely satisfying. What is certain, however, is that the distinction was either lost on or not particularly important to most people.

The movement of the planets and the rising and setting of the sun—events that happen in time—were vivid signs that the gods also existed in time. But this raises an obvious question: If the gods exist in time, more or less like us, how do they spend it? One of the more imaginative answers to this question appears in a rabbinic text from the fourth century:

> The day consists of twelve hours. During the first three [hours], the Holy One, blessed be He, sits and occupies Himself with the Torah. During the second three [hours], He sits and judges the whole world and when He sees that the world is so guilty as to deserve destruction, He stands from the seat of Justice and sits on the seat of Mercy. During the third three [hours], He sits and feeds the whole world, from the horned buffalo to the brood of vermin. During the fourth [three hours], He sits and plays with Leviathan, as it says, "There is Leviathan, who you formed to play there" [Psalms 104:26].[14]

The division of the human daytime into four three-hour periods is conventional in rabbinic literature. Other passages imagine God engaged in different activities, but all assume that God adheres to a schedule that befits the Creator. In this passage, after beginning the day with the study of Torah (arguably the most valued of all rabbinic activities), God does things that only God could: judging and feeding the world. God then has some downtime with the Leviathan, some kind of mythical beast that Psalms 104:26 expressly says God formed as a playmate. According to rabbinic passages, God prays or makes human matches, all on a rather precise schedule; he is even busy at night. Other rabbinic traditions draw a correspondence between the twelve hours of the day, the twelve tribes, and the twelve signs of the zodiac, all of which are woven together into the natural "order of the world." The Jewish liturgical poet Yannai casually refers to the signs of the zodiac, entirely confident that his cryptic references would be understood.[15]

Aside from the activities, there is another way that God's time and ours are different: God, unlike us, has a precise knowledge of time. Before wide access to accurate timekeeping devices, one's ability to keep track of time was rather hazy and could certainly not be pinned down to the minute or often hour. For the rabbis, this raised all kinds of complex legal issues in matters where precise time (particularly like the beginning of the Sabbath) mattered. The rabbis thus acknowledged that humans are imprecise timekeepers. God, however, is not. God embodies punctuality. Underlying this conception of heavenly punctuality is an essential belief about the nature of time. We can only strive, imperfectly, to emulate God's time. The rabbis imagine that one stratagem of God's adversary is to confuse the ordering of time.[16]

Divine time and human time are not strictly parallel lines that never intersect. The divine timescape, or the rhythms of divine life, sometimes irrupt into our own world. There are times at which heaven and earth meet, just as there are such places. Jews had long thought the Sabbath to be one such day. The Hebrew Bible itself connects its observance with the very creation of the world; the day is sacred because it was baked, as it were, into nature. The book of Jubilees, which was important for the authors of many of the Dead Sea Scrolls, extends this idea, envisioning the Sabbath as being part of a cosmically ordained, perfect calendar. In Late Antiquity, Jews observed the Sabbath (non-Jews testify, often hostilely, to continued Jewish observance), primarily because that was their ancestral custom and one that linked them to their families and communities. There is at least some Jewish evidence, however, that the Sabbath was seen as special precisely because its observance involved a particular kind of celestial congruity and imitation.[17]

This evidence is primarily found in Jewish liturgical poetry, or *piyyut* (plural: *piyyutim*), from the time, along with more incidental rabbinic comments. The practice of liturgical poetry was well-known and widely practiced throughout Late Antiquity. We know little of those who wrote piyyutim. The evidence suggests that they were at least acquainted with the rabbis and their literature, that they were deeply literate, and that they were commissioned by individual communities to create new liturgical compositions for the Sabbath and some special occasions. One of the recurring themes in these compositions is the angelic worship of God, which is also mentioned in some rabbinic texts. When Jews worship, according to these piyyutim, they join together with the angels who are also worshipping at that time. One would not want to show up late for the angelic worship service.[18]

Another way in which divine time was relevant, and probably the most important way for most people, was its relationship to auspicious and inauspicious days. The Romans thought that some days were "black" days that in their very nature were inauspicious, disfavored by divine beings. Writers from the time struggled to understand what made these days so bad. Plutarch, for example, offers a materialist explanation, that "black days" were a relic of archaic times when Romans would give themselves a breather after a holiday, "because affairs bring with them much that is troublesome and undesired." At the same time, though, he offers an alternative explanation that these days are dedicated to veneration of gods of the underworld. Whatever their true origin, by Late Antiquity it was commonly thought that days, like features in a landscape, had their own intrinsic qualities connected to the cosmos and the divine. Greeks shared the idea that some days were pure and others simply cursed.[19]

The Lunar Month

The new moon and the full moon, like dawn and twilight, are regular and easily visible markers of time. It is hardly surprising, then, that both were widely commemorated throughout antiquity. In several places, the

Hebrew Bible mentions that the appearance of the new moon was a time for communal sacrifice and feasting. The Greeks, as early as the *Odyssey*, saw the new moon as a particularly auspicious time to supplicate Apollo, in the festival known as the *Noumenia*. Several Greek festivals fell on the new moon. The regular appearance of the new moon was also a factor in the development of lunar and luni-solar calendrical systems throughout antiquity.[20]

Prior to the Roman conquests of the first century BCE, nearly all societies followed—for one purpose or another—a lunar or luni-solar calendar. The situation became somewhat more complicated after 8 BCE, when the Roman proconsul of Asia decreed that the Julian, or Roman, calendar (a solar calendar) would now be used. With some subtle modifications, the cities of Asia readily accepted this change. The imposition of the Roman calendar was clearly, and primarily, political. It was not only to be the calendar that governed administrative functions and the dating of documents but would also set the Roman imperial holidays that all cities were now expected to observe. Yet at the same time, the Roman calendar did not exactly displace the lunar calendar. Communities continued to observe their ancestral festivals, using whatever calendar they wanted. Many temples and city councils through the eastern Mediterranean continued to use lunar calendars. Even Romans never accepted their own solar calendar as the exclusive one. One Roman calendar from as late as 354 CE continues to note the phases of the moon, coordinated with the solar date.[21]

Calendars raise several intriguing questions about the nature of sacred time. The solar calendar is based on calculated rather than observed time and even then is only loosely tied to astronomical phenomenon (falling a quarter day behind each year). The lunar calendar can itself be calculated (as the Jewish calendar is today) or based on actual observation each month. In such calculated time schemes, detached from natural observation, what makes time special or sacred? Within calculated or observed time schemes, power matters. Groups such as the Roman Senate, temple priests, city councils, rabbis, and bishops all claimed for themselves the right to decree days as "holy." The Roman solar calendar, set by Roman imperial authorities, functioned as the overarching official calendar that set imperial holidays, thus helping to unite their

Empire through the observance of the same festivals on the same days. Every year an official list of state holidays was sent to the armies, to assure that the festivals—at which political allegiance was sworn—were uniformly kept. On the ground and running alongside it, though, were other calendars with their own sacred times, decreed by those who claimed—sometimes successfully and sometimes not—power for themselves.[22]

We know little about exactly how local calendars functioned, who set them, and how they did so. There is, however, an extended discussion in rabbinic literature on this topic, and even if it is largely fanciful—and most of it probably is—it sheds some light on the dynamics of the calendar and power. Rabbinic texts ignore the existence of a solar calendar, instead assuming only a lunar calendar. Presumably, this continued the use of the lunar calendar in the Jerusalem Temple, which, again presumably, was set by the priests. According to the rabbis, they were the ones who were now in charge of the Jewish calendar. Although they knew that one could calculate the beginning of the new lunar month through the conjunction (i.e., the time when the sun, moon, and earth are in a straight line), they rejected calculation in favor of observation. The rabbis detail an elaborate, court-centered process in which witnesses to the new moon are interrogated, the new month is declared by rabbinic fiat, and the news is spread via a system of beacons. The rabbis give themselves the power of intercalation, in which an extra month is added into the year in order to have months stay somewhat in the same season.[23]

One passage illustrates the process of checking the witnesses:

> Rabban Gamaliel possessed a tablet with the form of the shapes of the moon and hung it on the wall. He would show it to the nonexpert [witnesses] and say: "Did you see something like this, or like that?"
>
> Once two [witnesses] came and said: "In the morning, [we saw the moon] in the east, and in the evening in the west."
>
> Rabbi Yohanan ben Nuri said: "They are false witnesses!"
>
> When they came to Yavneh, Rabban Gamaliel accepted their testimony.

Another time, two came and said: "We saw it at its proper time, but in the night of the added day [the thirty-first day of the month] it did not appear," and Rabban Gamaliel accepted their testimony.

Rabbi Dosa ben Hyrcanus said: "They are false witnesses! How can they testify about a woman who has given birth that the next day her stomach is between her teeth?"

Rabbi Yehoshua said to him: "I see your word."[24]

This passage, first and foremost, ties determination of the calendar to expert knowledge. Moreover, as the story illustrates, experts could come to differing judgments. The two stories that follow both involve cases where, according to rabbinic astronomical understandings, the witnesses' testimonies were not coherent (i.e., if the new moon is sighted on the thirtieth day of the month, it must also be visible the next day). Even at the time of the Mishnah (ca. 200 CE), there is not yet a clear sense even among the rabbis themselves about what suffices as evidence for the new moon and who has the authority to adjudicate it.[25]

On the one hand, the rabbis tried to assert their own power to set the cultic calendar over that of the priests (who undoubtedly wished to continue to do so, even without a temple). On the other, they competed among themselves for this authority. Rabbis in Babylonia and Roman Palestine each jockeyed for the authority to declare the intercalated months. Although it would not take place until the ninth century, the move from a Jewish calendar based on observation to a fully predictable calculated calendar was in large part a last-ditch (and successful effort) by Babylonian rabbis to take power from Palestinian rabbis; if they could not have the power over the calendar, nobody could. Even within Palestine, though, rabbis competed for calendrical authority. Similarly, Macrobius, writing in Latin in modern-day Tunisia around 400 CE, records a story in which the Roman Senate opposed making public the sacrificial calendar, which was based on the sighting of the new moon. Control of the calendar is power.[26]

Power played a similarly important role for the bishops in setting the date of Easter. The question at the heart of this controversy was whether and to what extent Easter celebrations should be related to the observance of the Jewish Passover. Many bishops were keen on organizing the calendar so that Easter never coincided with the first day of Passover. As quickly became clear, though, at stake was not simply the relationship between Christianity and Judaism but the ordering of power relationships among the bishops. While the split between the Roman Catholic and Eastern Orthodox Churches would not occur until the eleventh century, the struggle over the calendar—cited as one of the major causes of this schism—had long and deep roots.[27]

Yet while rabbis and bishops fought each other and among themselves, issuing a confusing set of calendrical directives, most communities—whether city councils, Jewish synagogues, or groups of Christians—could still look to the sky on their own. The Roman solar calendar may have dictated some of the official holidays throughout the Empire, but the lunar cycle continued to play an important role throughout Late Antiquity in the cultic lives of these groups and individuals. In Late Antiquity, Jews apparently continued to observe the new moon as a festival day. The rabbis discuss the special liturgical features of the day, with one source suggesting that there was also a festive meal on it. There is also evidence that the Greek cities marked the new moon with a festive meal. Most intriguingly, though, is a tradition that associates the commemoration of the new moon specifically with women:[28]

> Women who have the custom of not working on the end of the Sabbath—this is not a custom.
>
> On Sabbath evening after the prayers—this is a custom.
>
> On Monday and Thursday—this is not a custom.
>
> [On Monday and Thursday] after the fast—this is a custom.
>
> On the day of intercalation—this is not a custom.
>
> [On the day of intercalation] from the afternoon prayers on—this is a custom.
>
> On the day of the new moon—this is a custom.[29]

Behind this tradition is a more general concern with the status of "customs" in rabbinic law: Are they "legitimate"? This passage seeks to distinguish legitimate customs of female abstention from work (which has its own thorny and technical definition) from customs that the rabbis believe are mistaken. Of most interest to us here is the very last clause, that there was a custom of Jewish women abstaining from work on the new moon. Is this report to be trusted, and if so, how prevalent was the custom and what was behind it?

There is no further evidence of these female customs from Late Antiquity. The custom of Jewish women observing the new moon in some special way, though, is attested in works from the early Middle Ages. One such work, *Pirke d'Rabbi Eliezer*, posits that the custom originated with the incident of the golden calf. When Aaron asks for their gold jewelry, "the women heard and refused to give their rings to their husbands but said to them: 'You want to make an abominable thing with no ability to save!' They did not listen [to the women]. And God gave reward to the women in this world and the next. And what reward did he give to the women in the next world and in this one? That they should observe the new moons, as it is written, 'who satisfies you with good as long as you live so that your youth is renewed like the eagle's' (Psalms 103:5)."[30] This tradition does not exactly state how the women were accustomed to observing the new moon, but it does link it back to a biblical story and might refer to the menstrual cycle. The idea that Jewish women have some special connection to the celebration of the new moon persists through the Middle Ages (and into the present).[31]

Other evidence, too, suggests that Jewish communities put importance on both the new moon and lunar dating. One inscription from Cyranaica (modern-day Libya) might testify to the Jewish community observing the new moon as both a festival and the beginning of a month. While this inscription probably dates from around 41 BCE, it at least suggests that Jewish communities outside of Palestine could have continued to observe new moon celebrations into Late Antiquity. Several Jewish inscriptions from Late Antiquity, especially epitaphs, explicitly note lunar dates. Both Roman and Christian sources also testify to Jewish observance of the new moon.[32]

Christian intellectuals condemned Christians who followed the Jewish calendar. They would undoubtedly have looked askance on Christians in any way "celebrating" the new moon, although it is unclear if there are any extant explicit condemnations. Ordinary Christians sometimes continued to date events, such as deaths, by the lunar calendar and to "observe" (in whatever form that took) Jewish holidays. It is less clear whether they observed special practices on the new moon, as their Jewish neighbors likely did, but it would not be surprising if evidence eventually emerges that they did.[33]

Written calendars ordered the different calendars that would govern everyday life, at least for the wealthy. In 354 CE, a rich Christian named Valentinus commissioned a calendar (or really what we might call an almanac) that tried to order his own life around the many calendars he had to navigate. The calendar section devoted a page to each month. Each month had five columns: (1) a letter noting the phase of the moon; (2) a letter denoting the day of the seven-day week; (3) a letter denoting the day of the eight-day Roman market week; (4) the day of the month as reckoned by Romans (e.g., the kalends, or first of the month; the *ides*, or thirteenth or fifteenth of the month; and the *nones*, which is counted back eight days before the ides of each month); and (5) important facts about the day, like whether it was a festival, imperial anniversary, or "unlucky day." Valentinus's almanac also contained several other sections, such as lists of important imperial birthdays, planets, astrological information, consuls, the Easter cycle, and the bishops of Rome. The calendar itself did not include the Christian dating, so in order to access important Christian dates Valentinus had to flip to other sections of his book. The version that survives—a copy from the Middle Ages—does not include any personal notations like family birthdays, but he may have included such dates as well (see figure 8.3).[34]

The mild calendrical anarchy that existed in Late Antiquity bothered the intellectuals. The rabbis, for example, clearly believed that all Jews throughout the world should celebrate their holidays on the same date, as determined by the rabbis. The idea of calendrical uniformity, greatly enabled by the adaptation of a calculated calendar, allowed Jews and Christians to do this. Throughout Late Antiquity, though, this idea was not widespread and was perhaps even actively resisted. Each community held on to its own right to set its lunar calendar through observation and to intercalate months as they saw fit. The visibility of the moon, and perhaps the informal exchange of information, assured that most

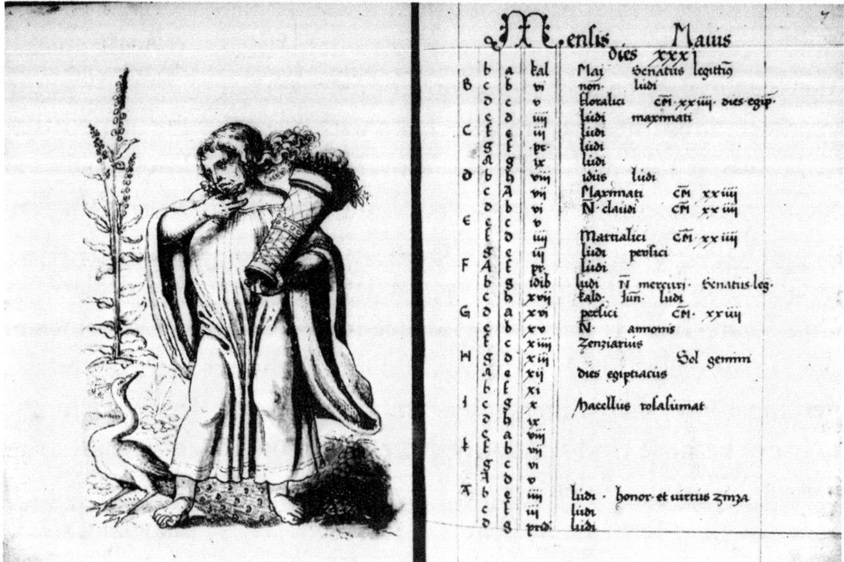

FIGURE 8.3. Codex-calendar of 354. This is a copy from the sixteenth century in which the illustrations were added. Austrian National Library (Cod. 3416). Public domain. https://digital.onb.ac.at/RepViewer/viewer.faces?doc=DTL_5676809&order=1&view=SINGLE.

communities would similarly date their lunar months. There would, however, be minor variations that in turn would lead to observing some holidays on slightly different days. To us, what might be surprising is that this probably did not bother many nonintellectuals. Sacred time, in this understanding, would have combined some notion of nature—as expressed in the cycle of the moon—with an idea that humans played a role too in establishing festivals.

The Week

There are no visible markers for the passing of weeks. Throughout history, human societies have thus marked these divisions differently, and there is nothing particularly natural or obvious about the seven-day week.

Israelites did use a seven-day week, as did the Jews who followed them. The seeds for understanding this division of time as significant, and the Sabbath as holy, are, of course, biblical. Neighboring cultures, almost certainly not coincidentally, also developed seven-day weeks. These were particularly important for astrological reasons. In some manifestations, the days are associated with gods and the planets that embody or represent them, whose movement can then be charted onto the constellations of the zodiac. Rabbinic sources emphasize the link between human and divine observance of the Sabbath; Jews are to do as God does on this naturally sacred day, a day that God declares as God's own. There is extensive evidence for wide Jewish observance of the Sabbath all through antiquity, and it is likely, but again uncertain, that most Jews shared this understanding of the day. The Sabbath was holy not because God arbitrarily decreed it to be so but because it was part of the natural order.

Greeks and Romans also knew of the seven-day, or planetary, week. Roman calendars in the first century CE often show awareness of the seven-day week (reconciling it to the eight-day week they also used, discussed later). In the second century, the author Cassius Dio explicitly ties the seven-day week to the planets and claims that, although created by the Egyptians, it was in general use. The seven-day week had most likely gained popularity due to its astrological connections.[35]

In Late Antiquity, though, the seven-day week was not the only one. There was also a Roman eight-day week, which was connected to the timing of markets. These eight-day weeks help to illustrate the paucity of our own binary distinctions between "sacred" and "profane" time for understanding Late Antiquity. Markets were a mainstay of economic life in antiquity. In cities, these market days would occur frequently, although the more rural the region the less common the market days. The Mishnah, probably reflecting popular practice of Galilee with its regional network of several small cities, assumes that there would be two market days each week, on Monday and Thursday. Well before Late Antiquity, Rome developed a system in which markets were held in different regional cities over an eight-day cycle. This was known as the *nundinae* cycle. Various customs and restrictions developed along with market days, such as festivities and limits on businesses that could interfere with market commerce.[36]

We might normally think of such market days as entirely "profane," but those in antiquity did not. Writers from Late Antiquity tell us that these market days were associated with Jupiter; they used to be days of festivals and sacrifices to the god. Inscriptions and other written sources additionally associate the gods Mercury and Saturn with these market days, but Jupiter himself presided in one city over "sales-tax-free monthly holidays on the fifteenth and thirtieth" of each month. Myths of the origin of the nundinae cycle tie it back to the rhythms of rural, archaic Rome. While the actual historical claims of these writers could well be wrong, it is likely that the market attendees themselves believed them. For most Roman marketgoers, the lines between commerce, veneration of ancestral gods, and assertions of their identity as Romans would have been fuzzy, perhaps not even recognizable. The markets contained meat from freshly butchered animal sacrifices as well, further reinforcing this association. To attend the market could thus activate a multilayered historical identity connected to the gods even when, as in Late Antique Rome, the markets took place daily rather than on an eight-day cycle.[37]

The idea that commerce, the sacred, and time were intertwined was not limited to Rome. Regions throughout the Roman Empire adopted the nundinae cycle to organize their markets. Market days in Greek cities similarly were not zones of pure commerce. The rabbis recognized and responded to this. They created an alternative explanation for the origin of the Monday and Thursday market days in Galilean cities. In their telling, the biblical scribe Ezra established them and ordained that the Torah be read publicly there so that Israel never has to go for more than a few days without hearing the recitation of the Torah. We do not know if most Jews at the markets would really have associated Torah reading, or Ezra, with the market, but it is not implausible that they too sought a narrative complex different from that of the Romans that tied the market days into their own identity and deities.[38]

Christians found themselves stuck between two competing impulses. On the one hand, they were attracted to the seven-day week, with its biblical roots and its difference from the Roman eight-day week. On the other hand, they were troubled by the planetary and astrological associations of the seven-day week. The solution was, ultimately, a simple one: use the seven-day week but change the names of the days. Augustine, for example, bemoans the fact that many Christians continued to use the traditional planetary names of the days when instead they should have been using (like the Jews, although he does not explicitly say this) the number of the day instead—for example, "Monday" should instead be called the "second weekday." The names of the weekdays, Augustine reminds his readers, are not used universally. Yet despite the condemnations by Augustine and other members of the Christian intelligentsia, most Christians continued to use (to this day) the traditional planetary names of the days.[39]

Sunday presented a different set of complications for Christians. The day began to take on increasing significance for Christians beginning in the second to third centuries. This was largely to distinguish Christian ritual gatherings from Jewish ones on the Sabbath (Saturday), which Christians acknowledged was the day of divine rest from creation. At the same time, Sunday acquired other associations, such as the first day of creation and the day of the resurrection of Christ. Since Christ was also associated with the sun, the continued term "Sunday" did not bother Christian writers as much as those for the other days. It was not, however, seen as a holiday until an edict by Constantine in 321 CE. Constantine's edict, of which only fragments survive, made Sunday a legal holiday, on which most official business was suspended (except for slave manumissions and emancipations, some of which were performed in churches). Predictably, Christian writers praised him for this act. The adoption of a seven-day official week did not entirely supplant the eight-day week, but it did subordinate it to a more Christian rhythm of time. Its real motivations, however, are difficult to recover. Was it a pious act made in response to the request of the bishops or an attempt to appease the worshippers of the god Sol Invictus (and maybe a reflection of Constantine's own continuing devotion to this god)? In any case, it took several further imperial laws over the course of subsequent decades to establish Sunday as a Christian, "holy" day.[40]

The Year and Festivals

Romans, Jews, and Christians all had a calendar of festivals that they observed annually. These festivals were established by fiat, whether by the Roman Senate, a Christian synod, or YHWH's directives in the Hebrew Bible. Some were justified according to the agricultural cycle (e.g., Sukkot or Tabernacles, which was associated with the harvest), others by historical commemoration (e.g., Easter or Passover). Whatever their particular origins, however, festivals—like other rituals—tend to take on a life and continuity of their own, divorced from a single, canonical "meaning." That is, people liked festivals; they broke up the monotony (and sometimes back-breaking labor) of the ordinary flow of time and they were often celebrated with particularly tasty food, sometimes supplied by others. They were thus apt to continue them, whether or not any particular meaning associated with them made sense. When a gap develops between a ritual and its meaning, it is more often the meaning that changes to justify the continuity of the festival.[41]

As with the deities themselves, annual festivals existed on several different levels. There were festivals devoted to the official gods of the Empire, which had a strong political valence. Municipalities had their own festivals whose celebrations were sometimes financed by endowments or gifts provided by patrons. Transregional groups, such as Jews, had their own calendar of festivals (even if they did not all observe them on exactly the same day). Smaller organizations, such as individual churches and voluntary associations, maintained their own annual calendars. Individual families kept track of their own special days, such as when to make their annual offering to the family *genius*. Within a city or town, one might easily witness the commemoration of several annual festivals each month, whether one participated in them or not.

For much of the twentieth century, scholars of religion tended to explain festivals according to the framework developed by Mircea Eliade, a professor at the University of Chicago. Eliade was himself a fascinating character, a member of the Romanian Iron Guard who ended up abandoning his native country for America after World War II. In any event, according to Eliade, we live primarily in "profane," or ordinary, time. Each moment is like every other undifferentiated moment. Since archaic times, we have remained trapped in history, alienated from the more organic and connected way that our ancestors lived. Yet we strive to return to that true, integrative "Reality." Festivals are our way of briefly tapping into that Reality to reconnect and rejuvenate. At their heart, these festivals, openings of the sacred into our profane time, are ritualized repetitions of basic, foundational myths. They are essentially sacred and cyclical, allowing us to tap into the more fundamental reality expressed by these myths. What makes the sacred sacred is that it is not the profane.[42]

Eliade's theories have been heavily critiqued. He waffles between understanding "Reality" as the way in which our earliest ancestors experienced the world and as something that is metaphysically Real. That is, scholars have often read him as saying that there really is a supernatural reality out there and that we strive to recover the moments that it was actually experienced by our distant ancestors. He uses several binary formulations (e.g., archaic vs. modern) that clearly flatten the many diverse ways that people have experienced and constructed time. The idea that the present and future are corruptions of a better past is also an essentially reactionary and conservative ideology that uncomfortably comports with that of the fascist groups that Eliade had joined in Romania.[43]

Yet Eliade's interpretive framework has some, albeit limited, utility for understanding how those in Late Antiquity may have experienced their festivals. For some people who observed Easter (like some of the festivals associated with Isis and Mithras) may have generated genuine feelings of connection to the idea of death and renewal. Passover could have evoked the feeling that one was "leaving Egypt," tapping back into both universal and particular narratives of enslavement followed by miraculous redemption. These kinds of emotional and mental experiences of long-dead individuals remain inaccessible to us. We can be relatively certain, though, that people experienced these festivals on different levels and with a wide degree of variation.

Rather than trying to list in tedious detail the many different festivals that would occur throughout Late Antiquity—for most of which, in any case, we have scant evidence—it will be more informative to examine in greater depth one striking festival, the annual festival of the Kalendae Ianuariae. In the Roman calendar, January, like every other month, began with the kalends. In 153 BCE the Romans arbitrarily chose this date as the time to install the new Roman consuls and thus the start of the new political year. By Late Antiquity, it had become a multiday festival well-known throughout the entire Roman Empire. According to the orator Libanius, writing in Antioch in the mid-fourth century CE, January 1 was marked by gift-giving, merrymaking, and revelry, along with the necessary sacrifices. The second day, he continues, people tended to stay home and treat their slaves and students gently. The third day was historically the most important one from the perspective of the imperial authorities, for it was when each Roman city, settlement, and army camp renewed its *vota publica*, vows of solidarity with the empire and emperor, with sacrifices.

The rabbis too were familiar with the Kalendae Ianuariae, one of the few Roman holidays they mention by name. It was, in their opinion, so tainted with idolatry that for the three days before and during it (and some say three days after) Jews should have no business dealings with Gentiles, for fear that they would use the goods or money acquired from them in their celebrations. The rabbis give two explanations for the origin of the Kalendae Ianuariae. The first is that it was the day that Adam realized with relief, after experiencing the winter solstice and its shortening days for the first time, that the days were getting longer again. The second explanation goes back to Roman history, as imagined by the rabbis. The Roman and Egyptian armies, locked in a consuming war, decided to settle their differences in favor of the side whose general killed himself. The Roman general Januarius, who was old and promised that his sons would get great honors, killed himself, and the Romans thereby prevailed. This explanation had the advantage of explaining why the next day, January 2, was subdued—it was a "black" day due to the mourning that followed Januarius's suicide.[44]

Here it is worth briefly returning to Eliade. When the rabbis tried to figure out the origins of the Kalendae Ianuariae, one of their explanations was very Eliadean: the festival evokes the beginning of cyclical time. Yet there is a bizarre twist to this interpretation. The rabbis are not justifying the celebration of the Kalendae Ianuariae by recourse to a myth of origins not known to the Romans; they are trying rather to recover, incorrectly, what the Romans are thinking. Lest one think that they could not imagine a holiday that was not attached to a primal moment, they without a beat offer a second justification, this one grounded in a historical military victory. The rabbis could imagine different rationales for festivals, all of which they treated equally. The question of no interest to them, of course, was how the Romans themselves actually saw their own holiday.

The Christian bishops, unlike the rabbis, were perfectly aware of the real meaning of the Kalendae Ianuariae—it was a holiday, after all, that most of them celebrated while growing up. This, however, made them like it even less than did the rabbis. In 404 CE, when January 1 fell on a Sunday, Augustine gave a *three-hour*-long sermon condemning the Kalendae Ianuariae; its length might have been intended to give his congregants less chance to mingle and drink with the "pagans." Instead of feasting and exchanging gifts, he says, Christians should be fasting—precisely the thing that they refused to do because it was the holiday of Kalendae Ianuariae. The truth, though, is that Augustine barely had enough material to preach specifically on the Kalendae Ianuariae. Rather, the holiday became an occasion to rail against all that was bad with paganism, idolatry, and assorted heresies. The Kalendae Ianuariae became not just one of many holidays on the Roman calendar but the pagan holiday par excellence, one that represented all of paganism. Augustine was only one of many bishops who inveighed against Christians participating in the Kalendae Ianuariae, almost certainly because many did throughout antiquity.[45]

The example of the Kalendae Ianuariae is intriguing because it illustrates many of the issues involved in "sacred time," especially as celebrated communally and ritually. Festivals, then and today, serve many functions. They can, like the Kalendae Ianuariae or Independence Day in the United States, be used to reinforce a shared national identity. As many scholars have suggested, the sociality and conviviality of festivals are essential, as one of their primary functions is to reinforce social bonds. The games and races of the Kalendae Ianuariae (or the parties of today's New Year's Eve) are an essential part of it, not an afterthought—festivals are by their very nature shared public marks of time. Yet despite Libanius's playing down of this fact, the core ritual at the heart of the festival is sacrifices, as the rabbis and bishops were only too aware and eager to emphasize. Any time was a good time to venerate the gods, but some times were better than others, at least for venerating certain gods in certain places and ways. It is the rabbis, with their incomplete knowledge (or perhaps willful ignorance) of Roman customs who drive this point home in their discussion. Clearly, there must be a reason behind both the timing and name of the Kalendae Ianuariae. The rabbinic discussion connects the holiday at once to a shared human experience at the beginning of time and to a particular (fictive) event in Roman history. Is the Kalendae Ianuariae really a festival that can universally be celebrated by all (and, in fact, the rabbis go on to argue about whether the prohibition of dealing with those who celebrate the Kalendae Ianuariae applies to all non-Jews, or only those who actively sacrifice), or is it a particularly Roman festival?[46]

A second-to-third-century inscription from Hierapolis, in Asia Minor, also illustrates the complexity of how individuals experienced sacred time. A man named Publius Aelius Glykon Zeuxianos Aelianus and his wife put up a limestone sarcophagus for them and their children. Glykon's name, along with that of his wife, Aurelia Amia, daughter of Amianos son of Seleukos, already hint at a complicated, but far from unique, combination of Greek and Roman identities. Neither of the names, though, suggests that they were Jewish, and the name Zeuxianos might indicate a continuing affinity to Zeus. Yet Glykon tells us in the Greek inscription on his tomb that he left two endowments. One is to the association of "purple-dyers" (probably a trade group dealing with the dyeing of materials for the clothes of the aristocracy), the other to the association of carpet-weavers. Interest from the endowment of the purple-dyers is to be distributed to its members each year "in the seventh month during the festival of Unleavened Bread." The interest from the endowment of the carpet-weavers is to be divided, with half distributed to its members on the "festival of Kalends on the eighth day of the fourth month and half during the festival of Pentecost." It is likely that the "festival of Unleavened Bread" is Passover, and that Pentecost is the Jewish holiday of Shavuot. Clearly, he is using a calendar that counts September as its first month; such a calendar could be the Jewish lunar calendar or a local, probably lunar, civic calendar. The reference to the "festival of Kalends on the eighth day of the fourth month" adds a further layer of confusion. January should be the fifth month in a calendar that begins in September, and it is unclear why kalends should be celebrated on the eighth day, not to mention whether it is a solar or lunar month. It seems unlikely but it is at least possible that the confusion was deliberate, an attempt by Glykon and Amia to assert a complex identity in which they were not forced even to choose a single understanding of sacred time.[47]

Growing up in a Jewish family in a largely Catholic town, my experience of Christmas was oppressive. It marked my difference. The omnipresent Christmas music and decorations, followed by the general closing-down of all stores on Christmas Day itself, I experienced as a sign that I did not belong. For my friends, it was all about the presents. Most of their parents, I am relatively certain, had mixed experiences of the holiday, but few saw it as a particularly auspicious time to appeal to God.

My own experience of Christmas has changed over the years, particularly now that I live in a mixed neighborhood that has a healthy Jewish presence. I still do not like the music on the radio, but I welcome the lights and decorations. Roving groups of young carolers make me smile. Before COVID-19, I liked to wander in the malls a bit during the season, just to experience the energy and bustle; maybe I will again one day, if the malls survive. Christmas Day feels to me much like a Sunday, although with fewer options for entertainment. In general, I enjoy the conviviality, even if I do not actively participate in it.

A person's experience of a festival, whether they participate in it or not, can be complex. It also need not be static. Festivals tend to stick (although it is interesting to trace how and why some do not), and thus the Kalendae Ianuariae morphed into our generally more secular New Year's Day. I suspect that in Late Antiquity, like today, the narrowly "sacred" aspect of a festival—that it is an auspicious time to communicate with deities—usually played a secondary role in people's observance of it. In a sense, and counterintuitively, they are so multidimensional and often so laden with ritual that one particular aspect cannot shine forth prominently. Especially when there are public games, free food, or dinner to prepare for the extended family.

In the fifth century and beyond, Christian leaders grew increasingly wrought over the nature of a distinctively Christian rhythm of time. They had turned their gaze away from the Jews, who continued to maintain their own distinctive calendar alongside other civic ones, and toward the tenacity of the Roman calendar. To their chagrin, they could make few inroads into Christian celebrations of traditional Roman holidays, even if these celebrations were empty of veneration of the traditional gods. New distinctly Christian festivals that revolved around the growing cult of the martyrs flooded the calendar—"hardly a day can be found in the circle of the year on which martyrs were not somewhere crowned," Augustine wrote—yet they did not displace the traditional holidays. They did slightly better when it came to encouraging Christians to use different, nonplanetary (and thus divine) names for the days of the week, but even there they fell far short of victory. Common practice and tradition, perhaps revalued, won over theology.[48]

Epilogue

THIS BOOK is a descriptive history that seeks to reframe the way in which we see the ancient world. Shifting our frame of reference from religious groups, identities, and institutions to the actual individuals who sought to deepen their relationships with supernatural beings to survive in a harsh and unforgiving world can open for us new ways of seeing the past. These relationships and the sophisticated strategies that people used to maintain them were neither "superstitious" nor "religious," at least in the way we normally use and understand those terms. They were part and parcel of living in an enchanted world, inextricable from the quotidian warp and woof of getting by in the world.

Histories are not written in a vacuum, and it would be naive to think that I was randomly drawn to these particular questions and approaches. I have always tried to bring to my source material an open, critical, and curious mind, willing to go wherever it took me. But I also recognize that I set out on this intellectual journey because I found something unsatisfying in previous histories. I honestly cannot say whether this dissatisfaction sprung from "purely" intellectual reasons or from a wider, more emotionally and psychologically motivated set of concerns. I can say that writing this book has helped me to see features of my own life and the communities in which I live with a new perspective.

I teach a class at Brown University called Happiness and the Pursuit of the Good Life, which brings positive psychology into conversation with religious thinkers. The goal of the class is to help students develop some tools for constructing for themselves a life of meaning and purpose after college. The class is huge, and I regularly turn away over a hundred students each semester.

I would like to think that the reason for the extraordinary demand for this course is that I am known as a skilled and loved teacher. I would be fooling myself, though. Classes similar to mine are increasingly taught at colleges across North America, and they all face more demand than they can accommodate. The class is popular because it strikes a chord with undergraduates, especially seniors who are aware of their own anxieties as they stare before them, with trepidation, at the rest of their lives.

We, as human beings, are built to be anxious, not happy. While some people are naturally happy, most of us—and I include myself in this group—muddle along, happy enough but always on the alert for things that can hurt us. A mistake, after all, can be fatal. We experience moments of great joy and moments of deep pain, but we tend ultimately to return to some genetically set mean. Anxiety and unhappiness are nothing new.

Yet there is something about the way that we live today that I think has increased these natural dispensations. We turn to science and rationalism at the expense of emotions. We value the efficiency of transactions over the humaneness of relationships. We pursue money and status at the expense of keeping families together. We create environments in which we compare ourselves to others and often feel underappreciated and treated unfairly. We increasingly live in worlds of small, ideologically consistent pockets and online echo chambers that encourage division over unity. My students are experiencing this growing feeling of alienation—magnified by their experience of the COVID-19 years—and they are frightened.

In the United States, we move consistently toward a culture that optimizes individual freedoms and economic opportunities over happiness and well-being. Maybe it is the right choice for us, but it comes at a cost that is all too human. Karl Marx and Max Weber long ago predicted this age of "disenchantment" and its ramifications. The accelerating march of progress, now so dramatically seen in the rise of AI, sometimes barely allows us to catch our collective breath and consider where we are going, why we want to go there, and whether we really want to go there after all. This is, of course, very hard to do as a collective, but it might be a bit easier to do as individuals.

Religious thinkers, and more recently scientists, have thought hard about the remedies to our anxieties. They tend to be remarkably simple: good relationships, feeling and expressing love and gratitude, and an ability to perceive challenges as opportunities. A sense of purpose, reinforced with meaningful work, also seems to help. Not terribly profound advice, but time-tested. The big question is not what we should strive for but *how* we might do so, especially when facing the stiff resistance of our own culture.

This book does not directly answer that question, but it does point a way. We have traveled back to a period normally known for its rigidity and intolerance as religious groups crystallized and fought each other, with sometimes fatal results. This story has many variations, but nearly all of them come back on some level to conflict. And in telling that story—again, and again, and again—we make it seem true and natural. The very story confines our ability to imagine a different world.

I have sought to tell a different story here, one that respects difference but foregrounds our shared fears and hopes, as human beings. The world of Late Antiquity was an enchanted one, one that was filled with invisible beings and forces that we could not control. To get by well in the world required the continual and careful cultivation of relationships both with other people and with these beings. Alone, one could not go far.

Progress has brought us magnificent achievements, and I would never want to live in the world that we have been exploring in these pages. But this exploration can show us alternative ways of being in the world. One does not need to be "religious" to think that there is more to the world than we can see and to feel a deeper sense of humility and gratitude. We can always be reminded that relationships need constant attention and cultivation and that any interaction—even some of the most transactional—can be made more human. Most of all, though, we can, and should, always remember that despite the varieties of labels that we apply to ourselves and others—national, ethnic, racial, political, religious, orientational—we share more than we don't. We need not love, or even like, those around us to strengthen our sense of empathy and to recognize that people come as frail individuals, not as representatives of a class or group. When we see people that way it can help us to be just a bit more as we wish to be. And that, maybe, is a move in the right direction.

ACKNOWLEDGMENTS

THIS BOOK has been long in the making. Along the way, I have incurred more debts than I can repay. This listing of thanks is incomplete and insufficient, but I hope it can serve as a token of my sincere gratitude.

This project was completed over three sabbaticals. These have been generously supported by Brown University and the Cogut Institute of the Humanities, where I also received some early feedback. I received additional support from a John Simon Guggenheim Foundation Fellowship, a National Endowment for the Humanities Public Scholars Fellowship, a Fulbright Scholars Fellowship, and the W. F. Albright Institute Seymour Gitin Distinguished Professorship. At Brown, research funds from the Program in Judaic Studies, the Office of the Vice President of Research, the Department of Religious Studies, and the Dorot chair have also been invaluable for my research and preparation of this manuscript.

For as long as I have been working on this book, I have also been directing the digital project *Inscriptions of Israel/Palestine* (http://inscriptionsisraelpalestine.org), or *IIP*. The intent of *IIP* was always to develop a way to utilize the diverse epigraphic material from Israel/Palestine, and it was invaluable to me throughout this project. This could not have been accomplished without the dedicated work of Gaia Lembi, Elli Mylonas, Charles Pletcher, Christine Roughan, and Christopher Zeichman, among others, and funding from the Goldhirsh-Yellin Foundation.

I have presented sections of this book to colleagues at Brown, at the University of Illinois Urbana-Champaign, and in the LEM (Laboratoire d'Études sur les Monothéismes) Groupe de Recherche en Études Juives in Paris. My sincere thanks to my hosts and to the participants of these sessions for their feedback.

While writing this book I repeatedly came up against questions for which I needed expert assistance. Over the years I annoyingly peppered many of my colleagues with requests that were either odd and out of context or stunningly stupid. In every case, though, they replied with patience and grace. I want especially to thank Yonatan Adler, John Bodel, Daniel Boyarin, Susan Ashbrook Harvey, Eric Orlin, Jeffrey Rubenstein, Michelle Salzman, and Zeev Weiss for sharing their expertise. Rubina Raja and Jörg Rüpke invited me to participate in a series of workshops on lived ancient religion that fundamentally shaped my thinking and this book. John Landry was exceptionally generous with his editorial advice.

Librarians have been equally helpful and patient with me. The Brown University Library supplied hard-to-find materials in a timely manner during a global pandemic. The librarians at the National Library of Israel, the W. F. Albright Institute, the American Academy in Rome, and the Vatican Library were also of great assistance.

My editor at Princeton University Press, Fred Appel, has supported this project from an early stage, with patience and sound advice. The Press's two anonymous referees offered critical advice that has greatly improved this book.

I am, as always, so grateful to my family, who have patiently encouraged me during this journey. I thank, with love, my mother, Felsa Satlow, and my siblings Vicki and Lester and their families. In her professional role as an international literary agent, Vicki has been extraordinarily generous with her advice and representation. My children, Daniel (and his wife Avital), Penina (and her husband Jeremy), and Jeremy have been sources of boundless amazement, pride, and good cheer. My wife, Jacqueline, remains my center and fulcrum. Without her, there is no telling in what dysfunctional direction I would have been flung.

I was in Italy in the throes of writing this book in the fall of 2023 when we learned of the massacre of October 7. That horror—and the knowledge as I write this that many victims remain captive in Gaza—has stayed with me every day since then.

"May we see the day when war and bloodshed cease, when a great peace will embrace the whole world."

ABBREVIATIONS

CIIP *Corpus Inscriptionum Iudaeae/Palaestinae : A Multi-lingual Corpus of the Inscriptions from Alexander to Muhammad,* edited by Hannah Cotton, Eran Lupu, Marfa Heimbach, Naomi Schneider, Jonathan Price. Berlin: De Gruyter, 2010-

CIL *Corpus Inscriptionum Latinarum.* Berolini: Apud G. Remerum, 1862-

CJ *The Codex of Justinian: A New Annotated Translation with Parallel Latin and Greek Text,* edited by Bruce W. Frier, based on a translation by Fred H. Blume. 3 vols. Cambridge: Cambridge University Press, 2016

CTH *Codex Theodosianus,* edited by Th. Mommsen and P. M. Meyer. Berlin, 1905

IEPH *Die Inschriften von Ephesos,* edited by Hermann Wankel. 8 vols. Bonn: Habelt, 1979–84

IIP *Inscriptions of Israel/Palestine,* edited by Michael L. Satlow. 2002–. http://inscriptionsisraelpalestine.org

IJO *Inscriptiones Judaicae Orientis,* edited by David Noy, H. Bloedhorn, and Alexander Panayotov. 3 vols. Tübingen: Mohr Siebeck, 2004

JIEW *Jewish Inscriptions of Western Europe,* edited by David Noy. 2 vols. Cambridge and New York: Cambridge University Press, 2005

P. Papyrus (the precise editions can be found in the "Checklist of Editions of Greek, Latin, Demotic, and Coptic Papyri, Ostraca, and Tablets" on Papyri.info: https://papyri.info/docs/checklist)

PSI *Papiri della Società Italiana,* https://psi-online.it/

SEG *Supplementum Epigraphicum Graecum*

NOTES

Introduction

1. Kotansky 1994, no. 18. The amulet does not mention the client's gender, but it was found in a grave with a female skeleton. It is uncertain whether "elephantiasis" (as it is written in Greek on the amulet) is equivalent to the disease that we call by that name.

2. Meyer and Smith 1999, no. 78 (=British Museum 10376).

3. Overview of "lived religion": Knibbe and Kupari 2020. The term "before religion" (Nongbri 2013) is also evocative in this respect.

4. "Age of anxiety": Dodds 1965.

5. Late Antiquity: P. Brown 1971; James 2008.

6. Rabbis' condemnation: Stuart Miller 2006. John Chrysostom: Wilken 1983. Method: S. Schwartz 2001, 2–3. Transformation of alms: Satlow 2010.

7. Religious borders: Boyarin 2004. Christian identity: Schott 2008, 1–9.

Chapter One: Imagining Late Antiquity

1. Cities: Liebeschuetz 2001; Humphries 2019.

2. Market days: de Ligt 1993, esp. 199–240; Mishnah *Megillah* 4:1. Public edicts: Begio 2016.

3. Late Antique coinage: S. Moorhead 2012.

4. "Be wary": Mishnah *Pirke Avot* 2:3. Arbitration: Gagos and van Minnen 1994, 30–46.

5. Country temples: *Codex Theodosianus* (ed. Mommsen and Meyer 1905; hereafter *CTh*) 16.10.16. Law of 408: *CTh* 16.10.19.1 (trans. Pharr 1952, 475).

6. Religious violence: Drake 2011.

7. Overview of education: Morgan 1998, 25–49.

8. Bathhouses: Maréchal 2020. Prayer: Babylonian Talmud, *Berakhot* 60a.

9. Blues and Greens: Alan Cameron 1976, with Whitby 2009.

10. Tertullian: trans. Glover 1966, 253–255. Rabbis: Yadin-Israel 2006.

11. Churches: Caseau 2022b. Synagogues: Hachlili 2014; Sivertsev 2024.

12. Processions: Brubaker and Wickham 2021.

13. On the smell of tanneries and other installations: Bartosiewicz 2003.

14. Burial and religious communities: Rebillard 2009, 13–36.

15. Slaves: Sommar 2020, 64–106.

16. Boethius: J. Moorhead 2009, 13–33.

17. Families: Nathan 2000.

Chapter Two: Religion and Identity in Late Antiquity

1. Minorca: Severus, *Letter on the Conversion of the Jews* 13 (ed. Bradbury 1996); Kraemer 2020, 43–74. France: Gregory of Tours, *History of the Franks* 5.11 (*distructamque a fundamentis*); E. Rose 2002. Laws: *CTh* 16.8.9; 16.8.20. Jewish violence: Horowitz 2006.

2. Christian violence: Gaddis 2005, 151–207; Dijkstra 2015. Exaggeration: Bremmer 2014.

3. Mason 2007; D. Schwartz 2007; S. Schwartz 2011; Satlow 2013; Boyarin 2018.

4. Erasure of Jews from the New Testament: Reinhartz 2014.

5. Jews and ethnicity: Cohen 1999; Gruen 2020. Stereotypes of Jews: Feldman 2001.

6. Theory of ethnicity: Barth 1969; Pohl 1998; J. Hall 2002. Free to present themselves: Cohen 1993. Isaac: *Inscriptions of Israel/Palestine* (Satlow 2002–; hereafter *IIP*) BETH0079. Siburesians: *Jewish Inscriptions of Western Europe* (Noy 2005; hereafter *JIEW*) 2, no. 527.

7. *Ioudaios*: *JIEW* 2, no. 567.

8. Ethnicity and religion: Millar 1998.

9. Cicero: *Pro Flacco* 69. Barbarians: Geary 1999.

10. Julian: *Against the Galileans* 306B (trans. Wright 1923), 3:407.

11. On this passage in context: Finkelstein 2018, 60–63.

12. Ethnic reasoning: Buell 2005. Jewish, Christian, Greek: Clement of Alexandria, *Stromata* 6.39.4, 41.2, 6. Anonymous letter: *Epistle to Diognetus* 5.4–9.

13. Augustine: Rebillard 2015.

14. Syrians to the Romans: Millar 1998; Andrade 2013, 125–147. Syriac Christian identity: Andrade 2019, 163–165.

15. Letter: Eusebius, *Life of Constantine* 4.13. Authenticity: Hall and Cameron 1999, 17–19, 313–314; Gross 2021. Identity and persecution: K. Smith 2016, 116–124, 152–153; Gross 2021.

16. Uncle-niece marriage: 2022 Rhode Island General Laws, Title 15, section 15-1-4; 305 N.Y. 486, 114 N.E.2d 4.

17. Antiochus's decrees: Mittag 2019 for overview of sources and debate.

18. Jerusalem tax: Mandell 1984 for review of evidence, even if her conclusions are not convincing. Tax: Goodman 1989.

19. Cassius Dio: *Roman History* 37.17.1. Domitian: Suetonius, *Domitian* 12.2. In general, see Goodman 1989.

20. Proselytes: Schremer 2012. Matrilineal principle: Cohen 1985.

21. Patriarchate: L. Levine 1979. Money: *CTh* 16.8.14 (399).

22. Summary of legislation: Linder 2006, 161–168.

23. *Religio*, *superstitio*, and *secta*: Linder 2006, 148–149. Law: *CTh* 16.8.8, on which see also Rotman 2021.

24. Knipfing 1923, no. 1, pp. 363–364 (=Papyrus [hereafter P.] Berlin, no. 124).

25. Decian persecution: Rives 1999.

26. Forged documents: Cyprian, *Epistle* 30. Decree of 305: Eusebius, *Martyrs of Palestine* 3.1, on which also see de Ste. Croix 1954. Martyrdom: Moss 2012.

27. Observer of traditional cults and Christians: *CTh* 12.1.112. Jews and debts: *CTh* 9.45.2.

28. Catholic: *CTh* 16.1.2 (380). Montanists: *CTh* 16.5.57 (415).

29. Bankers: *Papiri della Società Italiana* (hereafter *PSI*) XII 1265 (ed. Harland, Kloppenborg, and Ascough 2011, no. 248 = 3:518–524). Dionysian initiates: *Die Inschriften von Apameia (Bithynien) und Pylai* (Corsten 1987), 103 (ed. Harland, Kloppenborg, and Ascough 2011, no. 100 = 2.55–60). Donkey sacrifice: *Supplementum Epigraphicum Graecum* (hereafter *SEG*) 41:1612 (ed. Harland, Kloppenborg, and Ascough 2011, no. 281 = 3:503–506, dated 324 CE from Upper Egypt). Gladiators: Phillippi II 142/G562 (trans. and ed. Harland, Kloppenborg, and Ascough 2011, no. 70 = 1:330–332). More generally, see S. Wilson 1996.

30. Mithraism: Clauss 2000.

31. Initiation: Beck 2006, 41–44. Social hierarchies: Clauss 2000, 39–41. Quote: Beck 1996, 178. See also Gordon 1972.

32. Multiple identifications: Harland 2009, 156–157.

33. Cult of Theos Hypsistos as monotheists: Mitchell 1999, 2010 (with catalogs). Compare Belayche 2011.

34. Association with Jews: Cohen 1999, 140–174. God-fearers: Kraemer 2014. Donor list: Reynolds and Tannenbaum 1987.

35. Rabbinic conversion ceremony: Cohen 1999, 198–238; Lavie-Levkovitch 2018, esp. 25–79, 197–214. Like an Israelite: Babylonian Talmud, *Yevamot* 47b. Intermediate position: Palestinian Talmud, *Bikkurim* 1:4.

36. Catalog of inscriptions: Figueras 1990; Horbury 1997. Declaration of pride: J. Price 2023.

37. Voluntary associations: McCready 1996. Inscription: Wischmeyer 1980, quote from line 11.

38. Overview of development of Christian clergy: Torjesen 2008.

39. Relations between Jews and Christians: Kraemer 2023.

Chapter Three: Belief and Bureaucracy

1. Fears 1981, 8.

2. Jupiter Feretrius: Springer 1954; Jupiter Heliopolitanus: Winnefeld 1914; Fleischer 1973, 326–369. Overview: Wissowa 1902, 113–141.

3. Assimilation of gods: Avi-Yonah 1952.

4. Some rulers, such as Antiochus IV and Caligula, introduced cult statues into the Jewish temple in Jerusalem, probably assuming (wrongly and tragically) that the Jews would simply assimilate these divine manifestations to their own god. See Bilde 1978. Varro: quoted by Augustine, *de Consensu Evangelistarum* I, 22:30, and others (see Stern 1974–94, 1:209–211).

5. Divine names in the Bible: M. Segal 1955; M. Rose 1992; Ben-Sasson 2019, 67–124. A full survey is a desideratum.

6. Epithets for god and Jesus: Murray 1975, 354–363; M. Harris 1992.

7. Association of Sol with Jupiter: *Historia Augusta*, Elagabalus 1.5; Sunday: Eusebius, *Life of Constantine* 4.18; *CTh* 2.8.1. Sun as state god: Wallraff 2001. Constantine's "conversion": Drake 2006. It is possible that some Jews in Late Antiquity did conflate Sol Invictus with YHWH. See Friedheim 2009.

8. Roman Forum: Watkin 2009, 11–73; Gorski and Packer 2015; Kalas 2015, 1–22. Forums in other cities: e.g., Sepphoris (Avi-Yonah 1961; Z. Weiss 2019, 95, 97); Sardis (Yegül 1987, 50); and, of course, Pompeii, although for a slightly earlier period (Ball and Dobbins 2013). Power of statues: Mylonopoulos 2010, 1–19.

9. Last Roman Forum: Dark and Harris 2008. Temples to churches: Bagnall 2008.

10. Square: Mishnah *Ta'anit* 2:1; D. Levine 1999, 33–39.

11. Quote from Babylonian Talmud, *Bava Batra* 16a (Reish Laqish), and see also Targum Pseudo-Jonathan to Genesis 3:6; evil inclination as a figure: Rosen-Zvi 2011, 36–43; confusing Satan: Babylonian Talmud, *Rosh HaShanah* 16b; Satan as a woman: Babylonian Talmud, *Qiddushin* 81a; Yom Kippur: Babylonian Talmud, *Nedarim* 32b; Satan's angels: Tosefta *Avodah Zara* 1:3.

12. Daniel Schäfer 2020, 19–24.

13. Boyarin: Boyarin 2013, 26. Akatriel: Babylonian Talmud, *Berakhot* 7a; Schäfer 1981, §597 (p. 231). David: Schäfer 1981, §125–126 (p. 62). Lesser god: Schäfer 1981, §15 (p. 9). Polemics against Metatron: Babylonian Talmud, *Hagigah* 15a; *Sanhedrin* 38b. Yakir Paz (2019) argues that Metatron only becomes important in Palestine beginning in the seventh century.

14. Metatron in synagogues: Magness 2005. Metatron is directly addressed in other adjurations from the Cairo Genizah. Parallels to the formula recited here are found in three other

amulets from the Genizah: TS K1.168, lines 39–45 (Schiffman and Swartz 1992, 145–147); TS Or. 1080.15.81, lines 104–111, and TS 8.275, lines 1a/19–1b/8 (Schäfer and Shaked 1994–99, 1:164, 173). Metatron's adjuration to cut down all enemies: Schäfer and Shaked 1994–99, 1:129 (an amulet), and for "opening of the heart," i.e., improvement of learning and good memory, Naveh and Shaked 1993, 162. For other occurrences of Metatron in Genizah adjurations, see, for example, Schiffman and Swartz 1992, 99; Schäfer and Shaked 1994–99, 2:33, 88, 192, 219–220, 259, 3:121.

15. Tertullian, *Against Praxeas* 2 (trans. Souter 1920, 30). On trinitarianism, see especially Coakley 2007.

16. Origen, *Contra Celsum* 8.2; Wilken 1984, 176–179; Burnett 2021.

17. J. Russell 1981, 186–218; Pagels 1995. For an overview of scholarship, see D. Brown 2011. Antichrist: McGinn 1994, 57–78.

18. Exodus 14:19–22; 2 Kings 19:35. The Book of Watchers is 1 Enoch 1–36. Dead Sea Scrolls: Collins 2000 and Wassen 2007.

19. "Great minister": Babylonian Talmud, *Hagigah* 12b; Michael serving on altar: Babylonian Talmud, *Menahot* 110a; Gabriel and Dubiel: Babylonian Talmud, *Yoma* 77a; Michael, Raphael, Gabriel in amulets: Rebiger 2018. "If a person faces trouble": Palestinian Talmud, *Berakhot* 9:1, 13a; see also Bar-Ilan 2004.

20. Creation of angels: *Genesis Rabbah* 1:1, 78:1 (all angels except Michael and Gabriel created anew every day); Rebiger 2018; gender: Ahuvia 2021. On the pervasiveness of angels in early Jewish liturgical poetry, see Lieber 2010, 227–241.

21. Jacob: *Genesis Rabbah* 12:12.

22. Numerous as we are: Babylonian Talmud, *Berakhot* 6a. Demons and protection from them: Ronis 2022, 92–127.

23. Birth of Lilith: Babylonian Talmud, *Eruvin* 18b. Lilith attacking men sleeping alone: Babylonian Talmud, *Shabbat* 151b; quote: Shaked, Ford, and Bhayro 2013, 229. Zanay is probably to be associated with Zarnay, identified elsewhere as another kind of lilith (Shaked, Ford, and Bhayro 2013, 246–247).

24. Angels and demons in the New Testament: Luke 11:14–23, 2 Corinthians 11, Galatians 1:8 (but see also Colossians 2:18); D. Brown 2011. Evagrius and Augustine: Muehlberger 2013, 29–57.

25. Augustine, *City of God* 11.9, 11.19; Cline 2011, 137–165. Cult of Michael: Bonnet 1890; Chaniotis 2008; Jeffrey 2019. Condemnation of worship of angels: Council of Laodekeia, Canon 35. Inscription: Horsley and Luxford 2016, 170–175; chancel screen: Paweł Nowakowski, Cult of Saints, E01268, http://csla.history.ox.ac.uk/record.php?recid=E01268.

26. Demon of lust: *The Wisdom of the Desert Fathers*, Anthony 22 (trans. Ward 1975, 6), Moses 1 (trans. Ward 1975, 138). Demons as material: Gregory Smith 2008. Angelic guide: Muehlberger 2013, 88–118. Use of scripture: Brakke 2009, esp. 48–77.

27. Overview of John Chrysostom's demonology: Samantha Miller 2020, 46–79. Gregory of Nazianzus: G. Thomas 2019, 87–117. Images: Strickland 2003

28. The term "Gnosticism": K. King 2003. Valentinus: G. S. Smith 2020, esp. 17–29. Manicheans: BeDuhn 1995, quote at 433.

29. Eusebius, *Demonstratio Evangelica* 4.6 (trans. Ferrar 1920, 175), and Basil: "An angel attends everyone who believes in the Lord if we never chase him away by our evil deeds" (*Homily on Psalms* 33.5, trans. Way 1963, 257). This follows a long tradition: Plato (*Timaeus* 90a) discussed the existence of divine *daimones* who serve as individual guides. See also Puiggali 1983 on Philostratus's use of the term.

30. On angels and daimones, the classic study is Cumont 1915, which focuses on the issue of Semitic influence on conceptions of angels. Compare Sheppard 1982; Cline 2011, 48–76; Horsley and Luxford 2016. "Prayer for angels" inscription cited and discussed in Cline 2011, 72–73. Inscription of men: Petzl 1994, no. 38.

31. Euhemerism: Roubekas 2017.

32. Cicero: *Pro lege Manila* and Cole 2013. Antinoos: C. Jones 2010, 75–83, and more generally: Ekroth 1999. Boin 2015 on the term *divus* applied to a Christian emperor.

33. Philostratus, *The Life of Apollonius of Tyana*, quote at 8.31. Epigram: C. Jones 1980 (with some dispute about the reading). Compare Koskenniemi 1998.

34. On authenticity of Ephesians: deSilva 2022, 11–31; Ephesians 2:19; *Martyrdom of Polycarp* 18. Origen: *On Prayer* 6. "D N" on coins: Betjes 2022, 91. There was, however, some continuing opposition to the "cult of saints": see Jerome, *Contra Vigilantium* 6–8, and D. Hunter 1999.

35. Prayer to Mary: P. Rylands 470 (dated early by Shoemaker 2016, 68–73, and later by R. Price 2019). Gospel of Mary: Tuckett 2007 (who thinks it is probably about Mary Magdalene). Ephrem: Mellon Saint-Laurent 2022. Dormition narratives: Shoemaker 2016, 100–129. Later developments: Averil Cameron 2004.

36. Cult of the saints: P. Brown 1981. Ongoing debate: Constas 2002.

37. Acts of Paul and Thecla: Bremmer 1996. Cult of Thecla: Davis 2001.

38. Coherent theology: Marmorstein 1920; Schechter 1923, 170–198; Urbach 1975, 496–508. Merit: Kasher 1986. Midrash on Jacob: *Genesis Rabbah* 77:3 (note that the "angel" here is interpreted as a foe, even as, according to one rabbi earlier in this passage, the angel [*saro*] of his brother Esau). Amulets: e.g., Kotansky 1994, no. 52, lines 71–73 (a silver amulet found in a tomb in Beirut). Formula: Rist 1938. See also Taylor-Schechter Misc. 29.4.

39. M. Rubin 2009, 177–190; Rosenberg 2016; Kattan Gribetz 2018. On later development of the cult of Rachel: Sered 1995.

40. Babylonian Talmud, *Berakhot* 18b, introduced as a tannaitic tradition.

41. Overview of rabbinic eschatology and anthropology: Urbach 1975, 214–254.

42. The idea that mourners recite the *kaddish* in order to lessen the punishment of the dead is a medieval idea: Shyovitz 2015. Necromancy: Leviticus 19:31; Deuteronomy 18:9–12. Care of the dead: Sonia 2022. Graffiti: K. Stern 2018.

43. Care of the dead: Rebillard 2009, 37–41. Voluntary associations: Van Nijf 1997, 31–69; inscription: *Inscriptiones Graecae* (1903–) X/2.1 260 (=Ascough, Harland, and Kloppenborg 2012, no. 81)—the Greek word is simply μοι.

44. Inscription: *Corpus Inscriptionum Latinarum* (hereafter *CIL*) 6.14202, translation: "Epitaph Plaque," The British Museum, accessed January 2, 2024, https://www.britishmuseum.org/collection/object/G_1867-0508-35. On the *lares*, etc.: Orr 1978.

45. Inscription: *CIL* 6.20102 (in C. King 2020, 92); on these Roman festivals, see C. King 2020, 99–105. Curse tablet: Gager 1999, 171.

46. Discussion of the souls and angels in Origen: Ramelli 2017.

Chapter Four: The Intellectuals and the Making of "Religion"

1. Ginzburg 1980.

2. Overviews: Gupta 2014; Stutz 2020.

3. Enlil: *Myth of Enlil and Ninlil*: Black 2004, 165–190. Zeus: Hesiod, *Theogony*. Baal: M. Smith 2001, 54–66.

4. Myth and ritual: R. Segal 2004, esp. 61–78.

5. Orality and myths in antiquity: Edmunds 2005.

6. Scribes in antiquity: van der Toorn 2007, esp. 51–74; Schniedewind 2019, 70–94. On literacy in ancient Israel: Rollston 2010, 127–136.

7. Copying of myths by scribes: Schniedewind 2019, 141–164.

8. Hesiod: Millett 1984; the Bible and myth: Ballentine 2015.

9. Late Antique theater: Webb 2008.

10. Jews and theater: Bloch 2017. Miletus inscription: *Inscriptiones Judaicae Orientis* (Noy et al. 2004; hereafter *IJO*), no. 37.

11. Leda and the swan: Avigad 1957, 251; Avi-Yonah 1972. Forbidding of books and Greek: Tropper 2018. Coins: Babylonian Talmud, *Pesachim* 104a. Rehov: Millar 2011. "Mere ornament": Babylonian Talmud, *Avodah Zarah* 40b; Yadin-Israel 2006. Theater: Z. Weiss 2014, 211–221.

12. Critique of statues as material: Athenagoras, *Legatio pro Christianis* 16, and Finney 1994, 15–68; Nasrallah 2010. Actors: Fowden 1978. Demeas: Horsley 1992, 108; *Life of St. Benedict*, chap. 8. In general, see Kristensen 2013, 39–106.

13. Athlete for Christ: e.g., John Chrysostom, *Vainglory* 19. Theater: Tertullian, *de Spectaculis* 3.1–5.

14. John Chrysostom: *Ad populum Antiochenum* 17.9–10, 15.1; Vandenberghe 1955; Easterling and Miles 1999.

15. John and Libanius: Sozomen, *Historia ecclesiastica* 8.2; Julian's ban: *CTh* 13.3.5; Cribiore 2013, 229–237; Cribiore 2017.

16. Rhetorical function of theater: Easterling and Miles 1999; Lugaresi 2017. *Parrhesia*: Renswoude 2019, esp. 87–108.

17. Gospels as myths: Litwa 2019, 22–45. Gnostics and their myths: Brakke 2010, 52–89. On Epiphanius: Averil Cameron 2003; Jacobs 2016, 97–131.

18. Ravenna: Cristo 1975; Herrin 2020, 63–71.

19. Chrysostom and the poor: Mayer 2009, and more generally, P. Brown 2012.

20. Hasmonean and Herodian coins: Edelman 1995. "Half-Jew": Josephus, *Antiquities* 14.403.

21. The classic study of the Dura Europos synagogue mosaics is Goodenough 1953–68, vols. 9–11. Overview of synagogue mosaics: S. Schwartz 2001, 249–261; Bowersock 2006; Laderman 2021.

22. Hekhalot and myth: Idel 1990; Arbel 2003, 51–66.

23. Book of Zerubbabel: Himmelfarb 2017. Jews were unafraid to model their notion of the messiah as a replacement for the Byzantine emperor: Sivertsev 2011, 172–212.

24. Midrash: Kugel 1986; Mandel 2017, 222–288.

25. Babylonian Talmud, *Shabbat* 88b.

26. For more on this issue: Schäfer 1975.

27. Plato, *Protagoras* 324d; *Sophist* 242c8. On Plato's more complicated understanding of myth: Brisson 1998. For the persistence of this denigration of myth: Lincoln 1999, 47–75.

28. One example of Jews having mosaics that evoke classical myths: Zori 1966.

29. Greek skepticism: Whitmarsh 2015. Epicurus: Epicurus, *Letter to Menoeceus*. Rabbis and "Epicureans": Labendz 2003; Horace, *Satires* 1.5.100–104 (trans. Kline 2005). Overview: Bremmer 2007.

30. God is identified with an eternal reason (*logos*, Diogenes Laertius 44B) or intelligent designing fire or a breath (*pneuma*) that structures matter in accordance with its plan (Aetius, 46A). Stoicism: Algra 2009; Chrysippus: Cicero, *On the Nature of Gods* 1.15. More generally on Roman rationalization of religion: Rüpke 2012.

31. On Plotinus: Porphyry, *Life of Plotinus*; Hägg 2012, 368–379.

32. Unmoved mover: Aristotle, *Metaphysics* 1072b, with the discussion in Frede 1999, 49–51. "Providentially governs": Frede 1999, 53, and Plutarch, *Moralia* (*Stoic Self-Contradictions*) 1051e–f. The "One" as "monotheistic": Kenney 1991, 91–149.

33. Plotinus, *Ennead* II.9.38–39 (trans. Armstrong 1966–1988, 259); Hinduism: Pennington 2001.

34. God in each of us: Plotinus, *Ennead* VI.5.3. Porphyry, *On Abstinence*.

35. Harmonization: Berg 1999. Sallustius: *On the Gods and the Universe*, 16 (trans. Nock 1926, 29). Theurgy: Nock 1947; Shaw 1985. Iamblichus: Iamblichus, *de mysteriis*. Proclus: Chlup 2012. "Pagan" sacrifice: Harl 1990.

36. Cynics: Billerbeck 1996. Biography: P. Miller 1983, 17–44. Embodiment of divinity: Kirschner 1984, 106–109. Protect traditional practices: Fowden 1982; Bowersock 1990, 15–28. "Conversion": Nock 1933, 164–186. Aphrodisias sculptures: R. Smith 1990.

37. Endowments at Athens: Alan Cameron 1969, 11–12. Philosophers in Late Antiquity: P. Brown 1992, 35–70; Dillon 2005.

38. Hipparchia: Diogenes Laertius, *Lives* 6.96–97. Hypatia: Rist 1965; Watts 2017. Compare G. Clark 1993, 130–138.

39. Justin: Justin, *Dialogue with Trypho*, 2–3. Augustine: P. Brown 1967, 35–39.

40. Christianity is the "true philosophy": Augustine, *Contra Iulianum* 4.72; *de vera religione* 8.

41. P. Brown 1967, 88–100.

42. Origenist controversy: E. Clark 2014, 85–158. Augustine and free will: Greer 1996.

43. Arius: R. Williams 2002.

44. Origen: Origen, *Against Celsus* 8.12. Porphyry: Berchman 2005, 46–47.

45. Reception of Philo in antiquity: Runia 2002. Rabbis: Lapin 2012, 38–63. Trope of rabbis and philosophers: Danzig 2018. Similarities and differences: Hezser 2019.

46. Respect for Judaism: Feldman 2001, 149–153; Teitler 2017, 25–26. Jewish flourishing in Late Antiquity: Kraemer 2020, 2–42.

47. Hammurabi as propaganda: Claassens 2010; Satlow 2014a, 27.

48. On the making of law in the imperial court: Harries 1999, 36–55.

49. Application of Roman law: Matthews 2000, 10–30; Harries 2003; Mantovani 2016. Gaius, Paul, Ulpian: Mousourakis 2007, 170–178. Later codification: Liebs 2022.

50. Matthews 2000, 31–84.

51. The *Codex Theodosianus* and religious identity: Salzman 1993.

52. On the limits of application: Humphries 2020. Epiphanius and heresies: Averil Cameron 2003.

53. Rabbis: Satlow 2014a, 257–275.

54. Custom and law: Moskovitz 2019.

55. Mishnah: Tropper 2010. Rabbis as jurists: Hezser 1998.

56. Balberg 2017.

57. Hess 2002, 35–59.

58. Babylonian Talmud, *Betzah* 30a.

Chapter Five: Beyond Transaction

1. Plato: *Laws* 10, 885B, 905D.

2. Meaning of popular religion: Grig 2021.

3. Magic as an analytical category: Bohak 2008, 62. See also Ritner 1993, 3–28; Frankfurter 2019.

4. Exodus 22:17 (18), Deuteronomy 18:10 (note that these exact prohibitions were violated by Hezekiah's son Manasseh in 2 Chronicles 33:6), 1 Samuel 28:3–25.

5. Mishnah: Mishnah *Sanhedrin* 7:11. Cucumber story: Babylonian Talmud, *Sanhedrin* 68a.

6. Rabbis and magic: Babylonian Talmud, *Sanhedrin* 17a; Harari 2017, 353–460.

7. Ways of the Amorites: Bohak 2008, 382–385. Women: Babylonian Talmud, *Sanhedrin* 67a; Bar-Ilan 1993; Stratton 2007, 143–176.

8. Rabbinic discussion: Babylonian Talmud, *Sanhedrin* 67b.

9. Superstitio: Janssen 1979; Gordon 2008; Mucznik and Ovadiah 2014.

10. See especially Rives 2003. Paul: Paul, *Sententiae* 5.23.17 (trans. Rives 2003, 329). Acts 8:9–24, probably written in the early second century, accuses Simon of "practicing magic" without further specification. This is clearly meant to set up the end of the story, which shows him as an insincere follower of Peter and Christ.

11. Salzman 1987.

12. Theurgy: Nock 1947, whose own categories of "magic" and "religion" could use more precision. Proclus: Sheppard 1982. Augustine: *De civitate dei* 21.6 and *De doctrina Christiana* 2.20.30, 74F. Lactantius: *Institutiones divinae* 4.29.11–16.

13. Magic: Bohak 2008, 62.

14. *Ame Ha-aretz*: Ezra 10:2; Nehemiah 10:32; Furstenberg 2013. Varro: Augustine, *De civitate dei* 6.5.

15. Ginzburg: Ginzburg 1980, 112. Lived ancient religion: Stowers 2011, 2016; Albrecht et al. 2018; Gasparini et al. 2020.

16. Overview on sacrifice: Scheid 2007. Women: Hemelrijk 2006. The literature on sacrifice is massive. See the essays in Knust and Várhelyi 2011.

17. Pompeii: M. Robinson 2002. Julian: *Against Galileans* 299B–306A, on which see Finkelstein 2018, 76–77. Jewish altar: Bowersock 1999. Transformation of public sacrifice: Stroumsa 2009, 56–83; Salzman 2011.

18. On meat generally, Chandezon 2015. Price Edict of Diocletian: Giacchero and Istituto di Storia Antica e Scienze Ausiliarie dell'Università di Genova 1974 (pork: 4.1; worker: 7.1; scribe: 7.39). Paul: 1 Corinthians 8–10.

19. Deuteronomy 12:15–16, 21–25. There are animal bone deposits at Qumran that may be signs of sacrifice, or not: Mizzi 2016.

20. See, e.g., Mishnah *Hullin* 1:1–5, 2:1–7, 3:1. Covering the blood limited to nonsacrificial slaughtering: Mishnah *Hullin* 6:1; quote: Mishnah *Hullin* 2:10.

21. Butchers: Novick 2017. Stories: Palestinian Talmud, *Sheqalim* 7:5. The term *macellum* also appears in a story that describes Moses seeing R. Akiva's fate, of having his flesh weighted out in the meat market (Babylonian Talmud, *Menahot* 29b).

22. Vegetation offerings: Schultz 2016, esp. 64 and the sources listed there. Incense offerings: Caseau 2022b.

23. Altars with Jewish names: Bowersock 1999. Incense shovels: Meyers 2018. Tithes to priests: Satlow 2014b. On the continuing role of priests (both for and against): Z. Weiss 2012.

24. Caner 2006; Caseau 2022b, 334.

25. Women in synagogues: Brooten 1982; Rajak and Noy 1993. Greek and Roman: van Bremen 1996, 142–190; Hemelrijk 2012. Christian: Krawiec 2002, 73–91 (power as ascetics); Whiting 2023 (as benefactors).

26. Jewish: Lieber 2012, 337. The domestic religious practices of Christian women in Late Antiquity are poorly understood. See Maxwell 2006; Bowes 2007.

27. Synagogue inscription: Roth-Gerson 1987, ins. 9. Christian church inscriptions often noted donations and work that was completed and the name of the presiding church authority, without mentioning the names of donors: e.g., Gregg and Urman 1996, 68–69. Female donors to churches: Whiting 2023. Foundation deposits: Ariel 1987.

28. On votive lamps: Piranomonte 2009, 202 (Roman); Wiseman 1970; Slane and Sanders 2005 (Christian); Anderson 2007.

29. Models: van Straten 1981; Schörner 2015. Christian terracotta: Caputo 2024.

30. Naveh 1979; Keegan 2014, 86–114; K. Stern 2018, 35–79.

31. Septimus 2015, 21–35; Versnel 2015.

32. Sallust: *On the Gods and the World*, 16. Pliny: *Natural History* 28.3 (trans. Rackham 1968–1984, 9.). Hymns: F. Hahn 2007. Greek: Pulleyn 1997, 39–55 (for the earlier period).

33. Prayer: e.g., Cato, *On Agriculture* 134.

34. Marcus Aurelius: *Meditations* 9.40. Proclus, *Commentary on 2 Timaeus* 206.26–214.12 (trans. Baltzly 2009, 43–50). Prayer in inscriptions: Di Segni 2017.

35. Rabbinic account: Mishnah *Tamid* 5:1. Silence in sacrifices: Knohl 1995.

36. Prayer at Qumran: Eshel 1999; Falk 2000.

37. Swartz 2012.

38. General rabbinic approach to prayer: Langer 2003; Reif 2010. Whether Jews prayed (the *Amidah*): Langer 2004.

39. Early Christian prayer: Phillips 2018. History of the Eucharist: Bradshaw and Johnson 2012, 61–136.

40. Eucharist in Late Antiquity: Sheerin 2008. Women: Ambrose, *De sacramentis* 6.17.

41. Worrell 1930; Meyer and Smith 1999, 304–310. Quote: Meyer and Smith 1999, 305.

42. Rituals: Johnston 2001. Threshold: Bohak 2008, 318–319. Note that rituals connected to the writing of Torah scrolls begin to develop at this time and may be part of the same dynamic. See *Masekhet Soferim*.

43. Jewish amulet: Naveh and Shaked 1993, no. 16. Fuzzy boundaries: Boustan and Sanzo 2017. Magic bowls: Bohak 2019.

44. For an overview, see Mace 2018 and the essays in Johnston and Struck 2005; Luijendijk, Klingshirn, and Jenott 2019.

45. For an overview, see von Stuckrad 2000. On Jewish views, see especially Rubenstein 2007.

46. Manichaeans: P. Kellis I (Gr. 82–90), on which see Teigen 2021, 248–249. Christians: *PSI* I 22–24, on which see Bagnall 1993, 274. Horoscopes and other texts from Oxyrynchus suggest astrological rituals involving texts: Possiel 2020.

47. Graf 2005, 55–60, quote at 84; Fox 1987, 208–210; Pausanias, *Geography* 7.25.10. Ticket oracles: Frankfurter 1998, 159–162.

48. This is known as the *sortes Astrampsychi*, for which there are both medieval and (sparser) ancient examples. See Browne 1974; Naether 2010, esp. 299–310.

49. On earlier Jewish sortilege: 1 Maccabees 3:48 and van der Horst 2018. Augustine: *Confessions* 8.12. Scriptural sortilege: Klingshirn 2005. Story from Talmud: Babylonian Talmud, *Hullin* 95b, and more generally, Bolz 2012, 94–122; Picus 2017, 208–253. Cf. Babylonian Talmud, *Berakhot* 55b, where Rabbi Yochanan declares that one who wakes up with a verse in mind has experienced a "minor prophecy."

50. Apuleius quote: *Metamorphoses* 9.8 (trans. Ruden 2011, 190). Talmud: Babylonian Talmud, *Berakhot* 55a–56a, and on this passage, Alexander 1995. Christian views: Neil 2016.

51. Laws against necromancy: *CTh* 9.16.5 (357 CE)=*The Codex of Justinian* (ed. Frier 2016; hereafter *CJ*) 9.18.6. Visiting cemeteries: Babylonian Talmud, *Sanhedrin* 65b (and see Babylonian Talmud, *Hagigah* 3b); Palestinian Talmud, *Terumah* 1:1; more generally, Harari 2017, 416–431. Quote: *Sefer Ha-Razim* (Margolioth 1966, 76–77), trans. Harari 2017, 283–284. Go astray: Babylonian Talmud, *Berakhot* 59a.

52. Christian text: *Martyrdom of Pionius* 13.8–9, and on this text see also E. Gibson 2001. Jews on Jesus as necromancer: Schäfer 2007, 84–85.

53. Contagion: Frazer 1994, 26 (1.3.1); See further Ackerman 1991, 46–66.

54. Divine ownership: Tosefta *Qiddushin* 1:7; Gaius, *Institutes* 2:2–5; Y. Thomas 2004; Kochen 2008, 131–142.

55. Sacred: Rives 2012 (deals with an earlier period but the same idea is likely to have continued).

56. Niches: Goodman 1990; L. Levine 2000, esp. 355. Drawings: Satlow 2021.

57. Passage: Mishnah *Megillah* 3:1.

58. Holiness catches: Palestinian Talmud, *Megillah* 3:1, 73d.

59. Relics: Wiśniewski 2019, esp. 139. Cloth: McCulloh 1976.

60. Blessings: Caner 2006.

Chapter Six: Divine Mediators

1. Locke, *Letter concerning Toleration*. See further Kateb 2009.

2. Statistics: "Occupational Employment and Wages, May 2023: 21-2011 Clergy," U.S. Bureau of Labor Statistics, last modified April 3, 2024, https://www.bls.gov/oes/current/oes212011.htm#nat.

3. Spinoza: e.g., *Theologico-Political Treatise* chap. 18 (ed. Elwes 1951, 237); Elazar 1995.

4. Roman priests: Beard, North, and Price 1998, 1:186–196. Quote: Cassius Dio 53.17.8 (trans. Cary 1917, 239.

5. Rives 2007, 43–47. Polis religion: A. Jones 1966, 227–235; Sourvinou-Inwood 2000a and 2000b. Council accepting gifts: *Die Inschriften von Ephesos* (Wankel 1979–84; hereafter *IEph*) 27, on which Rogers 1991, esp. 99.

6. Pontifex: Kajanto 1981; Dijkstra and Van Espelo 2017.

7. This is not to say that Christians were uniformly hostile to the Roman Empire even in the second and third centuries. See G. Williams 1951, 6–8, for a survey of more positive views.

8. Drake 2000, 72–110; Rapp 2005, 154–169; Kashchuk 2014.

9. Augustine: *City of God* 5.24–26, on which see Dodaro 2004, 191–194; Hammer 2021, 98–101.

10. Patriarch: L. Levine 1979. Collection of funds: Lapin 2012, 21. Quote: *CTh* 16.8.29 (trans. Linder 1987, 321).

11. Exilarch: Beer 1970, 129–141; Herman 2012, 181–209.

12. Helena: Drijvers 1992, 39–72; Hillner 2023, 204–243. Theodora: Foss 2002. Dynamics of empresses exercising power: see Holum 1989, esp. 175–216.

13. Roman priesthood: Beard, North, and Price 1988, 1:186–196; Leone 2013, 87–99 (on *flamines* in North Africa); Greek priests: Sironen 2012 (Attica only). Aphrodisias: *Inscriptions of Aphrodisias* (Reynolds, Roueché, and Bodard 2007) 4, 5, 11, 12. Female priests: Hemelrijk 2006; Whiting 2023.

14. Satlow 2014b; Palestinian Talmud, *Sotah* 3:4, on which see Dalton 2020.

15. Overview of rabbinic tithes: Satlow 2014b. Boundaries of Israel: Tosefta *Shevi'it* 4:5. Inscription: *Corpus Inscriptionum Iudaeae/Palaestinae* (henceforth *CIIP*) *5.2, no.* 7793.

16. Satlow 2014b.

17. Jewish inscriptions that mention priestly status: *IIP* JAFF0050 (Jaffa); *IIP* KSUS0001 (Khirbet Susya); "Priestesses": *IIP* BETH0068 (Beit Shearim); Brooten 1982, 73–100.

18. Jewish priests in imperial legislation: *CTh* 16.2.2, see also 16.2.4; see further Irshai 2002.

19. Ascribed and achieved: Foladare 1969. Quote: Mishnah *Horayot* 3:8. Rabbinic competition with priests: Himmelfarb 2017.

20. Quote on clergy: *CJ* 1.3.51 (trans. Frier 2016, 133). Quote on priestly privilege: *CJ* 1.7.6 (trans. Frier 2016, 27); see also *CJ* 1.8.14. For a more technical discussion, Mossong 2022, 68–175.

21. Church hierarchy and Christian priests: Brent 1999, 310–330; G. Dunn 2013. Pontifices: Kajanto 1981, esp. 39–42; Dijkstra and Van Espelo 2017 (on later use of *pontifex maximus* by the pope).

22. Christian bishops accused of accepting gifts: Caner 2021, 141–149, 201–203. Christian bishops accepting "gifts" from non-Christians to look the other way: Vedeshkin 2018. On the complicated relationship between Christian clergy and money, see Salzman 2021. Traditional Egyptian priests, when not officiating (which was most of the time), also plied their ritual skills "privately." See Ritner 1993, 232.

23. Prophecy: Nissinen 2017. Cicero: *De haruspicum responso*, on which see Beard 2012.

24. Auspices and the Romans: Rüpke 2018, 152–156. Roman decree in Egypt deeming oracular activity "superstition": P. Yale inv. 299. Fear of unofficial prophecies: Suetonius, *Augustus* 31.1–2; Howley 2017, 219–220. Female prophets: Marx 2021, 103–107.

25. Julian's signs: Ammianus Marcellinus 23.1.5–7. Constantine's vision: Eusebius, *Life of Constantine* 1.28.2, on which see the state-of-the-field review in Flower 2012.

26. *SEG* 33:1013 (trans. Schnabel 2003, 163).

27. Belayche 2001, 124–129.

28. Overview of ritual entrepreneurship, or "freelance experts": Wendt 2016, 1–39.

29. Dreams: P. Miller 1994, esp. 77–91. Dream manual: Harris-McCoy 2012, 1–43. Rich dreamer: Artemidorus, *Oneirocritica* 1.76; mother: Artemidorus, *Oneirocritica* 1.79.

30. Minor prophecy: Babylonian Talmud, *Berakhot* 55a.

31. Rabbinic "dreambook": Babylonian Talmud, *Berakhot* 55a–57b, on which see Alexander 1995; Fishbane 2007; H. Weiss 2018.

32. Samaritan: Jews following their dreams: Palestinian Talmud, *Ma'aser Sheni* 4:6.

33. Tertullian, *de Anima* 45–48 (beans at 48).

34. Christian dreams: Le Goff 1988, 193–231; P. Miller 1994, 205–249; Stroumsa 1999. Demons and dreams: Brakke 2009, 115.

35. Condemnation of dream interpreters: Hippolytus, *Apostolic Tradition* 16.12. "Command of a dream": Rives 2007, 101–103.

36. Astrology in Late Antiquity: Mace 2018, 433–436.

37. Jewish debates: Babylonian Talmud, *Shabbat* 152a–b (on which see Rubenstein 2007). Christians: Hegedus 2007, 29–193.

38. *Sefer Ha-Razim*, preface (esp. lines 5–10; ed. Margolioth 1966, 143–150). See further Janowitz 2001, 85–106.

39. Chaldean: Rochberg-Halton 1984, esp. 115. Rabbis: Harari 2017, 446–459.

40. Prohibitions: *CTh* 9.16.4 (=*CJ* 9.18.5), 9.16.8, quote at *CTh* 9.16.12 (trans. Pharr 1952, 239). Christian condemnation and accommodation: Hegedus 2007, 139–182, 197–370.

41. Greek and Roman necromancy: Ogden 2001, with comments of Graf 2006. Legal condemnation: *CTh* 9.16.5. Biblical necromancy: Sonia 2022.

42. Roman and Greek: Ogden 2001, 149–159; Preisendanz 1973–74). 4.1928–2005. Egyptian: Pseudo-Manetho, *Apotelesmatica* 4.213. Jewish: Harari 2017, 426; *Sefer Ha-Razim*, lines 176–192 (ed. Margolioth 1966, 76–77). Christian: Pseudo-Clementine, *Homilies* 1.5, *Recognitions* 2.13; *Acts of Catherine* 4 and 11 (in text B) (ed. Viteau 1897, 26, 30–33). Accusations about Christian necromantic practices: Augustine, *De civitas dei* 18.53; *Martyrdom of Pionius* 13.8–9; *Against Celsus* 2.55.

43. Bringing up Titus, Balaam, and Jesus: Babylonian Talmud, *Gittin* 56b. Rav raising the dead: Babylonian Talmud, *Bava Metzia* 17b. Skulls: Levene 2006. Generally: Grypeou 2019.

44. Ancient literacy: Kaster 1988, 35–50; W. Harris 1989, esp. 285–322. Quantification is little more than guesswork. There is no reason to think that Jews or Christians had higher literacy rates: Hezser 2003.

45. Prices: Giacchero and Istituto di Storia Antica e Scienze Ausiliarie dell'Università di Genova 1974 (wages: 7.1; pulses: 1.1; oil: 3.1).

46. Social location of scribes: Frankfurter 1998, 238–264; Stemberger 2008; de Bruyn 2017, 68–88. Female scribes: Haines-Eitzen 1998; *Life of Macarius of Alexandria* (ed. Butler 1898) 1:150. Amulet maker: Leontios, *Life of Symeon*, in Krueger 1996, 165.

47. Scribal environment: Frankfurter 2019.

48. P. Brown 1971, 1982; J. Smith 1990.

49. Brown: P. Brown 1998. Suspicion of sources: E. Clark 2004, 89–92, 106–129; Kraemer 2020, 1–42. Women: Kraemer 2011, 3–28.

50. Philostratus, *Life of Apollonius* 1.2, 5–6, 8, 9, 19; 3.38; 4.10, 25, 45; 6.27, 43; 7.26, 38; 8.5, 26.

51. Philostratus, *Life of Apollonius* 1.2, 16; 3.41; 4.18–19, 24; 6.3, 11; 7.17, 34.

52. Apollonius and Christ: Lactantius, *Institutiones divinae* 5.3; John Chrysostom, *Adversus Judaeos* 5.3; Augustine, *Epistle* 138.4. Apollonius as noted philosopher: Ammianus Marcellinus 23.6.17 (where he calls Apollonius *amplissimus ille philosophus*). Inscription: C. Jones 1980.

53. "Holy" man: Holladay 1977. Neoplatonists and holy men: Fowden 1982.

54. Jewish difference: Philostratus, *Life of Apollonius* 5.33. On the difficulty of rabbinic biography: Green 1978. Honi and quotes: Mishnah *Ta'anit* 3:8 (parallel in Josephus, *Antiquities* 14.2.1 [21]).

55. Rabbis and holy men: D. Levine 2004; C. Safrai 2004. Dosa: Babylonian Talmud, *Ta'anit* 22a–23b; Kalmin 2003, 230–231.

56. Wonder-workers: Büchler 1922, 196–264; Bokser 1985; Satlow 2024. Dialogues: Herr 1971; Mokhtarian 2012.

57. The account is found in English translation, along with a fine study, in Krueger 1996. Quote at 154.

58. Account of Theodoret: Doran 1992, 69–84. See also Frankfurter 1990 on the continuity between stylites and other, non-Christian forms of piety in Syria.

59. Clark 1998. More generally: Coon 2011, esp. 95–119; Christensen and Gemeinhardt 2019. Collection of sources: Brock and Harvey 1998.

60. Early Jewish asceticism: Fraade 1986. Anthony: Brakke 1995, 201–265. Early Christian monasteries: Elm 1994, 227–252.

61. Plato on the body: Broadie 2001, 302–308. Neoplatonists and asceticism: Finn 2009, 9–33. Porphyry: G. Clark 2000, esp. 8–15; Tuominen 2021.

62. Monasteries and wealth: Bagnall 1993, 292–303; Caner 2021, 160–191. Ascetics and power: P. Brown 1998. Violent bishops: Fowden 1978.

63. Asceticism: Elm 1994, esp. 107–136; G. Clark 2002. Martyr narratives: the *Passion of Perpetua and Felicity* is among the more famous of these accounts. See also Moss 2012, esp. 122–144.

64. Philo: Fraade 1986; Kraemer 1989. Jewish ascetics: Boyarin 1991; Diamond 2004.

65. Presbyters in Egyptian temples: *P. Fayum* 39. Inscription: *IIP* JAFF0032. Women: Irenaeus, *Haereses* 1.13.2; Epiphanius, *Panarion* 49.2.1–50. Women at Christian altars: Gelasius, *Letters* 1.13, 22, 26; Eisen 2000, 1–46; Macy 2008, 49–88; Schenk 2017, 139–158.

66. Meaning of *presbyteros*: Meier 1973. *Presbyteroi* as clerics: *CJ* 1.3.8 (385) and 1.3.2 (357) on the privileges of clergy. Sex and priests: Canon of Elvira, canon 18.

67. Legally recognized list of clergy: *CJ* 1.3.6 (note inclusion of *exorcistas*), 1.3.5 (holy virgins); inscription: *IIP* EVRO0003; women: Eisen 2000, 116–142.

68. Synagogue offices: L. Levine 2000, 412–453. Women in the synagogues: Brooten 1982; Rajak and Noy 1993. Torah niches: L. Levine 2000, 355. Role of rabbis: Lapin 2012, esp. 151–167.

69. Romanos: Krueger 2014, 29–66. Yannai: Lieber 2010, 1–20. Similar techniques: Münz-Manor 2010. Augustine: *Retractationes* 19.1.

Chapter Seven: The Spiritual Landscape

1. Babylonian Talmud, *Gittin* 56b.

2. Biblical tension: Olyan 2018. Rabbinic tension: Gafni 1997, 58–78. Through a bit of exegetical trickery, the rabbis understand Sisera's army to have been drowned. See also Judges 5:21 and 4:15.

3. Bowls at doorsteps: Hunter 1996, 226, 231. Horse race: *Sefer Ha-Razim* 3.37–43. Location: J. Z. Smith 1978, 67–207.

4. Purity texts in the Bible: Leviticus 12–15. Overview and interpretations: Milgrom 2000; Douglas 2002, 42–58.

5. Moral impurity: Leviticus 18–19; Klawans 2000, 21–42.

6. Ephesus: *IEph* 213. Letter: P. *Mich* 5 244.17. Greek temples and purity: Lupu 2009, 14–15. Roman: Lennon 2014 (although mainly the Republic).

7. Ritual baths and purity: Amit and Adler 2010. Sepphoris: B. Gordon 2018.

8. Purity and the rabbis: Adler 2014. Handwashing: Furstenberg 2010. Purity, prayer, Torah study: Tosefta *Yadaim* 2:20; Babylonian Talmud, *Berakhot* 21b; Balberg 2014, 63–92.

9. Jesus and purity: J. Dunn 2002; Furstenberg 2008.

10. Christian views of Jewish purity: Tomson 2000. Christian concerns with purity: Meens 2000. Churches and water installations: Eusebius, *Church History* 10.4.39–40.

11. Lightning strikes: Musei Capitolini NCE 13 (Rome); Vatican Museums (inv. 252).

12. Banias gushing and early use: Berlin 1999.

13. Berlin: Berlin 1999. Caesarea Philippi: Wilson and Tzaferis 2007.

14. Mamre: Sozomen, *Church History* 2.4 (quote at 2.4.3, translation from Cline 2011, 114); Socrates, *Church History* 1.18; Eusebius, *Constantine* 3.51–53. Pilgrim's account: Piacenza Pilgrim, *Itinerarium* 30. Generally on Mamre, see Cline 2011, 106–118.

15. Holiness of Jerusalem: Sivan 2008, 187–229.

16. Refurbishing: Chastagnol 1969; Foschia 2009.

17. Roman understandings: Kiernan 2020, 222–271. Quote: Minucius Felix, *Octavius* 22.5. Christian transformation: Jensen 2022, esp. 90–107.

18. Consecration: Kiernan 2020, 10–14 (Arnobius is our primary source). Deconsecration: Kiernan 2020, 257–270.

19. Cult images: Gupta 2014, esp. 707–717. Social agent: D. Collins 2008, 95. Bionic: Spivey 1995, quote at 445. Avatars: Platt 2011, 136–137 (for an earlier period, but the analogy is still suggestive).

20. Epidaurus: Tomlinson 1983, 1–33. Asklepios and Christianity: Vikan 2016.

21. Rural temples and "shrines": Caseau 2003.

22. Importance of place: Markus 1994; Frankfurter 2010. Private shrines: Bowes 2008, esp. 106–120. Votive lamps: Anderson 2007 (lamps with Christian, Jewish, and "pagan" symbols were sometimes found in the same areas).

23. Lavatories: Babylonian Talmud, *Berakhot* 62a; *Shabbat* 67a. Theaters: Salminen 2016. More generally: Ronis 2019; Briata 2022; de Bruin 2022.

24. Relics: Yasin 2009, 151–209; Wiśniewski 2019, 203–213. More cautiously, McCulloh 1976.

25. Churches and basilicas: Perkins 1954.

26. Hagia Sophia: Dark and Kostenec 2019, 23–72. Ravenna: Deliyannis 2010, 61–104, 219–275. Pantheon: Thunø 2015, 233–235. Northern Mesopotamia: Kayaalp 2021, 21–152.

27. Caraher 2003, 123–128.

28. Law and gender: Grubbs 2001. Gender separation: Mathews 1971, 130–133; Aravecchia 2022, 215–216. Female modesty: e.g., *Didascalia Apostolorum* chap. 3; Ambrose, *On Virginity* 3.3 (10, 13). See also Berger 2006, 759–761 (on modesty in mixed assemblies).

29. Eusebius: *Church History* 10.3. Legal and other conceptions: Farag 2021, 18–27, 129–156.

30. Trombley 1993–94, 1.244–245 (on the Christian deconsecration of temples); Farag 2021, 12–13.

31. Synagogue origin: L. Levine 2000, 19–159. Inscription: *IIP* JERU0591.

32. Holy place: Fine 1997, 61–126. Dura Europos: L. Levine 2000, esp. 234–239

33. Parallel with Astypalaea: Jacoby 2001. Zodiacs and astrology: Gundel 1992, 23–39.

34. Synagogues as holy in rabbinic thought: Fine 1997, 61–94. Foundation deposits: Ariel 1987.

35. Selling synagogues: Mishnah *Megillah* 3:2–3.

36. Woman and sermon: *Leviticus Rabbah* 9:9. Inscriptions: Brooten 1982, 5–100. Galleries: Brooten 1982, 103–138. Synagogues: Zangenberg 2019.

37. *Mensa*: Jensen 2008.

38. MacMullen: MacMullen 2009, esp. 98–104. Catacombs: Stafford 2022.

39. Christian care of dead: Rebillard 2009, 140–175. Cult of martyrs: R. Price 2009; Caseau 2022b, 336–338.

40. Condemnation: MacMullen 2014.

41. Augustine, *Epistle* 22.6 (trans. Cunningham 1887, 240).

42. Council of Hippo, Greek Canon 20.

43. Roman: O. Robinson 1975. Nabatean: Alzoubi and Al Qudrah 2015, 5–7. For an earlier period: Zelnick-Abramovitz 2015.

44. Mines: *CTh* 9.17.1 (340 CE). Twofold crime: *CTh* 9.17.4. Next thing to sacrilege: *CTh* 9.17.5.

45. *Manes*: C. King 2020, esp. 148–179. *Parentalia*: C. King 2020, 149–160, 187. Individuals at tombs: Lewis 2013.

46. Tablet: Faraone and Rife 2007. Tombs: Haensch 2007, 216–217.

47. Communal burials: Bodel 2008; Ilan 2011 (pointing to great variety of burial patterns). Tomb inscriptions: e.g., *IIP* JAFF0065. Marking graves: Babylonian Talmud, *Moed Qatan* 5a–6b; Palestinian Talmud, *Shekalim* 1:1. Owning the gravesite: Babylonian Talmud, *Bava Batra* 112a; *IIP* JAFF0027.

48. Talmud: Babylonian Talmud, *Ta'anit* 16a (this statement, though, is missing from the parallel at Palestinian Talmud, *Ta'anit* 2:1). Cemeteries: Babylonian Talmud, *Ta'anit* 29a. Antioch: Triebel 2006. Jewish pilgrimage: Wilkinson 1990; Boustan 2005, 151–155; Hezser 2011, 385–388.

49. Beit Shearim: Avigad 1976, 83–115 (Catacomb 20). Rome: Rutgers 1995, 50–99.

50. Gafni 1997, 96–117.

Chapter Eight: Profane and Holy Time

1. Quote: Libanius, *Progymnasmata* 13.5 (trans. C. Gibson 2008, 436–441, with quote at 441). Chrysostom: John Chrysostom, *In Kalendas* 3. See further Graf 2015, 72–76.

2. Astrological assumptions: Mace 2018.

3. Israel has no *mazal*: *Genesis Rabbah* 15:5; Babylonian Talmud, *Shabbat* 156a–b (quote on 156a), on which see Rubenstein 2007; Gardner 2008. See also Harari 2017, 445–459. Israel does have a *mazal*: Babylonian Talmud, *Moed Qatan* 28a, and on this see Elman 2004, 43–52, who understands this sentiment to come from Persian sources. Somewhat earlier, Philo, *de Vita Contemplativa* 5, condemned the worship of the planets, but this seems to have been a veiled attack on the Egyptian cult of Serapis rather than a condemnation of astrology per se, which he elsewhere writes about approvingly. See Taylor and Hay 2012. Augustine condemns astrology: *Confessions* 4.3.3–6. Julius Firmicus Maternus: on whether he was a Christian when he wrote his tract on astrology, Forbes 1970, 7–9, 20; Mace 2018, 444–450. Generally: Cumont 1915, 166–170. Ambrosiaster, *Quaestiones Veteris et Novi Testamenti* 115.1, condemns astrology as opposed to being a Christian (Nihil tam contrarium Christiano, quam si arti matheseos adhibeat curam) on account of its acceptance of destiny (see also 5, 53–62, 64–66, 83). Augustine and fatalism: *De civitate dei* 5.1.

4. Chaldeans: Babylonian Talmud, *Berakhot* 64a; Augustine, *Confessions* 4.3.5. Augustus: Barton 1994, 42–43. Imperial legislation: *CTh* 9.16.4 (357), 9.16.6 (358), 9.16.8 (370), 9.16.12 (409), 16.5.62 (425). Epiphanius, *Panarion* 16.3.1–16.4.4, similarly condemns those who believe in fate.

5. Zodiacs in Roman Palestine: Hachlili 2002. Wider discussions can be found in H. Stern 1981 and Talgam 2014, esp. 268–281, 285–287, 439–501. Epiphanius accuses the Pharisees of believing in astrology and goes through the Greek and Hebrew terms for the signs of the zodiac (*Panarion* 16.2.1–5).

6. Didactic: Englard 2000. Helios and Metatron: Magness 2005. Rina Talgam (2014, 271–272) is skeptical but also suggests that the figure is a divine being subordinated to the supreme God (compare further Goodman 2003). On the role that images may have played in antiquity generally, see P. Brown 1999, in which Brown argues that they were visible portals into the ethereal world.

7. Overview of illustrated calendars: H. Stern 1981. Codices: Salzman 1990, esp. 269–272. For examples of illustrated months in mosaics, see Åkerström-Hougen 1974, esp. 72–82 (Argos), and Parrish 1979 (Tunisia). Ein Gedi inscription: Werlin 2015, 116 (*IIP* EING0003). Timekeeping devices, particularly those that used pegs, were known as *perapegmata*. For an extensive study of them, see Lehoux 2007, esp. 12–18, 147–491 (catalog).

8. Christian: Hegedus 2007, 197–200. Jewish example: Naveh and Shaked 1993, 152–157. Liturgical poetry: Lieber 2018, 132–140. Birthdays and *genius*: Feeney 2007, 148–149; see further Censorinus 2007, esp. 12–17.

9. Inscriptions marking dates of death: Meimaris and Kritikakou-Nikolaropoulou 2005. Christian death commemorations: *Martyrdom of Polycarp* 18 (on observing anniversary of Polycarp's death); see also Jensen 2008.

10. Sacrifices: Scheid 2007, 263. Several writers note special sacrifices that were made at night, but this notice may well have been generated by the very fact that they were unusual and directed to the chthonic gods. See Pausanias, *Phocis* 38.8; Petropoulou 2008, 35–36.

11. Jewish prayer: Kimelman 2006; Lieber 2020, 483–486. Rabbinic sources assume that individuals recited prayers privately, although that might well be more prescriptive than descriptive. See Babylonian Talmud, *Berakhot* 16b–17a. Imitation of the angels: *Hekhalot Rabbati* par. 173 (trans. Davila 2013, 92–93). There are also rabbinic countertraditions in which it is the angels who are imagined to be imitating humans. See, e.g., Babylonian Talmud, *Hullin* 91b. Mika Ahuvia (2021, 176–179) also points to a fascinating collection of quasi-rabbinic traditions that obliterate the meaning of time in heaven; every single moment is holy.

12. Time for prayer: Tertullian, *de Oratione* 25; *Apostolic Constitutions* 2.59 (sec. 7), 8.34, 36; Eusebius, *Commentarius in Psalmos* 64.10. After surveying the evidence, Robert Taft (1983, 56) concludes that the "morning hour of prayer was a service of thanks and praise for the new day and for salvation in Christ Jesus. . . . And vespers was the Christian way of closing it, thanking God for the day's graces, asking his pardon for the day's faults, and beseeching his grace and protection for a safe and sinless night." He links both to the fundamental "symbol" of light. See also Bradshaw 2008, 72–92, 111–123, and Phillips 1989, which discuss the evidence for additional services.

13. Quote: Pope Leo the Great, *Sermon* 27: *On the Nativity* 7.4 (trans. Feltoe 1890, 140).

14. Quote: Babylonian Talmud, *Avodah Zarah* 3b (trans. Gribetz 2020, 208).

15. God and time: Gribetz 2020, 188–227; *Genesis Rabbah* 100:9; Yannai: Lieber 2010, 308. See further Greenfield and Sokoloff 1989; Bohak and Geller 2013, 612 (line 11).

16. Precision: Kaye 2018, 32–55; Halbertal 2020, 171–203. Adversary: *Pesiqta d'Rav Kahana* 16:5 (ed. Mandelbaum 1962, 271).

17. Sabbath: Genesis 2:1–3; Exodus 20:8–11, 23:12, 31:12–17; Leviticus 23:3; Deuteronomy 5:12–15; Jubilees 50:1–13, and see Doering 1997. Non-Jewish sources for Jewish observance: Goldenberg 1979, 430–446.

18. Angels: *Hekhalot Rabbati* par. 173; Schäfer 2009, 254–256; Hamidović 2014; Ahuvia 2021, 135–138. Philip Alexander (2017) suggests that during the rabbinic period there were those who believed that they could, and should, try to ascend to the heavens during worship, to pray with the angels. Only in the early Middle Ages did the rabbis develop a more synergistic vision that imagined prayer together with the angels.

19. Black days: Plutarch, *Lucullus* 27.7; *Quaestiones Romanae* 25; Macrobius, *Saturnalia* 1.16.21–25; Broughall 1936, 163–166; Mikalson 1975.

20. Biblical sources: e.g., Numbers 10:10, 28:11–15; Ezekiel 45:17; 1 Samuel 20:5. *Odyssey*: *Odyssey* 10.306–307.

21. Decree of 8 BCE: Sherk 1969, 328–337 (no. 65)=*Inscriptiones Graecae ad res Romanas Pertinentes* (Cagnat et al. 1901–27) 4.1211; S. Stern 2012, 274–284; Thonemann 2015. Political

implications: S. Stern 2017. Plutarch (*Caes.* 26) notes the problem of reconciling lunar and solar calendars. The calendrical situation in Egypt was confused, as with nearly all things Egyptian, with several calendars simultaneously in use. See Depuydt 1997, 9–20.

22. Official calendar: Fink, Hoey, and Snyder 1940.

23. Rabbinic: S. Stern 2012.

24. Mishnah *Rosh HaShanah* 2:8.

25. Procedure: Mishnah *Rosh HaShanah* 1:7–3:1. Exclusion of heretics: 2:1–2. Messengers: 1:3. Bonfires in beacons: 2:3. There is, in a way that is typical of the Mishnah, some slipperiness between the Temple and the later rabbinic court at Yavneh. On this slipperiness, see Cohn 2013, 73–117.

26. Palestine vs. Babylonia: Gafni 1997, 96–117; Mishnah *Rosh HaShanah* 2:8–9; Palestinian Talmud, *Sanhedrin* 1:2, 19a (parallels Palestinian Talmud, *Nedarim* 7:14, 40a, and Babylonian Talmud, *Berakhot* 63a–b); S. Stern 2019. Move to calculated calendar: S. Stern 2001, 211–275; S. Stern 2016; Macrobius *Saturnalia* 1.15.9 (the scribe Gaius Flavius released the calendar despite the Senate's objections).

27. Passover and Easter: S. Stern 2001, 155–275; Rüpke 2011, 146–174.

28. Festive meal: Palestinian Talmud, *Ta'anit* 4:5, 68b; *Megilah* 1:2, 70b. Some Greek cities and groups observed the *noumenia*, the day of the new moon. See Mikalson 1975, 14–15, albeit for an earlier period.

29. Quote: Palestinian Talmud, *Ta'anit* 1:6, 64c (with parallel Palestinian Talmud, *Pesachim* 4:1, 30d). An additional custom of women abstaining from drinking for the nine days between the beginning of the month of Av until the commemoration of the destruction of the Temple is subsequently affirmed.

30. Golden calf: *Pirke d'Rabbi Eliezer* 44.

31. Women: Golby 1998.

32. Inscription: *Corpus Inscriptionum Graecarum* iii, 5361–5362, and see the discussion in S. Stern 2001, 120–121. Epitaphs: This is particularly pronounced in the cemetery in Zoora; see S. Stern 2001, 87–97, for examples and discussion. Jewish observance of new moon: Horace, *Satires* 1.9.67–70 (although earlier); on Christian texts: Thornton 1989 (although the article is problematic).

33. Christian condemnations: Wilken 1983, 92–93; Markus 1990, 99–103. For a Christian epitaph dated by the lunar calendar, see Bultrighini 2017, 190–193.

34. Calendar layout: Salzman 1990, 33–34.

35. *Perapegmata*: Degrassi 1963, 299–311; Lehoux 2007, 217–484. Personal inscriptions: Salzman 2004, 190–192; Cassius Dio: 37.18.1–2.

36. Markets: MacMullen 1970; Ker 2010.

37. Market activities: Macrobius, *Saturnalia* 1.16.5–6, 28–35. Inscriptions/Jupiter: MacMullen 1970, esp. 336, and *CIL* 3.184. Saturn: Plutarch, *Quaestiones Romanae* 42, 275b. Meat in markets: Belayche 2007; Scheid 2012, 90–93 (albeit for earlier period).

38. Ezra, Torah, and markets: Babylonian Talmud, *Bava Qama* 82a, and more generally (if problematically), Z. Safrai 1994, 239–243. Note the parallel with Macrobius, *Saturnalia* 1.16.35, who says that market days were used to promulgate Roman laws.

39. Condemnation: Augustine, *Enarrationes in psalmos* 93.3; Salzman 2004, 192–194. Note also the continued Christian use of Roman timekeeping terminology such as *kalends* (McGowan and Bradshaw 2018, 142).

40. Sunday: Rordorf 1968. Observance of Sabbath: *Apostolic Constitutions* 5.15. Constantine's edict: *CTh* 2.8.1 (321); *CJ* 3.12.2; Girardet 2007 (who follows Eusebius in understanding the Christian nature of this act). Subsequent legislation: *CTh* 2.18.1 (386), 2.8.20 (392), 2.8.25 (409).

41. The relationship between myth and ritual (including the rituals associated with festivals) has been much debated. For a perceptive introduction, see Versnel 1994.

42. Eliade: Eliade 1961, 68–113.

43. Critiques: Leach 1966; J. Smith 1972; McCutcheon 1997, 74–100.

44. Rabbinic discussion: Palestinian Talmud, *Avodah Zarah* 1:2 (with parallels).

45. Kalends: Augustine, *Sermon* 198 alum. (=Dolbeau 2009, 26.10), fasting: par. 6. The kalends had become, for all intents and purposes, a "public festival" in Late Antiquity. See Latham 2022.

46. Anthropologists have long noted the importance of sociality in festivals and other religious rituals. For an overview and an intriguing case study, see Leal 2016. See also Beard 1987, which argues that the Roman ritual calendar very much functioned as a way to assert Roman identity.

47. Inscription: *IJO*, no. 196 (2:414–422), "Grave of Glykon with Bequest to Purple-Dyers and Carpet-Weavers" (161–250 CE), with English translation at https://philipharland.com/greco-roman-associations/152-grave-of-glykon-involving-purple-dyers-and-carpet-weavers/#:~:text=Home-,%5B152%5D%20Grave%20of%20Glykon%20with%20Bequest%20to%20Purple%2DDyers,250%20CE)%20%E2%95%91%20Hierapolis%20%2D%20Phrygia&text=Limestone%20coffin%20(sarcophagus)%20located%20on,letter%20height%3A%204%20cm).

48. Practice: Markus 1990, 97–135, with translation of Augustine (*Sermon Denis* 13.1) on 99. On the Christian use of names for the days of the week, Pietri 1997.

BIBLIOGRAPHY

Ackerman, Robert. 1991. *The Myth and Ritual School: J.G. Frazer and the Cambridge Ritualists*. Theorists of Myth, vol. 2. New York: Garland.

Adler, Yonatan. 2014. "Tosefta Shabbat 1:14—'Come and See the Extent to Which Purity Had Spread': An Archaeological Perspective on the Historical Background to a Late Tannaitic Passage." In *Talmuda De-Eretz Israel*, edited by Steven Fine and Aaron Koller, 63–82. Boston: De Gruyter.

Ahuvia, Mika. 2021. *On My Right Michael, On My Left Gabriel: Angels in Ancient Jewish Culture*. Berkeley: University of California Press.

Åkerström-Hougen, Gunilla. 1974. *The Calendar and Hunting Mosaics of the Villa of the Falconer in Argos: A Study in Early Byzantine Iconography*. Skrifter utgivna av Svenska Institutet i Athen. 4° 23. Stockholm: Svenska Institutet i Athen.

Albrecht, Janico, Christopher Degelmann, Valentino Gasparini, Richard Gordon, Maik Patzelt, Georgia Petridou, Rubina Raja et al. 2018. "Religion in the Making: The Lived Ancient Religion Approach." *Religion* 48(4): 568–593. https://doi.org/10.1080/0048721X.2018.1450305.

Alexander, Philip S. 1995. "Bavli Berakhot 55a–57b: The Talmudic Dreambook in Context." *Journal of Jewish Studies* 4(1–2): 230–248. https://doi.org/10.18647/1801/JJS-1995.

Alexander, Philip. 2017. "The Heavenly World in Relation to Human Prayer and Service from a Rabbinic Perspective." In *Gottesdienst und Engel im antiken Judentum und frühen Christentum*, edited by Jörg Frey and Michael R. Jost, 167–181. Tübingen: Mohr Siebeck.

Algra, Keimpe. 2009. "Stoic Philosophical Theology and Graeco-Roman Religion." In *God and Cosmos in Stoicism*, edited by Ricardo Salles, 224–251. Oxford: Oxford University Press.

Alzoubi, Mahdi, and Hussein Al Qudrah. 2015. "Nabataean Practices for Tombs Protection." *Mediterranean Archaeology and Archaeometry* 15(3): 1–7.

Amit, David, and Yonatan Adler. 2010. "The Observance of Ritual Purity after 70 C.E.: A Re-evaluation of the Evidence in Light of Recent Archaeological Discoveries." In *"Follow the Wise": Studies in Jewish History and Culture in Honor of Lee I. Levine*, edited by Zeev Weiss, 121–143. Winona Lake, IN: Eisenbrauns.

Anderson, William. 2007. "Votive Customs in Early Byzantine Asia Minor." *Journal of the Australian Early Medieval Association* 3: 17–27. https://doi.org/10.3316/informit.769678811100961.

Andrade, Nathanael J. 2013. *Syrian Identity in the Greco-Roman World*. Cambridge: Cambridge University Press.

Andrade, Nathanael J. 2019. "Bardaisan of Edessa and Memories of Christian Persecution in the Near East." *Bulletin of the Institute of Classical Studies* 62(1): 86–105.

Aravecchia, Nicola. 2022. "Catechumens, Women, and Agricultural Laborers: Who Used the Fourth-Century Hall at the Church of 'Ain El-Gedida, Egypt?" *Journal of Late Antiquity* 15(1): 193–230. https://doi.org/10.1353/jla.2022.0006.

Arbel, Vita Daphna. 2003. *Beholders of Divine Secrets: Mysticism and Myth in the Hekhalot and Merkavah Literature*. Albany: State University of New York Press.

Ariel, Donald T. 1987. "Coins from the Synagogue at En Nashut." *Israel Exploration Journal* 37(2/3): 147–157.

Armstrong, Arthur Hilary, trans. 1966–1988. *Plotinus, Enneands II*. Loeb Classical Library, vol. 441. Cambridge, MA: Harvard University Press.

Ascough, Richard S., Philip A. Harland, and John Kloppenborg. 2012. *Associations in the Greco-Roman World: A Sourcebook*. Waco, TX: Baylor University Press.

Avigad, N. 1957. "Excavations at Beth She'arim, 1955: Preliminary Report." *Israel Exploration Journal* 7(4): 239–255.

Avigad, N. 1976. *Beth She'arim: Report on the Excavations during 1936–1940*. Vol. 3, *Catacombs 12–13*. New Brunswick, NJ: Rutgers University Press on behalf of the Israel Exploration Society and the Institute of Archaeology, Hebrew University.

Avi-Yonah, M. 1952. "Mount Carmel and the God of Baalbek." *Israel Exploration Journal* 2(2): 118–124.

Avi-Yonah, M. 1961. "A Sixth-Century Inscription from Sepphoris." *Israel Exploration Journal* 11(4): 184–187.

Avi-Yonah, Michael. 1972. "The Leda Sarcophagus from Beth She'arim." *Scripta Hierosolymitana* 24: 9–21.

Bagnall, Roger S. 1993. *Egypt in Late Antiquity*. Princeton, NJ: Princeton University Press.

Bagnall, Roger S. 2008. "Models and Evidence in the Study of Religion in Late Roman Egypt." In *From Temple to Church: Destruction and Renewal of Local Cultic Topography in Late Antiquity*, edited by Johannes Hahn, Stephen Emmel, and Ulrich Gotter, 23–41. Religions in the Graeco-Roman World, vol. 163. Leiden: Brill.

Balberg, Mira. 2014. *Purity, Body, and Self in Early Rabbinic Literature*. Berkeley: University of California Press.

Balberg, Mira. 2017. *Blood for Thought: The Reinvention of Sacrifice in Early Rabbinic Literature*. Berkeley: University of California Press.

Ball, Larry F., and John J. Dobbins. 2013. "Pompeii Forum Project: Current Thinking on the Pompeii Forum." *American Journal of Archaeology* 117(3): 461–492. https://doi.org/10.3764/aja.117.3.0461.

Ballentine, Debra Scoggins. 2015. *The Conflict Myth and the Biblical Tradition*. New York: Oxford University Press.

Baltzly, Dirk, ed. and trans. 2009. *Commentary on Plato's "Timaeus": Volume 4, Book 3, Part 2*. By Proclus. Cambridge: Cambridge University Press.

Bar-Ilan, Meir. 1993. "Witches in the Bible and in the Talmud." In *Approaches to Ancient Judaism: Historical, Literary, and Religious Studies*, edited by Herbert W. Basser and Simcha Fishbane, 7–32. N.s., vol. 5. South Florida Studies in the History of Judaism, vol. 82. Atlanta: Scholars Press.

Bar-Ilan, Meir. 2004. "Prayers of Jews to Angels and Other Mediators in the First Centuries CE." In *Saints and Role Models in Judaism and Christianity*, edited by Joshua Schwartz and Marcel Poorthuis, 79–95. Leiden: Brill.

Barth, Frederik, ed. 1969. *Ethnic Groups and Boundaries: The Social Organisation of Cultural Difference*. Boston: Little, Brown.

Barton, Tamsyn. 1994. *Ancient Astrology*. London: Taylor & Francis.

Bartosiewicz, László. 2003. "'There's Something Rotten in the State . . .': Bad Smells in Antiquity." *European Journal of Archaeology* 6(2): 175–195.

Beard, Mary. 1987. "A Complex of Times: No More Sheep on Romulus' Birthday." *Cambridge Classical Journal* 33: 1–15.

Beard, Mary. 2012. "Cicero's 'Response of the Haruspices' and the Voice of the Gods." *Journal of Roman Studies* 102: 20–39.

Beard, Mary, John North, and S. R. F. Price, eds. 1988. *Religions of Rome*. 2 vols. Cambridge: Cambridge University Press.

Beck, Roger. 1996. "The Mysteries of Mithras." In *Voluntary Associations in the Graeco-Roman World*, edited by S. G. Wilson and John S. Kloppenborg, 176–185. London: Routledge.

Beck, Roger. 2006. *The Religion of the Mithras Cult in the Roman Empire: Mysteries of the Unconquered Sun*. Oxford and New York: Oxford University Press.

BeDuhn, Jason David. 1995. "*Magical Bowls and Manichaeans*." In *Ancient Magic and Ritual Power*, edited by Marvin W. Meyer and Paul Mirecki. 419-434. New York: Brill.

Beer, Moshe. 1970. *Babylonian Exilarchate in the Arsacid and Sassanian Periods*. [In Hebrew.] Universiṭah Bar-Ilan sidrat meḥḳarim 'a.sh. meyased ha-Universiṭah u-nesi'ah ha-rishon Prof. Pinḥas Ḥurgin zal 8. Tel-Aviv: Devir.

Begio, Tommaso. 2016. "Epigraphy." In *The Oxford Handbook of Roman Law and Society*, edited by Paul J. du Plessis, Clifford Ando, and Kaius Tuori, 43–55. Oxford: Oxford University Press.

Belayche, Nicole. 2001. "'Partager la table des dieux': L'empereur Julien et les sacrifices." *Revue de l'histoire des religions* 218: 457–486.

Belayche, Nicole. 2007. "Religious Actors in Daily Life: Practices and Related Beliefs." In *A Companion to Roman Religion*, edited by Jörg Rüpke, 275–291. Blackwell Companions to the Ancient World. Ancient History. Malden, MA: Blackwell.

Belayche, Nicole. 2011. "Hypsistos: A Way of Exalting the Gods in Graeco-Roman Polytheism." In *The Religious History of the Roman Empire: Pagans, Jews, and Christians*, edited by J. A. North and S. R. F. Price, 139–174. Oxford: Oxford University Press.

Ben-Sasson, Hillel. 2019. *Understanding YHWH: The Name of God in Biblical, Rabbinic, and Medieval Jewish Thought*. Jewish Thought and Philosophy. Cham: Palgrave Macmillan.

Berchman, Robert M. 2005. *Porphyry against the Christians*. Studies in Platonism, Neoplatonism, and the Platonic Tradition, vol. 1. Leiden: Brill.

Berg, R. M. van den. 1999. "Plotinus' Attitude to Traditional Cult: A Note on Porphyry VP 10." *Ancient Philosophy* 19(2): 345–360. https://doi.org/10.5840/ancientphil199919232.

Berger, Teresa. 2006. "Women in Worship." In *The Oxford History of Christian Worship*, edited by Geoffrey Wainwright and Karen B. Westerfield Tucker, 755–768. Oxford: Oxford University Press.

Berlin, Andrea M. 1999. "The Archaeology of Ritual: The Sanctuary of Pan at Banias/Caesarea Philippi." *Bulletin of the American Schools of Oriental Research* 315: 27–45. https://doi.org/10.2307/1357531.

Betjes, Sven. 2022. *The Mind of the Mint: Continuity and Change in Roman Imperial Coin Design from Augustus to Zeno (31 BCE–491 CE)*. Nijmegen: Radboud University Nijmegen.

Bilde, Per. 1978. "The Roman Emperor Gaius (Caligula)'s Attempt to Erect His Statue in the Temple of Jerusalem." *Studia Theologica* 32(1): 67–93.

Billerbeck, M. 1996. "The Ideal Cynic from Epictetus to Julian." In *The Cynics*, edited by R. Bracht Branham and Marie-Odile Goulet-Caze, 205–221. Berkeley: University of California Press. https://doi.org/10.1525/9780520921986-011.

Black, Jeremy A. 2004. *The Literature of Ancient Sumer*. Oxford: Oxford University Press.

Bloch, René S. 2017. "Part of the Scene: Jewish Theater in Antiquity." *Journal of Ancient Judaism* 8(2): 150–169.

Bodel, John. 2008. "From Columbaria to Catacombs: Collective Burial in Pagan and Christian Rome." In *Commemorating the Dead*, edited by Laurie Brink, Deborah Green, and Richard Saller, 177–242. Berlin: De Gruyter. https://doi.org/10.1515/9783110211573.

Bohak, Gideon. 2008. *Ancient Jewish Magic: A History*. Cambridge and New York: Cambridge University Press.

Bohak, Gideon. 2019. "Jewish Amulets, Magic Bowls, and Manuals in Aramaic and Hebrew." *Guide to the Study of Ancient Magic*, edited by David Frankfurter, 388–415. Leiden: Brill.

Bohak, Gideon, and Mark Geller. 2013. "Babylonian Astrology in the Cairo Genizah." In *Envisioning Judaism, Studies in Honor of Peter Schäfer*, edited by Ra'anan S. Boustan, Klaus Herrmann, Reimund Leicht, Annette Yoshiko Reed, and Giuseppe Veltri, 1: 607–622. Tübingen: Mohr Siebeck.

Bohak, Gideon, Yuval Harari, and Shaul Shaked. 2011. *Continuity and Innovation in the Magical Tradition*. Leiden: Brill.

Boin, Douglas. 2015. "Late Antique *Divi* and Imperial Priests of the Late Fourth and Early Fifth Centuries." In *Pagans and Christians in Late Antique Rome: Conflict, Competition, and Coexistence in the Fourth Century*, edited by Michele Renee Salzman, Marianne Sághy, and Rita Lizzi Testa, 139–161. The Wiles Lectures. New York: Cambridge University Press. https://doi.org/10.1017/CBO9781316274989.

Bokser, Baruch M. 1985. "Approaching Sacred Space." *Harvard Theological Review* 78(3–4): 279–299.

Bolz, Stephanie L. 2012. "Rabbinic Discourse on Divination in the Babylonian Talmud." PhD dissertation, University of Michigan. Deep Blue. http://deepblue.lib.umich.edu/handle/2027.42/93902.

Bonnet, Max, ed. 1890. *Narratio de Miracvlo a Michaele Archangelo Chonis Patrato: Adiecto Symeonis Metaphrastae De Eadem Re Libello*. Paris: Librairie Hachette et cie.

Boustan, Ra'anan S. 2005. *From Martyr to Mystic: Rabbinic Martyrology and the Making of Merkavah Mysticism*. Texts and Studies in Ancient Judaism, vol. 112. Tübingen: Mohr Siebeck.

Boustan, Ra'anan, and Joseph E. Sanzo. 2017. "Christian Magicians, Jewish Magical Idioms, and the Shared Magical Culture of Late Antiquity." *Harvard Theological Review* 110(2): 217–240. https://doi.org/10.1017/S0017816017000050.

Bowersock, G. W. 1990. *Hellenism in Late Antiquity*. Jerome Lectures, vol. 18. Ann Arbor: University of Michigan Press.

Bowersock, G. W. 1999. "The New Inscription from Rāsūn in Jordan." *Syria* 76: 223–225.

Bowersock, G. W. 2006. *Mosaics as History: The Near East from Late Antiquity to Islam*. Cambridge: Cambridge University Press.

Bowes, Kimberly Diane. 2007. "'Christianization' and the Rural Home." *Journal of Early Christian Studies* 15(2): 143–170. https://doi.org/10.1353/earl.2007.0029.

Bowes, Kimberly Diane. 2008. *Private Worship, Public Values, and Religious Change in Late Antiquity*. Cambridge: Cambridge University Press.

Boyarin, Daniel. 1991. "Internal Opposition in Talmudic Literature: The Case of the Married Monk." *Representations* 36: 87–113.

Boyarin, Daniel. 2004. *Border Lines: The Partition of Judaeo-Christianity*. Divinations. Philadelphia: University of Pennsylvania Press.

Boyarin, Daniel. 2013. "Is Metatron a Converted Christian?" *Judaïsme Ancien—Ancient Judaism* 1: 13–62.

Boyarin, Daniel. 2018. *Judaism: The Genealogy of a Modern Notion*. Key Words in Jewish Studies. New Brunswick, NJ: Rutgers University Press.

Bradbury, Scott, ed. and trans. 1996. *Severus of Minorca: Letter on the Conversion of the Jews*. Oxford: Clarendon Press.

Bradshaw, Paul F. 2008. *Daily Prayer in the Early Church: A Study of the Origin and Early Development of the Divine Office*. Eugene, OR: Wipf & Stock.

Bradshaw, Paul F., and Maxwell E. Johnson. 2012. *The Eucharistic Liturgies: Their Evolution and Interpretation*. Collegeville, MN: Liturgical Press.

Brakke, David. 1995. *Athanasius and the Politics of Asceticism*. Oxford Early Christian Studies. Oxford: Clarendon Press.

Brakke, David. 2009. *Demons and the Making of the Monk: Spiritual Combat in Early Christianity*. Cambridge, MA: Harvard University Press.

Brakke, David. 2010. *The Gnostics: Myth, Ritual, and Diversity in Early Christianity*. Cambridge, MA: Harvard University Press.

Bremmer, Jan N. 1996. *The Apocryphal Acts of Paul and Thecla*. Studies on the Apocryphal Acts of the Apostles, vol. 2. Kampen: Kok Pharos.

Bremmer, Jan N. 2007. "Atheism in Antiquity." In *The Cambridge Companion to Atheism*, edited by Michael Martin, 11–26. Cambridge Companions to Philosophy. New York: Cambridge University Press.

Bremmer, Jan N. 2014. "Religious Violence between Greeks, Romans, Christians, and Jews." In *Violence in Ancient Christianity: Victims and Perpetrators*, edited by Albert C. Geljon and Riemer Roukema, 8–30. Supplements to Vigiliae Christianae, vol. 125. Boston: Brill.

Brent, Allen. 1999. *The Imperial Cult and the Development of Church Order: Concepts and Images of Authority in Paganism and Early Christianity before the Age of Cyprian*. Supplements to Vigiliae Christianae, vol. 45. Leiden: Brill.

Briata, Ilaria. 2022. "Demons and Scatology: Cursed Toilets and Haunted Baths in Late Antique Judaism." In *Demons in Early Judaism and Christianity: Characters and Characteristics*, edited by Hector M. Patmore and Josef Lössl, 256–272. Ancient Judaism and Early Christianity, vol. 113. Leiden: Brill.

Brisson, Luc. 1998. *Plato the Myth Maker*. Chicago: University of Chicago Press.

Broadie, Sarah. 2001. "Soul and Body in Plato and Descartes." *Proceedings of the Aristotelian Society* 101(1): 295–308. https://doi.org/10.1111/j.0066-7372.2003.00032.x.

Brock, Roger. 2015. "Law and Citizenship in the Greek Poleis." In *The Oxford Handbook of Ancient Greek Law*, edited by Edward Monroe Harris and Mirko Canevaro. https://doi.org/10.1093/oxfordhb/9780199599257.013.15.

Brock, Sebastian P., and Susan Ashbrook Harvey. 1998. *Holy Women of the Syrian Orient*. Updated ed. with a new preface. Transformation of the Classical Heritage, vol. 13. Berkeley: University of California Press.

Brooten, Bernadette J. 1982. *Women Leaders in the Ancient Synagogue: Inscriptional Evidence and Background Issues*. Brown Judaic Studies, vol. 36. Atlanta: Scholars Press.

Broughall, M. S. 1936. "The Pattern of the Days in Ancient Rome." *Greece & Rome* 5(15): 160–176.

Brown, Derek R. 2011. "The Devil in the Details: A Survey of Research on Satan in Biblical Studies." *Currents in Biblical Research* 9(2): 200–226.

Brown, Peter Robert Lamont. 1967. *Augustine of Hippo: A Biography*. Berkeley: University of California Press.

Brown, Peter Robert Lamont. 1971. "The Rise and Function of the Holy Man in Late Antiquity." *Journal of Roman Studies* 61: 80–101.

Brown, Peter Robert Lamont. 1981. *The Cult of Saints: Its Rise and Function in Latin Christianity*. Haskell Lectures on History of Religions, n.s., vol. 2. Chicago: University of Chicago Press.

Brown, Peter Robert Lamont. 1992. *Power and Persuasion in Late Antiquity: Towards a Christian Empire*. The Curti Lectures. Madison: University of Wisconsin Press.

Brown, Peter Robert Lamont. 1998. "The Rise and Function of the Holy Man in Late Antiquity, 1971–1997." *Journal of Early Christian Studies* 6(3): 353–376.

Brown, Peter Robert Lamont. 1999. "Images as a Substitute for Writing." In *East and West: Modes of Communication, Proceedings of the First Plenary Conference at Merida*, edited by Euangelos K. Chrysos and I. N. Wood, 15–34. Transformation of the Roman World, vol. 5. Leiden: Brill.

Brown, Peter Robert Lamont. 2012. *Through the Eye of the Needle: Wealth, the Fall of Rome, and the Making of Christianity in the West, 350–550 AD*. Princeton, NJ: Princeton University Press.

Browne, Gerald M. 1974. *The Papyri of the Sortes Astrampsychi*. Beiträge Zur Klassischen Philologie, vol. 58. Meisenheim am Glan: A. Hain.

Brubaker, Leslie, and Chris Wickham. 2021. "Processions, Power, and Community Identity: East and West." In *Empires and Communities in the Post-Roman and Islamic World, c. 400–1000 CE*, edited by Walter Pohl and Rutger Kramer, 121–187. Oxford Studies in Early Empires. New York: Oxford University Press.

Büchler, Adolf. 1922. *Types of Jewish-Palestinian Piety from 70 B.C.E. to 70 C.E: The Ancient Pious Men*. Jews' College. Publications, no. 8. London: University Press.

Buell, Denise Kimber. 2005. *Why This New Race: Ethnic Reasoning in Early Christianity*. Gender, Theory, and Religion. New York: Columbia University Press.

Bultrighini, Ilaria. 2017. "Notes on Days of the Week and Other Date-Related Aspects in Three Greek Inscriptions of the Late Roman Empire." *Zeitschrift für Papyrologie und Epigraphik* 201: 187–196.

Burnett, D. Clint. 2021. *Christ's Enthronement at God's Right Hand and Its Greco-Roman Cultural Context*. Beihefte zur Zeitschrift für die Neutestamentliche Wissenschaft, vol. 242. Berlin: De Gruyter.

Butler, Cuthbert, trans. 1898. *The Lausiac History*. By Palladius. Texts and Studies: Contributions to Biblical and Patristic Literature, vol. 6, nos. 1–2. Cambridge: Cambridge University Press.

Cagnat, René, Jules François, Georges Lafaye, and Victor Henry, eds. 1901–27. *Inscriptiones Graecae ad res Romanas Pertinentes*. Paris.

Caldwell, Richard S., trans. 1987. *Hesiod's Theogony*. Cambridge: Focus Information Group.

Cameron, Alan. 1969. "The Last Days of the Academy at Athens." *Proceedings of the Cambridge Philological Society* 15(195): 7–29.

Cameron, Alan. 1976. *Circus Factions: Blues and Greens at Rome and Byzantine*. Oxford: Clarendon Press.

Cameron, Averil. 2003. "How to Read Heresiology." *Journal of Medieval and Early Modern Studies* 33(3): 471–492.

Cameron, Averil. 2004. "The Cult of the Virgin in Late Antiquity: Religious Development and Myth-Making." *Studies in Church History* 39: 1–21.

Caner, Daniel. 2006. "Towards a Miraculous Economy: Christian Gifts and Material Blessings in Late Antiquity." *Journal of Early Christian Studies* 14(3): 329–377.

Caner, Daniel. 2021. *The Rich and the Pure: Philanthropy and the Making of Christian Society in Early Byzantium*. Transformation of the Classical Heritage, vol. 62. Oakland: University of California Press. https://doi.org/10.1525/9780520381599.

Caputo, Clementina. 2024. "Christian Terracotta Figurines from el-Ashmunein in the Museo Egizio, Turin." *Rivista del Museo Egizio* 8: 36–49.

Caraher, William R. 2003. "Church, Society, and the Sacred in Early Christian Greece." PhD dissertation, Ohio State University. ProQuest. https://www.proquest.com/docview/305308513/abstract/5930870EB04949CCPQ/1.

Cary, Earnest, trans. 1917. *Roman History. Volume VI, Books 51–55*. By Dio Cassius. Loeb Classical Library, vol. 83. Cambridge, MA: Harvard University Press.

Caseau, Béatrice. 2003. "The Fate of Rural Temples in Late Antiquity and the Christianisation of the Countryside." In *Recent Research on the Late Antique Countryside*, edited by William Bowden, Luke Lavan, and Carlos Machado, 105–144. Late Antique Archaeology, vol. 2. Leiden: Brill.

Caseau, Béatrice Chevallier. 2022a. "Early Christian Rejection of Incense Sacrifice (2–5th c)." In *Sensing Divinity*. Hal-03862187. https://hal.sorbonne-universite.fr/hal-03862187.

Caseau, Béatrice Chevallier. 2022b. "Spaces of Roman Religion and Christianity in Late Antiquity." In *The Oxford Handbook of Religious Space*, edited by Jeanne Halgren Kilde, 327–343. Oxford: Oxford University Press. https://doi.org/10.1093/oxfordhb/9780190874988.013.24.

Censorinus. 2007. *The Birthday Book*. Chicago: University of Chicago Press.

Chandezon, Christophe. 2015. "Animals, Meat, and Alimentary By-Products." In *A Companion to Food in the Ancient World*, edited by John Wilkins and Robin Nadeau, 133–146. Oxford: John Wiley & Sons. https://doi.org/10.1002/9781118878255.ch13.

Chaniotis, Angelos. 2008. "The Conversion of the Temple of Aphrodite at Aphrodisias in Context." In *From Temple to Church: Destruction and Renewal of Local Cultic Topography in Late Antiquity*, edited by Stephen Emmel, Johannes Hahn, and Ulrich Gotter, 243–274. Religions of the Graeco-Roman World Series, vol. 163. Leiden: Brill.

Chastagnol, André. 1969. "La restauration du temple d'Isis au 'Portus Romae' sous le règne de Gratien." *Bulletin de la Société nationale des antiquaires de France* 1967(1): 47–55. https://doi.org/10.3406/bsnaf.1969.11709.

Chlup, Radek. 2012. *Proclus: An Introduction*. New York: Cambridge University Press.

Christensen, Maria Munkholt, and Peter Gemeinhardt. 2019. "Holy Women and Men as Teachers in Late Antique Christianity." *Zeitschrift für Antikes Christentum / Journal of Ancient Christianity* 23(2): 288–328. https://doi.org/10.1515/zac-2019-0015.

Claassens, S. J. 2010. "The So-Called 'Mesopotamian Law Codes': What's in a Name?" *Journal for Semitics* 19(2): 481–498. https://doi.org/10.10520/EJC101161.

Clark, Elizabeth A. 1998. "Holy Women, Holy Words: Early Christian Women, Social History, and the 'Linguistic Turn.'" *Journal of Early Christian Studies* 6(3): 413–430. https://doi.org/10.1353/earl.1998.0042.

Clark, Elizabeth A. 2004. *History, Theory, Text Historians and the Linguistic Turn*. Cambridge, MA: Harvard University Press.

Clark, Elizabeth A. 2014. *The Origenist Controversy: The Cultural Construction of an Early Christian Debate*. Princeton Legacy Library. Princeton, NJ: Princeton University Press.

Clark, Gillian. 1993. *Women in Late Antiquity: Pagan and Christian Lifestyles*. Oxford: Clarendon Press; New York: Oxford University Press.

Clark, Gillian, trans. 2000. *Porphyry, On Abstinence from Killing Animals*. Ithaca, NY: Cornell University Press.

Clark, Gillian. 2002. "Women and Asceticism in Late Antiquity: The Refusal of Status and Gender." In *Asceticism*, edited by Vincent L. Wimbush and Richard Valantasis, 33–48. New York: Oxford University Press.

Clauss, Manfred. 2000. *The Roman Cult of Mithras: The God and His Mysteries*. Edinburgh: Edinburgh University Press.

Cline, Rangar. 2011. *Ancient Angels: Conceptualizing Angeloi in the Roman Empire*. Religions in the Graeco-Roman World, vol. 172. Leiden: Brill.

Coakley, Sarah. 2007. "Introduction: Disputed Questions in Patristic Trinitarianism." *Harvard Theological Review* 100(2): 125–138. https://doi.org/10.1017/S0017816007001472.

Cohen, Shaye J. D. 1985. "The Origins of the Matrilineal Principle in Rabbinic Law." *AJS Review* 10(1): 19–53. https://doi.org/10.1017/S0364009400001185.

Cohen, Shaye J. D. 1993. "'Those Who Say They Are Jews and Are Not': How Do You Know a Jew in Antiquity When You See One?" In *Diasporas in Antiquity*, edited by Shaye J. D. Cohen and Ernest S. Frerichs, 1–46. Brown Judaic Studies. Atlanta, GA: Scholars Press.

Cohen, Shaye J. D. 1999. *The Beginnings of Jewishness: Boundaries, Varieties, Uncertainties*. Hellenistic Culture and Society, vol. 31. Berkeley: University of California Press.

Cohn, Naftali. 2013. *The Memory of the Temple and the Making of the Rabbis*. Divinations. Philadelphia: University of Pennsylvania Press.

Cole, Spencer. 2013. *Cicero and the Rise of Deification at Rome*. Cambridge: Cambridge University Press.

Collins, Derek. 2008. *Magic in the Ancient Greek World*. Blackwell Ancient Religions. Hoboken: Wiley.

Collins, John J. 2000. "Powers in Heaven: God, Gods, and Angels in the Dead Sea Scrolls." In *Religion in the Dead Sea Scrolls*, edited by John J. Collins and Robert A Kugler, 9–28. Grand Rapids, MI: Eerdmans.

Constas, Nicholas. 2002. "An Apology for the Cult of Saints in Late Antiquity: Eustratius Presbyter of Constantinople, On the State of Souls after Death (CPG 7522)." *Journal of Early Christian Studies* 10(2): 267–285. https://doi.org/10.1353/earl.2002.0017.

Coon, Lynda L. 2011. *Sacred Fictions: Holy Women and Hagiography in Late Antiquity*. Philadelphia: University of Pennsylvania Press.

Corsten, Thomas, ed. 1987. *Die Inschriften von Apameia (Bithynien) und Pylai*. Bonn: R. Habelt.

Corpus Inscriptionum Iudaeae/Palaestinae: A Multi-lingual Corpus of the Inscriptions from Alexander to Muhammad. 2010–. Edited by Hannah Cotton, Eran Lupu, Marfa Heimbach, Naomi Schneider, Jonathan Price. Berlin: De Gruyter.

Corpus Inscriptionum Latinarum. 1862–. Berolini: Apud G. Remerum.

Cribiore, Raffaella. 2013. *Libanius the Sophist: Rhetoric, Reality, and Religion in the Fourth Century*. Townsend Lectures/Cornell Studies in Classical Philology, vol. 63. Ithaca: Cornell University Press.

Cribiore, Raffaella. 2017. "Why Did Christians Compete with Pagans for Greek Paideia?" In *Pedagogy in Ancient Judaism and Early Christianity*, edited by Karina Martin Hogan, Matthew Goff, and Emma Wasserman, 359–373. Atlanta: Scholars Press.

Cristo, Stuart. 1975. "The Art of Ravenna in Late Antiquity." *The Classical Journal* 70(3): 17–29.

Cumont, Franz. 1915. "Les anges du paganisme." *Revue de l'histoire des religions* 72: 159–182.

Cunningham, J. G. 1887. *Augustine. The Confessions and Letters*. A Select Library of the Nicene and Post-Nicene Fathers of the Christian Church, vol. 1. Edinburgh: T&T Clark.

Dalton, Krista. 2020. "Teaching for the Tithe: Donor Expectations and the Matrona's Tithe." *AJS Review* 44(1): 49–73.

Danzig, Gabriel. 2018. "What to Say When You Don't Have a Good Answer: Rabbi Hoshaya and the Philosopher." *Revue des études juives* 177(3): 281–296.

Dark, K. R., and A. L. Harris. 2008. "The Last Roman Forum: The Forum of Leo in Fifth-Century Constantinople." *Greek, Roman, and Byzantine Studies* 48(1): 57–69.

Dark, K. R., and Jan Kostenec. 2019. *Hagia Sophia in Context: An Archaeological Re-examination of the Cathedral of Byzantine Constantinople*. Oxford: Oxbow Books.

Davila, James. 2013. *Hekhalot Literature in Translation: Major Texts of Merkavah Mysticism*. Leiden: Brill.

Davis, Stephen J. 2001. *The Cult of Saint Thecla: A Tradition of Women's Piety in Late Antiquity*. Oxford Early Christian Studies. Oxford: Oxford University Press.

De Bruin, Tom. 2022. "Demons and Vices in Early Christianity." In *Demons in Early Judaism and Christianity*, edited by Hector M. Patmore and Josef Lössl, 130–154. Leiden: Brill. https://doi.org/10.1163/9789004518148_008.

De Bruyn, Theodore. 2017. *Making Amulets Christian: Artefacts, Scribes, and Contexts*. Oxford Early Christian Studies. Oxford: Oxford University Press.

Degrassi, Attilio. 1963. *Inscriptiones Italiae. Volumen XIII, Fasti et Elogia. Fasciculus II, Fasti anni numani et iuliani, accedunt ferialia, menologia rustica, parapegmata*. Incriptiones Italiae Academiae italicae consociatae edidervnt, vol. 13. Rome: Instituto poligrafico dello stato, Libreria dello stato.

De Ligt, Luuk. 1993. *Fairs and Markets in the Roman Empire: Economic and Social Aspects of Periodic Trade in a Pre-industrial Society*. Amsterdam: Gieben.

Deliyannis, Deborah Mausk. 2010. *Ravenna in Late Antiquity*. Cambridge: Cambridge University Press.

Depuydt, Leo. 1997. *Civil Calendar and Lunar Calendar in Ancient Egypt*. Orientalia Lovaniensia Analecta, vol. 77. Leuven: Peeters.

deSilva, David. 2022. *Ephesians*. Cambridge: Cambridge University Press.

De Ste. Croix, G. E. M. 1954. "Aspects of the 'Great' Persecution." *Harvard Theological Review* 47(2): 75–113.

Diamond, Eliezer. 2004. *Holy Men and Hunger Artists: Fasting and Asceticism in Rabbinic Culture*. Oxford and New York: Oxford University Press.

Dignas, Beate, and R. R. R. Smith. 2012. *Historical and Religious Memory in the Ancient World*. Oxford: Oxford University Press.

Dijkstra, Jitse H. F. 2015. "Religious Violence in Late Antique Egypt Reconsidered: The Cases of Alexandria, Panopolis and Philae." *Journal of Early Christian History* 5(2): 24–48. https://doi.org/10.1080/2222582X.2015.11877325.

Dijkstra, Roald, and Dorine Van Espelo. 2017. "Anchoring Pontifical Authority: A Reconsideration of the Papal Employment of the Title *Pontifex Maximus*." *Journal of Religious History* 41(3): 312–325. https://doi.org/10.1111/1467-9809.12400.

Dillon, John. 2005. "Philosophy as a Profession in Late Antiquity." In *The Philosopher and Society in Late Antiquity: Essays in Honour of Peter Brown*, edited by Andrew Smith and Karin Alt, 1–17. Swansea: Classical Press of Wales.

Dio, Cassius. 1917. *Roman History. Volume VI, Books 51–55*. Translated by Earnest Cary. Loeb Classical Library, vol. 83. Cambridge, MA: Harvard University Press.

Di Segni, Leah. 2017. "Expressions of Prayer in Late Antique Inscriptions in the Provinces of Palaestina and Arabia." In *Prayer and Worship in Eastern Christianities, 5th to 11th Centuries*, edited by Brouria Bitton-Ashkelony and Derek Krueger, 63–88. Abingdon and New York: Routledge.

Dodaro, Robert. 2004. *Christ and the Just Society in the Thought of Augustine*. Cambridge: Cambridge University Press.

Dodds, E. R. 1965. *Pagan and Christian in an Age of Anxiety: Some Aspects of Religious Experience from Marcus Aurelius to Constantine*. Cambridge: Cambridge University Press.

Doering, Lutz. 1997. "The Concept of the Sabbath in the Book of Jubilees." In *Studies in the Book of Jubilees*, edited by Matthias Albani, Jörg Frey, and Armin Lange, 179–205. Tübingen: Mohr Siebeck.

Dolbeau, François. 2009. *Augustine, Vingt-six sermons au peuple d'Afrique*. Collection des études Augustiniennes, vol. 147. Paris.

Doran, Robert. 1992. *The Lives of Simeon Stylites*. Kalamazoo, MI: Cistercian Publications.

Douglas, Mary. 2002. *Purity and Danger: An Analysis of Concepts of Pollution and Taboo*. New York and London: Routledge.

Drake, H. A. 2000. *Constantine and the Bishops: The Politics of Intolerance*. Ancient Society and History. Baltimore: Johns Hopkins University Press.

Drake, H. A. 2006. "The Impact of Constantine on Christianity." In *The Cambridge Companion to the Age of Constantine*, edited by Noel Lenski, 111–136. Cambridge: Cambridge University Press.

Drake, H. A. 2011. "Intolerance, Religious Violence, and Political Legitimacy in Late Antiquity." *Journal of the American Academy of Religion* 79(1): 193–235.

Drake, H. A., and Emily Albu, eds. 2006. *Violence in Late Antiquity: Perceptions and Practices*. Aldershot, UK, and Burlington, VT: Ashgate.

Drijvers, Jan Willem. 1992. *Helena Augusta: The Mother of Constantine the Great and the Legend of Her Finding of the True Cross*. Brill's Studies in Intellectual History, vol. 27. Boston and Leiden: Brill.

Dunn, Geoffrey D. 2013. "The Clerical *Cursus Honorum* in the Late Antique Roman Church." *Scrinium* (Saint Petersburg, Russia) 9(1): 120–133. https://doi.org/10.1163/18177565-90000074.

Dunn, James D. G. 2002. "Jesus and Purity: An Ongoing Debate." *New Testament Studies* 48(4): 449–467. https://doi.org/10.1017/S0028688502000279.

Easterling, Pat, and Richard Miles. 1999. "Dramatic Identities: Tragedy in Late Antiquity." In *Constructing Identities in Late Antiquity*, edited by Richard Miles, 105–121. London and New York: Routledge.

Edelman, Diana Vikander. 1995. "Tracking Observance of the Aniconic Tradition through Numismatics." In *The Triumph of Elohim: From Yahwisms to Judaisms*, edited by Diana Vikander Edelman, 185–225. Kampen: Peeters Publishers.

Edmunds, Lowell. 2005. "Epic and Myth." In *A Companion to Ancient Epic*, edited by John Miles Foley, 31–44. Malden, MA: Blackwell.

Eisen, Ute E. 2000. *Women Officeholders in Early Christianity: Epigraphical and Literary Studies*. Collegeville, MN: Liturgical Press.

Ekroth, G. 1999. "Pausanias and the Sacrificial Rituals of Greek Hero-Cults." In *Ancient Greek Hero Cult: Proceedings of the Fifth International Seminar on Ancient Greek Cult, Organized by the Department of Classical Archaeology and Ancient History, Göteborg University, 21–23 April 1995*, edited by Robin Hägg, 147–158. Skrifter utgivna av Svenska Institutet i Athen, 8° = Acta Instituti Atheniensis Regni Sueciae, Series in 8° 16. Stockholm: Svenska Institutet i Athen.

Elazar, Daniel J. 1995. "Spinoza and the Bible." *Jewish Political Studies Review* 7(1/2): 5–19.

Eliade, Mircea. 1961. *The Sacred and the Profane: The Nature of Religion*. New York: Harper & Row.

Elm, Susanna. 1994. *Virgins of God: The Making of Asceticism in Late Antiquity*. Oxford Classical Monographs. Oxford: Oxford University Press.

Elman, Yaakov. 2004. "Acculturation to Elite Persian Norms and Modes of Thought in the Babylonian Jewish Community of Late Antiquity." *Neti'ot Ledavid: Jubilee Volume for David Weiss Halivni*, edited by Yaakov Elman, Ephraim Bezalel Halivni, and Zvi Arie Steinfeld, 31–56. Jerusalem: Orhot.

Elsner, Jaś. 2000. "From the Culture of Spolia to the Cult of Relics: The Arch of Constantine and the Genesis of Late Antique Forms." *Papers of the British School at Rome* 68 (November): 149–184. https://doi.org/10.1017/S0068246200003901.

Elwes, R. H. M., trans. 1951. *Spinoza, Ethics: Ethica Ordine Gemoetrico Demonstrata*. Auckland: Floating Press.

Englard, Y. 2000. "The Eschatological Significance of the Zodiac Panels in the Mosaic Pavements of Ancient Synagogues in Israel." [In Hebrew.] *Cathedra* 98: 33–48.

Eshel, Esther. 1999. "Prayer in Qumran and the Synagogue." In *Gemeinde Ohne Tempel: zur Substituierung und Tranformation des Jerusalemer Tempels und seines Kults im Alten Testament, antiken Judentum und frühen Christentum*, edited by Beate Ego, Armin Lange, Peter Pilhofer, and Kathrin Ehlers, 323–334. Wissenschaftliche Untersuchungen zum Neuen Testament, vol. 118. Tübingen: Mohr Siebeck.

Falk, Daniel K. 2000. "Qumran Prayer Texts and the Temple." In *Sapiential, Liturgical and Poetical Texts from Qumran*, edited by Maurice Baillet, Daniel K. Falk, Florentino Garcia Martinez, and Eileen M. Schuller, 106–126. Leiden: Brill.

Farag, Mary K. 2021. *What Makes a Church Sacred?: Legal and Ritual Perspectives from Late Antiquity*. Transformation of the Classical Heritage, vol. 63. Oakland: University of California Press.

Faraone, Christopher A., and Joseph L. Rife. 2007. "A Greek Curse against a Thief from the Koutsongila Cemetery at Roman Kenchreai." *Zeitschrif für Papyrologie und Epigraphik* 160: 141–157.

Fears, J. Rufus. 1981. "The Cult of Jupiter and Roman Imperial Ideology." *Aufstieg und Niedergang der Römischen Welt: Religion II* 17(1): 3–141.

Feeney, D. C. 2007. *Caesar's Calendar: Ancient Time and the Beginnings of History*. Berkeley: University of California Press.

Feldman, Louis H. 2001. *Jew and Gentile in the Ancient World: Attitudes and Interactions from Alexander to Justinian*. Princeton, NJ: Princeton University Press.

Feltoe, Charles Lett. 1890. "The Letters and Sermons of Leo the Great Bishop of Rome." In *A Select Library of Nicene and Post-Nicene Fathers of the Christian Church, Second Series*, vol. 12, edited by Philip Schaff and Henry Wace. New York: The Christian Literature Company.

Ferrar, W. J., trans. 1920. *Eusebius of Caesarea: Demonstratio Evangelica*. Translations of Christian Literature, Series I, Greek Texts. New York: Macmillan.

Figueras, Pau. 1990. "Epigraphic Evidence for Proselytism in Ancient Judaism." *Immanuel* 24/25: 194–206.

Fine, Steven. 1997. *This Holy Place: On the Sanctity of the Synagogue during the Greco-Roman Period*. Christianity and Judaism in Antiquity Series, vol. 11. Notre Dame, IN: University of Notre Dame Press.

Fink, Robert Orwill, Allan Spencer Hoey, and Walter Fifield Snyder. 1940. *The Feriale Duranum*. New Haven: Yale University Press.

Finkelstein, Ari. 2018. *The Specter of the Jews: Emperor Julian and the Rhetoric of Ethnicity in Syrian Antioch*. The S. Mark Taper Foundation Imprint in Jewish Studies. Berkeley: University of California Press.

Finn, Richard. 2009. *Asceticism in the Graeco-Roman World*. Key Themes in Ancient History. Cambridge: Cambridge University Press.

Finney, Paul Corby. 1994. *The Invisible God: The Earliest Christians on Art*. New York: Cambridge University Press.

Fishbane, Simcha. 2007. "'Every Dream Becomes Valid Only by Its Interpretation': Dreams, Dream Interpretations and Dream Interpreters in the Babylonian Talmud." *Deviancy in Early Rabbinic Literature*, edited by Simcha Fishbane, 177–212. Leiden: Brill.

Fleischer, Robert. 1973. *Artemis von Ephesos und verwandte Kultstatuen aus Anatolien und Syrien*. Études préliminaires aux religions orientales dans l'Empire romain, vol. 35. Leiden: Brill.

Flower, Richard. 2012. "Visions of Constantine." *Journal of Roman Studies* 102: 287–305.

Foladare, Irving S. 1969. "A Clarification of 'Ascribed Status' and 'Achieved Status.'" *The Sociological Quarterly* 10(1): 53–61. https://www.tandfonline.com/doi/abs/10.1111/j.1533-8525.1969.tb02061.x.

Forbes, Clarence A., ed. 1970. *Firmicus Maternus : The Error of the Pagan Religions*. Ancient Christian Writers, the Works of the Fathers in Translation, vol. 27. New York: Newman.

Foschia, Laurence. 2009. "The Preservation, Restoration, and (Re)Construction of Pagan Cult Places in Late Antiquity, with Particular Attention to Mainland Greece (Fourth–Fifth Centuries)." *Journal of Late Antiquity* 2(2): 209–223. https://doi.org/10.1353/jla.0.0052.

Foss, C. 2002. "The Empress Theodora." *Byzantion* 72(1): 141–176.

Fox, Robin Lane. 1987. *Pagans and Christians*. New York: Knopf.

Fowden, Garth. 1978. "Bishops and Temples in the Eastern Roman Empire A.D. 320–435." *The Journal of Theological Studies* 29(1): 53–78.

Fowden, Garth. 1982. "The Pagan Holy Man in Late Antique Society." *Journal of Hellenic Studies* 102: 33–59.

Fraade, Steven D. 1986. "Ascetical Aspects of Ancient Judaism." In *Jewish Spirituality*, edited by Arthur Green, 253–288. New York: Crossroad.

Frankfurter, David T. M. 1990. "Stylites and Phallobates: Pillar Religions in Late Antique Syria." *Vigiliae Christianae* 44(2): 168–198. https://doi.org/10.2307/1584330.

Frankfurter, David. 1998. *Religion in Roman Egypt: Assimilation and Resistance*. Princeton, NJ: Princeton University Press.

Frankfurter, David M. 2010. "Where the Spirits Dwell: Possession, Christianization, and Saints' Shrines in Late Antiquity." *Harvard Theological Review* 103(1): 27–46.

Frankfurter, David M. 2019. "Ancient Magic in a New Key: Reviving an Exotic Discipline in the History of Religions." In *Guide to the Study of Ancient Magic*, edited by David M. Frankfurter, 3–20. Leiden: Brill.

Frazer, James George. 1994. *The Golden Bough: A Study in Magic and Religion*. Oxford World's Classics. Oxford: Oxford University Press.

Frede, Michael. 1999. "Monotheism and Pagan Philosophy in Late Antiquity." In *Pagan Monotheism in Late Antiquity*, edited by Polymnia Athanassiadi and Michael Frede, 41–67. Oxford: Clarendon Press; New York: Oxford University Press.

Friedheim, Emmanuel. 2002. "Quelques remarques sur l'introduction du culte de Jupiter Héliopolitain à Emmaüs-Nicopolis à l'époque romaine." *Revue biblique* 109(1): 101–108.

Friedheim, Emmanuel. 2009. "Sol Invictus in the Severus Synagogue at Hammath Tiberias, the Rabbis, and Jewish Society: A Different Approach." *Review of Rabbinic Judaism* 12(1): 89–128.

Frier, Bruce W., ed. 2016. *The Codex of Justinian: A New Annotated Translation with Parallel Latin and Greek Text*. Based on a translation by Fred H. Blume. 3 vols. Cambridge: Cambridge University Press.

Furstenberg, Yair. 2008. "Defilement Penetrating the Body: A New Understanding of Contamination in Mark 7.15." *New Testament Studies* 54(2): 176–200. https://doi.org/10.1017/S0028688508000106.

Furstenberg, Yair. 2010. "The Rabbinic View of Idolatry and the Roman Political Conception of Divinity." *The Journal of Religion* 90(3): 335–366.

Furstenberg, Yair. 2013. "Am-Ha-Aretz in Tannatic Literature and Its Social Context." [In Hebrew.] *Zion* 78(3): 287–319.

Gaddis, Michael. 2005. *There Is No Crime for Those Who Have Christ: Religious Violence in the Christian Roman Empire*. Transformation of the Classical Heritage, vol. 39. Berkeley: University of California Press.

Gafni, Isaiah M. 1997. *Land, Center and Diaspora: Jewish Constructs in Late Antiquity*. Journal for the Study of the Pseudepigrapha, supplement series vol. 21. Sheffield, UK: Sheffield Academic Press.

Gager, John G. 1999. *Curse Tablets and Binding Spells from the Ancient World*. New York: Oxford University Press.

Gagos, Traianos, and P. van Minnen. 1994. *Settling a Dispute: Toward a Legal Anthropology of Late Antique Egypt*. Ann Arbor: University of Michigan Press.

Gardner, Gregg E. 2008. "Astrology in the Talmud: An Analysis of Bavli Shabbat 156." In *Heresy and Identity in Late Antiquity*, edited by Eduard Iricinschi and Holger M. Zellentin, 314–338. Tübingen: Mohr Siebeck.

Gasparini, Valentino, Maik Patzelt, Rubina Raja, Anna-Katharina Rieger, Jörg Rüpke, and Emiliano Rubens Urciuoli. 2020. "Pursuing Lived Ancient Religion." In *Lived Religion in the Ancient Mediterranean World*, edited by Valentino Gasparini, Maik Patzelt, Rubina Raja, Anna-Katharina Rieger, Jörg Rüpke, and Emiliano Rubens Urciuoli, 1–8. Berlin: De Gruyter.

Geary, Patrick J. 1999. "Barbarians and Ethnicity." In *Late Antiquity: A Guide to the Postclassical World*, edited by G. W. Bowersock, Peter Robert Lamont Brown, and Oleg Grabar, 107–129. Harvard University Press Reference Library. Cambridge, MA: Belknap Press.

Giacchero, Marta, and Istituto di Storia Antica e Scienze Ausiliarie dell'Università di Genova. 1974. *Edictum Diocletiani et collegarum de pretiis rerum venalium in integrum fere restitutum e latinis graecisque fragmentis*. Genova: Istitituto di Storia Antica e Scienze Ausiliarie dell'Università di Genova.

Gibson, Craig, trans. 2008. *Libanius's Progymnasmata: Model Exercises in Greek Prose Composition and Rhetoric*. Writings from the Greco-Roman World, vol. 27. Atlanta: Society of Biblical Literature.

Gibson, E. Leigh. 2001. "Jewish Antagonism or Christian Polemic: The Case of the Martyrdom of Pionius." *Journal of Early Christian Studies* 9(3): 339–358. https://doi.org/10.1353/earl.2001.0041.

Ginzburg, Carlo. 1980. *The Cheese and the Worms: The Cosmos of a Sixteenth-Century Miller*. Baltimore: Johns Hopkins University Press.

Girardet, Klaus M. 2007. "Vom Sonnen-Tag zum Sonntag: Der dies solis in Gesetzgebung und Politik Konstantins d. Gr." *Zeitschrift für Antikes Christentum / Journal of Ancient Christianity* 11(2): 279–310. https://doi.org/10.1515/ZAC.2007.015.

Glover, T. R., trans. 1966. *Apology; De spectaculis*. By Tertullian. Loeb Classical Library, vol. 250. Cambridge, MA: Harvard University Press.

Golby, Amanda. 1998. "Women and the New Moon." In *Hear Our Voice*, edited by Sybil Sheridan, 119–127. Columbia: University of South Carolina Press.

Goldenberg, Robert. 1979. "The Jewish Sabbath in the Roman World up to the Time of Constantine the Great." *Aufstieg und Niedergang der Römischen Welt* II 19/2: 414–479.

Goodenough, E. R. 1953–68. *Jewish Symbols in the Greco-Roman Period*. Bollingen series vol. 37. New York: Pantheon.

Goodman, Martin. 1989. "Nerva, the *Fiscus Judaicus*, and Jewish Identity." *Journal of Roman Studies* 79 (November): 40–44. https://doi.org/10.2307/301179.

Goodman, Martin. 1990. "Sacred Scripture and 'Defiling the Hands.'" *Journal of Theological Studies* 41(1): 99–107.

Goodman, Martin. 2003. "The Jewish Image of God in Late Antiquity." In *Jewish Culture and Society under the Christian Roman Empire*, edited by Richard L. Kalmin and Seth Schwartz, 133–145. Leuven: Peeters.

Gordon, Benjamin D. 2018. "The Ritual Baths: Introduction and Catalog." In *The Architecture, Stratigraphy, and Artifacts of the Western Summit of Sepphoris*, edited by Eric M. Meyers, 391–418. University Park, PA: Eisenbrauns.

Gordon, R. L. 1972. "Mithraism and Roman Society: Social Factors in the Explanation of Religious Change in the Roman Empire." *Religion* 2(2): 92–121. https://doi.org/10.1016/0048-721X(72)90042-5.

Gordon, R. L. 2008. "*Superstitio*, Superstition and Religious Repression in the Late Roman Republic and Principate (100 BCE–300 CE)." *Past & Present* 199 (S3): 72–94. https://doi.org/10.1093/pastj/gtm060.

Gorski, Gilbert, and James E. Packer. 2015. *The Roman Forum: A Reconstruction and Architectural Guide*. New York: Cambridge University Press.

Graf, Fritz. 2005. "Rolling the Dice for an Answer." In *Mantikê: Studies in Ancient Divination*, edited by Sarah Iles Johnston and Peter T. Struck, 55–98. Religions in the Graeco-Roman World, vol. 155. Leiden: Brill.

Graf, Fritz. 2006. "Greek and Roman Necromancy." *Classical World* 99(4): 459–460.

Graf, Fritz. 2015. *Roman Festivals in the Greek East: From the Early Empire to the Middle Byzantine Era*. Cambridge: Cambridge University Press.

Green, William Scott. 1978. "What's in a Name? The Problematic of Rabbinic 'Biography.'" In *Approaches to Ancient Judaism*, edited by William Scott Green, 77–96, Missoula: Scholars Press.

Greenfield, J. C., and M. Sokoloff. 1989. "Astrological and Related Omen Texts in Jewish Palestinian Aramaic." *Journal of Near Eastern Studies* 48(3): 201–214.

Greer, Rowan A. 1996. "Augustine's Transformation of the Free Will Defence." *Faith and Philosophy* 13(4): 471–486. https://doi.org/10.5840/faithphil199613445.

Gregg, Robert C., and Dan Urman. 1996. *Jews, Pagans, and Christians in the Golan Heights: Greek and Other Inscriptions of the Roman and Byzantine Eras*. South Florida Studies in the History of Judaism, vol. 140. Atlanta: Scholars Press.

Gribetz, Sarit Kattan. 2018. "Zekhut Imahot: Mothers, Fathers, and Ancestral Merit in Rabbinic Sources." *Journal for the Study of Judaism* 49(2): 263–296. https://doi.org/10.1163/15700631-12491201.

Gribetz, Sarit Kattan. 2020. *Time and Difference in Rabbinic Judaism*. Princeton, NJ: Princeton University Press.

Grig, Lucy. 2021. "Reconsidering 'Popular Religion' for a New Era." *Studies in Late Antiquity* 5(1): 139–149.

Gross, Simcha. 2021. "Being Roman in the Sasanian Empire: Revisiting the Great Persecution of Christians under Shapur II." *Studies in Late Antiquity* 5(3): 361–402.

Grubbs, Judith Evans. 2001. "Virgins and Widows, Show-Girls and Whores: Late Roman Legislation on Women and Christianity." In *Law, Society, and Authority in Late Antiquity*, edited by Ralph W. Mathisen, 220–241. Oxford: Oxford University Press.

Gruen, Erich S. 2020. *Ethnicity in the Ancient World—Did It Matter?* Berlin and Boston: De Gruyter.

Grypeou, Emmanouela. 2019. "Talking Heads: Necromancy in Jewish and Christian Accounts from Mesopotamia and Beyond." *Collectanea Christiana Orientalia* 16: 1–30. https://doi.org/10.21071/cco.v16i0.1100.

Gundel, Hans Georg. 1992. *Zodiakos: Tierkreisbilder im Altertum: kosmische Bezüge und Jenseitsvorstellungen im antiken Alltagsleben*. Kulturgeschichte der antiken Welt, vol.54. Mainz am Rhein: P. von Zabern.

Gupta, Nijay K. 2014. "'They Are Not Gods!' Jewish and Christian Idol Polemic and Greco-Roman Use of Cult Statues." *The Catholic Biblical Quarterly* 76(4): 704–719.

Hachlili, Rachel. 2002. "The Zodiac in Ancient Jewish Synagogal Art: A Review." *Jewish Studies Quarterly* 9(3): 219–258.

Hachlili, Rachel. 2014. *Ancient Synagogues—Archaeology and Art: New Discoveries and Current Research*. Leiden: Brill.

Haensch, Rudolf. 2007. "Inscriptions as Sources of Knowledge for Religions and Cults in the Roman World of Imperial Times." In *A Companion to Roman Religion*, edited by Jörg Rüpke, 207–218. Blackwell Companions to the Ancient World. Ancient History. Malden, MA: Blackwell.

Hägg, Tomas. 2012. *The Art of Biography in Antiquity*. Cambridge and New York: Cambridge University Press.

Hahn, Cynthia. 2010. "What Do Reliquaries Do for Relics?" *Numen* 57(3/4): 284–316.

Hahn, Frances Hickson. 2007. "Performing the Sacred: Prayers and Hymns." In *A Companion to Roman Religion*, edited by Jörg Rüpke, 262–276. Blackwell Companions to the Ancient World. Ancient History. Malden, MA: Blackwell.

Haines-Eitzen, Kim. 1998. "'Girls Trained in Beautiful Writing': Female Scribes in Roman Antiquity and Early Christianity." *Journal of Early Christian Studies* 6(4): 629–646.

Halbertal, Moshe. 2020. *The Birth of Doubt: Confronting Uncertainty in Early Rabbinic Literature*. Brown Judaic Studies, vol. 366. Providence, RI: Brown Judaic Studies.

Hall, Jonathan M. 2002. *Hellenicity: Between Ethnicity and Culture*. Chicago: University of Chicago Press.

Hall, Stuart George, and Averil Cameron, trans. 1999. *Eusebius, Life of Constantine*. Oxford: Clarendon Press.

Hamidović, David. 2014. "Du culte des anges aux développements liturgiques du Shema dans le judaïsme ancien." *Judaïsme Ancien—Ancient Judaism* 2: 135–156.

Hammer, Dean. 2021. "Books 4 & 5: Roman Religion and Just Power." In *The Cambridge Companion to Augustine's City of God*, edited by David Vincent Meconi, 81–101. Cambridge: Cambridge University Press.

Harari, Yuval. 2017. *Jewish Magic before the Rise of Kabbalah*. Translated by Batya Stein. Raphael Patai Series in Jewish Folklore and Anthropology. Detroit: Wayne State University Press.

Harl, K. W. 1990. "Sacrifice and Pagan Belief in Fifth- and Sixth-Century Byzantium." *Past & Present* 128: 7–27.

Harland, Philip A. 2009. *Dynamics of Identity in the World of the Early Christians: Associations, Judeans, and Cultural Minorities*. New York: T & T Clark.

Harland, Philip A., John S. Kloppenborg, and Richard S. Ascough, eds. 2011. *Greco-Roman Associations: Texts, Translations, and Commentary*. Beihefte zur Zeitschrift für die neutestamentliche Wissenschaft und die Kunde der älteren Kirche, vols. 181, 204, 246. Berlin and New York: De Gruyter.

Harries, Jill. 1999. *Law and Empire in Late Antiquity*. Cambridge: Cambridge University Press.

Harries, Jill. 2003. "Creating Legal Space: Settling Disputes in the Roman Empire." In *Rabbinic Law in Its Roman and Near Eastern Context*, edited by Catherine Hezser, 63–82. Texts and Studies in Ancient Judaism, vol. 97. Tübingen: Mohr Siebeck.

Harris, Murray J. 1992. *Jesus as God: The New Testament Use of Theos in Reference to Jesus*. Grand Rapids, MI: Baker Book House.

Harris, William V. 1989. *Ancient Literacy*. ACLS Fellows' Publications. Cambridge, MA: Harvard University Press.

Harris-McCoy, Daniel E., trans. 2012. *Artemidorus' "Oneirocritica": Text, Translation, and Commentary*. Oxford: Oxford University Press.

Hegedus, Tim. 2007. *Early Christianity and Ancient Astrology*. Patristic Studies, vol. 6. New York: P. Lang.

Hemelrijk, Emily A. 2006. "Priestesses of the Imperial Cult in the Latin West: Benefactions and Public Honour." *L'antiquité classique* 75(1): 85–117. https://doi.org/10.3406/antiq.2006.2593.

Hemelrijk, Emily A. 2012. "Public Roles for Women in the Cities of the Latin West." In *A Companion to Women in the Ancient World*, edited by Sharon L. James and Sheila Dillon, 478–490. Hoboken: John Wiley.

Herman, Geoffrey. 2012. *A Prince without a Kingdom: The Exilarch in the Sasanian Era*. Texts and Studies in Ancient Judaism, vol. 150. Tübingen: Mohr Siebeck.

Herr, Moshe David. 1971. "The Historical Significance of the Dialogues between Sages and Roman Dignitaries." *Scripta Hierosolymitana* 22: 123–150.

Herrin, Judith. 2001. "Women in Purple: Rulers of Medieval Byzantium." Electronic resource. *ACLS Humanities E-Book*. https://hdl.handle.net/2027/heb02950.

Herrin, Judith. 2020. *Ravenna: Capital of Empire, Crucible of Europe*. Princeton, NJ: Princeton University Press.

Hess, Hamilton. 2002. *The Early Development of Canon Law and the Council of Serdica*. Oxford Early Christian Studies. Oxford: Oxford University Press.

Hezser, Catherine. 1998. "The Codification of Legal Knowledge in Late Antiquity: The Talmud Yerushalmi and Roman Law Codes." In *The Talmud Yerushalmi and Graeco-Roman Culture*, edited by Peter Schäfer, 1: 581–641. Tübingen: Mohr Siebeck.

Hezser, Catherine. 2003. "Jewish Literacy and the Use of Writing in Late Roman Palestine." In *Jewish Culture and Society under the Christian Roman Empire*, edited by Richard L. Kalmin and Seth Schwartz, 149–195. Leuven: Peeter.

Hezser, Catherine. 2011. *Jewish Travel in Antiquity*. Texte und Studien zum antiken Judentum, vol. 144. Tübingen: Mohr Siebeck.

Hezser, Catherine. 2019. "Rabbis as Intellectuals in the Context of Graeco-Roman and Byzantine Christian Scholasticism." In *Scholastic Culture in the Hellenistic and Roman Eras: Greek, Latin, and Jewish*, edited by Sean A. Adams, 169–185. Berlin and Boston: De Gruyter.

Hillner, Julia. 2023. *Helena Augusta: Mother of the Empire*. Women in Antiquity. New York: Oxford University Press.

Himmelfarb, Martha. 2017. "'Greater Is the Covenant with Aaron' (Sifre Numbers 119): Rabbis, Priests, and Kings Revisited." In *The Faces of Torah: Studies in the Texts and Contexts of Ancient Judaism in Honor of Steven Fraade*, edited by Michal Bar-Asher Siegal, Tzvi Novick, and Christine Hayes, 339–350. Göttingen: Vandenhoeck & Ruprecht.

Holladay, Carl R. 1977. *Theios Aner in Hellenistic-Judaism: A Critique of the Use of This Category in New Testament Christology*. Dissertation series—Society of Biblical Literature, vol. 40. Missoula, MT: Scholars Press.

Holum, Kenneth G. 1989. *Theodosian Empresses*. Berkeley: University of California Press.

Horbury, William. 1997. "A Proselyte's 'Heis Theos' Inscription near Caesarea." *Palestine Exploration Quarterly* 129(2): 133–137.

Horowitz, Elliott S. 2006. *Reckless Rites: Purim and the Legacy of Jewish Violence*. Jews, Christians, and Muslims from the Ancient to the Modern World. Princeton, NJ: Princeton University Press.

Horsley, G. H. R. 1992. "The Inscriptions of Ephesos and the New Testament." *Novum Testamentum* 34(2): 105–168. https://doi.org/10.2307/1561039.

Horsley, G. H. R., and Jean M. Luxford. 2016. "Pagan Angels in Roman Asia Minor: Revisiting the Epigraphic Evidence." *Anatolian Studies* 66: 141–183.

Howley, Joseph A. 2017. "Book-Burning and the Uses of Writing in Ancient Rome: Destructive Practice between Literature and Document." *Journal of Roman Studies* 107: 213–236.

Humphries, Mark. 2019. *Cities and the Meanings of Late Antiquity*. Brill Research Perspectives. Leiden: Brill.

Humphries, Mark. 2020. "The Rhetorical Construction of a Christian Empire in the *Theodosian Code*." In *Rhetoric and Religious Identity in Late Antiquity*, edited by Richard Flower and Morwenna Ludlow, 145–159. Oxford Scholarship Online. Oxford: Oxford University Press.

Hunter, David G. 1999. "Vigilantius of Calagurris and Victricius of Rouen: Ascetics, Relics, and Clerics in Late Roman Gaul." *Journal of Early Christian Studies* 7(3): 401–430. https://doi.org/10.1353/earl.1999.0061.

Hunter, Erica C. D. 1996. "Incantation Bowls: A Mesopotamian Phenomenon?" *Orientalia* 65(3): 220–233.

Idel, Moshe. 1990. "Enoch Is Metatron." *Immanuel: A Journal of Religious Thought and Research in Israel* 25: 220–240.

Ilan, Tal. 2011. "'Kever Israel': Since When Do Jews Bury Their Dead Separately and What Did They Do Beforehand?" In *Halakhah in Light of Epigraphy*, edited by Albert I. Baumgarten, Hanan Eshel, Ranon Katzoff, and Shani Tzoref, 241–254. Göttingen: Vandenhoeck & Ruprecht.

Inscriptiones Graecae. 1903–. Berlin.

Irshai, Oded. 2002. "Confronting a Christian Empire: Jewish Culture in the World of Byzantium." In *Cultures of the Jews*, edited by David Biale, 181–221. New York: Schocken.

Jacobs, Andrew S. 2016. *Epiphanius of Cyprus: A Cultural Biography of Late Antiquity*. Christianity in Late Antiquity, vol. 2. Berkeley: University of California Press.

Jacoby, Ruth. 2001. "The Four Seasons in Zodiac Mosaics: The Tallaras Baths in Astypalaea, Greece." *Israel Exploration Journal* 51(2): 225–230.

James, Edward. 2008. "The Rise and Concept of 'Late Antiquity.'" *Journal of Late Antiquity* 1(1): 20–30.

Janowitz, Naomi. 2001. *Magic in the Roman World: Pagans, Jews, and Christians*. London and New York: Routledge.

Janssen, L. F. 1979. "'Superstitio' and the Persecution of the Christians." *Vigiliae Christianae* 33(2): 131–159.

Jeffrey, Hugh. 2019. "Eight Hundred Years of the Cult of the Archangels at Aphrodisias/Stauropolis: Modern and Ancient Narratives." In *Trends and Turning Points: Constructing the Late Antique and Byzantine World*, edited by Matthew Kinloch and Alex MacFarlane, 205–228. Leiden: Brill.

Jensen, Robin Margaret. 2000. *Understanding Early Christian Art*. London: Taylor & Francis.

Jensen, Robin M. 2008. "Dining with the Dead: From the *Mensa* to the Altar in Christian Late Antiquity." In *Commemorating the Dead: Texts and Artifacts in Context. Studies of Roman, Jewish and Christian Burials*, edited by Laurie Brink and Deborah Green, 107–143. Berlin: De Gruyter.

Jensen, Robin M. 2022. *From Idols to Icons: The Emergence of Christian Devotional Images in Late Antiquity*. Berkeley: University of California Press.

Johnston, Sarah Iles. 2001. "Sacrifice in the Greek Magical Papyri." In *Magic and Ritual in the Ancient World*, edited by Paul Allen Mirecki and Marvin W. Meyer, 344–358. Religions in the Graeco-Roman World, vol. 141. Leiden: Brill.

Johnston, Sarah Iles, and Peter T. Struck. 2005. *Mantikê: Studies in Ancient Divination*. Religions in the Graeco-Roman World, vol. 155. Leiden: Brill.

Jones, Arnold H. M. 1966. *The Greek City: From Alexander to Justinian*. Oxford: Clarendon Press.

Jones, Christopher P. 1980. "An Epigram on Apollonius of Tyana." *The Journal of Hellenic Studies* 100: 190–194. https://doi.org/10.2307/630745.

Jones, Christopher P. 2010. *New Heroes in Antiquity: From Achilles to Antinoos*. Revealing Antiquity, vol. 18. Cambridge, MA: Harvard University Press.

Julian. 1923. *Against the Galilaeans*. In *Letters, Epigrams. Against the Galilaeans. Fragments*. Translated by Wilmer C. Wright. Cambridge, MA: Harvard University Press.

Kajanto, Iiro. 1981. "'Pontifex Maximus' as the Title of the Pope." *Arctos: Acta Philologica Fennica* 15: 37–52.

Kalas, Gregor. 2015. *The Restoration of the Roman Forum in Late Antiquity: Transforming Public Space*. Austin: University of Texas Press.

Kalmin, Richard. 1998. "Relationships between Rabbis and Non-Rabbis in Rabbinic Literature of Late Antiquity." *Jewish Studies Quarterly* 5(2): 156–170.

Kalmin, Richard Lee. 2003. "Holy Men, Rabbis, and Demonic Sages in Late Antiquity." In *Jewish Culture and Society under the Christian Roman Empire*, edited by Richard L. Kalmin and Seth Schwartz, 213–249. Leuven: Peeters.

Kashchuk, Oleksandr. 2014. "The Attitude of the Pro-Arian Bishops towards the Emperor in the Period of Reception of the Nicene Christology (325–381)." *Vox Patrum* 34: 137-155. https://czasopisma.kul.pl/index.php/vp/article/view/3614/3561.

Kasher, Aryeh. 1986. "Miracle, Faith, and the Merit of the Ancestors: On the Development of Concepts in Rabbinic Literature." [In Hebrew.] *Jerusalem Studies in Jewish Thought* 5: 15–22.

Kaster, Robert A. 1988. *Guardians of Language: The Grammarian and Society in Late Antiquity*. The Transformation of the Classical Heritage, vol. 11. Berkeley: University of California Press.

Kateb, George. 2009. "Locke and the Political Origins of Secularism." *Social Research* 76(4): 1001–1034.

Kayaalp, Elif Keser. 2021. *Church Architecture of Late Antique Northern Mesopotamia*. Oxford Studies in Byzantium. Oxford: Oxford University Press.

Kaye, Lynne. 2018. *Time in the Babylonian Talmud: Natural and Imaginative Times in Jewish Law and Narrative*. Cambridge: Cambridge University Press.

Keegan, Peter. 2014. *Graffiti in Antiquity*. London: Routledge.

Kenney, John Peter. 1991. *Mystical Monotheism: A Study in Ancient Platonic Theology*. Hanover, NH: Brown University Press, published by the University Press of New England.

Ker, James. 2010. "'Nundinae': The Culture of the Roman Week." *Phoenix* 64(3/4): 360–385.

Kiernan, Philip. 2020. *Roman Cult Images: The Lives and Worship of Idols from the Iron Age to Late Antiquity*. New York: Cambridge University Press. https://doi.org/10.1017/9781108766555.

Kimelman, Reuven. 2006. "Rabbinic Prayer in Late Antiquity." In *The Cambridge History of Judaism*, vol. 4, *The Late Roman-Rabbinic Period*, edited by Steven T. Katz, 573–611. Cambridge: Cambridge University Press.

King, Charles. 2020. *The Ancient Roman Afterlife: Di Manes, Belief, and the Cult of the Dead*. Ashley and Peter Larkin Series in Greek and Roman Culture. Austin: University of Texas Press.

King, Karen L. 2003. *What Is Gnosticism?* Cambridge, MA: The Belknap Press of Harvard University Press.

Kirschner, Robert. 1984. "The Vocation of Holiness in Late Antiquity." *Vigiliae Christianae* 38(2): 105–124. https://doi.org/10.2307/1583058.

Klawans, Jonathan. 2000. *Impurity and Sin in Ancient Judaism*. Oxford: Oxford University Press.

Kline, A., trans. 2005. "Horace: The Satires." Poetry in Translation. https://www.poetryintranslation.com/PITBR/Latin/HoraceSatiresBkISatV.php.

Klingshirn, William E. 2005. "Christian Divination in Late Roman Gaul: The *Sortes Sangallenses*." In *Mantikê: Studies in Ancient Divination*, edited by Sarah Iles Johnston and Peter T. Struck, 99–128. Religions in the Graeco-Roman World, vol. 155. Leiden: Brill. https://doi.org/10.1163/9789047407966_005.

Knibbe, Kim, and Helena Kupari. 2020. "Theorizing Lived Religion: Introduction." *Journal of Contemporary Religion* 35(2): 157–176. https://doi.org/10.1080/ 13537903.2020.1759897.

Knipfing, John R. 1923. "The Libelli of the Decian Persecution." *Harvard Theological Review* 16(4): 345–390.

Knohl, Israel. 1995. *The Sanctuary of Silence: The Priestly Torah and the Holiness School*. Minneapolis: Fortress Press.

Knust, Jennifer Wright, and Zsuzsanna Várhelyi, eds. 2011. *Ancient Mediterranean Sacrifice*. New York and Oxford: Oxford University Press.

Kochen, Madeline. 2008. "'It Was Not for Naught That They Called It *Hekdesh*': Divine Ownership and the Medieval Charitable Foundation." *Jewish Law Association Studies* 18: 13–142.

Koskenniemi, Erkki. 1998. "Apollonius of Tyana: A Typical Θεῖος Ἀνήρ?" *Journal of Biblical Literature* 117(3): 455–467. https://doi.org/10.2307/3266442.

Kotansky, Roy. 1994. *Greek Magical Amulets: The Inscribed Gold, Silver, Copper, and Bronze Lamellae. Part I: Published Texts of Known Provenance*. Papyrologica Coloniensia 22/1. Wiesbaden: Springer Fachmedien Wiesbaden.

Kraemer, Ross Shepard. 1989. "On the Meaning of the Term 'Jew' in Greco-Roman Inscriptions." *Harvard Theological Review* 89(1): 35–53.

Kraemer, Ross Shepard. 2011. *Unreliable Witnesses: Religion, Gender, and History in the Greco-Roman Mediterranean*. New York: Oxford University Press.

Kraemer, Ross Shepard. 2014. "Giving Up the Godfearers." *Journal of Ancient Judaism* 5(1): 61–87.

Kraemer, Ross Shepard. 2020. *The Mediterranean Diaspora in Late Antiquity: What Christianity Cost the Jews*. New York: Oxford University Press.

Kraemer, Ross Shepard. 2023. "Social Relations between Jews and Christians in the Mediterranean Diaspora in Late Antiquity." In *The Social Worlds of Ancient Jews and Christians: Essays in Honor of L. Michael White*, edited by Jaimie Gunderson, Anthony G. Keddie, and Douglas Boin, 202–222. Leiden: Brill.

Krawiec, Rebecca. 2002. *Shenoute and the Women of the White Monastery: Egyptian Monasticism in Late Antiquity*. New York: Oxford University Press.

Kristensen, Troels Myrup. 2013. *Making and Breaking the Gods: Christian Responses to Pagan Sculpture in Late Antiquity*. Aarhus Studies in Mediterranean Antiquity (ASMA), vol. 12. Aarhus: Aarhus University Press.

Krueger, Derek. 1996. *Symeon the Holy Fool: Leontius's Life and the Late Antique City*. Transformation of the Classical Heritage, vol. 25. Berkeley: University of California Press.

Krueger, Derek. 1997. "Writing as Devotion: Hagiographical Composition and the Cult of the Saints in Theodoret of Cyrrhus and Cyril of Scythopolis." *Church History* 66(4): 707–719. https://doi.org/10.2307/3169209.

Krueger, Derek. 2014. *Liturgical Subjects: Christian Ritual, Biblical Narrative, and the Formation of the Self in Byzantium*. Divinations. Philadelphia: University of Pennsylvania Press.

Kugel, James L. 1986. "Early Interpretation: The Common Background of Late Forms of Biblical Exegesis." In *Early Biblical Interpretation*, edited by James L. Kugel and Rowan A. Greer, 9–106. Library of Early Christianity, vol. 3. Philadelphia: Westminster Press.

Labendz, Jenny R. 2003. "'Know What to Answer the Epicurean': A Diachronic Study of the 'Apiqoros in Rabbinic Literature." *Hebrew Union College Annual* 74: 175–214.

Laderman, Shulamit. 2021. "Jewish Art in Late Antiquity: The State of Research in Ancient Jewish Art." *Brill Research Perspectives in Religion and the Arts* 4(3): 1–80. https://doi.org/10.1163/24688878-12340013.

Langer, Ruth. 2003. "The 'Amidah as Formative Rabbinic Prayer." In *Identität durch Gebet: Zur gemainschaftsbildenden Funktion institutionalisierten Betens in Judentum und Christentum*, edited by Albert Gerhards, Andrea Doeker, and Peter Ebenbauer, 127–156. Paderborn: F. Schöningh.

Langer, Ruth. 2004. "Early Rabbinic Liturgy in Its Palestinian Milieu: Did Non-Rabbis Know the 'Amidah?" In *When Judaism and Christianity Began*, edited by Alan J. Avery-Peck, Daniel Harrington, and Jacob Neusner, 2: 423–439. Leiden: Brill.

Lapin, Hayim. 2012. *Rabbis as Romans: The Rabbinic Movement in Palestine, 100–400 CE*. Oxford and New York: Oxford University Press.

Latham, Jacob A. 2022. "The Re-invention of the Kalends of January in Late Antiquity: A Public Festival between 'Pagans' and Christians." *Journal of Late Antiquity* 15(1): 69–110.

Lavie-Levkovitch, Moshe. 2018. *The Rabbinic Conversion of Judaism: The Unique Perspective of the Bavli on Conversion and the Construction of Jewish Identity*. Leiden: Brill.

Le Goff, Jacques. 1988. *The Medieval Imagination*. Chicago: University of Chicago Press.

Leach, Edmund R. 1966. "Sermons by a Man on a Ladder." *The New York Review of Books*. 7(6): 28–31.

Leal, João. 2016. "Festivals, Group Making, Remaking and Unmaking." *Ethnos* 81(4): 584–599.

Lehoux, Daryn. 2007. *Astronomy, Weather, and Calendars in the Ancient World: Parapegmata and Related Texts in Classical and Near Eastern Societies*. Cambridge: Cambridge University Press.

Lennon, Jack J. 2014. *Pollution and Religion in Ancient Rome*. Cambridge: Cambridge University Press.

Leone, Anna. 2013. *The End of the Pagan City: Religion, Economy, and Urbanism in Late Antique North Africa*. Oxford: Oxford University Press.

Levene, Dan. 2003. *A Corpus of Magic Bowls: Incantation Texts in Jewish Aramaic from Late Antiquity*. The Kegan Paul Library of Jewish Studies. London: Kegan Paul.

Levene, Dan. 2006. "Calvariae Magicae: The Berlin, Philadelphia, and Moussaieff Skulls." *Orientalia* 75(4): 359–379.

Levine, David. 1999. "Who Participated in the Fast-Day Ritual in the City Square? Communal Fasts in Third- and Fourth-Century Palestine." [In Hebrew.] *Cathedra* 94: 33–54.

Levine, David. 2004. "Holy Men and Rabbis in Talmudic Antiquity." In *Saints and Role Models in Judaism and Christianity*, edited by Joshua Schwartz and Marcel Poorthuis, 45–57. Leiden: Brill.

Levine, Lee I. 1979. "The Jewish Patriarch (Nasi) in Third Century Palestine." *Aufstieg und Niedergang der Römischen Welt* II 19/2: 649–688.

Levine, Lee I. 1982. *Ancient Synagogues Revealed*. Jerusalem: Israel Exploration Society.

Levine, Lee I. 2000. *The Ancient Synagogue: The First Thousand Years*. New Haven: Yale University Press.

Lewis, Nicola Denzey. 2013. "Roses and Violets for the Ancestors." In *The Gift in Antiquity*, edited by Michael L. Satlow, 122–136. Somerset: John Wiley & Sons. https://doi.org/10.1002/9781118517895.ch9.

Lieber, Laura S. 2010. *Yannai on Genesis: An Invitation to Piyyut*. Monographs of the Hebrew Union College, vol. 36. Cincinnati: Hebrew Union College Press.

Lieber, Laura S. 2012. "Jewish Women: Texts and Contexts." In *A Companion to Women in the Ancient World*, edited by Sharon L. James and Sheila Dillon, 329–342. Hoboken: John Wiley & Sons.

Lieber, Laura S. 2018. *Jewish Aramaic Poetry from Late Antiquity: Translations and Commentaries*. Études sur le judaïsme médiéval, vol. 75. Leiden: Brill.

Lieber, Laura S. 2020. "Jewish Prayer, Liturgy, and Ritual." In *A Companion to Late Ancient Jews and Judaism: Third Century BCE to Seventh Century CE*, edited by Naomi Koltun-Fromm and Gwynn Kessler, 477–494. Hoboken: John Wiley & Sons.

Liebeschuetz, J. H. W. G. 2001. *Decline and Fall of the Roman City*. Oxford: Oxford University Press.

Liebs, Detlef. 2022. "The Code System: Reorganizing Roman Law and Legal Literature in the Late Antique Period." In *Jurists and Legal Science in the History of Roman Law*, edited by Fara Nasti and Aldo Schiavone, 261–285. London and New York: Routledge.

Lincoln, Bruce. 1999. *Theorizing Myth: Narrative, Ideology, and Scholarship*. Chicago: University of Chicago Press.

Linder, Amnon, ed. 1987. *The Jews in Roman Imperial Legislation*. Detroit: Wayne State University Press; Jerusalem: Israel Academy of Sciences and Humanities.

Linder, Amnon. 2006. "The Legal Status of the Jews." In *The Cambridge History of Judaism*, vol. 4, *The Late Roman-Rabbinic Period*, edited by Steven T. Katz, 128–173. The Cambridge History of Judaism, vol. 4. Cambridge: Cambridge University Press.

Litwa, M. David. 2019. *How the Gospels Became History*. New Haven: Yale University Press.

Lugaresi, Leonardo. 2017. "Rhetoric against the Theatre and Theatre by Means of Rhetoric in John Chrysostom." In *Rhetorical Strategies in Late Antique Literature: Images, Metatexts, and Interpretation*, edited by Alberto J. Quiroga Puertas, 117–148. Leiden: Brill.

Luijendijk, AnnMarie, William E. Klingshirn, and Lance Jenott, eds. 2019. *My Lots Are in Thy Hands: Sortilege and Its Practitioners in Late Antiquity*. Religions in the Graeco-Roman World, vol. 188. Leiden: Brill.

Lupu, Eran. 2009. *Greek Sacred Law: A Collection of New Documents (NGSL)*. 2nd ed. with a postscript. Religions in the Graeco-Roman World, vol. 152. Leiden: Brill.

Mace, Hannah. 2018. "Astrology and Religion in Late Antiquity." In *A Companion to Religion in Late Antiquity*, edited by Josef Lossl and Nicholas Baker-Brian, 433–451. Hoboken: John Wiley & Sons. https://doi.org/10.1002/9781118968130.ch20.

MacMullen, Ramsay. 1964. "Nationalism in Roman Egypt." *Aegyptus* 44(3/4): 179–199.
MacMullen, Ramsay. 1970. "Market-Days in the Roman Empire." *Phoenix* 24(4): 333–341.
MacMullen, Ramsay. 2009. *The Second Church: Popular Christianity A.D. 200–400*. Society of Biblical Literature Writings from the Greco-Roman World Supplement Series, vol. 1. Atlanta: Society of Biblical Literature.
MacMullen, Ramsay. 2014. "The End of Ancestor Worship: Affect and Class." *Historia: Zeitschrift für Alte Geschichte* 63(4): 487–513.
Macy, Gary. 2008. *The Hidden History of Women's Ordination: Female Clergy in the Medieval West*. Oxford: Oxford University Press.
Magness, Jodi. 2005. "Heaven on Earth: Helios and the Zodiac Cycle in Ancient Palestinian Synagogues." *Dumbarton Oaks Papers* 59: 1–52. https://doi.org/10.2307/4128749.
Mandel, Paul D. 2017. *The Origins of Midrash: From Teaching to Text*. Supplements to the Journal for the Study of Judaism, vol. 180. Leiden: Brill.
Mandelbaum, Bernard, ed. 1962. *Pesikta de'Rav Kahana*. New York: Jewish Theological Seminar of America.
Mandell, Sara. 1984. "Who Paid the Temple Tax When the Jews Were under Roman Rule?" *Harvard Theological Review* 77(2): 223–232. https://doi.org/10.1017/S0017816000014309.
Mantovani, Dario. 2016. "More than Codes: Roman Ways of Organising and Giving Access to Legal Information." In *The Oxford Handbook of Roman Law and Society*, edited by Paul J. du Plessis, Clifford Ando, and Kaius Tuori, 23–42. Oxford: Oxford University Press.
Maréchal, Sadi. 2020. *Public Baths and Bathing Habits in Late Antiquity: A Study of the Evidence from Italy, North Africa and Palestine A.D. 285–700*. Late Antique Archaeology. Supplementary Series, vol. 6. Boston and Leiden: Brill.
Margolioth, Mordecai. 1966. *Sepher ha-razim, hu sefer keshafim mi-teḳufat ha-Talmud*. Jerusalem: Ḳeren Yehudah leb u-Mini Epshtein she-ʻal yad ha-Aḳademyah le-Madaʻe ha-Yahadut be-Artsot ha-Berit.
Markus, R. A. 1990. *The End of Ancient Christianity*. Cambridge: Cambridge University Press.
Markus, R. A. 1994. "How on Earth Could Places Become Holy? Origins of the Christian Idea of Holy Places." *Journal of Early Christian Studies* 2(3): 257–271.
Marmorstein, Arthur. 1920. *The Doctrine of Merits in Old Rabbinical Literature*. Jews' College, London. Publication no. 7. London: Oxford University Press.
Marx, Heidi. 2021. *Sosipatra of Pergamum: Philosopher and Oracle*. New York: Oxford University Press. https://doi.org/10.1093/oso/9780190618858.001.0001.
Mason, Steve. 2007. "Jews, Judaeans, Judaizing, Judaism: Problems of Categorization in Ancient History." *Journal for the Study of Judaism* 38(4–5): 457–512. https://doi.org/10.1163/156851507X193108.
Mathews, Thomas F. 1971. *The Early Churches of Constantinople: Architecture and Liturgy*. University Park, PA: Pennsylvania State University Press.
Matthews, John. 2000. *Laying Down the Law: A Study of the Theodosian Code*. New Haven: Yale University Press.
Maxwell, Jaclyn. 2006. "Lay Piety in the Sermons of John Chrysostom." In *Byzantine Christianity*, edited by Derek Krueger, 19–38. A People's History of Christianity, vol. 3. Minneapolis: Fortress Press.
Mayer, Wendy. 2009. "John Chrysostom on Poverty." In *Preaching Poverty in Late Antiquity: Perceptions and Realities*, edited by Pauline Allen, Bronwen Neil, and Wendy Mayer, 69–118. Leipzig: Evangelische Verlagsanstalt.
McCready, Wayne O. 1996. "*Ekklēsia* and Voluntary Associations." In *Voluntary Associations in the Graeco-Roman World*, edited by S. G. Wilson and John S. Kloppenborg, 59–73. London: Routledge.

McCulloh, John M. 1976. "The Cult of Relics in the Letters and 'Dialogues' of Pope Gregory the Great: A Lexicographical Study." *Traditio* 32(1): 145–184. https://doi.org/10.1017/S0362152900005493.

McCutcheon, Russell. 1997. *Manufacturing Religion: The Discourse on Sui Generis Religion and the Politics of Nostalgia*. New York: Oxford University Press.

McGinn, Bernard. 1994. *Antichrist: Two Thousand Years of the Human Fascination with Evil*. San Francisco: Harper.

McGowan, Anne, and Paul F. Bradshaw. 2018. *The Pilgrimage of Egeria: A New Translation of the "Itinerarium Egeriae" with Introduction and Commentary*. Collegeville, MN: Liturgical Press.

Meens, Rob. 2000. "'A Relic of Superstition': Bodily Impurity and the Church from Gregory the Great to the Twelfth-Century Decretists." In *Purity and Holiness: The Heritage of Leviticus*, edited by Marcel Poorthuis and Joshua Schwartz, 281–293. Jewish and Christian Perspectives Series, vol. 2. Leiden: Brill.

Meier, John P. 1973. "'Presbyteros' in the Pastoral Epistles." *The Catholic Biblical Quarterly* 35(3): 323–345.

Meimaris, Yiannis E., and Kalliope I. Kritikakou-Nikolaropoulou. 2005. *Inscriptions from Palaestina Tertia: The Greek Inscriptions from Ghor es-Safi (Byzantine Zoora)*. Vol. 1. Athens: National Hellenic Research Foundation.

Mellon Saint Laurent, Jeanne Nicole. 2022. "St. Ephrem's Mary: Icon of Wonder, Icon of Beauty." In *The Church and Her Scriptures: Essays in Honor of Patrick J. Hartin*, edited by Catherine Brown Tkacz and Douglas Kries, 61–86. Eugene, OR: Wipf and Stock.

Meyer, Marvin W., and Richard Smith. 1999. *Ancient Christian Magic: Coptic Texts of Ritual Power*. Mythos Series. Princeton, NJ: Princeton University Press.

Meyers, Eric M. 2018. "Ceramic Incense Shovels." In *The Architecture, Stratigraphy, and Artifacts of the Western Summit of Sepphoris*, edited by Eric M. Meyers, Carol L. Meyers, and Benjamin D. Gordon, 644–652. Duke Sepphoris Report, vol. 3. University Park, PA: Eisenbrauns.

Mikalson, Jon D. 1975. *The Sacred and Civil Calendar of the Athenian Year*. Princeton, NJ: Princeton University Press.

Milgrom, Jacob. 2000. "The Dynamics of Purity in the Priestly System." In *Purity and Holiness: The Heritage of Leviticus*, edited by Marcel Poorthuis and Joshua Schwartz, 27–32. Jewish and Christian Perspectives Series, vol. 2. Boston and Leiden: Brill.

Millar, Fergus G. B. 1998. "Ethnic Identity in the Roman Near East, 325–450: Language, Religion, and Culture." *Mediterranean Archaeology* 11: 159–176.

Millar, Fergus G. B. 2011. "Inscriptions, Synagogues and Rabbis in Late Antique Palestine." *Journal for the Study of Judaism* 42(2): 253–277. https://doi.org/10.1163/157006311X544382.

Miller, Patricia Cox. 1983. *Biography in Late Antiquity: A Quest for the Holy Man*. The Transformation of the Classical Heritage, vol. 5. Berkeley: University of California Press.

Miller, Patricia Cox. 1994. *Dreams in Late Antiquity: Studies in the Imagination of a Culture*. Princeton, NJ: Princeton University Press.

Miller, Samantha L. 2020. *Chrysostom's Devil: Demons, the Will, and Virtue in Patristic Soteriology*. Downer's Grove: InterVarsity Press.

Miller, Stuart S. 2006. *Sages and Commoners in Late Antique 'Ereẓ Israel: A Philological Inquiry into Local Traditions in Talmud Yerushalmi*. Texte und Studien zum antiken Judentum, vol. 111. Tübingen: Mohr Siebeck.

Millett, Paul. 1984. "Hesiod and His World." *The Cambridge Classical Journal* 30: 84–115. https://doi.org/10.1017/S006867350000465X.

Mitchell, Stephen. 1999. "The Cult of Theos Hypsistos between Pagans, Jews, and Christians." In *Pagan Monotheism in Late Antiquity*, edited by Polymnia Athanassiadi and Michael Frede, 81–148. Oxford: Clarendon Press.

Mitchell, Stephen. 2010. "Further Thoughts on the Cult of Theos Hypsistos." In *One God: Pagan Monotheism in the Roman Empire*, edited by Stephen Mitchell and Peter van Nuffelen, 167–208. Cambridge and New York: Cambridge University Press.

Mittag, Peter Franz. 2019. "Antiochus IV Epiphanes's Policy toward the Jews." In *Intolerance, Polemics, and Debate in Antiquity: Politico-Cultural, Philosophical, and Religious Forms of Critical Conversation*, edited by George H. van Kooten and Jacques van Ruiten, 186–204. Boston and Leiden: Brill.

Mizzi, Dennis. 2016. "The Animal Bone Deposits at Qumran: An Unsolvable Riddle?" *Journal of Ancient Judaism* 7(1): 51–70. https://doi.org/10.30965/21967954-00701005.

Mokhtarian, Jason Sion. 2012. "Empire and Authority in Sasanian Babylonia: The Rabbis and King Shapur in Dialogue." *Jewish Studies Quarterly* 19(2): 148–180.

Mommsen, Th., and P. M. Meyer, eds. 1905. *Codex Theodosianus*. Berlin.

Moorhead, John. 2009. "Boethius' Life and the World of Late Antique Philosophy." In *The Cambridge Companion to Boethius*, edited by John Marenbon, 1–33. Cambridge: Cambridge University Press.

Moorhead, Sam. 2012. "The Coinage of the Later Roman Empire, 364–498." In *The Oxford Handbook of Greek and Roman Coinage*, edited by William E. Metcalf, 601–632. Oxford and New York: Oxford University Press.

Morgan, Teresa. 1998. *Literate Education in the Hellenistic and Roman Worlds*. Cambridge and New York: Cambridge University Press.

Moskovitz, Leib. 2019. "Rabbinic Law." In *The Oxford Handbook of Biblical Law*, edited by Pamela Barmash, 451–470. Oxford Handbooks Online. New York: Oxford University Press.

Moss, Candida R. 2012. *Ancient Christian Martyrdom: Diverse Practices, Theologies, and Traditions*. The Anchor Yale Bible Reference Library. New Haven: Yale University Press.

Mossong, Isabelle. 2022. *Der Klerus des spätantiken Italiens im Spiegel epigraphischer Zeugnisse: Eine soziohistorische Studie*. Berlin: De Gruyter.

Mousourakis, G. 2007. *A Legal History of Rome*. London and New York: Routledge.

Mucznik, Sonia, and Asher Ovadiah. 2014. "'*Deisidaimonia, Superstitio* and *Religio*: Graeco-Roman, Jewish, and Early Christian Concepts." *Liber Annus: Studium Biblicum Franciscanum* 64: 417–440.

Muehlberger, Ellen. 2013. *Angels in Late Ancient Christianity*. New York: Oxford University Press.

Münz-Manor, Ophir. 2010. "Liturgical Poetry in the Late Antique Near East." *Journal of Ancient Judaism* 1(3): 336–361.

Murray, Robert. 1975. *Symbols of Church and Kingdom: A Study in Early Syriac Tradition*. London: Cambridge University Press.

Mylonopoulos, Jannis, ed. 2010. *Divine Images and Human Imaginations in Ancient Greece and Rome*. Religions in the Graeco-Roman World, vol. 170. Leiden: Brill.

Naether, Franziska. 2010. *Die Sortes Astrampsychi: Problemlösungsstrategien durch Orakel im römischen Ägypten*. Orientalische Religionen in der Antike, vol. 3. Tübingen: Mohr Siebeck.

Nasrallah, Laura S. 2010. *Christian Responses to Roman Art and Architecture: The Second-Century Church amid the Spaces of Empire*. Cambridge and New York: Cambridge University Press.

Nathan, Geoffrey. 2000. *The Family in Late Antiquity: The Rise of Christianity and the Endurance of Tradition*. London: Routledge.

Naveh, Joseph. 1979. "Graffiti and Dedications." *Bulletin of the American Society of Oriental Research* 235: 27–30.

Naveh, Joseph, and Shaul Shaked. 1993. *Magic Spells and Formulae: Aramaic Incantations of Late Antiquity*. Jerusalem: Magnes Press.

Neil, Bronwen. 2016. "Studying Dream Interpretation from Early Christianity to the Rise of Islam." *Journal of Religious History* 40(1): 44–64. https://doi.org/10.1111/1467-9809.12262.

Nissinen, Martti. 2017. *Ancient Prophecy: Near Eastern, Biblical, and Greek Perspectives*. Oxford: Oxford University Press.

Nock, Arthur Darby, ed. 1926. *Sallustius concerning the Gods and the Universe*. Cambridge: Cambridge University Press.

Nock, Arthur Darby. 1933. *Conversion: The Old and the New in Religion from Alexander the Great to Augustine of Hippo*. Donnellan Lectures 1931. Trinity College, Dublin, Ireland. Oxford: Clarendon Press.

Nock, Arthur Darby. 1947. "The Emperor's Divine Comes." *Journal of Roman Studies* 37(1–2): 102–116.

Nongbri, Brent. 2013. *Before Religion: A History of a Modern Concept*. New Haven: Yale University Press.

Novick, Tzvi. 2017. "I Am Not a Butcher." *Journal of Ancient Judaism* 8(1): 112–144.

Noy, David, ed. 2005. *Jewish Inscriptions of Western Europe*. 2 vols. Cambridge and New York: Cambridge University Press.

Noy, David, H. Bloedhorn, and Alexander Panayotov, eds. 2004. *Inscriptiones Judaicae Orientis*. 3 vols. Tübingen: Mohr Siebeck.

Ogden, Daniel. 2001. *Greek and Roman Necromancy*. Princeton, NJ: Princeton University Press.

Olyan, Saul. 2018. "The Territoriality of YHWH in Biblical Texts." In *Strength to Strength: Essays in Appreciation of Shaye J. D. Cohen*, edited by Michael L. Satlow, 45-52. Brown Judaic Studies, vol. 363. Providence, RI: Brown Judaic Studies.

Orr, David G. 1978. "Roman Domestic Religion: The Evidence of the Household Shrines." *Aufstieg und Niedergang der Römischen Welt* 16.2: 1557-1591. https://doi.org/10.1515/9783110851335-016

Pagels, Elaine H. 1995. *The Origin of Satan*. New York: Random House.

Palladius. 1898. *The Lausiac History. Translated by Cuthbert* Butler. Texts and Studies: Contributions to Biblical and Patristic Literature, vol. 6, nos. 1–2. Cambridge: Cambridge University Press.

Parrish, David. 1979. "Two Mosaics from Roman Tunisia: An African Variation of the Season Theme." *American Journal of Archaeology* 83(3): 279–285.

Paz, Yakir. 2019. "Metatron Is Not Enoch: Reevaluating the Evolution of an Archangel." *Journal for the Study of Judaism* 50(1): 52–100. https://doi.org/10.1163/15700631-12501239.

Pennington, Brian K. 2001. "Constructing Colonial Dharma: A Chronicle of Emergent Hinduism, 1830–1831." *Journal of the American Academy of Religion* 6(3): 577–603.

Perkins, J. B. Ward. 1954. "Constantine and the Origins of the Christian Basilica." *Papers of the British School at Rome* 22: 69–90. https://doi.org/10.1017/S0068246200006541.

Petropoulou, M. Z. 2008. *Animal Sacrifice in Ancient Greek Religion, Judaism, and Christianity, 100 BC–AD 200*. Oxford Classical Monographs. Oxford: Oxford University Press.

Petzl, Georg. 1994. *Die Beichtinschriften Westkleinasiens*. Epigraphica Anatolica, vol. 22. Bonn: R. Habelt.

Pharr, Clyde, trans. 1952. *The Theodosian Code and Novels, and the Sirmondian Constitutions*. Princeton, NJ: Princeton University Press.

Phillips, L. Edward. 1989. "Daily Prayer in the 'Apostolic Tradition' of Hippolytus." *Journal of Theological Studies* 4(2): 389–400.

Phillips, L. Edward. 2018. "Early Christian Prayer." In *The Oxford Handbook of Early Christian Ritual*, edited by Risto Uro, Juliette J. Day, Rikard Roitto, and Richard E. DeMaris, 570–586. Oxford and New York: Oxford University Press.

Picus, Daniel Max. 2017. "Ink Sea, Parchment Sky: Rabbinic Reading Practices in Late Antiquity." PhD dissertation, Brown University.

Pietri, Charles. 1997. "Le temps de la semaine à Rome et dans l'Italie chrétienne (IVe-VIe siècle)." *Publications de l'École Française de Rome* 234(1): 201–235.

Piranomonte, Marina. 2009. "Religion and Magic at Rome: The Fountain of Anna Perenna." In *Magical Practice in the Latin West: Papers from the International Conference Held at the University of Zaragoza, 30 Sept.–1st Oct. 2005*, edited by Marco Simón and R. L. Gordon, 191–213. Religions in the Graeco-Roman World, vol. 168. Boston: Brill. https://doi.org/10.1163/ej.9789004179042.i-676.

Platt, Verity J. 2011. *Facing the Gods: Epiphany and Representation in Graeco-Roman Art, Literature and Religion*. Greek Culture in the Roman World. Cambridge: Cambridge University Press.

Pliny. 1968–1984. *Natural History*. Translated by Harris Rackham. Loeb Classical Library, vol. 418. Cambridge, MA: Harvard University Press.

Pohl, Walter. 1998. "Telling the Difference: Signs of Ethnic Identity." In *Strategies of Distinction: The Construction of Ethnic Communities, 300–800*, edited by Walter Pohl and Helmut Reimitz, 17–69. The Transformation of the Roman World, vol. 2. Leiden: Brill.

Possiel, Scott. 2020. "More than Text: Approaching Ritual Papyri from Oxyrhynchus as Inscribed Objects." *Archiv für Religionsgeschichte* 21–22(1): 175–200. https://doi.org/10.1515/arege-2020-0009.

Preisendanz, Karl, ed. 1973–74. *Papyri Graecae Magicae*. 2 vols. Stuttgart: Teubner.

Price, Jonathan J. 2023. "Jewish Proselytes in Inscriptions: An Update and Reassessment." In *Religion und Epigraphik: Kleinasien, der griechische Osten und die Mittelmeerwelt: Festschrift zum 65. Geburtstag von Walter Ameling*, edited by Walter Ameling, Dagmar Hofmann, Andreas Klingenberg, and Klaus Zimmermann, 119–135. Bonn: Dr. Rudolf Habelt.

Price, Richard. 2009. "Martyrdom and the Cult of the Saints." In *The Oxford Handbook of Early Christian Studies*, edited by Susan Ashbrook Harvey and David G. Hunter, 808–825. Oxford: Oxford University Press. https://doi.org/10.1093/oxfordhb/9780199271566.003.0040.

Price, Richard. 2019. "The Virgin as Theotokos at Ephesus (ad 431) and Earlier." In *The Oxford Handbook of Mary*, edited by Chris Maunder, 67–77. Oxford: Oxford University Press.

Proclus. 2009. *Commentary on Plato's Timaeus, Part 2, Proclus on the World Soul*. Edited by Dirk Baltzly. Cambridge: Cambridge University Press.

Puiggali, Jacques. 1983. "La démonologie de Philostrate." *Revue des sciences philosophiques et théologiques* 67(1): 116–130.

Pulleyn, Simon. 1997. *Prayer in Greek Religion*. Oxford Classical Monographs. Clarendon Press: Oxford.

Rackham, Harris, trans. 1968–1984. *Natural History*. By Pliny Loeb Classical Library, vol. 418. Cambridge, MA: Harvard University Press.

Rajak, Tessa, and David Noy. 1993. "*Archisynagogoi*: Office, Title and Social Status in the Greco-Jewish Synagogue." *Journal of Roman Studies* 83(83): 75–93. https://doi.org/10.2307/300979.

Ramelli, Ilaria L. E. 2017. "Origen and the Platonic Tradition." *Religions* 8(2): 21. https://doi.org/10.3390/rel8020021.

Rapp, Claudia. 2005. *Holy Bishops in Late Antiquity the Nature of Christian Leadership in an Age of Transition*. The Joan Palevsky Imprint in Classical Literature. Berkeley: University of California Press.

Rapp, Claudia. 2007. "Holy Texts, Holy Men, and Holy Scribes: Aspects of Scriptural Holiness in Late Antiquity." In *The Early Christian Book*, edited by William E. Klingshirn and Linda Safran, 194–222. CUA Studies in Early Christianity. Washington, DC: Catholic University of America Press.

Rebiger, Bill. 2007. "Angels in Rabbinic Literature." *Deuterocanonical and Cognate Literature Yearbook*: 629–644.

Rebiger, Bill. 2018. "Engel und Dämonen im rabbinischen Denken und in der jüdischen Magie." *Chilufim: Zeitschrift für jüdische Kulturgeschichte* 25: 3–38.

Rebillard, Éric. 2009. *The Care of the Dead in Late Antiquity*. Cornell Studies in Classical Philology, vol. 59. Ithaca: Cornell University Press.

Rebillard, Éric. 2015. "Late Antique Limits of Christianness: North Africa in the Age of Augustus." In *Group Identity and Religious Individuality in Late Antiquity*, edited by Éric Rebillard and Jörg Rüpke, 293–317. CUA Studies in Early Christianity. Washington DC: Catholic University of America Press. https://doi.org/10.2307/j.ctt15zc8w0.2.

Reif, Stefan. 2010. "Prayer in Liturgy." In *The Oxford Handbook of Jewish Daily Life in Roman Palestine*, edited by Catherine Hezser, 545–565. Oxford: Oxford University Press.

Reinhartz, Adele. 2014. "The Vanishing Jews of Antiquity—By Adele Reinhartz." *The Marginalia Review of Books* (blog). June 24, 2014. https://themarginaliareview.com/vanishing-jews-antiquity-adele-reinhartz.

Renswoude, Iren van. 2019. *The Rhetoric of Free Speech in Late Antiquity and the Early Middle Ages*. Cambridge: Cambridge University Press.

Reynolds, J., and R. F. Tannenbaum. 1987. *Jews and Godfearers at Aphrodisias: Greek Inscriptions with Commentary*. Proceedings of the Cambridge Philological Society Ser., vol. 12. Cambridge: Cambridge Philological Society.

Reynolds, Joyce, Charlotte Roueché, and Gabriel Bodard. 2007. *Inscriptions of Aphrodisias*. https://insaph.kcl.ac.uk/iaph2007.

Rist, John M. 1965. "Hypatia." *Phoenix* 19(3): 214–225.

Rist, Martin. 1938. "The God of Abraham, Isaac, and Jacob: A Liturgical and Magical Formula." *Journal of Biblical Literature* 57(3): 289–303.

Ritner, Robert Kriech. 1993. *The Mechanics of Ancient Egyptian Magical Practice*. Studies in Ancient Oriental Civilization, vol. 54. Chicago: Oriental Institute of Chicago.

Rives, James B. 1999. "The Decree of Decius and the Religion of Empire." *Journal of Roman Studies* 89: 135–154. https://doi.org/10.2307/300738.

Rives, James B. 2003. "Magic in Roman Law: The Reconstruction of a Crime." *Classical Antiquity* 22(2): 313–339. https://doi.org/10.1525/ca.2003.22.2.313.

Rives, James B. 2007. *Religion in the Roman Empire*. Blackwell Ancient Religions. Malden, MA: Blackwell.

Rives, James B. 2012. "Control of the Sacred in Roman Law." In *Law and Religion in the Roman Republic*, edited by O. E. Tellegan-Couperus, 165–180. Leiden: Brill. https://doi.org/10.1163/9789004219205_010.

Robinson, Mark. 2002. "Domestic Burn Offerings and Sacrifices at Roman and Pre-Roman Pompeii, Italy." *Vegetation History and Archaeobotany* 11: 93–100.

Robinson, Olivia. 1975. "The Roman Law on Burials and Burial Grounds." *Irish Jurist* 10(1): 175–186.

Rochberg-Halton, F. 1984. "New Evidence for the History of Astrology." *Journal of Near Eastern Studies* 43(2): 115–140. https://doi.org/10.1086/373070.

Rogers, Guy M. 1991. "Demosthenes of Oenoanda and Models of Euergetism." *Journal of Roman Studies* 81: 91–100.

Rollston, Chris A. 2010. *Writing and Literacy in the World of Ancient Israel: Epigraphic Evidence from the Iron Age*. Archaeology and Biblical Studies, vol. 11. Leiden: Brill.

Ronis, Sara. 2019. "A Seven-Headed Demon in the House of Study: Understanding a Rabbinic Demon in Light of Zoroastrian, Christian, and Babylonian Textual Traditions." *AJS Review* 43(1): 125–142.

Ronis, Sara. 2022. *Demons in the Details: Demonic Discourse and Rabbinic Culture in Late Antique Babylonia*. Berkeley: University of California Press.

Rordorf, Willy. 1968. *Sunday: The History of the Day of Rest and Worship in the Earliest Centuries of the Christian Church*. Philadelphia: Westminster Press.

Rose, E. M. 2002. "Gregory of Tours and the Conversion of the Jews of Clermont." In *The World of Gregory of Tours*, edited by Kathleen Mitchell and I. N. Wood, 307–320. Cultures, Beliefs, and Traditions, vol. 8. Leiden: Brill.

Rose, Martin. 1992. "Names of God in the OT." In *Anchor Bible Dictionary*, edited by David Noel Freedman, 4: 1001–1011. New York: Doubleday.

Rosenberg, Michael. 2016. "Sexual Serpents and Perpetual Virginity: Marian Rejectionism in the Babylonian Talmud." *Jewish Quarterly Review* 106(4): 465–493. https://doi.org/10.1353/jqr.2016.0035.

Rosen-Zvi, Ishay. 2011. *Demonic Desires: Yetzer Hara and the Problem of Evil in Late Antiquity*. Divinations. Philadelphia: University of Pennsylvania Press.

Roth-Gerson, Lea. 1987. *ha-Ketovot ha-Yeṿaniyot mi-bate-ha-keneset be-Erets-Yiśra'el*. Jerusalem: Yad Yitzchak ben Zvi.

Rotman, Youval. 2021. "Between Ethnos and Populus: The Boundaries of Being a Jew." In *Rome: An Empire of Many Nations: New Perspectives on Ethnic Diversity and Cultural Identity*, edited by Jonathan J. Price, Margalit Finkelberg, and Yuval Shaḥar, 203–222. Cambridge and New York: Cambridge University Press.

Roubekas, Nickolas P. 2017. *An Ancient Theory of Religion: Euhemerism from Antiquity to the Present*. Routledge Monographs in Classical Studies. Abingdon: Routledge.

Rubenstein, Jeffrey L. 2007. "Talmudic Astrology: *Bavli Šabbat* 156a-b." *Hebrew Union College Annual* 78: 109–148.

Rubin, Miri. 2009. *Mother of God: A History of the Virgin Mary*. New Haven: Yale University Press.

Ruden, Sarah, trans. 2011. *Apuleius, The Golden Ass*. New Haven: Yale University Press.

Runia, David T. 2002. "One of Us or One of Them? Christian Reception of Philo the Jew in Egypt." In *Shem in the Tents of Japhet: Essays on the Encounter of Judaism and Hellenism*, edited by James L. Kugel, 203–222. Leiden: Brill.

Rüpke, Jörg. 2011. *The Roman Calendar from Numa to Constantine: Time, History, and the Fasti*. Hoboken: John Wiley & Sons.

Rüpke, Jörg. 2012. *Religion in Republican Rome: Rationalization and Ritual Change*. Empire and After. Philadelphia: University of Pennsylvania Press.

Rüpke, Jörg. 2018. *Pantheon: A New History of Roman Religion*. Princeton, NJ: Princeton University Press.

Russell, Jeffrey Burton. 1981. *Satan: The Early Christian Tradition*. Ithaca: Cornell University Press.

Russell, Norman. 2005. *The Doctrine of Deification in the Greek Patristic Tradition*. Oxford: Oxford University Press.

Rutgers, Leonard Victor. 1995. *The Jews in Late Ancient Rome: Evidence of Cultural Interaction in the Roman Diaspora*. Religions in the Graeco-Roman World, vol. 126. Leiden: E. J. Brill.

Safrai, Chana. 2004. "Rabbinic Holy Men." In *Saints and Role Models in Judaism and Christianity*, edited by Joshua Schwartz and Marcel Poorthuis, 59–78. Leiden: Brill.

Safrai, Zeev. 1994. *The Economy of Roman Palestine*. London and New York: Routledge.

Salminen, Joona. 2016. "The City of God and the Place of Demons: City Life and Demonology in Early Christianity." In *Spaces in Late Antiquity: Cultural, Theological and Archaeological Perspectives*, edited by Juliette Day, Raimo Hakola, Maijastina Kahlos, and Ulla Tervahauta, 106–117. Abingdon: Routledge.

Salzman, Michele R. 1987. "'Superstitio' in the 'Codex Theodosianus' and the Persecution of Pagans." *Vigiliae Christianae* 41(2): 172–188. https://doi.org/10.2307/1584108.

Salzman, Michele Renee. 1990. *On Roman Time: The Codex-Calendar of 354 and the Rhythms of Urban Life in Late Antiquity*. The Transformation of the Classical Heritage, vol. 17. Berkeley: University of California Press.

Salzman, Michele Renee. 1993. "The Evidence for the Conversion of the Roman Empire to Christianity in Book 16 of the 'Theodosian Code.'" *Historia: Zeitschrift für Alte Geschichte* 42(3): 362–378.

Salzman, Michele Renee. 2004. "Pagan and Christian Notions of the Week in the 4th Century CE Western Roman Empire." In *Time and Temporality in the Ancient World*, edited by Ralph M. Rosen, 185–211. Philadelphia: University of Pennsylvania Museum of Archaeology.

Salzman, Michele R. 2011. "The End of Public Sacrifice: Changing Definitions of Sacrifice in Post-Constantinian Rome and Italy." In *Ancient Mediterranean Sacrifice*, edited by Jennifer Wright Knust and Zsuzsanna Várhelyi, 167–185. New York: Oxford University Press.

Salzman, Michele R. 2021. "Simony and the State: Politics and Religion in the Later Roman Empire." In *Late-Antique Studies in Memory of Alan Cameron*, edited by William V. Harris and Anne Hunnell Chen, 198–219. Boston: Brill.

Satlow, Michael L., ed. 2002–. *Inscriptions of Israel/Palestine*. http://inscriptionsisraelpalestine.org.

Satlow, Michael L. 2010. "'Fruit and the Fruit of Fruit': Charity and Piety among Jews in Late Antique Palestine." *Jewish Quarterly Review* 100(2): 244–277.

Satlow, Michael L. 2013. "Jew or Judaean?" In *"The One Who Sows Bountifully": Essays in Honor of Stanley K. Stowers*, edited by Caroline Johnson Hodge, Saul M. Olyan, Daniel Ullucci, and Emma Wasserman, 165–175. Brown Judaic Studies. Providence, RI: Brown Judaic Studies.

Satlow, Michael L. 2014a. *How the Bible Became Holy*. New Haven: Yale University Press.

Satlow, Michael L. 2014b. "Markets and Tithes in Roman Palestine." In *Gift Giving and the "Embedded" Economy in the Ancient World*, edited by Filippo Carlà and Maja Gori, 315–335. Akademiekonferenzen, vol. 17. Heidelberg: Universitätsverlag Winter.

Satlow, Michael L. 2021. "The Status of Torah in Late Antiquity." In *Torah: Functions, Meanings, and Diverse Manifestations in Early Judaism and Christianity*, edited by William M. Schniedewind, Jason M. Zurawski, and Gabriele Boccaccini, 459–472. Atlanta: SBL Press.

Satlow, Michael L. 2024. "Personal Representations of the Holy." In *The Routledge Handbook of Jews and Judaism in Late Antiquity*, edited by Catherine Hezser, 203–215. Abingdon and New York: Routledge.

Schäfer, Peter. 1975. *Rivalität Zwischen Engeln und Menschen: Untersuchungen z. Rabbin. Engelvorstellung*. Berlin: De Gruyter.

Schäfer, Peter. 1981. *Synopse zur Hekhalot-Literatur*. Texte und Studien zum antiken Judentum, vol. 2. Tübingen: J. C. B. Mohr.

Schäfer, Peter. 2007. *Jesus in the Talmud*. Princeton, NJ: Princeton University Press.

Schäfer, Peter. 2009. *The Origins of Jewish Mysticism*. Princeton, NJ: Princeton University Press.

Schäfer, Peter. 2020. *Two Gods in Heaven: Jewish Concepts of God in Antiquity*. Princeton, NJ: Princeton University Press.

Schäfer, Peter, and Shaul Shaked. 1994–99. *Magische Texte aus der Kairoer Geniza*. Texte und Studien zum antiken Judentum, vol. 42, 64, 72. Tübingen: J. C. B. Mohr.

Schechter, S. 1923. *Some Aspects of Rabbinic Theology*. New York: Macmillan.

Scheid, John. 2007. "Sacrifices for Gods and Ancestors." In *A Companion to Roman Religion*, edited by Jörg Rüpke, 263–271. Blackwell Companions to the Ancient World. Ancient History. Malden, MA: Blackwell.

Scheid, John. 2012. "Roman Animal Sacrifice and the System of Being." In *Greek and Roman Animal Sacrifice: Ancient Victims, Modern Observers,* edited by Christopher A. Faraone and F. S. Naiden, 84–95. Cambridge: Cambridge University Press.

Schenk, Christine. 2017. *Crispina and Her Sisters: Women and Authority in Early Christianity.* Minneapolis: Fortress Press.

Schiffman, Lawrence H., and Michael D. Swartz. 1992. *Hebrew and Aramaic Incantation Texts from the Cairo Genizah: Selected Texts from Taylor-Schechter Box Kl.* Semitic Texts and Studies, vol. 1. Sheffield: JSOT Press.

Schnabel, Eckhard J. 2003. "Divine Tyranny and Public Humiliation: A Suggestion for the Interpretation of the Lydian and Phrygian Confession Inscriptions." *Novum Testamentum* 45(2): 160-188. https://www.jstor.org/stable/1561015.

Schniedewind, William M. 2019. *The Finger of the Scribe: How Scribes Learned to Write the Bible.* Oxford Scholarship Online. New York: Oxford University Press.

Schörner, Günther. 2015. "Anatomical ex votos." In *A Companion to the Archaeology of Religion in the Ancient World,* edited by Rubina Raja and Jörg Rüpke, 397–411. Malden, MA: Wiley Blackwell.

Schott, Jeremy. 2008. *Christianity, Empire, and the Making of Religion in Late Antiquity.* Divinations. Philadelphia: University of Pennsylvania Press.

Schremer, Adiel. 2012. "Thinking about Belonging in Early Rabbinic Literature: Proselytes, Apostates, and 'Children of Israel', or: Does It Make Sense to Speak of Early Rabbinic Orthodoxy?" *Journal for the Study of Judaism in the Persian, Hellenistic and Roman Period* 43(2): 249–275.

Schultz, Celia E. 2016. "Roman Sacrifice, Inside and Out." *Journal of Roman Studies* 106: 58–76. https://doi.org/10.1017/S0075435816000319.

Schwartz, Daniel R. 2007. "'Judaean' or 'Jew'? How Should We Translate *Ioudaios* in Josephus?" In *Jewish Identity in the Greco-Roman World,* edited by Jörg Frey, Daniel R. Schwartz, and Stephanie Gripentrog, 3–27. Leiden: Brill.

Schwartz, Seth. 2001. *Imperialism and Jewish Society, 200 B.C.E. to 640 C.E.* Core Textbook. Jews, Christians, and Muslims from the Ancient to the Modern World. Princeton, NJ: Princeton University Press.

Schwartz, Seth. 2011. "How Many Judaisms Were There?: A Critique of Neusner and Smith on Definition and Mason and Boyarin on Categorization." *Journal of Ancient Judaism* 2(2): 208-238.

Segal, M. H. 1955. "El, Elohim, and Yhwh in the Bible." *Jewish Quarterly Review* 46(2): 89–115. https://doi.org/10.2307/1452792.

Segal, Robert A. 2004. *Myth: A Very Short Introduction.* Oxford: Oxford University Press.

Septimus, Yehuda. 2015. *On the Boundaries of Talmudic Prayer.* Texts and Studies in Ancient Judaism, vol. 161. Tübingen: Mohr Siebeck.

Sered, Susan Starr. 1995. "Rachel's Tomb: The Development of a Cult." *Jewish Studies Quarterly* 2(2): 103–148.

Shaked, Shaul, James Nathan Ford, and Siam Bhayro. 2013. *Aramaic Bowl Spells: Jewish Babylonian Aramaic Bowls.* Vol. 1. Magical and Religious Literature of Late Antiquity, vol. 1. Leiden: Brill.

Shaw, Gregory. 1985. "Theurgy: Rituals of Unification in the Neoplatonism of Iamblichus." *Traditio* 41: 1–28.

Sheerin, Daniel. 2008. "Eucharistic Liturgy." In *The Oxford Handbook of Early Christian Studies,* edited by Susan Ashbrook Harvey and David G. Hunter, 711–743. Oxford: Oxford University Press. https://doi.org/10.1093/oxfordhb/9780199271566.003.0036.

Sheppard, Anne. 1982. "Proclus' Attitude to Theurgy." *Classical Quarterly* 32(1): 212–224.

Sherk, Robert K. 1969. *Roman Documents from the Greek East: Senatus Consulta and Epistulae to the Age of Augustus*. Baltimore: Johns Hopkins University Press.

Shoemaker, Stephen J. 2016. *Mary in Early Christian Faith and Devotion*. New Haven: Yale University Press.

Shyovitz, David I. 2015. "'You Have Saved Me from the Judgment of Gehenna': The Origins of the Mourner's Kaddish in Medieval Ashkenaz." *AJS Review* 39(1): 49–73.

Sironen, Erkki. 2012. "Heidnische Priester in Attika vom dritten bis zum fünften Jahrhundert nach Christus." In *Civic Priests*, edited by Marietta Horster and Anja Klöckner, 209–218. Religionsgeschichtliche Versuche und Vorarbeiten, vol. 58. Berlin and Boston: De Gruyter. https://doi.org/10.1515/9783110258080.209.

Sivan, Hagith. 2008. *Palestine in Late Antiquity*. Oxford: Oxford University Press.

Sivertsev, Alexei. 2011. *Judaism and Imperial Ideology in Late Antiquity*. Cambridge: Cambridge University Press.

Sivertsev, Alexei. 2024. "Synagogues and Churches as the Centers of Local Communities." In *The Routledge Handbook of Jews and Judaism in Late Antiquity*, edited by Catherine Hezser, 111–125. Abingdon: Routledge.

Slane, Kathleen W., and Guy D. R. Sanders. 2005. "Corinth: Late Roman Horizons." *Hesperia: The Journal of the American School of Classical Studies at Athens* 74(2): 243–297.

Smith, Geoffrey S. 2020. *Valentinian Christianity: Texts and Translations*. Berkeley: University of California Press.

Smith, Gregory A. 2008. "How Thin Is a Demon?" *Journal of Early Christian Studies* 16(4): 479–512. https://doi.org/10.1353/earl.0.0229.

Smith, Jonathan Z. 1972. "The Wobbling Pivot." *Journal of Religion* 52(2): 134-149.

Smith, Jonathan Z. 1978. *Map Is Not Territory: Studies in the History of Religions*. Studies in Judaism in Late Antiquity, vol. 23. Leiden: Brill.

Smith, Jonathan Z. 1990. *Drudgery Divine: On the Comparison of Early Christianities and the Religions of Late Antiquity*. Jordan Lectures in Comparative Religion, vol. 14. Chicago: University of Chicago Press.

Smith, Kyle. 2016. *Constantine and the Captive Christians of Persia: Martyrdom and Religious Identity in Late Antiquity*. Transformation of the Classical Heritage, vol. 57. Berkeley: University of California Press.

Smith, Mark S. 2001. *The Origins of Biblical Monotheism: Israel's Polytheistic Background and the Ugaritic Texts*. New York: Oxford University Press.

Smith, R. R. R. 1990. "Late Roman Philosopher Portraits from Aphrodisias." *Journal of Roman Studies* 80: 127–177. https://doi.org/10.2307/300284.

Sommar, Mary E. 2020. *The Slaves of the Church: A History*. Oxford: Oxford University Press.

Sonia, Kerry M. 2022. "Contested Divination: Biblical Necromancy and Competition among Ritual Specialists in Ancient Israel." In *New Perspectives on Ritual in the Biblical World*, edited by Laura Quick and Melissa Ramos, 103–116. Library of Hebrew Bible/Old Testament Studies, vol. 702. London: Bloomsbury.

Souter, Alexander, trans. 1920. *Against Praxeas*. By Tertullian. Translations of Christian Literature, Series II, Latin Texts. London: Society for Promoting Christian Knowledge and New York: Macmillan.

Sourvinou-Inwood, Christiane. 2000a. "Further Aspects of *Polis* Religion." In *Oxford Readings in Greek Religion*, edited by Richard Buxton, 38–55. Oxford: Oxford University Press.

Sourvinou-Inwood, Christiane. 2000b. "What Is *Polis* Religion?" In *Oxford Readings in Greek Religion*, edited by Richard Buxton, 13–37. Oxford Readings in Classical Studies. Oxford: Oxford University Press.

Spivey, Nigel. 1995. "Bionic Statues." In *The Greek World*, edited by Anton Powell, 442-460. London: Routledge.

Springer, Lawrence A. 1954. "The Cult and Temple of Jupiter Feretrius." *Classical Journal* 50(1): 27–32.

Stafford, Grace. 2022. "Between the Living and the Dead: Use, Reuse, and Imitation of Painted Portraits in Late Antiquity." *Journal of Roman Archaeology* 35(2): 683–712. https://doi.org/10.1017/S1047759422000319.

Stemberger, Günter. 2008. "Sages, Scribes, and Seers in Rabbinic Judaism." In *Scribes, Sages and Seers: The Sage in the Eastern Mediterranean World*, edited by Leo G. Perdue, 295–310. Forschungen zur Religion und Literatur des Alten und Neuen Testaments, vol. 219. Göttingen: Vandenhoeck and Ruprecht.

Stern, H. 1981. "Les calendriers romains illustriés." *Aufstieg und Niedergang der Römischen Welt* 12(2): 432–475.

Stern, Karen B. 2018. *Writing on the Wall: Graffiti and the Forgotten Jews of Antiquity*. Princeton, NJ: Princeton University Press.

Stern, Menachem. 1974–94. *Greek and Latin Authors on Jews and Judaism*. 3 vols. Jerusalem: Hebrew University Press.

Stern, Sacha. 2001. *Calendar and Community: A History of the Jewish Calendar, Second Century BCE–Tenth Century CE*. Oxford: Oxford University Press.

Stern, Sacha. 2012. "The Rabbinic New Moon Procedure: Context and Significance." In *Living the Lunar Calendar*, edited by Jonathan Ben-Dov, Wayne Horowitz, and John M. Steele, 211–230. Oxford: Oxbow Books.

Stern, Sacha. 2016. "A Primitive Rabbinic Calendar Text from the Cairo Genizah." *Journal of Jewish Studies* 67(1): 68–90.

Stern, Sacha. 2017. "The Jewish Aramaic Tombstones from Zoar." *Journal of Jewish Studies* 68(1): 158–179.

Stern, Sacha. 2019. *The Jewish Calendar Controversy of 921/2 CE*. Time, Astronomy, and Calendars, vol. 7. Leiden: Brill.

Stowers, Stanley. 2011. "The Religion of Plant and Animal Offerings versus the Religion of Meanings, Essences, and Textual Mysteries." In *Ancient Mediterranean Sacrifice*, edited by Jennifer Wright Knust and Zsuzsanna Várhelyi, 35–56. New York: Oxford University Press.

Stowers, Stanley. 2016. "Why Expert versus Nonexpert Is Not Elite versus Popular Religion: The Case of the Third Century." In *Religious Competition in the Greco-Roman World*, edited by Nathaniel P. DesRosiers and Lily C. Vuong, 139–154. Atlanta: SBL Press.

Stratton, Kimberly B. 2007. *Naming the Witch: Magic, Ideology, & Stereotype in the Ancient World*. Gender, Theory, & Religion. New York: Columbia University Press.

Strickland, Debra Higgs. 2003. *Saracens, Demons & Jews: Making Monsters in Medieval Art*. Princeton, NJ: Princeton University Press.

Stroumsa, Guy G. 2009. *The End of Sacrifice: Religious Transformations in Late Antiquity*. Chicago: University of Chicago Press.

Stutz, Jonathan. 2020. "Mocking Parades and the Place of Pagan Statuary in Late Antique Alexandria." *Zeitschrift für Antikes Christentum / Journal of Ancient Christianity* 24(2): 270–288. https://doi.org/10.1515/zac-2020-0022.

Swartz, Michael D. 2012. "Liturgy, Poetry, and the Persistence of Sacrifice." In *Was 70 CE a Watershed in Jewish History?*, edited by Daniel R. Schwartz and Zeev Weiss, 393–412. Leiden: Brill.

Taft, Robert F. 1983. *The Liturgy of the Hours in the Christian East: Origins, Meaning, Place in the Life of the Church*. Kerala: KCM Press.

Talgam, Rina. 2014. *Mosaics of Faith: Floors of Pagans, Jews, Samaritans, Christians, and Muslims in the Holy Land*. Treasures of the Past. Jerusalem: Yad Ben-Zvi Press.

Taylor, Joan E., and David Hay. 2012. "Astrology in Philo of Alexandria's *De Vita Contemplativa*." *ARAM Periodical* 24: 293–309. https://doi.org/10.2143/ARAM.24.0.3009278.

Teigen, Håkon Fiane. 2021. *A Manichaean Church at Kellis*. Nag Hammadi and Manichaean Studies, vol. 100. Leiden: Brill.

Teitler, H. C. 2017. *The Last Pagan Emperor: Julian the Apostate and the War against Christianity*. Oxford: Oxford University Press.

Tertullian. 1920. *Against Praxeas*. Translated by Alexander Souter. Translations of Christian Literature, Series II, Latin Texts. London: Society for Promoting Christian Knowledge and New York: Macmillan.

Thomas, Gabrielle. 2019. *The Image of God in the Theology of Gregory of Nazianzus*. Cambridge: Cambridge University Press.

Thomas, Yan. 2004. "*Res Religiosae*: On the Categories of Religion and Commerce in Roman Law." In *Law, Anthropology, and the Constitution of the Social: Making Persons and Things*, edited by Alain Pottage, Martha Mundy, and Chris Arup, 40–72. Cambridge: Cambridge University Press.

Thonemann, Peter. 2015. "The Calendar of the Roman Province of Asia." *Zeitschrift für Papyrologie und Epigraphik* 196: 123-141.

Thonemann, Peter. 2020. *An Ancient Dream Manual: Artemidorus' "The Interpretation of Dreams."* Oxford: Oxford University Press.

Thornton, T. C. G. 1989. "Jewish New Moon Festivals, Galatians 4:3–11 and Colossians 2:16." *The Journal of Theological Studies* 40(1): 97–100.

Thunø, Erik. 2015. In *The Pantheon: From Antiquity to the Present*, edited by Tod A. Marder and Mark Wilson Jones, 231–254. Cambridge: Cambridge University Press.

Tomlinson, R. A. 1983. *Epidauros*. Austin: University of Texas Press.

Tomson, Peter J. 2000. "Jewish Purity Laws as Viewed by the Church Fathers and by the Early Followers of Jesus." In *Purity and Holiness: The Heritage of Leviticus*, edited by Marcel Poorthuis and Joshua Schwartz, 73–91. Jewish and Christian Perspectives Series, vol. 2. Leiden: Brill.

Torjesen, Karen Jo. 2008. "Clergy and Laity." In *The Oxford Handbook of Early Christian Studies*, edited by David G. Hunter and Susan Ashbrook Harvey. Oxford Handbooks in Religion and Theology. Oxford: Oxford University Press. https://doi.org/10.1093/oxfordhb/9780199271566.003.0020.

Triebel, Lothar. 2006. "Die Angebliche Synagoge der Makkabäischen Märtyrer in Antiochia Am Orontes." *Zeitschrift für Antikes Christentum / Journal of Ancient Christianity* 9(3): 464–495. https://doi.org/10.1515/ZAC.2005.012.

Trombley, Frank R. 1993–94. *Hellenic Religion and Christianization, c. 370–529*. Religions in the Graeco-Roman World, vol. 115. Leiden: Brill.

Tropper, Amram. 2010. "The State of Mishnah Studies." In *Rabbinic Texts and the History of Late-Roman Palestine*, edited by Martin Goodman and Philip S. Alexander, 91–115. Proceedings of the British Academy, vol. 165. Oxford: Published for the British Academy by Oxford University Press.

Tropper, Amram. 2018. "Banning Greek: A Rabbinic History." *Journal for the Study of Judaism in the Persian, Hellenistic, and Roman Period* 49(1): 108–142.

Tuckett, C. M. 2007. *The Gospel of Mary*. Oxford Early Christian Gospel Texts. Oxford: Oxford University Press.

Tuominen, Miira. 2021. "The Role of Laws in Porphyry's Arguments against Animal Sacrifice." In *Animals and the Law in Antiquity*, edited by Saul M. Olyan and Jordan D. Rosenblum, 121–141. Brown Judaic Studies, vol. 368. Providence, RI: Brown Judaic Studies.

Urbach, Efraim Elimelech. 1975. *The Sages, Their Concepts and Beliefs*. Publications of the Perry Foundation in the Hebrew University of Jerusalem. Jerusalem: Magnes Press, Hebrew University.

Van Bremen, Riet. 1996. *The Limits of Participation: Women and Civic Life in the Greek East in the Hellenistic and Roman Periods*. Dutch Monographs on Ancient History and Archaeology, vol. 15. Amsterdam: J. C. Gieben.

Vandenberghe, Bruno H. 1955. "Saint Jean Chrysostome et les spectacles." *Zeitshcrift für Religions- und Geseitesgeschichte* 7(1): 34–46.

Van der Horst, Pieter W. 2018. "Sortes Biblicae Judaicae." In *My Lots Are in Thy Hands: Sortilege and Its Practitioners in Late Antiquity*, edited by AnnMarie Luijendijk, William E. Klingshirn, and Lance Jenott, 154–172. Religions in the Graeco-Roman World, vol. 188. Leiden: Brill.

Van der Toorn, K. 2007. *Scribal Culture and the Making of the Hebrew Bible*. Cambridge, MA: Harvard University Press.

Van Nijf, Onno. 1997. *The Civic World of Professional Associations in the Roman East*. Dutch Monographs on Ancient History and Archaeology, vol. 17. Amsterdam: J. C. Gieben.

Van Straten, Folkert T. 1981. "Gifts for the Gods." In *Faith, Hope and Worship: Aspects of Religious Mentality in the Ancient World*, edited by H. S. Versnel, 65–151. Leiden: Brill.

Van Straten, Folkert T. 1995. "Catalogue II: Votive Reliefs." In *Hierà kalá: Images of Animal Sacrifice in Archaic and Classical Greece*, edited by Folkert T. Van Straten, 275–332. Religions in the Graeco-Roman World, vol. 127. Leiden: Brill. https://doi.org/10.1163/9789004283459_008.

Vedeshkin, Mikhail. 2018. "Bribe and Punishment: To the Question of Persistence of Pagan Cults in Late Antiquity." *SHOLE. Filosofskoe antikovedenie i klassičeskaâ tradiciâ* 12(1): 259–275.

Versnel, Hendrik. 1994. "What Is Sauce for the Goose Is Sauce for the Gander: Myth and Ritual, Old and New." In *Inconsistencies in Greek and Roman Religion, Volume 2: Transition and Reversal in Myth and Ritual*, edited by Henk Versnel, 15–88. Studies in Greek and Roma Religion, vol. 6/2. Leiden: Brill.

Versnel, Hendrik S. 2015. "Prayer and Curse." In *The Oxford Handbook of Ancient Greek Religion*, edited by Esther Eidinow and Julia Kindt, 447–462. Oxford: Oxford University Press.

Vikan, Gary. 2016. "From Asclepius to Simeon: Votives and Sacred Healing in Late Antiquity." In *Religious Competition in the Greco-Roman World*, edited by Nathaniel P. DesRosiers and Lily C. Vuong, 247–258. Atlanta: SBL Press.

Viteau, Joseph-Eugène. 1897. *Passions des saints Écaterine et Pierre d'Alexandrie, Barbara et Anysia*. Paris: É. Bouillon.

Von Stuckrad, Kocku. 2000. "Jewish and Christian Astrology in Late Antiquity: A New Approach." *Numen* 47(1): 1–40.

Wallraff, Martin. 2001. "Constantine's Devotion to the Sun after 324." *Studia Patristica* 34: 256–269.

Wankel, Hermann, ed. 1979–84. *Die Inschriften von Ephesos*. 8 vols. Bonn: Habelt.

Ward, Benedicta, trans. 1975. *The Wisdom of the Desert Fathers: The Apophthegmata Patrum*. Fairacres, vol. 48. Oxford: SLG Press.

Wassen, Cecilia. 2007. "Angels in the Dead Sea Scrolls." *Deuterocanonical and Cognate Literature Yearbook* 2007: 499–523.

Watkin, David. 2009. *The Roman Forum*. Wonders of the World. London: Profile Books.

Watts, Edward J. 2017. *Hypatia: The Life and Legend of an Ancient Philosopher*. New York: Oxford University Press.

Way, Sister Agnes Clare, trans. 1963. *Saint Basil: Exegetic Homilies*. The Fathers of the Church: A New Translation, vol. 46. Washington, DC: Catholic University of America Press.

Webb, Ruth. 2008. *Demons and Dancers: Performance in Late Antiquity*. Cambridge, MA: Harvard University Press.

Weiss, Haim. 2018. "'All the Dreams Follow the Mouth': Dreamers and Interpreters in Rabbinic Literature." In *Perchance to Dream: Dream Divination in the Bible and the Ancient Near East*, edited by Esther J. Hamori and Jonathan Stökl, 193–203. Atlanta: SBL Press.

Weiss, Zeev. 2012. "Were Priests Communal Leaders in Late Antique Palestine? The Archaeological Evidence." In *Was 70 CE a Watershed in Jewish History? On Jews and Judaism before and after the Destruction of the Second Temple*, edited by Daniel R. Schwartz and Zeev Weiss, 91–111. Leiden: Brill.

Weiss, Zeev. 2014. *Public Spectacles in Roman and Late Antique Palestine*. Cambridge, MA: Harvard University Press.

Weiss, Zeev. 2019. "Sepphoris: The City and Its Hinterland in Roman Times." In *Judaea/Palaestina and Arabia: Cities and Hinterlands in Roman and Byzantine Times*, edited by Achim Lichtenberger, Oren Tal, and Zeev Weiss, 95–107. Heidelberg: Propylaeum.

Wendt, Heidi. 2016. *At the Temple Gates: The Religion of Freelance Experts in the Roman Empire*. New York: Oxford University Press.

Werlin, Steven H. 2015. *Ancient Synagogues of Southern Palestine, 300–800 C.E.: Living on the Edge*. Leiden: Brill.

Whitby, Michael. 2009. "The Violence of the Circus Factions." In *Organised Crime in Antiquity*, edited by Keith Hopwood, 229–253. Swansea: Classical Press of Wales.

Whiting, Marlena. 2023. "Female Patronage in Late Antiquity: Titles and Rank of Women Donors in Sixth- and Seventh-Century Palaestina and Arabia." In *The Public Lives of Ancient Women (500 BCE–650 CE)*, edited by Lucinda Dirven, Martijn Icks, and Sofie Remijsen, 291–318. Leiden: Brill. https://brill.com/display/title/63940.

Whitmarsh, Tim. 2015. *Battling the Gods: Atheism in the Ancient World*. New York: Arthur A. Knopf.

Wilken, Robert Louis. 1983. *John Chrysostom and the Jews: Rhetoric and Reality in the Late 4th Century*. The Transformation of the Classical Heritage, vol. 4. Berkeley: University of California Press.

Wilken, Robert Louis. 1984. *The Christians as the Romans Saw Them*. New Haven: Yale University Press.

Wilkinson, John. 1990. "Jewish Holy Places and the Origins of Christian Pilgrimage." In *The Blessings of Pilgrimage, edited by Robert G. Ousterhout, 41–53*. Illinois Byzantine Studies, vol. 1. Urbana: University of Illinois Press.

Williams, George Huntston. 1951. "Christology and Church-State Relations in the Fourth Century." *Church History* 20(3): 3–33. https://doi.org/10.2307/3161893.

Williams, Rowan. 2002. *Arius: Heresy and Tradition*. Rev. ed. Grand Rapids, MI: Eerdmans.

Wilson, John F., and Vassilios Tzaferis. 2007. "An Herodian Capital in the North: Caesarea Philippi (Panias)." In *The World of the Herods: Volume 1 of the International Conference "The World of the Herods and the Nabataeans" Held at the British Museum, 17–19 April 2001*, edited by Nikos Kokkinos, 131–143. Stuttgart: Franz Steiner.

Wilson, S. G. 1996. "Voluntary Associations: An Overview." In *Voluntary Associations in the Graeco-Roman World*, edited by S. G. Wilson and John S. Kloppenborg, 1–15. London: Routledge.

Winnefeld, H. 1914. "Zur Geschichte des Syrischen Heliopolis." *Rheinisches Museum für Philologie* 69: 139–159.

Wischmeyer, Wolfgang. 1980. "Die Aberkiosinschrift als Grabepigramm." *Jahrbuch für Antike und Christentum* 23: 22–47.

Wiseman, James. 1970. "The Fountain of the Lamps." *Archaeology* 23(2): 130–137.

Wiśniewski, Robert. 2016. "Pagans, Jews, Christians, and a Type of Book Divination in Late Antiquity." *Journal of Early Christian Studies* 24(4): 553–568. https://doi.org/10.1353/earl.2016.0043.

Wiśniewski, Robert. 2019. *The Beginnings of the Cult of Relics*. Oxford: Oxford University Press.

Wissowa, Georg. 1902. *Religion und Kultus der Römer*. Handbuch der klassischen Altertumswissenschaft, vol. 5. Munich: C. H. Beck.

Worrell, Wiliam H. 1930. "A Coptic Wizard's Hoard." *American Journal of Semitic Languages and Literatures* 46(4): 239–262.

Wright, Wilmer Cave, trans. 1923. *Letters. Epigrams. Against the Galilaeans. Fragments.* By Julian. Loeb Classical Library, vol. 157. Cambridge, MA: Harvard University Press.

Yadin-Israel, Azzan. 2006. "Rabban Gamliel, Aphrodite's Bath, and the Question of Pagan Monotheism." *Jewish Quarterly Review* 96(2): 149–179.

Yasin, Ann Marie. 2009. *Saints and Church Spaces in the Late Antique Mediterranean: Architecture, Cult, and Community*. Greek Culture in the Roman World. Cambridge: Cambridge University Press.

Yegül, Fikret. 1987. "Roman Architecture at Sardis." In *Sardis: Twenty-Seven Years of Discovery: Papers Presented at a Symposium Sponsored by the Archaeological Institute of America, Chicago Society, and the Oriental Institute of the University of Chicago, Held at the Oriental Institute March 21, 1987*, edited by Eleanor Guralnick, 46–61. Chicago: Chicago Society of the Archaeological Institute of America.

Zangenberg, Jürgen. 2019. "Will the Real Women Please Sit Down: Interior Space, Seating Arrangements, and Female Presence in the Byzantine Synagogue of Horvat Kur in Galilee." In *Gender and Social Norms in Ancient Israel, Early Judaism and Early Christianity: Texts and Material Culture*, edited by Michaela Bauks, Katharina Galor, and Judith Hartenstein, 91–117. Journal of Ancient Judaism, Supplements, vol. 28. Göttingen: Vandenhoeck and Ruprecht.

Zelnick-Abramovitz, Rachel. 2015. "Whose Grave Is This? The Status of Grave Plots in Ancient Greece." *Dike—Rivista di Storia del Diritto Greco ed Ellenistico* 18: 51–95. https://doi.org/10.13130/1128-8221/8029.

Zori, N. 1966. "The House of Kyrios Leontis at Beth Shean." *Israel Exploration Journal* 16(2): 123–134.

INDEX

Note: Page numbers in italic type indicate illustrations.

A NOTE ON THE TYPE

This book has been composed in Arno, an Old-style serif typeface in the classic Venetian tradition, designed by Robert Slimbach at Adobe.